Chile and the Great Depression:

The Politics of Underdevelopment, 1927-1948

D1520643

Chile and the Great Depression:
The Politics of Underdevelopment, 1927-1948

by

MICHAEL MONTEÓN

Center for Latin American Studies Press

ARIZONA STATE UNIVERSITY

Published by ASU Center for Latin American Studies Press
Arizona State University
Center for Latin American Studies
PO Box 872401
Tempe, AZ 85287-2401

Published in the United States of America.

Cover design by Stefanie L. Bobar
Editing, book design, index, and typesetting by Evelyn Smith de Gálvez
Computer consulting by Sebastian J. Bronner, CPU, Mesa, Arizona
Printing by Thomson-Shore, Dexter, Michigan

Library of Congress Cataloging-in-Publication Data

Monteón, Michael
Chile and the Great Depression: the politics of underdevelopment,
1927-1948 / by Michael Monteón.
    p.   cm.
Includes bibliographical references and index.
ISBN 0-87918-090-0 (alk. paper)
    1. Chile—Economic conditions—1918-1970. 2. Chile—Politics
and government—1920-1970.   I. Title.
HC192.M6588   1998
320.983'09'04—dc21   98-18509
                                                  CIP

For Betty, whose love and tolerance
were essential
to writing this work

Contents

Tables and Graphs

Table

Graph

Figures

Acronyms and Organizations

AGECh. The Guild Association of Chilean Employees. Agrupación Gremial de Empleados de Chile.

ASECh. Chilean Employees Association. Asociación de Empleados de Chile.

Chilean Council of Provisions. Junta de Abastecimiento.

Chilean Electric Company. Compañía Chilena de Electricidad.

CGT. General Confederation of Labor. Confederación General de Trabajadores.

CNS. Chilean National Confederation of Syndicates. Confederación Nacional de Sindicatos de Chile.

Controller General. Controlaría General.

COPEC. Chilean Oil Company. Compañía de Petroleos de Chile.

CORFO. Development Corporation, literally the Corporation for the Development of Production. Corporación de Fomento de la Producción.

COSACh. Chilean Nitrate Corporation. Corporación de Salitre de Chile.

CRAC. Confederation of the Republic for Social Action. Confederación Republicana de Acción Social.

CTCh. Chilean Labor Confederation. Confederación de Trabajadores de Chile.

Currency Exchange Commission. Comisión de Control de Operaciones de Cambio.

Employees Social Security Agency. Caja de Previsión de Empleados Particulares.

ENDESA. National Electric Company. Empresa Nacional de Electricidad, Sociedad Anónima.

FECh. Chilean Student Federation. Federación de Estudiantes de Chile.

FOCh. Chilean Labor Federation. Federación Obrera de Chile.

FTC. (United States) Federal Trade Commission.

La Moneda. The presidential palace and administration building.

LAN. Chilean National Airlines. Lineas Aereas Nacionales.

MEMCh. Movement for the Emancipation of Chilean Women. Movimiento Pro-Emancipación de las Mujeres de Chile.

Ministry of Development. Ministerio de Fomento.

Ministry of Finance. Ministerio de Hacienda.

Ministry of Welfare. Ministerio de Bienestar.

MNS. Nacis or National Socialist Movement of Chile. Movimiento Nacional Socialista de Chile.

NAP. New Public Action. Nueva Acción Política.

National Defense League of Small Farmers. Liga Nacional de Defensa de Campesinos Pobres.

National Mining Society. Sociedad Nacional de Minería.

OCIAA. (United States) Office of the Coordinator of Inter-American Affairs.

People's Liberation Alliance. Alianza Popular Libertadora.

People's Socialist Vanguard. Vanguardia Popular Socialista.

SNA. National Agricultural Society. Sociedad Nacional de Agricultura.

SNM. National Mining Society. Sociedad Nacional de Minería.

SOFOFA. Society for Industrial Development. Sociedad de Fomento Fabril. In many works in English, this is called the National Society of Manufacturers.

State Mortgage Bank. Caja de Crédito Hipotecario.

Acknowledgments

I wish to thank some of the many institutions and people who have helped with the research and writing of this book. Many of my greatest debts are a decade or more in the past. Still, it is not too late to acknowledge financial support from the American Philosophical Association, the National Research Council's Ford Foundation Grants for Minorities program, the Academic Senate and the Chancellor's Office of the University of California, San Diego, the Herbert Hoover Library Fellowship program, and the Brookings Institution.

I owe some very special debts to those individuals in Santiago, Chile, who helped me acquire research material that was otherwise unavailable. The staff of the National Archives of Chile allowed me to go hunting in warehouses where documents were held prior to the construction of a new archive. The assistance of Ana María Malinorich de Agüero made my archival hunt twice as productive as it would otherwise have been. She photocopied materials while protests were being staged against the dictatorship. The friendship I received from the Garreaud family and a constellation of young historians, Sol Serrano, Isabel Torres D. and the group at FLACSO, kept my spirits up in those often bleak days.

Of my colleagues in the United States I cannot say enough. Ramón Eduardo Ruiz gave the initial manuscript the red-pencil editing it badly needed. His excellent advice has been essential to seeing this project through. When things looked especially bleak, Chancellor Richard Atkinson, now President of the University of California, provided support and counsel. Christine Hünefeldt, Eric Van Young, and Paul Drake read drafts critically and added their own insights to helping me formulate what I was trying to say. William Beezley, Michael Conniff, Ramón Gutiérrez, John Hart, and Peter Smith showed real solidarity in helping me to see the project to completion. The conclusion was originally written as a paper for the University of California Conference of Latin American Historians in Riverside, 1996; I am grateful for the comments on that draft by Ronald Chilcote, Gilbert Joseph, and Michael Bernstein. Other scholars, contacted by my department in various academic reviews and by this press, gave me both of sense of what was missing and what was worthwhile. Under the rules of the game of academic reviewing, I can only offer an impersonal, thank you.

I also have debts with the personnel at Arizona State University, Center for Latin American Studies. I want to single out Lynn Stoner, during her tenure as Director, for her enthusiastic support for the project, and Tod Swanson, current Director, for seeing the project through to completion. Stefanie Bobar often provided reassurance when events did not look the best. Evelyn E. Smith de Gálvez was everything an author would want from an editor, conscientious, patient, and intelligent in her suggestions.

Introduction:

Underdevelopment and Political authority

I began this book on Chile with some basic questions about how and why a nation remains "underdeveloped." I wanted some answers to the causes of underdevelopment. Are poverty, technical backwardness, political instability, and repeated economic crises in Latin American nations the result of factors outside each nation's control or do they arise out of domestic politics and social structures in the region? There is, of course, no single answer and, in many respects, no complete answer. In the course of writing, I found as most historians do, that events often defy theory yet make little sense without being placed in some larger context that provides insight into a fundamental pattern of change. Also, the reasons that may explain what happened in Chile may not be true of all Latin America.

Still, we need an interpretative scheme, based on research, to make sense of any set of events. My search for it had an eclectic result. In this work, I juxtapose ideas from very different schools of thought on the causes of underdevelopment and political conflict. Underdevelopment has often been characterized in terms of a nation's internal conditions: a rural and illiterate population; a poorly developed industrial base; and/or a few rich ruling over an impoverished mass. Another approach is to discuss a nation's prospects for creating a dynamic economy with a rising standard of living. A third, more culturally focused, view compares underdeveloped nations to those that are considered advanced, modern, and technically progressive, that is, to the United States, western Europe, and Japan. The very terminology of *developed* and *underdeveloped* is inescapably loaded with ideological assumptions. An intellectual tradition, especially among Marxists, explains Latin America's underdevelopment in terms of its relationship with external actors. These may be described as powerful capitalists or governments, as multinational corporations or financial forces, but the basic assumption is that these external actors determine what happens within a Latin American nation. Those working in this tradition often treat Chile as a case study in neocolonialism, or economic imperialism, or *dependency*. It is described in terms of its incorporation, that is, its trade and political interaction, with the dominant powers of the capitalist world. Underdeveloped nations such as Chile are interpreted through the long history of imperialism and neocolonialism, which continue trading raw materials for manufactures long after they acquire political independence. In this neocolonial scheme, Chile's political life and economic possibilities conform to decisions made by external actors over which it has little influence and no control. Underdevelopment cannot be overcome until a nation's reliance on foreign capital and markets is fundamentally altered.

Another extensive body of literature emphasizes the domestic history and political evolution of an individual nation. In this view, Chile's problems are largely of its own making: the country's political and economic leaders made poor choices that retarded economic growth and reduced constructive, social changes. Their conduct, in Karl Polany's famous phrase, retards "the great transformation" that sets a nation on the road to a dynamic, capitalist economy.[1]

Another possible interpretation is that each nation moves at its own pace along a continuum of economic development. Chile entered the twentieth century farther behind on that continuum than more prosperous nations, and so, has had to accomplish tasks other nations completed earlier even as it tries not to fall further behind. It takes time and a series of learning experiences to generate everything from political parties to engineering schools required in a modern, industrial economy.[2]

Put very simply, explanations that stress foreign factors pay particular attention to relations of international power. When did foreign corporations begin to invest in Chile? What did they build? How did their decisions affect the rest of the economy? Did they become a central factor in domestic politics? Did they use their influence with their home governments to improve their economic position in Chile? Responses to these questions, in turn, are used to explain the rise of nationalist sentiment: a rejection of foreign investment, a desire for domestic industry, and even a cultural wish to free the nation of foreign influence. There is no avoiding the importance of foreign corporations in Chile's economy; among their activities, they dominated copper, the nation's lifeline by the 1930s. Their presence and behavior stimulated nationalist sentiment not only on the left but among political moderates and even on the right. Of course, it may be true of nations as it is of individuals, externalizing blame frees the nation from looking too closely at itself. In sharp contrast, those who emphasize that Chile's problems have developed from within its borders, stress the internal politics and culture of the country and downplay or ignore external forces in its history.

This work assumes that Chile's underdevelopment is a result of both external and internal factors, and of contingency. Decisions made by foreign governments, especially the government of the United States, affected Chilean political leaders and the stability of the country's political system and economy.

One significant effect of the Great Depression was that it rolled through nations great and small in ways none could control. Within Chile, the crash of 1929-32 forced politicians of every stripe to become more nationalistic. Unlike some *dependistas* [authors who ascribe to the ideas of "dependency."], I did not find that this surge in nationalist rhetoric was accompanied by a break with international capitalism. Chile's industry, to take one major sector, grew during the 1930s but evolved in a setting of continued bargaining between Chilean and foreign interests.

The details, therefore, of how the Great Depression altered the political economy of Chile is the central subject of this work. Its central argument is that the Great Depression stimulated the growth of industry, a larger political public, and a more active government but that Chile remained underdeveloped and dependent. Its economy grew slowly, but the basic pace of economic change was set by external factors, even by decisions of foreign governments, and not by government policies and Chilean capitalists. This external vulnerability shaped internal possibilities: within the country, its leaders created a new set of rules and regulations devoted to achieving political stability and to prioritizing issues of patronage over those of development. They tried, of course, to make their decisions seem in the service of both stability and development. Chile's political system was structurally complex but fragile. The nation had an electoral system in which a substantial minority of adult men could vote, but it had entered the era of mass politics early in the century. Those who could not vote could take to the streets and had begun to acquire a political identity. A variety of political parties vied for office so that much of the nation's politics turned on creating party coalitions. But the patronage required to sustain such coalitions was difficult to maintain because the government had a weak fiscal base that was extremely susceptible to changes in foreign trade. After the Crash, political leaders spent most of their time trying to survive in office and had little energy, and sometimes, little idea how to refinance an economy in crisis and revive a demoralized society. These are issues I first explored in a study of Chile during the nitrate era, 1880-1930, when the economy and society were reshaped by an export boom based on nitrates and copper.[3]

My analysis in the earlier study turned on the relation of an export economy to the political system. The British dominated the nitrate sector in the northern provinces, but the taxes on that sector sustained the Parliamentary Regime. This Regime, which begins after a civil war in 1891, had a multiparty system dominated by the national legislature. An upper class based in landholding, merchant activities, and finance controlled the legislature through patronage. Chilean politics had a number of characteristics that set it apart from the rest of Latin America. In the nineteenth century, it was not a nation of *caudillos*, of strongmen who ruled with ad hoc armies. Despite civil wars in 1851, 1859, and 1891, the same Constitution, albeit reformed over time, remained the law of the land from 1833 until 1925. The military remained in its barracks throughout the Parliamentary era. The system was relatively stable and attempted, over time, to incorporate new elements into politics.

Elections were held, suffrage was gradually extended to new social elements, and the press was relatively free of censorship. By the second decade of the twentieth century, the left could form its own parties. The economic underpinnings of the system began to collapse during World War I as belligerents discovered how to produce nitrate from industrial processes. Then in 1920, the postwar economic crisis generated the election of Arturo Alessandri Palma. President Alessandri broadened the government's appeal by proposing new labor laws and public projects and by including members of the middle class in his cabinet. A hostile legislature blocked his projects while the society still suffered the effects of the postwar depression. The system broke down in the coup of 1924 and, despite valiant party efforts to revive it, collapsed completely when a military strongman, Carlos Ibáñez del Campo, rose to power in 1927.

This particular crisis is a familiar one in Latin American history. An export economy expands the prospects and income of a domestic elite, the oligarchy, and the breakdown of elite governance invites the military into the executive office. Ibáñez was both an autocrat and a reformer, for he continued many of the trends begun by Alessandri. He also sustained his government with heavy foreign borrowing. The economic collapse of 1931 simultaneously ended the nitrate era and the nation's eligibility for foreign loans. Chile suffered the sharpest economic collapse of any American republic, some argue of any independent nation of the era. Substantial portions of the society were reduced to near starvation. Public demonstrations drove Ibáñez from office. Uncertainty permeated every social stratum. The republic fell into a general crisis of demonstrations, of coups and attempted coups, and of strikes and riots. Communists believed this was the crisis before revolution; conservatives thought it presaged "social dissolution." Both were wrong. But a sense of crisis that appeared during the Depression continued to influence the nation well into the 1940s. The government and the economy gradually recovered and the civilian, constitutional system that began in 1932 endured until 1973.

Those familiar with the literature on political change, economic systems and political economy will recognize the influence of *dependista* authors and of the Economic Commission on Latin America on the questions I ask, if not the answers I found.[4] I also owe considerable debts to Albert Hirschman, Hyman Minsky, and Amartya Sen—three specialists of capitalist economic theory.[5] I have tried to incorporate some of the insights of social anthropologists and historical sociologists such as Benedict Anderson, Nathan Gellner, and Charles Tilly.[6]

In the rest of this introduction, I will present five elements for an analysis of Chile's evolution between 1927 and 1948. Those who write on issues of foreign trade and comparative development often speak in terms of the *center* and the *periphery*. If the term *peripheral* has any historical significance, then Chile was and is a peripheral nation. It had always been a minor part of the Spanish empire. During the nineteenth century, it remained a small, poor nation selling wheat, copper, silver, and nitrates to the rest of the world. Its evolution was strongly conditioned by the cultural and demographic legacies of the colonial era as well as the market opportunities created by the expansion of the Atlantic economy when Great Britain was the dominant creditor, market center, and industrial power of the capitalist world. During World War I, as was the case in much of the rest of South America, it turned from relying primarily on Great Britain to developing closer ties and a dependent relationship with the United States. The United States became Chile's chief creditor, its major investor, and the dominant market for Chilean exports.

Hirschman, in a work in the late 1940s, anticipated some of the later generalizations of the dependistas and the first element of my analysis, when he noted that there was an asymmetrical relationship between Latin American nations and the United States. Each Latin American nation desperately needed to enhance its trade, and its credit line derived from trade, with the United States, while the overall economy of the United States was not vulnerable to any decision taken in Latin America. Of all Latin American countries, Chile was second only to Mexico in relying on the United States as a trading partner. While the value of trade had fallen during the Depression, the percentage of Chile's trade with the United States actually increased, from 34 to 40 percent on imports and 32 to 44 percent on exports.[7]

Throughout this book, there is evidence of how the U.S. government and U.S. corporations pressured Chile on issues relating to trade, the foreign debt, and commercial rules. This pressure often complicated the Chilean political leaders' efforts to gain domestic support and, in 1931, played a role in destroying at least one administration. U.S. economic diplomacy was not only central to trade and economic issues, but it also set conditions on the government's behavior and affected the country's internal politics and social history. Although they did not always lose in these negotiations, Chilean political leaders argued from a very weak position.

A second element of analysis evaluates the relation between the government of Chile and the dominant capitalists in the country. The latter included U.S. companies running the Chilean copper and nitrate mines as well as an array of foreign companies with interests in manufacturing, trade, and finance. In the literature of Latin American economic history, the 1930s comprise the famous period of development "from within," when countries turned away from exports and favored import substitution industrialization (often abbreviated ISI). Much has been written about why ISI failed to provide the dynamism expected of it. I argue that a close analysis of how Chile's economy changed in the 1930s, especially regarding the state regulation of markets, does not lead to any dramatic claims for industrialization;

industry grew, but it was not the motor of Chile's recovery.[8] Most importantly, industrial expansion did not provide a means to reduce Chile's dependence on U.S. corporations and on trade and credit from the United States.

Foreign capitalists and the Chilean government struck all kinds of bargains. They often acted in concert with western European firms to create cartels that controlled large portions of Chile's trade. In many instances, I find that within these cartels, U.S. mining companies were allowed by the Chilean government to bargain on behalf of "Chilean" interests. When unhappy with Chile's regulations, U.S. companies lobbied the State Department, and other U.S. ministries, to pressure Santiago for changes.

By comparison with their foreign counterparts, Chilean capitalists had relatively weak financial and political resources. In his Marxist analysis of Third World economies, Paul Baran coined the term *comprador* [a word referring to the traders of colonial Macao] to characterize the role of national capitalists in a neocolonial situation.[9] These middlemen exploited domestic opportunities at the price of never challenging their basically subordinate role. Some have argued that as dependent economies evolve, foreign and domestic interests become intertwined.[10] My own view is closer to Baran's. My work adds something to this discussion by emphasizing the need of peripheral capitalists for a state capable of bargaining on their behalf. Chilean society had changed to the point that businessmen counted on the state to keep labor in line. They also needed the government to serve as an agent vis à vis foreign firms, who usually were many times larger and had far greater financial and technical resources. Elements of Chile's business class became more nationalistic, supporting a more active government in a number of realms. For example, Chilean businessmen supported the creation of a national oil company to replace the two foreign firms that supplied the nation's fuels. At the same time, Chilean capitalists resented any government intrusion in their business and labor practices, any increase in taxes, and any confrontation that threatened to drive foreigners out of Chile. Although it is little studied, the increase in state authority cannot be understood without first examining the role of domestic capitalists.

A third issue is the relationship between the form of government and its sources of income, a subject that still needs elaboration in the historical literature of Latin America. Who pays taxes? Who receives revenues? Who gets special favors? And, how are the answers to these questions related to the form and function of government? Such questions are particularly relevant to Chile in the 1930s. As the economic crisis of 1929-32 became a fiscal crisis, official improvisation generated new laws, some of which remained in the commercial code of the country long after the 1930s.

Here, my analysis owes much to economists who study rent-seeking behavior. Their work argues that private interests often try to use government to reduce costs and improve their position in the marketplace. A common example is one of tariffs, where specific sectors lobby the government for protection. If successful, they derive a "rent" from the consumers confined to the national market. Moreover, once the law codifies such an advantage, the beneficiaries will spend resources —even fight—to preserve it. Similarly, politically influential interests will use their power to shift the costs of government to those who are less powerful. Thus, rent-seeking behavior is accompanied by "rent-avoidance," which can take the form of everything from dodging income taxes to smuggling.[11]

This was certainly the case in Chile. The international collapse of nitrate sales reduced the nation's income and its government revenues. Political leaders saw foreign interests, especially the large companies in mining and utilities, as sources of untapped revenue, and treated them accordingly. The regulatory and tax powers of the government were deployed as never before, and in the process generated new winners and losers. Although the government had suffered a fiscal crisis, it could still pass out favors and hope for support in return. Government regulation in the form of tax increases, price controls, currency controls, and exemptions from regulations generated a black market and widespread tax avoidance.

It is hardly surprising to find a public demand for state action accompanied by a refusal to pay higher taxes. In Chile, this rentier attitude arose from the long history of state power which owed little to the consent of the governed. Writers on underdevelopment have noted that post-colonial governments in Latin America and elsewhere tend to be bureaucratic, insolvent, conservative, and hierarchical.[12] Indeed, rentier attitudes are not peculiar to Latin America. Writing on Iran under the Shah, an economist called it a "rentier state," which "receive[d] on a regular basis substantial amounts of external rent . . . paid by foreign individuals, concerns or governments."[13] I analyze how a rentier attitude had developed within Chile prior to the Great Depression and how it persisted through the crisis. It was one of the reasons why, despite what had happened in the late 1920s, the government renewed a cycle of intemperate borrowing in 1939. It is hard to escape the fact that the revival of civilian, constitutional rule in Chile after 1932 had at its center a silence about the persistent shortage of revenues for the tasks facing the government. Party leaders across the ideological spectrum preferred to insist on what the government should do and skipped over how the government would raise the money.

The fourth element of my analysis relates changes in the political economy to the public sphere. Chile had a vigorous political press, which quickly recovered its voice once Ibáñez was overthrown. More than half of all adults could read and write; laborers, feminists, as well as the political parties recruited support through their newspapers and pamphlets. The nation had seen its first round of class conflict—urban demonstrations, riots in the major cities and mining areas, and official massacres—in the first two decades of the century. Despite and, in some instances, in response to the breakdown of the Parliamentary Regime, the public continued to evolve a widening sense of citizenship. In 1931, after the fall of Ibáñez, political parties, labor associations, and professional guilds proliferated. These groups contested Chile's future in a series of key elections, leading to the re-election of Alessandri in 1932, and to the rise of the Popular Front and the victory of its presidential candidate, Pedro Aguirre Cerda, in 1938.

In analyzing the relation between elections and the public, I again found Hirschman an excellent guide. In his study of the origin of the public sphere in eighteenth-century England, Jürgen Habermas tells us how a public is constructed from the interaction of government and the media.[14] But it is Hirschman who, in his *Exit, Voice, and Loyalty*, provides the logic of political "voice." In that work, now twenty years old, Hirschman compared behaviors within economic and political markets. He noted that economists tend to see unhappy voters as something like unhappy customers who can "exit" the market when they do not like what they see. In most political situations, however, those who are dissatisfied tend to voice their complaints rather than depart. Exit in the political market—that is, leaving a party, union, or even a nation-state—is usually a last resort. A key element in all politics is leaders appeal to group loyalty to get participants to agree to a less-than-optimal situation.[15] How does this relate to a political economy? Hirschman insisted that institutional arrangements affect how people see their choice of exit and voice; certain arrangements, particularly the lack of internal democratic practices within an organization, can promote exit or boycott.

Chile, in the 1930s, experienced a threat to the system of government as a whole. It became common for political figures on the right and on the left not only to oppose policies but to urge resistance and rebellion. Paramilitary units became common. There was a persistent threat of military coups. The state had too few resources to command much loyalty. It is, in this setting, understandable that Chilean leaders put stability before development. They used the expansion of government into new activities to revive clientalism, and so garner support and diffuse the opposition.

The terms of political loyalty and opposition were fluid in the 1930s. Ibáñez left for exile, returned, conspired, and left again. Other political figures switched parties, merged parties with paramilitary movements, and did their best to label opponents traitors. When the consequences of exit, voice, and loyalty are unclear, as they were in the 1930s, political life can career toward violence, justified by a polarizing rhetoric. Policies affecting the political economy could quickly change, ruining expectations based on earlier rules. This dynamic relationship between the public sphere and the economy opened the possibility that change would take a redistributive direction.

Unfortunately, the spade work to discuss the role of gender in this relationship—a monumental task in itself and requiring sources other than those relating to governments, firms, and the general economy —has only recently begun. Where sources and recent scholarship permit, I note the obviously patriarchal character of the society and the relation of women to economic and political outcomes. Gender roles, as historians of the subject remind us, must have defined what people thought was appropriate behavior at every level of politics and economics, but the capacity of women to change much of anything was extremely limited and therefore not central to my narrative.[16]

The final aspect of this analysis, the geographic relations of power within Chile, is subordinated to the others. By 1930, Santiago was a primary city in political and economic terms that defined the nation's dominant culture. The way in which this supremacy was exercised by those who held national office or held power within the economy is an important part of the story. Many of the key tragedies of the era occurred in the provinces and were then reinterpreted in the capital. The capital's version of events became the nation's viewpoint; I have tried to demonstrate that this version, often deeply flawed, ignored what was happening in the copper and coal mines and the frontier.

This narrative of Chile's underdevelopment describes a number of asymmetrical relationships: the U.S. government was far more powerful than and largely indifferent to Chile; foreign capitalists had greater resources than Chilean capitalists; the rich, within Chile, still held the principal reins of national power and used them to control the laboring population; and Santiago had emerged triumphant over any region or coalition of provinces. But these were contested relationships: the Chilean government became less passive in dealing with the United States and other nations; it also made substantial demands on foreign companies; and the working poor and the middle class began a long campaign to redistribute control and income within the economy. An emerging and fragile constitutional order had to reconcile intensified public demands with an economy in crisis and an often insolvent government. Chile emerged from the Great Depression with a politics of economic nationalism and a nation-state still dependent on the United States.

As the working class and the middle class participated more openly and effectively in the political system, Chile became a case study of a "populist dilemma." How was this under-financed and often besieged state to satisfy new public demands without provoking the exit of foreign interests and domestic capitalists? If foreign interests pulled out of Chile or retaliated by reducing Chile's access to foreign markets, the economy would collapse further and worsen domestic conflict. If wealthy Chileans became too alienated they would "exit" by calling upon the military, by arming themselves, or doing both to bring down the regime. The dilemma not did end there. As some interests were accommodated by government action and others were not, a crucial difference began to appear between the middle class and the rest of the laboring population. The expansion of government increased the bureaucracy and generated inflation; it turned out that meeting the demands of the middle class meant postponing many of the needs of the working poor.

I do not read the present into the past. Chile faced different choices and somewhat distinct conflicts between the 1920s and the 1940s than it has faced from the 1970s to the present. Still, it is true that the past is prologue, that the history of Chilean politics and underdevelopment certainly began before the breakdown of the socialist experiment of the Popular Unity presidency of the early 1970s. No one who looks at this earlier period can help but be struck by the continuities. The political order by the late 1940s included a left, a right, and something like a middle-class center. They were at odds with one another, unable to hold a ruling coalition of parties together for very long and unable to agree on how to deal with such persistent problems as inflation, poverty, and the nation's vulnerability to downturns in its export economy. These problems were at the heart of the polarizing politics of the late 1960s and early 1970s. The left, often spoke of the Popular Front era, as a failure that could not be repeated. In examining the period of the Great Depression, we are also examining a history of a political order that broke down in 1973 and led to the longest dictatorship in Chilean history.

Endnotes

1. Karl Polanyi, *The Great Transformation: The Political and Economic Origins of Our Time* (Boston: Beacon Press, 1944).

2. I will not summarize bibliographies of contrasting points of view, but one can begin with the excellent first chapter of Victor Bulmer-Thomas, *The Economic History of Latin America since Independence* (Cambridge: Cambridge University Press, 1994), which stresses a modernization point of view. Cristóbal Kay, *Latin American Theories of Development and Underdevelopment* (New York: Routledge, 1989), chaps. 1 and 2 provide a very readable summary of dependency and Marxist perspectives. I attempted to wrestle with the contrasting points of view and what was useful in each in, "Latin America, Underdevelopment, and the Rentier State," *Crítica* 2:2 (Fall, 1990), a version in Spanish appeared in *Economía* 13:25 (June, 1990).

3. Michael Monteón, *Chile in the Nitrate Era: The Evolution of Economic Dependence, 1880-1930* (Madison: University of Wisconsin Press, 1982).

4. For the classic statements of dependency theory, see Fernando Henrique Cardoso and Enzo Faletto, *Dependency and Development in Latin America* (Berkeley: University of California Press, 1979), and André Gunder Frank, *Capitalism and Underdevelopment in Latin America: Historical Studies of Chile and Brazil* (New York: Monthly Review Press, 1967). See also, Raúl Prebisch, *The Economic Development of Latin America and Its Principal Problems* (New York: United Nations, 1949). Joseph Love has a superb survey of Prebisch's work, "Raúl Prebisch and the Origins of the Doctrine of Unequal Exchange," in J.L. Dietz and J.H. Street, eds., *Latin America's Economic Development: Institutionalist and Structuralist Perspectives* (Boulder: Lynne Rienner Publishers, 1987). The Commission was once called ECLA, Economic Commission on Latin America; its Spanish acronym was CEPAL. It is now called ECLAC, Economic Commission on Latin America and the Caribbean.

5. Albert Hirschman, *National Power and the Structure of Foreign Trade* (Berkeley: University of California Press, 1980, original published in 1945) and *Exit, Voice, and Loyalty: Responses to Decline in Firms, Organizations and States* (Cambridge: Cambridge University Press, 1970); Hyman Minsky, *Can "It" Happen Again? Essays on Instability and Finance* (New York: M.E. Sharpe, Inc., 1982); and Amartya Sen, *Poverty and Famines: An Essay on Entitlement and Deprivation* (Oxford: Oxford University Press, 1981).

6. Benedict Anderson, *Imagined Communities: Reflections on the Origin and Spread of Nationalism* (London: Verso, 1983); Ernest Gellner, *Nations and Nationalism* (Oxford: Blackwell, 1983); and Charles Tilly, *Coercion, Capital, and European States, AD 990-1990* (Cambridge, MA: Basil Blackwell, 1990.)

7. Hirschman, *National Power*, 98.

8. In this respect, my argument supports some of the work of others on this era. See Bulmer-Thomas, op. cit.

9. Paul A. Baran, *The Political Economy of Growth* (New York: Monthly Review Press, 1967, orig. 1957).

10. Peter B. Evans, *Dependent Development: The Alliance of Multinational, State and Local Capital in Brazil* (Princeton: Princeton University Press, 1979).

11. For a basic anthology on rent-seeking behavior, see James M. Buchanan, Robert D. Tollison, and Gordon Tullock, *Toward a Theory of the Rent-Seeking Society* (College Station: Texas A&M University Press, 1980). Mancur Olson, *The Rise and Decline of Nations: Economic Growth, Stagflation, and Social Rigidities* (New Haven: Yale University Press, 1982) provides an excellent application of rent-seeking theory to the issues of national development.

12. I elaborate this discussion of politics and issues in economic development in "Latin America, Underdevelopment, and the Rentier State."

13. Hossein Mahdavy, "The Problems of Economic Development in Rentier States: The Case of Iran," in M.A. Cook. ed., *Studies in the Economic History of the Middle East from the Rise of Islam to the Present Day* (London: Oxford University Press, 1970), 428.

14. Jürgen Habermas, *The Structural Transformation of the Public Sphere: An Inquiry into a Category of Bourgeois Society*, trans. by Thomas Burger (Cambridge, Mass.: MIT Press, 1989).

15. Hirschman, *Exit, Voice, and Loyalty*, especially chap. 7, "A Theory of Loyalty," 76-105.

16. See, Joan Scott, "Gender: A Useful Category of Historical Analysis," *American Historical Review* 91: 5 (December 1986): 1059-75.

1

Chile and the
Financial Pyramid

It turns out that the fundamental instability of a
capitalist economy is a tendency to explode—to
enter into a boom or "euphoric state."

Hyman Minsky, *Can "It" Happen Again?*[1]

Chile never played an important role in the Spanish Empire nor did it define any key moments in the history of Latin American nation-states. Still, Chileans, by the 1920s, developed a strong sense of nationalism and pride. In contrast to their neighbors, they had held regular elections since the 1830s, under-girded by a complex civic culture and a multi-party system. The military was not central to politics. Beginning in the 1880s, the economy grew dramatically, fueled by nitrate and copper exports. Despite extremes of wealth and poverty, reformers sought the integration of a growing population into political life. The number of registered voters expanded from 49 thousand in 1873 to 122.5 thousand in 1885. In a population of 2.5 million, almost 20 percent of the adult male population was eligible to vote.[2] Reformers invoked the ideals of liberalism and spoke in favor of continuing the expansion of the suffrage. From 1880 to 1900, the number of government jobs increased from 3 to 13 thousand; by 1925, excluding the military and railroad workers, the government employed 28 thousand—many of them school teachers.[3]

Within the context of Latin American societies, Chile appeared a temperate place. The odd shape of the country, some one-hundred-fifty miles at its widest and two-thousand miles long, might have led to pronounced regionalism. But most people lived in the central and extensive valley, where the Spanish conquistadors had put down their deepest roots. The highly centralized government was a republic, with a national judiciary, a bicameral legislature, and an executive branch; but it had no provincial legislatures. All provincial intendants and governors were appointed by the president, with congressional approval. Municipal aldermen [*alcaldes*] were the only locally elected officials.

The capital, Santiago, only fifty miles from the coast, was over a mile above sea level, with a spectacular view of the Andes. By the 1920s, it was several times the size of the next major population center, and it was the nation's financial center, having replaced Valparaiso, the port that had boomed in the age of British capital but was largely ignored by U.S. entrepreneurs.

Agriculture remained the major source of employment. Like many other areas in Latin America, Chile's countryside was divided into large estates and small farms. The haciendas [often called *fundos*] dominated rural markets and were chiefly devoted to growing wheat and raising cattle; some had developed an increasingly sophisticated viticulture in the region near Santiago. Small farms clustered around the major cities and around larger estates. The *inquilino*, a type of tenant farmer, and peons or casual laborers were the most common forms of rural employees. Rural production was severely hampered by the Andes and the shortage of water in most of the country.

From the 1840s on, Chile's export economy, which was administered by laws issued from Santiago, had been located in the northern or southern provinces. From 1840 to 1870, the north (later labeled Norte Chico) was a copper-mining zone, and the south, around the city of Concepción, was a frontier zone devoted to wheat production. In the 1870s, Chileans moved into the Atacama Desert, to areas owned by Bolivia and Peru that exported sodium nitrate [*salitre*]. At the end of the decade, Bolivia, Chile and Peru looked to these nitrate deposits to offset the consequences of a financial downturn in the Atlantic economy. The outcome of this competition was the War of the Pacific (1879-83), in which Chile conquered the nitrate provinces, taking Antofagasta from Bolivia and Tarapacá from Peru. Nitrate, used as a fertilizer or to make gunpowder, became Chile's economic cornerstone until the early 1920s.

There are several well-established characteristics of the nitrate era prior to the crisis of the Parliamentary Regime in the 1920s. The economy grew at about three percent per year, but this barely outpaced the increase in population. Productivity was especially low in agriculture, a recent attempt to measure it fails to show any increase between 1880 and 1910 and finds only a 33 percent increase over the next twenty years. One cannot, however, blame agriculture alone for the poor performance: mining productivity fell through the nitrate era and manufacturing was at about the same level in the mid-1920s as in 1880.[4] As Table 1.1 demonstrates, government spending was a key economic sector well before the 1920s. Prior to the nitrate boom, government expenditures almost equaled 39 percent of agricultural output—no small amount. By 1910, however, they exceeded agricultural output and remained greater for the rest of the era. While Arturo Alessandri and Carlos Ibáñez built the state dramatically in the 1920s, they were working within a political system that was already committed to public spending as an economic stimulus.

In Chile, like much of rest of the Atlantic world, the 1920s were years of harsh adjustments. Politically, the Parliamentary Regime, dating from the civil war of 1891 and based on nitrate exports, was exhausted.

Table 1.1: Economic Growth in the Nitrate Era, 1870-1930
(In millions of 1908-1910 pesos)

Year	Agriculture	Mining	Government Expenditure	Index,Labor Productivity (1930=100)	Annual Rate, GDP (per cap. %)
1870	131	32	52	107	1.3
1880	157	82	87	95	1.8
1890	275	208	191	126	1.1
1900	232	283	194	90	1.1
1910	260	441	333	85	1.1
1920	334	301	389	92	1.4
1930	473	612	569	100	1.4

Source: Gert Wagner, "Trabajo, producción y crecimiento. La economía chilena, 1860-1930" (Santiago: Pontifícia Universidad Católica de Chile, Instituto de Economía, Documento de Trabajo no. 150, octubre 1992). Production figures based on series B, constant pesos from 1908-1910, cuadros. 1.2, AGR5, TC6.[5]

It was unable to respond to the demands for relief from the depression following World War I or to demands to changes laws governing labor and social welfare. The balance of trade remained positive, but similar to other nations of the time Chile's government did not calculate the importance of the balance of payments. Despite a surge of exports in the mid- to late-1920s, the economy seemed sluggish.[6] The nation was only beginning to address the social consequences of export-oriented expansion: the rapid growth of cities accompanied by housing shortages, a deterioration of real wages, and the continuing misery in the countryside. Until 1924, the small political class could pretend that these difficulties would go away. Then the political order began to unravel.

The Dream of Ibáñez

The names of two men intertwine in this history of crisis and political renewal that runs from the 1920s into the 1940s: Arturo Alessandri Palma and Carlos Ibáñez del Campo. Of modest origins, both made their careers denouncing oligarchic rule. Both championed the rise of professionalism and the middle class and claimed to be protectors of the working class. When he seized power, Ibáñez recruited some of Alessandri's supporters who claimed they were promoting Alessandrismo without Alessandri.[7] The events during and after 1924 put them at odds and they came to detest and distrust one another. Ibáñez owed one of his most important promotions to Alessandri, and repaid the debt by twice forcing him from the presidency. Alessandri hated Ibáñez with a single-minded intensity. Their battles contributed to the end of the Parliamentary Regime and the beginning of a new political order. They shaped the rhetoric of their time and were central to many of the political moments of three decades: the 1920s, 1930s, and 1940s.

The phrase *Parliamentary Regime* is something of a misnomer since the government was not run by a prime minister and the president did not serve at the will of Congress. But it covers the period from 1891 until 1924. In the earlier year, a congressional rebellion overthrew President José Manuel Balmaceda. The president had spent nitrate revenues freely in a drive to diversify the nation's economy, improve its infrastructure, and institute the beginnings of a state industrial policy. Congress demanded a system of accountability and an end to presidential control of the polls. The president held his ground, opposing what he saw as a pack of spoils men in league with British capital. The rebels used the new navy, went to the nitrate fields, seized the government's major source of income, and used it to build an army of nitrate laborers equipped with new weapons. Balmaceda's forces lost in two very one-sided battles. The president, rather than surrender, entered the Argentine Embassy, wrote a farewell accusing his opponents of selling out the nation, and then committed suicide. The victors curtailed executive authority. Congress rewrote election laws, placing local officials in control who used their powers to promote their own parties.[8] Congress also acquired the ability to depose any cabinet member—a right it often used. Chieftains, in Chile's multi-party system, forged congressional coalitions as they fought over patronage. It became extremely difficult for any president to implement policies consistently.[9] Thus, the result of curtailing autocratic behavior and improving the role of Congress became political drift, endless fights over spoils, and eventual widespread political cynicism. In reaction, Congress rehabilitated Balmaceda's reputation. By 1920, the Parliamentary Regime was an object of public contempt. Even in elite editorials, the defeated "dictator" of 1891 had become the "martyred president."

Elections after 1891 involved government intervention at the polls, bribery on a massive scale, and the use of legislative certification to remove unwanted victors. There were 383 thousand registered voters in 1920. Only literate adult males could vote and, of those inscribed, about 57 percent (164 thousand) went to the polls.[10] Nineteenth-century conflicts over the role of the Church and the centralization of national authority in Santiago continued into the twentieth century and were complicated by increasing demands for social legislation on behalf of a struggling middle class and an impoverished work force. By the onset of World War I, an urban public interested in issues of development and social justice confronted an entrenched political class that seemed unassailable in its control of money and legislative coalitions.[11]

Arturo Alessandri's election to the presidency in 1920 was another blow to the Parliamentary Regime.[12] He was a lawyer and a Liberal, whose career began in the 1890s and who had served in Congress and in the cabinet. Nevertheless, he was considered an outsider by the Chilean upper class. He had made his mark running for senator in the nitrate region in 1915, when his tirades against elite control earned him the title, "the Lion of Tarapacá." He won the presidency on a reform ticket, but he was inaugurated only after holding rallies that threatened the government with massive violence if his victory was not upheld. After his inauguration, his opponents, led by the Conservatives and the upper crust of the Liberals, dominated the Senate and prevented the passage of bills he proposed that would raise taxes, protect labor, and improve highways and schools. The postwar depression and the legislative impasse led Alessandri to increase government borrowing and print more money, generating inflation and intensifying class conflicts over real wages. The peso's value in 1924 was less than half of what it had been in 1910; prices rose almost 140 percent in the same period.[13]

On September 5, 1924, junior army officers, hit by the rising cost of living and furious over the inability of the government to pass a budget, staged a bloodless coup. Alessandri would later admit, in a piece of disingenuousness, that he had supported the military men in their initial demands, which coincided with his own, and was then surprised and betrayed by the officers' "exaltation" and refusal to return to the barracks. He had tried to use the soldiers against Congress and the attempt had backfired.[14] The officers presented themselves as servants of the nation; they demanded their pay increase and the passage of new labor laws. The Parliamentary Regime was over. Alessandri went into exile. The junior officers who led the coup gave way to their superiors. A junta composed of flag-rank officers turned rightist, disappointing the more liberal military movement, leaving the public disillusioned, and splitting the ranks of the army. To fend off an internal crisis, the army recalled Alessandri and restored him to office in 1925—scarcely six months after his exile began.

A new Constitution was promulgated that very year. It did not expand the suffrage but concentrated on the relative powers of the president and Congress. The president no longer needed congressional permission to make cabinet appointments or changes. Congress could, however, "impugn" a cabinet minister, that is, accuse and convict him of unconstitutional conduct. The president had acquired the authority to sponsor bills relating to the government budget; and he alone could name military officers for promotion, subject to approval of Congress.[15] Separation of Church and state was established.[16] As one scholar has noted, this last change left the Conservative Party without its major ideological plank. It also left the middle-class Radical Party without its plank, which opposed the Conservatives on Church-related issues.[17] All future political fights would occur in a more "secularized" landscape, thus moving discussion leftward.

When Alessandri tried to use his presidential powers, a crisis erupted within his cabinet. The soldiers had returned to the barracks, but Ibáñez as Minister of War made it plain that he thought the army now had a permanent voice in government. An indication of the extent of authority the military had acquired was evident in the official interpretation of the army massacre of 1200 striking nitrate miners at the site of La Coruña in Antofagasta. Alessandri was forced to support the army's account of events.[18] Then another stalemate developed in Congress. The president, in order to build legislative support, asked for the resignation of all his cabinet members. He appeared to be returning to the parliamentary game of building congressional coalitions by awarding ministries to various parties—a situation in which each minister felt entitled to dole out jobs to his party. Ibáñez calmly replied that he would not resign; he owed his position to the "revolution" of 1924. Considering this, Alessandri decided that since he could not control his own cabinet, he would not remain. He packed his bags and left Chile for Europe.

The political parties mounted a reaction to military rule in general, and Ibáñez, in particular. Ibáñez was maneuvering to run for the presidency.[19] The parties, especially on the right, still had formidable bases of power. The juntas in 1924 and 1925 rewrote some social and economic rules; but they made no attack on property.[20] The political parties, and their aging leaders, were still in place. Established interests, operating as party subgroups and based in agriculture, finance, and international trade, could still frustrate any changes that threatened their positions.[21] While acknowledging the enhanced authority of the military, they decided to back a member of the elite, Emilio Figueroa Larraín, for the presidency. On October 24, 1925, Figueroa Larraín was elected president. But Ibáñez remained as Minister of War and, by 1927, had become Minister of the Interior, the most important cabinet position. Controlling the police and a major section of the bureaucracy, Ibáñez easily embroiled the weak Figueroa in a political scandal. When Figueroa resigned in April 1927, Ibáñez became interim head of state, ran a rigged election, and became president with 98 percent of the vote.

Inaugurated on July 21, 1927, Ibáñez ruled with a combination of selective repression and populist achievements. He eliminated the leftist Chilean Federation of Labor [FOCh or Federación Obrera de Chile] while promulgating some of its objectives. Labor organizations lost their institutional autonomy and were reorganized into state-regulated syndicates. Formally, all such syndicates belonged to a state-administered Confederation of the Republic for Social Action [CRAC, Confederación Republicana de Acción Social]. The agency openly borrowed its organizational structure from Mussolini.[22] Ibáñez ruthlessly put down anarchists and communists, sending many into an internal exile in isolated outposts of Chile's far north or south or to the Easter Islands. He exiled opponents of any stripe: financial speculator Gustavo Ross Santa María, who had tried to warn President Figueroa that Ibáñez was dangerous, was sent packing.[23] Several of Alessandri's key supporters, including Agustín Edwards, the banker, newspaper publisher, and diplomat, were also forced abroad. At the same time, Ibáñez pursued much of Alessandri's program and recruited Alessandristas into the new government. Ibáñez belonged to no party, seeing himself as above partisanship.

Ibáñez was a product of his time, a man with a military background and an autocratic personality. He came from a rural gentry with little money, and therefore wielded no social power. His life in the military was, until 1920, one of provincial postings and lousy pay. While on assignment in El Salvador in 1912, he met and married his first wife. While senator for Tarapacá, Alessandri met Ibáñez, who was then head of police in the provincial capital, Iquique. Alessandri had promoted Ibáñez to assignments in Santiago in 1920. There, the colonel, now a widower, found an environment in which a few determined men made a major difference. He believed in loyalty and punished any dissent. He had no interest in literature or the arts. An admirer of Mussolini and Primo de Rivera, he copied some of their rhetoric and many of their practices. He styled himself a modernizing *caudillo*, a man who welcomed technological change. (He helped create Chile's air force.) He despised the elite of the Parliamentary Regime, but as president in 1927, married into it. An ornate ceremony was held. From one of the nation's most aristocratic families, his new wife, Graciela Letelier Velasco, was twenty-five years younger than he.[24] He recruited talent from the middle class and claimed to be building a meritorious society. He surrounded himself with educated men, hungry for government employment, and opened bureaucratic doors for young professionals.

There was a readiness to restructure government. His government supported the new over the old, the middle class over what it considered a decrepit oligarchy, and the interests of the United States over those of Great Britain. And, finally, he styled himself the patriotic and patriarchal provider, who bestowed public works on a scale never before seen in Chile. His program concentrated on highways, warehouses, and other elements of the commercial infrastructure. It kept unemployment low; real wages were rising in 1928 and 1929.

The general success of Ibáñez' achievements and the way in which the public accepted the loss of freedom of speech and assembly caught all elements of the political system by surprise. Unlike his contemporary in Mexico, Plutarco Elías Calles, Ibáñez did not have to deal with any militant rural movements. Like Augusto Leguía, the caudillo of Peru who imposed civic peace on Lima in the 1920s, Ibáñez successfully coopted elements of the established parties and combined them with support from the military. Unlike Leguía, he retained the Congress.[25] Legislators kept their positions and perks; but real power moved to the presidency and to Ibáñez' inner circle.

Even before he became president, while still in the cabinet, Ibáñez had made his corporatism clear: government existed "to organize the productive forces that are the only solid basis for regenerating a national economy."[26] It was the state that would reform society and the economy. The creation of an income tax, which Alessandri had first proposed, changes in the rules of labor recruitment, and the state-imposed labor syndicates meant that the wealthy might be held accountable to governmental authority.[27] (In fact, they were not forced to account for very much.) In 1927, Ibáñez' first year as chief executive, the national government spent 23 million pesos; but by 1930, his last full year in office, that figure rose to 83.5 million.[28]

Without a massive increase in taxes (the income tax was minimal) or a substantial gain in export earnings, the country remained at the margins of an international economy. Ibáñez beat the nationalist drum consistently but knew very well that Chile's future lay in cooperating with the United States. He always accompanied his public utterances with private assurances to foreign corporations that basic property rights would remain unchanged. During a visit to the United States, his Minister of Hacienda, Pablo Ramírez, urged closer ties between Chile and U.S. businessmen by stating, "We now need capital, lots of capital at reasonable rates of interest, in order to develop and expand our unfettered industries."[29] Playing this game of international investment required brokering favors to domestic interests while not offending foreign ones to the point that they withdrew. His program included greater regulation of utilities, airlines, and the oil industry. He tried to subsidize a diversification of exports. A comprehensive plan was drawn up at the end of 1929 to build up viticulture, with government subsidized vats for wine (as storehouses), new rail links, and even pipelines to major terminals at Valparaiso, San Antonio, and Talcahuano.[30] He offered other subsidies to producers of vegetable oil and rice, to southern lumber interests, and to northern fishermen.[31] In all this lay the beginnings of an idea Alessandri had not entertained: Chile could not rely on mining forever and should use its mining income to provide for that inevitability. The last president to propose such a policy had been José Manuel Balmaceda.

Ibáñez and the United States

Chile, like much of Latin America at the end of the nineteenth century, had based an expanding economy and society on foreign trade. It exchanged its minerals for manufactures, capital goods, and the coal and oil needed to keep its mines and small factories working.[32] The Crash of 1929-31 closed the nitrate mines and forced the copper companies to cut production sharply. Industry and agriculture contracted; the entire economy spiraled downward. Chile's populace was poor even in prosperous times: in 1931, beggary was commonplace. Families roamed the countryside subsisting on wild greens. The government put many of the unemployed in urban warehouses; even then, thousands remained homeless.

In global surveys of the depression's impact, Chile headed the list of nations with the greatest loss of income. Nitrates had been 42 percent and copper, 40 percent of all exports; together they accounted for 40 percent of the total national output. Between 1929 and 1932, the total value of exports fell 42 percent, that of imports 87 percent. Total gross domestic product dropped almost 36 percent.[33] However, comparing Chile to the rest of the globe is rather meaningless; any meaningful comparisons must be to other Latin American nations. The same League of Nations' data cited above notes that in these years, the exports of Argentina, Brazil, and Mexico all fell more than 60 percent (Mexico's dropped 66 percent); imports for each country declined 70-75 percent.[34] One could argue that Chile's exports made up a larger share of its total economy. But total trade was just as important to Argentina as it was to Chile.[35] So, the severity in Chile's experience cannot be explained exclusively through an index of trade. As we shall see, it was the relationship between trade and the structure of the economy, on the one hand, and trade and the structure of government, on the other, that explains why Chile endured a much sharper collapse than above-mentioned nations. Reviewing the statistics in the 1980s, Angus Maddison gave a more conservative estimate of Chile's downturn during the Crash: it was only 26.5 percent. In his calculations, however, this was still considerably worse than the regional average of 13.5 percent and that of the other nations previously mentioned: Argentina, 14.8 percent; Brazil, 1.2 percent; and Mexico, 19 percent.[36]

The collapse, in Chile as elsewhere, caught politicians and businessmen completely by surprise. They shared the global illusions of late 1929 that the depression would last only a year or two, during which time they could survive on borrowed funds. The depression of 1919-21 was the guide. As World War I ended, the prices of nitrate and copper plunged, but rose again in the mid-1920s. The same had been true of earlier depressions; the world market for minerals always had recovered.

The 1930s would be different. Changes in the global economy during the 1920s increased competition, reducing prices and profitability. In the copper sector, output rose during the war and continued to rise in the 1920s, not only in Chile but also in Europe, the western United States, Mexico, and Peru. The surge ended with a glut on the market. Chilean copper production was a quarter of the world's supply in 1929; exports were two and one-half times what they had been in 1917. But by 1932 the value of copper exports had dropped to 15 percent of its 1929 level. Sales to the United States alone dropped from US$56 to 6 million.[37]

The collapse of the nitrate sector was even worse. From the War of the Pacific until 1914, sodium nitrate, or salitre, had been the world's major source of non-organic nitrogen. The world war isolated Chile from its major customer, Germany, which began producing synthetic nitrogen on a large scale. After the war, other nations built hydroelectric plants that produced nitrogen as a by-product. The world nitrate market grew but Chile's share declined: from 56 percent in 1913, when it sold 430 thousand metric tons; to 37 percent in 1918; and to 23 percent in 1929, when it sold 444 thousand metric tons.[38] The Crash and a global oversupply of fertilizers reduced nitrate exports; by 1932 they were only 26 percent of what they had been three years before.

The nitrate sector had benefitted Chileans in a number of ways. At the end of the War of the Pacific in 1883, British companies dominated the sector. Although British managers remained important to the industry until the Crash, Chileans gradually bought stock until, by the early 1920s, they owned a majority of nitrate company shares. Nitrate exports influenced the fiscal policy of the government and affected the general economy. From 1880 until the late 1920s, a tax on nitrate exports provided a major part of the government's revenues from 1880 until the late 1920s. An analysis of nitrate-generated income found that the government's export duty claimed about a third of the total, another third went to the costs of production, and the rest to the mine owners. A reasonable guess is that Chile, in terms of taxes and money spent by the nitrate sector, gained about 55 percent of all income generated by the trade.[39] Whenever the trade-based duties fell short, the government printed up more money, thereby devaluing the currency, or borrowed abroad. So, its international line of credit was closely tied to nitrate prosperity. The development of the nitrate zone stimulated the creation of industry and the expansion of agriculture. The success of nitrates attracted new foreign investment into other exports: the aforementioned copper, wool, iron ore, and borax.

World War I and its aftermath altered Chile's prospects.[40] As a result of the war, the United States replaced Britain as the world's industrial and commercial power. The major capitalists of the United States and Europe accelerated their experimentation with cartels in order to reduce risks. During the war, British merchant banks, principally the Baring Brothers and the Rothschilds, were unable to play their traditional role as Chile's lenders of last resort. The Morgan financial group and the First National City Bank, both based in New York, replaced them. From that point forward, Chile relied first on New York and second on London for government loans and private financing. Trade follows finance. By the end of the war, the United States had displaced Britain as Chile's major trading partner. This was a trend characteristic of all Latin America: by 1929, the United States had over 25 percent of the region's imports compared to 12 percent for Britain.[41]

The impact of cartels evolved over a longer period. The British interests that dominated the nitrate trade in the 1880s and 1890s had cooperated, periodically, with one another to reduce output and raise prices. The chief speculator in that era, John T. North, won notoriety for coordinating these "pools." But these efforts were usually short-lived. Chile's nitrate duty was tied to the volume of exports. Therefore, the government countered the cartel policies by selling off deposits, which raised output and led to the formation of new companies. Gradual improvements in technology also gave new producers an incentive to capture market shares by undercutting the pool price. As older deposits wore out and new machinery was deployed, the center of the industry moved from Tarapacá Province to the one south of it, Antofagasta Province. After World War I, the prospects of an international nitrate cartel, combined with possible gains from new U.S. technology, drew the Guggenheims into a gamble that altered the structure of the entire sector.

The Guggenheims were then in their second generation as successful American entrepreneurs; Daniel Guggenheim, the eldest of seven brothers, still ran a firm that began as a merchant fortune. In the 1880s, the brothers plunged into American silver mining in Colorado and Nevada, and in the 1890s, expanded to Mexico. Early in the twentieth century, they added copper mining to their interests even as they became important players in the mining trust of the American Smelting and Refining Company. By the early 1920s, their assets amounted to perhaps US$200 million.[42]

They had invested in Chile's copper mines as a means of competing with the Rockefellers, who dominated the American Smelting and Refining Company. They played a crucial role in the large-scale development of El Teniente mine in Rancagua Province. In 1915, they drew together El Teniente and mines in Mexico and the United States, and formed the Kennecott Copper Corporation. Under a separate corporate scheme, they also owned Chuquicamata, an open-pit mine in Antofagasta, which they developed during war. By the 1920s, as Chile's share of the world copper market jumped from almost nothing two decades before to about 15 percent, the Guggenheims had become major investors in American Smelting, which they used to refine their ore.[43]

By the early 1920s, the Guggenheims and another U.S. firm, Anaconda, dominated the industry: the Guggenheims had Chuqui, which was run as the Chile Exploration Company; through Kennecott, they controlled El Teniente, which was operated under the name of the of the Braden Copper Company; and Anaconda owned Potrerillos, run as Andes Copper Mining Company.[44] These firms were part of a consolidation of capital in the United States, which was then projected abroad. By the 1920s, 130 of the 300 thousand non-financial corporations in the United States controlled US$54.7 billion or 80 percent of all the capital listed on the New York Stock Exchange. Two hundred corporations, including the largest financial conglomerates, held US$67.1 billion, almost half of all the corporate wealth and 19 percent of all assets in the United States.[45] Any one of these corporations had access to greater financial resources, administrative skills, and technological talent than was available to the government of Chile. Unlike the British, who had built their economic bases in Chile over a century and through a number of merchant and mining firms, U.S. capital invaded through a few major enterprises. The Guggenheims and Anaconda intended their Chilean holdings to complement their global copper strategies. Then in 1923, the Guggenheims sold Chuquicamata to Anaconda and gambled heavily on income from nitrates. They hoped that by adapting the technology used in copper mining, they could completely dominate nitrate production. Instead, this maneuver compounded the nitrate sector's already evident problems and helped bring down the Chilean government.

* * *

Ibáñez' dream provoked a reaction from foreign and domestic capitalists. They supported his repression of the left, even as they resisted enforcement of any labor laws. They accepted his offer of government subsidies to particular sectors, but rejected more government regulation of trade. Chilean businessmen supported his nationalism; they wanted a state that would help them gain a larger share of the market.[46] Neither Ibáñez nor domestic capitalists wanted autarky; their goals involved establishing new rules within a dependent economy. For Chilean financiers, industrialists, and agricultural exporters, Ibáñez was successful because he controlled labor while strengthening their ability to bargain with entities such as Standard Oil of New Jersey and Kennecott.

Ibáñez sought foreign investment. His government was part of a regional trend, substituting an enhanced capacity to borrow as an alternative to higher taxes. But Ibáñez also had hopes of enlarging Chile's domestic industrial base and, in imitation of caudillos elsewhere, of adorning his administration with state-led initiatives in airlines and oil. In pursuing such hopes, he counted on foreign loans. Foreign companies, particularly those from the United States, repeatedly demanded that he scale down his nationalist ambitions and back away from more regulations and higher taxes. Contests followed in which Ibáñez lost confrontations over key sectors but sometimes won those on regulations or taxes. He tried, for example, to get the copper and nitrate companies to use Chilean coal and shipping. They refused, and with backing from the U.S. government, forced him to back away from his position. But he succeeded in imposing an income tax on Anaconda and Kennecott that almost tripled government revenues from copper.[47]

One of the most important confrontations was over electricity. Under a 1925 law, Chileans were supposed to own and operate all domestic power. The president could make exceptions, and did, for Chile's largest utility, the British-owned Chilean Electric Company, Limited [Compañía Chilena de Electricidad]. It produced power for Santiago and Valparaiso, some 85 percent of the nation's total electric supply. In 1920, it generated 59 million kilowatt hours for Santiago; by 1929, it was producing 234 million.[48] But the high costs of expanding service discouraged the British. Municipal governments used electricity without paying for it, and, despite inflation, authorities repeatedly denied the tramway, a Chilean Electric subsidiary, any rate increases. In 1929, Chilean Electric sold out to the South American Power Company for US$50 million. South American Power was a subsidiary of the U.S.-based American and Foreign Power Company, Inc., which in turn was owned by General Electric and was taking over utilities in parts of Mexico and in Buenos Aires and Rio de Janeiro at about the same time.[49] Tired of arguing with the British, the Ibáñez government at first welcomed the sale. It soon began arguing with the Americans over the same issues: rate increases and municipal bills. The president tried to grandstand on the issue by appointing a congressional committee to investigate the sale. The committee's recommendation was that Chile imitate Germany and begin nationalization of all utilities.[50]

Ibáñez used the recommendation to pressure the company for money; he wanted US$8 million in company improvements and a US$2 million loan to the national government. He won, and in addition to these demands, also gained a consolidation of millions of dollars in municipal electric bills into a long-term loan. In return, the government agreed the company could charge its fees in gold pesos and increase its electric and tramway rates to cover any currency depreciation.[51] The agreement, so happily announced, led to fifteen years of conflicts between the company and successive administrations.

The government also pursued nationalist policies toward airlines and the oil companies. The U.S. merchant and investment firm of William

R. Grace had created Pan American Grace Airways, an extension of its involvement in shipping. It secured mail contracts from the U.S. government to underwrite its efforts. In 1929, it won a ten-year contract to fly mail from Panama to Chile, Argentina, and Uruguay; it then demanded permission to land in Chile. Even U.S. Embassy officials criticized its high-handed behavior.[52] Chilean officials wanted Grace to pay generously for landing rights. They demanded that the new airline serve travelers within Chile (the government especially sought links to the isolated north) and construct a domestic network of airports. The Chief of the Army Aviation Corps, Lt. Colonel Arturo Merino Benítez, proposed an agenda that would have had Grace build Chilean facilities then pull out as a national airline was formed.[53] U.S. Ambassador William Culbertson intervened and forced the Ibáñez administration to back down, arguing that airlines should no more be expected to build airports than shipping lines are expected to build ports.[54]

Ibáñez wanted a national oil company. All oil and gasoline were imported; Shell-Mexico, a British company, and West India Oil Company, a subsidiary of Standard Oil of New Jersey, controlled the market. One estimate said it cost over 50 million pesos a month to pay for gasoline for Santiago's new stock of imported cars and cover the cost of heating oil; this amount was about 40 percent of all Chilean imports.[55] Ibáñez first tried to attract foreign competition to reduce prices. He made direct overtures to Antony Gibbs, but the British firm refused to bid.[56] He then explored the possibility of establishing the country's first refinery and converting Chilean coal to gasoline. These efforts also failed.

Finally, he tried to create a government monopoly, believing its profits could eventually be used to build a refinery and enable Chile to buy its own transport equipment for rails and shipping. Standard Oil already faced a government-run oil company in Argentina. It panicked and demanded help from the U.S. State Department, claiming its US$150 million investment in all of Latin America was threatened by economic nationalism. The State Department was gearing up for a major confrontation with Ibáñez when his government collapsed.[57]

The most bizarre quarrel between foreign capital and the government involved General Motors and the Ibáñez' family. General Motors had established a small assembly plant in Santiago and a distribution network of dealerships. In 1930, it demanded immediate payment on all orders and forced car dealers into bankruptcy if they failed to comply.

One of these, Brasadelli and Manni, claimed it had been hit by a double claim for a single loan and that GM had altered its books.[58] The dealership retaliated by calling upon the best-connected lawyer of the era, Osvaldo Koch, the president's son-in-law.

Koch served as Minister of Justice between 1927 and 1930 but had been forced out in a scandal involving influence peddling. He continued in his other government post as editor of *La Nación*, the official newspaper, and took up a private practice that specialized in helping those needing a favor from a judge. In the eyes of the U.S. Ambassador, he was a cross between "Horatio Alger Jr. and Al Capone."[59] To help Brasadelli and Manni, Koch sued GM for fraud, claiming 18 million pesos in damages. Through use of his judicial connections, GM's assets were seized and its chief executive dragged out of bed at midnight and interrogated in a holding cell for two days. U.S. businessmen in Santiago were scandalized; the State Department and the U.S. Embassy in Santiago demanded an apology and a guarantee that there would be no further attacks on GM

The sides were drawn: the foreign, corporate giant against Chile. Throughout Latin America, newspapers denounced Yankee misbehavior. But General Motors approached other U.S. corporations and got support from the Guggenheims, who warned Ibáñez that the publicity in New York was hurting Chile's credit rating. The Guggenheims and Ibáñez were in the middle of reorganizing the nitrate sector through the formation of the Corporación de Salitre de Chile [COSACh], a corporate monopoly with semi-official status. Rather than risk the success of this venture, Ibáñez forced his son-in-law to drop the case.[60]

In his last two years in office, Ibáñez gambled Chile's future on the nitrate monopoly and an expansion of the government's debt. His policies in each area were related to the growing crisis in the export economy and illustrate how Ibáñez' plans depended on ties to the United States.

The Guggenheims had sold Chuqui in order to buy the Anglo-Chilean Consolidated Nitrate Corporation from British and Chilean investors. They used the company's resources to build the Maria Elena, a new refinery in Antofagasta Province. In 1927, they merged with Lautaro Nitrate Company, then controlled by Yugoslav immigrants. The combined operation, still called Anglo-Chilean but incorporated in the United States, started building another plant, the Pedro de Valdivia, near Tocopilla (also in Antofagasta Province). The company expected to finish the plant in two years. To cover its costs, Anglo-Chilean floated a US$32 million bond in New York through the National City Company, the largest U.S. bank in Chile.[61]

The Guggenheims assumed that, with new technology they had developed, they would soon dominate the nitrate industry. They expected profits as high as 30 percent.[62] Then, as prices fell they attempted to create a Chilean-based cartel to rescue the conglomerate. The cartel would assign export market shares and production quotas to all the salitre companies. They pressured the Ibáñez government to drop the nitrate export duty and adopt a tax based on the industry's profits.[63] When this proved inadequate, the idea of a cartel within Chile gave way to one involving a new Chilean corporation that would act on behalf of all producers in negotiating with the fertilizer companies in Europe. This was the origin of COSACh. The Guggenheims named E.A. Cappelen Smith, who already ran their Chilean nitrate interests, as negotiator and general manager. By early 1930, he was in charge of the overall consolidation of the sector.

Fearful that Chile would lose the fertilizer market to synthetic competition, Ibáñez agreed to the Guggenheim's plans and sent his Minister of Finance, Pablo Ramírez, a major nitrate speculator, to bargain on behalf of the government.[64] The new corporation was formed in New York in March 1931. Its agreement with Ibáñez stipulated that the government would own half of all COSACh shares, four of the twelve seats on the board of directors, a guaranteed income, and other benefits. In return, the government lost all say in management. The Guggenheims received the largest portion of the remaining stock, buried their nitrate debts in COSACh's general obligations, and gained executive control of the board. COSACh, capitalized at US$375 million, began with a US$219 million debt and with no working capital. It was the largest Guggenheim-controlled firm and the largest corporation in South America.[65]

Among its other consequences, the creation of COSACh completed the exile of the British in the nitrate industry. The British were already withdrawing from Chile: their investments in 1930 amounted to £72 million, about £7 million less than in 1926. Most of the British investment was in Chilean government bonds, the nitrate industry, and nitrate railroads.[66] They were left with no role in COSACh and had none in the copper sector; trade links dating to the nineteenth century disappeared. The firm of Antony Gibbs and Sons, an adviser to the Guggenheims, now found itself cut out of the conglomerate.[67] A British banker complained, in February 1930, "of the almost complete American monopoly of the Nitrate and Copper interests," which purchased supplies only from the United States.[68] The new corporation concentrated all production in Antofagasta Province. Of the 80 non-Guggenheim plants, only three still operated in early 1931; abandoned factories or salitreras dotted the nitrate provinces.[69] By mid-1930, Tarapacá's major port, Iquique, was flooded with unemployed nitrate miners. The government did what had been done in other downturns and moved the workers south to the warehouses of Valparaiso and Santiago and sent some into the countryside.

The government did not want an explosive social situation in a regional port. A government unemployment agency reported it had sent 50,413 people out of the north; of these, 24,328 were unemployed men.[70] Wages in the nitrate zone dropped an average of 40 percent from the previous year.[71] Several thousand remained in the North, including hundreds of white-collar workers dismissed from the nitrate plants and merchant houses. The government maintained them by illegally raiding Chile's Social Security Fund [Caja Social].[72]

Ibáñez knew that industrial consolidation would cut jobs but counted on the government's income from COSACh and access to U.S. credit to sustain a public works program that would absorb the displaced.[73] The Guggenheims, in turn, expected COSACh to give them substantial leverage in an international cartel. In June 1930, the "Chilean" delegation headed by Guggenheim executives took part in negotiations that created the European Nitrogen Agreement [Convention de l'Industrie de l'Azote (CIA)]. The key firms taking part were I.G. Farben, heading the German Nitrogen Syndicate; Norsk Hydro, dominating the Scandinavian producers; and English Industrial Chemical. Considered a model for its time, CIA was soon overwhelmed by the world glut in nitrogen and fell apart in June 1931.[74]

As the nitrate sector collapsed, Ibáñez turned to his remaining economic crutch, foreign banks. Chile was part of a global expansion of public debt, in which New York banks played the central role. This boom started when New York financiers became the brokers of German debts, a development tied to the complexities of Germany's war-time reparations. Once they discovered how easy it was to sell these bonds in the United States, they began brokering loans for governments around the world. The United States shipped money out at record rates; in 1928 alone, long-term capital investments abroad amounted to US$3.2 billion. Europe received the largest share of U.S. capital, followed by Canada; Latin America was third.[75] Latin American regimes, with the exception of Mexico, which had suspended its debt payments during the Revolution, mortgaged their future to build public works and patronage networks. In 1921, U.S. buyers held US$187.4 million in Latin American national government bonds and another US$42 million in Latin American corporate issues; in 1930, they held over US$1.5 billion in government bonds and nearly US$700 million in corporate bonds. By 1930, total U.S. investment in the region was estimated by the U.S. Department of Commerce at between US$5.1 and US$5.3 billion.[76] There are a few observations worth making about the pattern of investment. The largest surge in buying government bonds came in the years 1926-28, coinciding with Ibáñez' rise to power—he hit the market at the best moment. Twenty percent of the European securities sold in the U.S. were issued by private corporations; but U.S. investors held only two percent of their Latin American portfolio in corporate bonds. The U.S. credit market was not a source of financing for native industrial development. Finally, most U.S. investment in Latin America was direct: private sector purchase of already existing companies or creation of new ones. The pattern of U.S. capital flows split into 68 percent in direct investments and 32 percent in portfolio. The pattern in Chile was almost exactly that average: 63 percent was direct, most of it in mining; and 37 percent in securities.[77]

The risks surrounding this lending frenzy were compounded by the influence of the gold standard. In the nineteenth century, the gold standard, in the form of the British pound, had provided the price stability and monetary security to expand trade and international investment.[78] But in the 1920s, the return to the gold standard by the major powers deflated prices almost everywhere, and had an especially sharp impact on agricultural and mineral products.[79] Worse, the United States was simultaneously the world's chief creditor and, partly through high tariffs, running a trade surplus that it turned into gold. As a result, countries found it very difficult to repay loans or balance trade deficits.[80] Gold was accumulating in a few countries. Out of the world's total gold stocks of US$11.5 billion in 1931, the United States had US$5 billion and France had US$2.3 billion. As one student of the period noted, the movement of gold was "perverse": it flowed from developing to already developed zones.[81]

Chile tried to play by the international rules. Edwin Walter Kemmerer, the famous "money doctor" of Princeton University, came to Santiago in 1925 and designed a central bank and rediscount system that put the gold standard at its center.[82] The decision led to greater monetary stability but left the internal credit structure extremely vulnerable to forces outside the nation's control. Any imbalance in trade would automatically lead to monetary contraction. Falling prices for primary products pushed Chile to cover the shortfall with foreign borrowing. When New York banks had begun lending massive sums abroad, more or less in 1924, they had tried to calculate their risks. But in the final stages of global credit expansion, that is from late 1928 to early 1930, these loans became *Ponzis*. Charles A. Ponzi, an Italian immigrant, has acquired a place in economic history for the simplicity of his scheme. Operating out of Boston in the early twentieth century, he promised higher returns than anyone else. He never invested the money; he instead attracted new investors and used their funds to pay any withdrawals. The scheme worked until someone demanded proof of his investment genius. In essence, a *Ponzi* consists of any financial arrangement in which assets and income cannot possibly cover obligations.[83]

A few in the United States warned against irresponsible lending. Among them, Herbert Hoover, then Secretary of Commerce, complained publicly; but he stopped when bankers warned him he was meddling in their affairs.[84] When Hoover made his pre-inaugural trip to South America, he went to Chile in 1928 and praised Ibáñez, who, in turn, bragged of his access to New York credit.[85]

By then, Ibáñez was breaking Chilean financial laws, but only Alessandri and his circle protested and their objections were issued in exile.[86] I discuss the total pattern of Ibáñez' borrowing in the last section of this chapter. Here, it is noted that in the figures that Ibáñez published, the government debt rose from 2.6 million gold pesos in 1922 to 4.1 in 1930, and debt service from 177 million to 279 million a year.[87] By consolidating some older loans, the percentage of government revenue devoted to debt service dropped from 47 to 24.[88] There were two problems in all this, Ibáñez was lying about the extent of the government's real obligations and there was little relationship between the source of credit (the United States) and how the money was being spent. The public works were not generating any foreign currency; income to pay for them would have to come from the mining sector. And then, its terms of trade—what Chile could import compared with what it could export—dropped a disastrous 45 percent between 1929 and 1932. This was a collapse worse than any other industrializing Latin American nation.[89] The government had no idea what was happening to the flow of capital. Reflecting fiscal practice of the time, it did not track the nation's balance of payments as opposed to its balance of trade. The trade balance was positive until 1931; but payments were obviously not, as money drained out of the nation.[90] The payments included profits paid to foreign investors and sums for foreign services such as insurance, shipping, and interest on business loans.[91] A hidden vulnerability existed in the nation's pattern of trade and finance.

In all, an unequal partnership evolved between the Ibáñez government and U.S. capital. Each side got what it wanted. Ibáñez received money without having to pay the political cost of raising taxes. He increased the size of the government, spending substantially on refitting the military and building highways. He called the result a "nationalist" government, and many middle-class lawyers and bureaucrats in his administration agreed. The Ministry of Finance became a stronghold of young engineers, called the *cabros* or "boys" of Pablo Ramírez, who were determined to reform state administration and introduce modern economic planning. Some of their efforts bore fruit. Changes in the state railways reduced its drain of the treasury, but at the cost of 5.7 thousand jobs.[92] By one estimate, in 1929, Chile and Uruguay ranked first in Latin America in terms of the weight of public spending on the economy.[93]

But this nationalism, while expanding the state, did little to influence foreign capital. U.S. interests at the end of the decade controlled Chile's copper and nitrates, its major telephone company, Santiago's electric and tramway company, and the nation's most important iron smelter. The country imported most of its capital goods from the United States and relied on imported oil supplied by Standard Oil of New Jersey and the British-owned Shell-Mexico Company. By the end of the decade, foreigners, led by U.S. investors, owned 46 percent of all industrial capacity.[94] Not surprisingly, despite their many quarrels with the government, most foreign businessmen were quite happy with the general tone and purpose of the administration.

The Crash

Until the Crash, Ibáñez could placate domestic interests with higher tariffs and more public works. Chile had increased its tariffs on manu-

Table 1.2: Real Wages in Chile, 1928-1931
(Jan. 1928=100)

Month	1928	1929	1930	1931
Jan.	100	129	140	109
Feb.	83	102	131	101
Mar.	99	115	130	
April	97	125	153	
May	100	121	123	
June	111	130	131	
July	95	135	116	
Aug.	102	122	123	
Sept.	110	134	115	
Oct.	113	134	115	
Nov.	114	142	125	
Dec.	133	165	115	
Ave.	105	130	127	105

Source: *Boletín de la Sociedad de Fomento Fabril*, 47:5 (May 1931), 339.

factures in 1916 and 1921. Ibáñez, in 1928, raised tariffs 15 percent on manufactures and agricultural goods, creating substantive protection. The rate on imported manufactures varied between 35 to 50 percent ad valorem, and the law allowed the president to use higher import revenues to subsidize the expansion of domestic manufactures.[95] Agricultural duties rose 45 percent. Landowners won an unpopular increase in the beef tariff.[96] Domestic prices increased, especially in Santiago; but there was little public complaint. The left had been silenced and almost everyone had a job. The middle class gained through the expansion of the bureaucracy and the growing financial sector in Santiago, while the public-works program helped raise real wages to record levels in 1929 (see Table 1.2 for real wage data). Wages rose 50 and 60 percent in 1928 and 1929, while prices rose only about 10 percent.[97]

The collapse of the nitrate economy rippled through the entire nation. COSACh-motivated consolidation drove unemployed workers into the nitrate ports and to the warehouses in Santiago. A commercial slump hit Valparaiso, which always had handled supplies to the nitrate provinces, and firms there were ruined.[98] The impact of the gold standard and export decline reduced the money supply. A squeeze on rural credit and farm prices led to a crisis in the countryside just as the unemployed nitrate workers arrived in small, southern towns looking for work. Government income fell and, by the last quarter of 1930, Ibáñez reluctantly cut back several departments and reduced pay in those remaining. Short-term extensions of credit became common in all sectors.[99]

As a result of Ibáñez' labor regulations, the labor movement had neither independent unions nor a militant leadership to face the crisis. Around 1926, the movement had 125 thousand members in a loose network of unions.[100] By 1929, there were about 29 thousand laborers and 8.5 thousand white-collar workers as members of the officially sanctioned syndicates.[101] Ibáñez' determination to control labor mobilization paralleled efforts by leaders in western Europe and the United States, where repression and the depression of older industries reduced the size of the union movements in the 1920s.[102] The administration argued that state-supported labor syndicates were a necessary correction to "the failure of liberal principles" and an antidote to communism. In general, these policies succeeded and by 1929, even labor organizations that recognized the class character of society, such as the Cooperative Committee of Valparaiso Syndicates, openly espoused their intention to avoid class conflict and promote "harmony between capital and labor."[103] At El Teniente, the Kennecott Corporation ran company unions and a paternalistic social welfare system that tried to tie men to the mine by rewarding marriage.[104]

Ibáñez defended his labor policies as, "simultaneously repressive and just."[105] The government, through inspectors in the Labor Department, tried to eliminate the worst abuses in company stores and labor-recruiting practices, and it imposed safety regulations in some of the largest factories and mines.[106] Among the government's most popular measures was the requirement that 75 percent of all laborers in major enterprises be Chilean.[107] Labor-management relations were affected but not transformed. The Labor Department was always undermanned and rarely confronted management. Government regulations avoided the countryside, where conditions were as brutal as ever and the authority of landlords was enforced by the new national police, the *carabineros*. An outraged congressman noted in 1930 a trend for rural laborers accused of theft or union militancy to die under carabinero torture.[108] Reports from provincial administrators in 1929 indicate that political parties had stopped appealing to laborers.[109]

Authorities often declared strikes to be illegal. A strike among bakers in Tocopilla ended in March 1929 when the governor arrested leaders, shut down the syndicates, and confiscated their funds.[110] The official attitude was one of patron to labor clients. Social justice was not on the agenda. Government-approved syndicates were passive in 1930, even though their membership was experiencing drastic declines in wages and sky-rocketing unemployment. This does not mean, of course, that all labor militancy stopped. Recent research claims that some anarcho-syndicalists, who had survived the repression of 1927, mobilized dock workers in the late 1920s.[111]

Ibáñez deprived any potential opposition of a chance to mobilize when, in 1930, he simply appointed the existing Congress with some minor changes in personnel. He justified this maneuver by claiming that the cancellation of elections saved the country an unnecessary expense. As the crisis descended, Ibáñez attempted a political alliance that united labor, the middle class, and his bureaucratic support (including major elements of the army) against the oligarchy. In May 1931, he proposed new labor legislation with more generous provisions on hours and basic wages. The Chambers of Commerce and the Society for Industrial Development [Sociedad de Fomento Fabril or SOFOFA] vigorously protested.[112] He counted on salary increases and new hardware to maintain military support. Among other achievements, he had turned the Chilean air force into the fifth largest in the world.[113] The official labor syndicates went along, but not the middle class. Allied with conservatives, the middle class in Santiago brought the government down.

Understanding what was at stake requires a brief glance at the social composition of the labor force and the extent to which the middle class was able or willing to change the political direction of the country. The census of 1930 listed only 29 percent of the population in the active work force. This amounted to a million men and 185 thousand women. The major sectors of employment were 40 percent in agriculture and fishing, 23 percent in industry, almost 12 percent in commerce, and 6 percent in mining. The only noticeable change from the 1920 census was that in the earlier counting, 30 percent were listed in industry. The broad category of commerce, some 147 thousand people, included most of the private sector middle class as well as newspaper boys and women selling herbs in the central town markets. Forty thousand men were involved in "administration" of some kind, an additional 20 thousand in the national defense, and 12 thousand in the "liberal professions." This last category also included over 14 thousand women, of whom 11.6 thousand were school teachers.[114]

Women received about half the wages the men earned, even when they gained comparable employment, which was not common. As an example, they were banned from working in the El Teniente Copper Mine.[115] They suffered from a patriarchal bias that labeled any woman who worked "sexually promiscuous."[116] Society viewed their wages as supplementary, even though it was common that women headed households. In the cities, they were concentrated in domestic service and factories. Because of low wages and income instability, they were often forced into casual prostitution, but that traditional behavior ran into increased regulation in the 1920s. The military junta in 1925 had passed the Law in Defense of the Race, providing for medical inspection of prostitutes and linking the campaign against prostitution with efforts against other social diseases such as alcoholism.[117] In the countryside, their labor was often not even registered in the census.[118]

For reasons that are not entirely clear, women became a smaller part of the active labor force between 1890 and 1930, and especially declined in numbers in Santiago's factories: there were 135 thousand of them in industry in 1907 and only 70 thousand in that category in 1930. Recent scholarship points to the increasing cult of domesticity and motherhood that the state and the media promoted.[119] There is evidence that here, as well, the census failed to record reality. Women remained most of the manufacturing labor force in food, textiles, and clothing. Another factor was the expansion of home work, a "putting-out" system, in which women stayed home and sewed shoes and clothing from pieces provided by a contractor.[120]

If the census is interpreted with an eye to maximizing its size, the middle class, including dependents, numbered 200 thousand. It comprised less than 15 percent of the economically active population and 5 percent of all Chileans and was concentrated in Santiago and Valparaiso.[121] Although its income was smaller, its social roles resembled the European middle class.[122] Given Chile's small manufacturing sector, most of the white-collar workers relied on the government, large commercial enterprises, retailing, and the professions to earn a living.

Although it has been asserted that the middle class lacked class-consciousness, it seems to have acted with as much class solidarity as labor, if not more.[123] It supported public schooling and state subsidies to the university. Because the government was their largest employer, members of the middle class also supported reforms that increased the role and size of the state; they strongly backed government intervention in the economy. Professional associations lobbied for state credit to various industries and for higher tariffs on manufactures.[124] The middle class also relied on regulations to limit access to the professions; by the late 1920s, anyone not educated in Chile had difficulty entering the practice of law or medicine. But the middle-class voice in professional guilds, political parties, and other civic organizations was not strong enough, either in terms of numbers or financial power, to greatly influence government or the elite. Nevertheless, by the 1920s, their contribution to public discussion was evident.

The middle class had enthusiastically supported Arturo Alessandri, and its members were grouped around the Radical and Liberal parties, although a few younger members dared to join the Democrats. Young professionals became significant clients of the political system, but they did not dominate it. They pinned their hopes on universal male suffrage to remove the oligarchy from office, provide the path to moral regeneration and social reform, and improve general living standards. Within Santiago, where all the parties had their headquarters, the middle class shared a resentment of the elite with the working class. The middle class was bound, however, to be a political swing group for, of course, a truly massive labor movement would have threatened its income and position as well as that of the elite.

Ibáñez, coming from the ranks of junior army officers, found it easy to recruit middle-class support by enunciating the themes of social order, economic growth, and national development.[125] An American scholar of Chilean rural society in this era referred to the 1920s as a "social revolution" led by military officers whose social origins were in the "lower middle class."[126] But Ibáñez failed to turn the middle class into a loyal clientele. Despite his admiration for Mussolini, he never created a political party. The middle class thus continued its public participation through guilds and parties created before 1927, institutions that Ibáñez intimidated but never controlled. In the panic of the Great Depression, they turned against him.

* * *

Even after the Crash began, Ibáñez' friends in business, banking, and foreign corporations, as well as a public anticipating economic improvements, wanted to believe him. To maintain a favorable press, he started the first government newspaper and censored other publications. The rest of the world seemed in collapse, but the manager of Antony Gibbs and Sons in Valparaiso concluded that Chile had "gold reserves to cover 100% of notes issued."[127] A U.S. attache, writing in January 1931, summarized the prognosis of his commercial contacts as one of "restricted production" in the mines, "sustained low agricultural prices" and "increasingly difficult money markets." Even so, he thought "the situation is not so serious as to warrant alarm." The "situation" seemed much better than "the 1920 decline as there now exists much better organization and control of currency, credit, government finance, and industry."[128] The branch manager of the Bank of London and South America in Valparaiso reported in April, "With a strong Government paying close care to the proper administration of public affairs and finances, there is a basic confidence in the future welfare of the Republic."[129]

Month by month, the government slipped into insolvency. In 1929, an illusion of prosperity was sustained by covering the foreign debt service with new loans. Even then, exports fell so far below imports that the Central Bank began shipping gold to cover the difference.[130] The National City Bank and the Rothschilds had loaned Ibáñez almost US$50 million in 1929 alone, but in April 1930, Chile placed bonds on the New York market for US$25 million dollars.[131] These loans were not enough. In September 1930, a compliant Congress granted Ibáñez permission to issue discountable non-interest bearing treasury certificates to cover quarterly shortfalls, with the expectation that they would be redeemed within a year.[132] In 1931, as long-term loans evaporated and mineral prices fell, the government borrowed 570 million pesos (about US$45.6) on very short terms.[133] Chile had accelerated its debt treadmill. The government also used the "floating debt," that is obligations to domestic suppliers, to keep its programs going. It stopped paying some salaries and most contractors. The amounts owed did not appear on the public records thanks to creative accounting by the Ministry of Finance, which simply ignored, for periods of time, obligations of the Department of Public Works.[134] The expansion of credit during the 1920s was not limited to public loans. Land had always been the basis of domestic credit, and rural producers had steadily borrowed to increase production to meet the demand for grain, wine, and meat in the major metropoli of Santiago, Valparaiso, and Concepción, and in the northern mining towns. Estate owners and small farmers had survived 1930 on short-term credit at 10 percent, and then the prices for their products plummeted 50 percent in one year, a drop much sharper than that of manufactures.[135] In 1931, the total agricultural debt was over 6 billion pesos. The interest alone amounted to over half of the country's agricultural income.[136] Facing general foreclosure, landowners demanded a moratorium on debt collections by the State Mortgage Bank [Caja de Crédito Hipotecario]. Instead, the government canceled export premiums, raised rural railroad rates, and eliminated other subsidies.[137]

By the end of 1930, any hope that copper would replace lost nitrate revenues ended with the passage of the Smoot-Hawley Tariff in the United States. The copper market shrank to one-third its size in 1928.[138] Ruling through decrees, the president trimmed salaries and demanded "loans" from government workers. Not only was the government running out of money, but also a severe shortage of hard currency loomed as the country imported beyond its means. In desperation, Ibáñez raised all tariffs a minimum of 20 to 25 percent and protected manufactures with duties averaging 71 percent. The Society for Industrial Development drew up the list of items to be protected.[139]

The country's use of foreign loans reached an inevitable conclusion. The decisive blow came in May 1931, when Ibáñez sought another US$25 million short-term loan in New York and asked the Rothschilds to participate. They refused and demanded payment on £1 million loan that was due. Chile's Finance Minister took umbrage, accusations flew back and forth, and a financial relationship with roots in the previous century came to an end.[140] Gold and foreign exchange bills drained out at a rapid pace. In mid-June 1931, Ibáñez deferred payment on the foreign debt.[141] The domestic capital market collapsed. Valparaiso had imitated New York and allowed stock purchases based on little collateral, that is, buying on margin. As the crisis in exports and foreign borrowing deepened, margin calls were not met, forcing a sell-off by brokers. Prices fell an average of 38 percent in early 1931, nitrate stocks fell 56 percent, and shipping shares fell 68 percent. Too late, in April 1931 Ibáñez banned all margin trading.[142]

An opposition was slow to mobilize. It had centered on a coterie of Alessandristas, most of them abroad with the former president. Alessandri's group had been plotting a coup against Ibáñez since January 1928. Although its efforts ended in a farce, the conspiracy is significant because of the people it brought together: Gustavo Ross Santa María, Marmaduke Grove, and Enrique Bravo Ortiz all played important roles in the 1930s. Ross, a successful financial speculator, had probably provided Alessandri with his basic income while the two were in exile. Grove had been a leader in the coup of 1924 and was instrumental in building the Chilean air force from 1925 to 1927. Then he and Ibáñez had a falling out. Grove seems to have been too much of a nationalist to stomach Ibáñez' deals with the Guggenheims and foreign investors. While in Europe to buy military hardware, Grove went into voluntary exile and joined Alessandri's conspiracy.[143] Bravo, a former general, had been Alessandri's Minister of War. The group was financed by Ross and Agustín Edwards, another exile and owner of Chile's principal newspaper, *El Mercurio*.

In March 1931, his informers in Europe convinced Ibáñez that the Alessandristas would attack soon. As a preemptive move, he had the carabineros raid the Alessandri home in Santiago at two o'clock one morning. Alessandri's wife was home and suffered such a shock that her health deteriorated. The former president's two older sons and several of his nephews were imprisoned on Easter Island.[144] Alessandri never forgave Ibáñez for this raid.

The Alessandristas' plan sounded as if it came from the nineteenth century. It called for winning over the Chacabuco Regiment in Concepción, Chile's major southern city, and using those troops to move northward against the government. The conspirators rented a private plane in Buenos Aires and flew Grove, Bravo, and some others to Concepción, where the police caught them all. Bravo and Grove were given fifteen years on Easter Island, but security was so lax that the two escaped.[145] The arrest of the Alessandristas left the initiative to ad hoc alliances in the capital and to the students at the university.

As the economic crisis deepened, Ibáñez evoked emergency powers and tried to recoup support by reorganizing his cabinet. This shuffle of ministerial posts gave opponents an opening, and they demanded his resignation.[146] On July 10, Ibáñez attempted and failed to form a cabinet from among Chile's established parties. Conservatives and Liberals demanded that he give up his emergency powers before they would play along. Finally he agreed, and on July 13, Juan Esteban Montero Rodríguez became Minister of the Interior and Welfare; Pedro Blanquier Teylletche took over Finance. Montero immediately ended press censorship and allowed Ibáñez' opponents to return. Then on July 18, Blanquier revealed that the government was insolvent, with a total national debt, external and internal, of about 3 billion pesos (about US$240 million) and an indirect debt, owed principally for state guarantees on municipal and other obligations, of 1.2 billion pesos (about US$96 million). The government's official figures in 1930 had claimed that revenues and expenditures were balanced at 1.1 billion pesos each. Another 414 million pesos was owed on an advance against the government's next foreign loan; 85 million pesos were due on Treasury notes already issued. Ninety million pesos in payments were due immediately. The government had five million pesos on hand.[147] Immediate cuts in the budget were ordered.

Feeling betrayed by his new cabinet, Ibáñez dissolved it on July 21. He complained that the Montero-Blanquier cabinet had ignored his demand "to avoid disorder" and any "increase in the general misery just for the sake of balancing the budget." The cuts, in his opinion, were to blame for anarchy, the parade of "the red flag" in the streets of Santiago, and a student movement "misled by the rhetoric of politicians and Communists," who now sang the international red anthem.[148] He altered his cabinet two more times in a matter of hours, ending with military men at its head. Ibáñez' demagogic conclusions bore little resemblance to reality. He had succeeded in demobilizing the Communists. The students organizing the street demonstrations against him were being financed by conservative opponents—the very "oligarchy" he had promised to displace.[149] Those demonstrating had only one objective: to get rid of the "dictator." This was street politics, led by young enthusiasts who sensed the regime was mortal and the moment belonged to the audacious. Conservatives complained of the fantastic increase in the foreign debt; but most demonstrators were far more worried about rising unemployment and the disappearance of future opportunity.[150]

The students became the shock troops. They organized a civic guard, occupied the university, published their own propaganda, and, when confronted by the carabineros, shot it out with the police. At least one group of them came from the middle-class ANEC, or National Association of Catholic Students [Asociación Nacional de Estudiantes Católicos]. It consisted of a who's who of future leaders: Manuel Antonio Garretón, Ignacio Palma, Bernardo Leighton, Ricardo Boizard, and Eduardo Frei Montalva.[151] On July 24, there were a series of confrontations in which a medical intern and a young attorney died. The next day, the professional guilds of doctors, lawyers, and engineers voted to support the student strike and to demand Ibáñez' resignation. By the end of the 25th, between 100 and 250 demonstrators and a few police were dead; an even larger number of people were wounded.[152] Ibáñez surrounded La Moneda with troops and machine gun nests, and appeared ready to hold out.[153] But on Sunday, knowing he had lost the confidence of even his closest advisors, he handed a request for "a leave of absence" to a congressional leader. He and his family then fled to Argentina.

The President of the Senate, Pedro Opazo Letelier, became acting president and asked Montero to become Minister of the Interior. When Opazo resigned, Montero became vice president and acting chief executive. Congress met and formally voted on Ibáñez' request. The Senate was in favor but the House of Deputies said no. In the meantime, the carabineros abandoned their patrols, and the public was treated to university students, male and female, directing traffic. A holiday air prevailed.[154]

The middle class had demonstrated its political importance. Ibáñez had done more than any other executive to recruit its support, and he was the first president to suffer the consequences of its opposition. But politicians, antedating the 1924 coup, held the institutional initiative. Montero began a massive cut in public spending by limiting government salaries while promising no dismissals. Montero announced that Chile could not pay the foreign debt, and he became the first of a series of executives, who, in the next year and a half, discovered just how difficult it had become to govern Chile.

* * *

Events in Chile were not unique. In 1930-31, fifteen Latin American governments fell. These included elected, civilian regimes and military despots. The common denominator was the depression.[155] Latin American governments in this period shared an indifference to budgetary reality. They spent whatever was available to garner political support. When foreign loans were easy to get, it seemed foolish not to use them.

Chile was also part of the larger economic pattern. One of the sobering lessons of the Great Depression is that bankers and presidents did not really understand or control the economies that they oversaw. No government in the advanced countries had discussed the international debt in realistic terms. After World War I, politicians promised the unobtainable—financial stability and rapid recovery—while also trying a return to liberal capitalism. Capitalists wanted prices to rise without raising wages, changing the existing distribution of wealth, or increasing government control over the economy.[156] In one of the more famous essays on the Great Depression, an economic historian argued that international trade requires a "lender of last resort."[157] Perhaps so, but no lender, making a rational calculation of benefits, would have put any more money into Chile. By resorting to foreign loans, the Chilean government had avoided the painful costs and political crisis of a declining nitrate sector and an over reliance on export earnings. Its need to borrow matched the short-sighted goals of international lenders. But the *Ponzi* scheme had run its course. One question remained: who would pay the bill?

Endnotes

Abbreviations Used in Notes

BOLSA. Archive of the Bank of London and South America. University of London, London, U.K.

Chile. Archivo Nacional. Name of Ministry consulted follows. Santiago, Chile.

FO. Archives of the Foreign Office. Public Record Office, Kew Gardens, U.K.

France-MAE. Ministere des Affaires Etrangeres. Archives Diplomatiques. L'Amerique, 1918-1940 (B). Quai D'Osay, Paris, France.

Gibbs. Antony Gibbs and Sons Archive. Guildhall Library, London, U.K.

Hoover Papers. Papers of President Herbert Hoover. Hoover Presidential Library, West Branch, Iowa, United States.

MID. Military Intelligence Division of the War Department, abbreviation used under RG 165.

RG. Record Group in the National Archives, Washington, D.C. United States. Numbers used as follows:

RG 59:   Department of State. Records Relating to Internal Affairs of Another Nation.

RG 84:   Department of State. Post Records of Embassies.

RG 151:   Department of Commerce.

RG 165:   War Department.

* * *

Endnotes to Chapter 1.

1. Hyman Minsky, *Can "It" Happen Again? Essays on Instability and Finance* (New York: M.E. Sharpe, Inc., 1982), xvii, 118.

2. National Census of 1885 put the male population of Chile over the age of 15 at 699,700, p. 83. For voting data, see Germán Urzúa Valenzuela, *Historia política de Chile y su evolución electoral (desde 1810 a 1992)* (Santiago: Editorial Jurídica de Chile, 1992), 222, 265. For characterizations of the electorate and its development, see Samuel J. Valenzuela, *Democratización via reforma: la expansión del sufragio en Chile* (Buenos Aires: Ediciones del IDES, 1985), and Maurice Zeitlin, *The Civil Wars in Chile (or the Bourgeois Revolutions that Never Were)* (Princeton: Princeton University Press, 1984).

3. Fernando Bravo Valdivieso, Francisco Bulnes Serrano, and Gonzalo Vial Correa, *Balmaceda y la guerra civil* (Santiago: Editorial Fundación, 1991), 105.

4. Gert Wagner, "Trabajo, producción y crecimiento. La economía chilena, 1860-1930" (Santiago: Pontifícia Universidad Católica de Chile, Instituto de Economía, Documento de Trabajo no. 150, octubre 1992), cuadro L4.

5. I decided to use Wagner's series B, since it sits in the middle of the nitrate era and avoids the distortions of using a very small base of the peso in the 1860s and those caused by Ibáñez' borrowing in the late 1920s—his series A and C, respectively. This is certainly the most sophisticated effort yet to calculate the impossible.

6. Specialists will note that I do not agree with the interpretation, or rather apologia, of Patricio Bernedo, "Prosperidad economica bajo Carlos Ibáñez del Campo, 1927-1929," *Historia* 24 (1989), 5-105, about the Ibáñez era. He considers the traditional portrait of a free-spending administration inaccurate, basing his conclusions on newspapers and government banking reports, and ignores the balance of payments and misinterprets the importance of debt funding in the era of "unprecedented prosperity" he so much admires.

7. Ricardo Boizard B., *Patios Interiores* (Santiago: Nascimento, 1948), 70-72.

8. Recent scholarship includes, Patricia Arancibia Clavel, Pablo Bravo Díaz, and [Departamento de Historia et al., Universidad Finis Terrae], *1891 visto por sus protagonistas* (Santiago: Editorial Fundación, 1991), 100, 191; and Maurice Zeitlin, *The Civil Wars in Chile*, 206-16.

9. Gonzalo Vial Correa, Pablo Valderrama Hoyl, David Vásquez Vargas, *Historia del Senado de Chile* (Santiago: Editorial Andrés Bello, 1995), 119-45; Bernardino Bravo Lira, "Chile 1925-1932: De la nueva constitución al nuevo régimen de gobierno," La contraloria General de la República, *50 años de vida institucional (1927-1977)* (Santiago, 1977, separata), 34-37; and H.E. Bicheno, "Anti-Parliamentary Themes in Chilean History," *Government and Opposition* 7, no. 3 (Summer 1972), 360-61.

10. Urzúa V., op. cit., 310.

11. Karen L. Remmer, *Party Competition in Argentina and Chile: Political Recruitment and Public Policy, 1890-1930* (Lincoln: University of Nebraska Press, 1984), 131; and Gonzalo Fernández, "Orden, libertad e igualdad, valores básicos de la evolución democrática en Chile hasta 1925," *Estudios sociales* 10:36 (second trimester, 1983), 79-80.

12. Gonzalo Vial Correa, *Historia de Chile (1893-1973): historia del Régimen Parlamentario (1891-1920)* and *Arturo Alessandri y los golpes militares (1920-1925)*, 3 vols. Vol. 1-3 (Santiago: Editorial Fundación, 1981-86).

13. Wagner, op. cit., cuadro F2.

14. The president's basic account is Arturo Alessandri Palma, *Recuerdos de Gobierno* (Santiago Editorial Nascimento, 1967), 1: chaps. 12, 13. See especially 12, pp. 283-366. To read his more pithy accounts that I find revealing, see *Historia de América bajo la dirección superior de Ricardo Levene, Rectificaciones al Tomo IX* (Santiago: Imprenta Universitaria, 1941), 42-49. The term *exaltado* appears in Armando Donoso, *Conversaciones con don Arturo Alessandri* (Santiago: Biblioteca Ercilla, 1934), 85; for the account here, 79-97.

15. Ricardo A. Yocelevsky R., "El desarrollo de los partidos políticos chilenos hasta 1970," *Cuadernos de Trabajo*, no. 102. Santiago: FLACSO [Facultad Latinoamericana de ciencias sociales], 1986), 29-30.

16. Brian H. Smith, *The Church and Politics in Chile: Challenges to Modern Catholicism* (Princeton, N.J.: Princeton University Press, 1982), 73.

17. Boizard B., Ricardo, *La Democracia Cristiana en Chile; un mundo que nace entre dos guerras* (Santiago de Chile: Editorial Orbe, 1963, 3d ed.), 98-99.

18. Brian Loveman, *Chile: the Legacy of Hispanic Capitalism* 2d ed. (Oxford: Oxford University Press, 1988), 220; and Alejandro Chélen Rojas, *Trayectoria del socialismo: apuntes para una historia crítica del socialismo chileno* (Buenos Aires: Editorial Astral, 1967), 47.

19. Gonzalo Vial Correa, *Historia de Chile (1891-1973): la dictadura de Ibáñez (1925-1931)*, vol.4 (Santiago: Editorial Fundación, 1996), 65.

20. For an interesting, conservative argument that the military movement was a failed revolutionary one, see Crescente Donoso Letelier, "Notas sobre el orígen, acatamiento y desgaste del régimen presidencial: 1925-1973," *Historia* 13 (1976), 347. For the view that nothing fundamental had changed, see Oscar Bermúdez Miral, *El drama político de Chile* (Santiago: Editorial Tegualda, 1947), 20.

21. Jorge Tapia-Videla, "The Chilean Presidency in a Developmental Perspective," *The Journal of Interamerican Studies and World Affairs* 19:4 (Nov. 1977), 459-61, 463.

22. Homero Ponce Molina, *Historia del movimiento asociativo laboral chileno (primer tomo: período 1838-1973)* (Santiago: Editorial ALBA, 1986), 111. The best new research on Ibáñez and labor is, Jorge Rojas Flores, *El sindicalismo y el estado en Chile (1924-1936)* (Santiago: Colección Nuevo Siglo, 1986), 26-33. See also Crisóstomo Pizarro, *La huelga obrera en Chile, 1890-1970* (Santiago: Ediciones Sur, 1971), 96-100.

23. Vial Correa, *Historia de Chile (1891-1973): la dictadura de Ibáñez (1925-1931)*, 4:111.

24. Ibid. See plate vi for photos of the wedding.

25. A summary of the Calles' administration is, Enrique Krauze, Jean Meyer, and Cayetano Reyes, *Historia de la revolución mexicana, 1924-1928* vol. 10, *La reconstrucción económica* (Mexico: El Colegio de mexico, 1977). On this point, see chap. 4. A very readable account of Leguía is, Robert Marrett, *Peru* (London: Praeger Publishers, 1969), chap. 11.

26. Adolfo Ibáñez Santa María, "Los ingenieros, el estado y la política en Chile, Del Ministerio de Fomento a la Corporación de Fomento, 1927-1939," *Historia* 18 (1983), 47.

27. RG 59: 825.5123/39, Atwood, 22 July 1935.

28. RG 84: 815. (Santiago, 1931), Bowman, 28 July 1931.

29. Bernedo, op. cit., 102, quoting *La Nación*, 16 Apr. 1929.

30. Chile. Fomento (1930). Oficios con Antecedentes, v. 479, no. 5, Dept. de Agricultura, Director General, 16 diciembre 1929.

31. Chile. Fomento (1929). Oficios con Antecedentes, v. 333, no.8; Defensa Fiscal, no. 905, 1 junio 1929; and Fomento (1930). Oficios con Antecedentes, v. 484, no. 10; Comité del Fondo de Auxilio a la Exportación de Trigo, no. 93, julio 1930; and v. 489, no. 15, Ministerio de Bienestar Social, no. 1878, 11 noviembre 1930.

32. The first pages of this section draw heavily from, *Chile in the Nitrate Era: The Evolution of Economic Dependence, 1880-1930* (Madison: University of Wisconsin Press, 1982). Those interested in particular issues for the 1920s should consult that work for references. The focus here is on the beginning of Chile's crisis in the 1930s rather than, as in the earlier study, the end of the nitrate era.

33. League of Nations. Economic Intelligence Service, *Review of World Trade, 1937* (Geneva: Publications Department of the League of Nations, 1938), 24, 73.

34. J. Gabriel Palma, "Chile 1914-1935: de la economía exportadora a la sustitutiva de importaciones," *Nueva historia: revista de historia de Chile* 2:7 (Jan.-Mar. 1983), 180.

35. Victor Bulmer-Thomas, *The Economic History of Latin America since Independence* (Cambridge: Cambridge University Press, 1994), 195.

36. Angus Maddison, *Two Crises: Latin America and Asia, 1929-38 and 1973-83* (Paris: Development Centre of the Organisation for Economic Co-operation and Development [OECD], 1985), 84.

37. Markos Mamalakis and Clark Winton Reynolds, *Essays on the Chilean Economy* (Homewood, Il: Richard D. Irwin, Inc., 1965), 363; and Ignacio

Aliaga Ibar, *La economía de Chile y la industria del cobre (algunas reflexiones sobre la post-guerra)* (Santiago: Universidad de Chile, published dissertation, 1946), 173, 195-96.

38. *La Nación* (Santiago), 13 Oct. 1930.

39. Markos J. Mamalakis, *The Growth and Structure of the Chilean Economy: From Independence to Allende* (New Haven: Yale University Press, 1976), 55-56; and Santiago Macchiavello Varas, *El problema de la industria del cobre en Chile y sus proyecciones económicas y sociales* (Santiago: Imprenta Fiscal de la Penitenciaria, 1923), 2:108.

40. See Bill Albert, *South America and the First World War: The Impact of the War on Brazil, Argentina, Peru, and Chile* (Cambridge: Cambridge University Press, 1988), especially chap. 3.

41. The notable exception was Argentina. Leslie Bethell, "Britain and Latin America in Historical Perspective," in Bulmer-Thomas, ed., *Britain and Latin America: A Changing Relationship* (New York: Cambridge University Press, The Royal Institute of International Affairs, 1989), 16. A more general survey is, Rory Miller, *Britain and Latin America in the Nineteenth and Twentieth Centuries* (New York: Longman, 1993). Trade figure is from the League of Nations, *World Trade, 1937,* 24-25.

42. Standard works on the Guggenheims are, Harvey O'Connor, *The Guggenheims: The Making of an American Dynasty* (New York: Covici, 1937), and Edwin P. Hoyt, Jr., *The Guggenheims and the American Dream* (New York: Funk and Wagnells, 1967). The relation of the Guggenheims evolution and their role in Chile is summarized in, Thomas F. O'Brien, "'Rich beyond the Dreams of Avarice': The Guggenheims in Chile," *Business History Review 63* (Spring 1989), 125-31 and his, *The Revolutionary Mission: American Enterprise in Latin America, 1900-1945* (Cambridge: Cambridge University Press, 1996), 177.

43. Thomas Miller Klubock, "Class, Community, and Gender in the Chilean Copper Mines: The El Teniente Miners and Working Class Politics, 1904-1951," 2 vols. (Ph.D. diss., Yale University, 1993), 1:48-50, 57.

44. Clark Winton Reynolds, "Development Problems of an Export Economy: The Case of Chile and Copper," in Mamalakis and Reynolds, *Essays on the Chilean Economy,* 218. Reynolds leaves the mistaken impression that Kennecott was not a Guggenheim interest.

45. Gardiner C. Means, "The Growth in the Relative Importance of the Large Corporation in American Economic Life," in Frederic C. Lane and Jelle C. Riemersma, eds., *Enterprise and Secular Change: Readings in Economic History* (Homewood, IL: Richard D. Irwin, Inc., 1953), 128.

46. Those who have read my earlier work may note an important revision of my view of Ibáñez. In *Chile in the Nitrate Era*, I argued that his economic nationalism was without substance. Further research into the archives has led me to change my opinion.

47. Monteón, *Chile in the Nitrate Era*, 167-68.

48. Chile. Interior (1930), v. 7661. Dirección General de Servicio Eléctricos; and José M. Seguel C., *La industria eléctrica ante la legislación chilena* (Santiago: Imprenta de los Talleres Leblanc, 1941), 17, 135, 137.

49. RG 59: Chile 825.6463-Elec. Bond and Share Co./69, enclosure, unreleased article by C.E. Calder. American Foreign Power was set up to run the foreign holdings of GE's general investment arm, Electric Bond and Share Company; it invested in 11 Latin American nations. For its overall holdings and operations in Mexico, see Thomas F. O'Brien, *The Revolutionary Mission: American Enterprise in Latin America, 1900-1945* (New York: Cambridge University Press, 1996), 36, 286-87.

50. Chile. Interior (1930), v. 7661. memorándum sobre el Contrato Eléctrico. Antecedentes.

51. RG 59: Chile 825.6463-Elec. Bond and Share Co./69, enclosure, unreleased article by C.E. Calder; RG 165: War Dept., MID 2347-0-35/1, Wooten, no. 376, 19 Jan. 1930; and Chile. Archivo Interior (1930), v. 7661. Press Comments, *La Nación*, 8 Feb. 1930.

52. RG 165: War Dept., MID 2054-106/78, Wooten 326, 15 Oct. 1929, and MID 2563-48/2, Wooten, no. 338, 26 Nov. 1929.

53. RG 165: War Dept., MID 2563-48/2, Wooten, no. 338, 26 Nov. 1929.

54. Chile. Archivo Relaciones Exteriores (1930), v. 91. Culbertson to Ministro de Relaciones Exteriores, 29 July 1930; Culbertson cites his newspaper clippings in his unpublished autobiography, "Ventures in Time and Space," vol. 2, chap. 16, p. 22, Culbertson Papers, cont. 98.

55. BOLSA, B28/6, Santiago, 5 Apr. 1930; based on a monthly averaging of the annual imports for 1929 and 1930, in *Anuario estadístico, 1930*, comercio exterior.

56. Gibbs, L64.22, Ms. 16,822/31, Valpo, 8 June 1931.

57. RG 59: 8235.6362/54, Culbertson, no. 734, 13 Jan. 1931, enclosure no. 1, Edward J. Craig, Anaconda Representative in Santiago, memo, 24 Dec. 1930; 825.6363/72, Stimson to Thurston and Wilson, memo, 26 Oct. 1931; and 825.6363 /82, Stimson to Wilson, memorandum, 23 Nov. 1931.

58. RG 59: 325.1121-Bethune/7, Culbertson telegram 22 Mar. 1931; and *La Nación*, 22 Mar. 1931.

59. RG 59: 325.1121-Bethune/31, Culbertson, no. 819, 27 Mar. 1931, enclosure no. 1, memo, 24 Mar. 1931 on Koch.

60. *La Nación*, 26 Mar. 1931; and RG 59: 325.1121 Bethune/33, memo of conversation with Don Oscar Blanco Viel [sic], First Secretary of Chilean Embassy, and 325.1121-Bethune/39, Culbertson, no. 823, 30 Mar. 1931.

61. RG 84: 600 (Valparaiso, 1930), "Annual Review of Chilean Commerce and Industries for 1929," Don Jay Berry, 22 Feb. 1930.

62. O'Brien, "'Rich beyond the Dreams of Avarice,'" 144-45.

63. RG 84: 600 (Valparaiso, 1930), "Annual Review of Chilean Commerce and Industries for 1929," Don Jay Berry, 22 Feb. 1930.

64. His role is discussed in FO 371-17508, Sir R. Michell to Sir John Simon, 9 Feb. 1934, "List of Leading personalities in Chile."

65. Monteón, *Chile in the Nitrate Era*, 170. See also O'Brien, "'Rich beyond the Dreams of Avarice','" 152-54. This article was incorporated into a chapter which emphasizes the role of COSACh in the rise of anti-Ibáñez sentiment and economic nationalism in Chile in O'Brien, *The Revolutionary Mission*, 188-96.

66. RG 59: 825.00-General conditions, Culbertson, no. 656G, 13 Oct. 1930, "Report on General Conditions."

67. Gibbs, MS 11.470, v. 29, Valparaiso, 11 Dec. 1929 and 6 Aug. 1930.

68. BOLSA, B11/5, W.C. Maycock to Chairman, 25 Feb. 1930.

69. Chile. Hacienda (1931), v. 2. Antecedentes de Oficios. Nitrate Railway Directors to Chilean Ambassador in London, 16 Apr. 1931.

70. Chile. Interior (1931), v. 7868. Ministerio de Bienestar Social, Inspección General del Trabajo, Departamento de Asociaciones, 18 Mar. 1931.

71. *Boletín de la Sociedad de Fomento Fabril*, 47:5 (May 1931),339.

72. Chile. Interior (1931), v. 7915. Telegram from Intendant in Iquique, 18 Feb. 1931.

73. Carlos Sáez Morales, *Recuerdos de un soldado: el ejército y la política* (Santiago: Biblioteca Ercilla, 1934), 2:110.

74. RG 59: 825.6374/1054, "Report on Compañía de Salitre de Chile," Div. of Latin American Affairs, Dept. of State, 16 Sept. 1932; and *Volkischer Beobachter*, 8 Aug. 1935 (State Department translation), in RG 59: 825.6374/1265, Dodd, no. 2257, 28 Aug. 1935.

75. Lewis E. Ellis, *Republican Foreign Policy, 1921-1933* (New Brunswick: Rutgers University Press, 1968), 200; Heywood W. Fleisig, *Long Term Capital*

Flows and the Great Depression: The Role of the United States, 1927-1933
(New York: Arno Press, 1975), 152; Council on Foreign Relations, *The United
States in World Affairs: An Account of American Foreign Relations, 1931,*
written by Walter Lippman in collaboration with William O. Scroggs (New
York: Harper and Brothers, 1932), 134-36; Stephen V.O. Clarke, *Central Bank
Cooperation, 1924-1931* (New York: Federal Reserve Bank of New York,
1967), 22-23; J. Fred Rippy, *Globe and Hemisphere: Latin America's Place
in the Postwar Foreign Relations of the United States* (Chicago: H. Regnery
Co., 1958), 40; and Gilbert Ziebura, *World Economy and World Politics,
1924-1931: From Reconstruction to Collapse,* Bruce Little, trans. (Oxford:
Oxford University Press, 1990), 54. A basic text on the thinking of U.S.
corporations in the era is, Joseph S. Tulchin, *The Aftermath of War: World War
I and U.S. Policy Toward Latin America* (New York: New York University Press,
1971).

76. Council on Foreign Relations, *The United States in World Affairs, 1930,*
24.

77. Ibid., 50-51.

78. Charles Morgan-Webb, *The Rise and Fall of the Gold Standard* (New York:
The MacMillan Company, 1934), 53-55; Gustav Cassell, *The Downfall of the
Gold Standard* (New York: Augustus M. Kelley, 1966; reprint of 1936 ed.),
3-6; and Council on Foreign Relations, *The United States in World Affairs,
1931,* 211-12.

79. Milton Friedman and Anna Jacobson Schwartz, *A Monetary History of the
United States, 1867-1960* (Princeton: Princeton University Press, 1963), 297-
98; and Williams, "The Crisis of the Gold Standard,"in *Enterprise and Secular
Change: Readings in Economic History,* edited for the American Economic
Association and the Economic History Association by Frederic C. Lane and
Jelle C. Riemersma (Homewood, IL: R.D. Irwin, 1953), 400.

80. Morgan-Webb, op. cit., 101-102; D.E. Moggridge, *Return to Gold 1925:
The Formulation of Economic Policy and Its Critics* (Cambridge: Cambridge
University Press, 1969), 81-82; Ellis, op. cit., 23; Derek H. Aldcroft, *From
Versailles to Wall Street* (London: Allen Lane, 1977), 192; William E. Leucht-
enburg, *The Perils of Prosperity, 1914-1932* (Chicago: The University of
Chicago Press, 1958), 179-81, 198-99; and David S. Landes, *The Unbound
Prometheus: Technological change and Industrial Development in Western
Europe from 1750 to the Present* (Cambridge: Cambridge University Press,
1969), 362-69.

81. R.G. Hawtrey, *The Gold Standard in Theory and Practice* (London:
Longmans, Green and Co., 1947, 5th ed.), 117, 119; and Cassell, op. cit., 59-61.
Most of this section was already written when I read the work that promises

to be the definitive analysis on gold for the next generation, that of Barry Eichengreen, *Golden Fetters: The Gold Standard and the Great Depression, 1919-1939* (Oxford: Oxford University Press, 1992), especially chap. 7.

82. Paul W. Drake, "La misión Kemmerer a Chile: Consejeros norteamericanos, estabilización y endeudamiento, 1925-1932," *Cuadernos de historia* 4 (July 1984), 31-59. Drake has written a comparative history on the Kemmerer banking missions, *The Money Doctor in the Andes: the Kemmerer Missions, 1923-1933* (Durham, N.C.: Duke University Press, 1989).

83. This argument is most clearly presented in Hyman P. Minsky, op. cit. Other works by Minsky that have influenced this study are: *John Maynard Keynes* (New York: Columbia University Press, 1975), and *Stabilizing an Unstable Economy* (New Haven: Yale University Press, 1986). On issues of the relation of monetary values to global price instability, see Paul Davidson, *Money and the Real World* (London: MacMillan Press, 1978, 2d ed.), and *International Money and the Real World* (London: MacMillan Press, 1982).

84. Herbert Hoover, then Secretary of Commerce, made the effort. Joseph Brandes, *Herbert Hoover and Economic Diplomacy: Department of Commerce Policy* (Pittsburgh: University of Pittsburgh Press, 1962), 198; and Joan Hoff Wilson, *American Business and Foreign Policy, 1920-1933* (Lexington: University Press of Kentucky, 1971), 111.

85. Hoover Papers, Pres., Box 1006, Folder on Foreign Affairs, Financial Correspondence, 1929, July-December, Grosvenor Jones to Sec. Lamont, 13 July 1929, and C&T, Box 166, folder on Latin America trip, Addresses: Central and South America, p. 30, speaking to Carlos Ibáñez, 11 Dec. 1928, and *El Sol* (Santiago), 10 Aug. 1931.

86. RG 151: Commerce Dept., 640 (Chile 1921-1948), Assistant Vice President, National City Bank, NY, to Secretary of State, 2 Mar. 1929.

87. A gold peso was worth 6 British pence or 12.5 U.S. cents.

88. RG 59: 825.51/322, Culbertson, no. 538, 8 Aug. 1930, enclosure 8.

89. Angus Maddison, *Two Crises: Latin America and Asia, 1929-38 and 1973-83* (Paris: Development Centre of the Organisation for Economic Co-operation and Development, 1985), 87.

90. League of Nations, *World Trade, 1934*, 60-66.

91. Carlos Marichal, *A Century of Debt Crises in Latin America: From Independence to the Great Depression, 1820-1930* (Princeton: Princeton University Press, 1989), 187.

92. On Ramírez, see Luis Correa Prieto, *El presidente Ibáñez, la política y los politicos: apuntes para la historia* (Santiago: Editorial Orbe, 1962), 82. Patricio Silva points to this government as the origin of government technocrats, "State, Public Technocracy, and Politics in Chile, 1927-1941," *Bulletin*

of Latin American Research 13:3 (Sept. 1994), 284-85. On railways, see Vial Correa, *Historia de Chile (1891-1973): la dictadura de Ibáñez (1925-1931)*, 181-91, 275-75.

93. Bulmer-Thomas, *The Economic History of Latin America*, 182.

94. Henry W. Kirsch, *Industrial Development in a Traditional Society: The Conflict of Entrepreneurship and modernization in Chile* (Gainesville: The University Presses of Florida, 1977), 87.

95. Bernedo, op. cit., 76.

96. RG 151: Commerce Dept., Bureau of Foreign and Domestic Commerce, Commercial Attaches: Santiago. Randall, Special Report no. 7, 16 Sept. 1931; RG 59: 625.003/129, Don Jay Berry, 20 Nov. 1930; and FO 371-14216 (A8336/817/9), Chilton, 10 Dec. 1930.

97. Chile. Interior (1940), v. 10203. Comisariato General de Subsistencias y Precios, Departamento Técnico.

98. RG 59: 825.00-General Conditions, Culbertson, no. 656G, 13 Oct. 1930, Report on General Conditions.

99. RG 84: 600 (Valparaiso, 1930), "Review of Commerce and Industries for the Quarter Ending September 30," Don Jay Berry, 22 Oct. 1930.

100. The classic source on figures for the early labor movement is, Moíses Poblete Troncoso, "Labor Organizations in Chile," *Bulletin of Labor Statistics* (United States Government Printing Office), no. 461 (Oct. 1928). He claims as many as 136 thousand in the Chilean Workers Federation or FOCh.

101. Rojas Flores, *El sindicalismo*, 58.

102. Jan Dhondt, "Government, Labour and Trade Unions," *The Great Depression Revisited. Essays on the Economics of the Thirties*, van der Wee, ed. (The Hague: Nijhoff, 1972), 250; and Maier, *Recasting Bourgeois Europe*, 9-10.

103. Rojas Flores, *El sindicalismo*, 60, quoting from *El Progreso* (Valparaiso), 28 diciembre 1929.

104. Klubock, op. cit., 1:93, 99-106.

105. Chile. Interior (1929), v. 7371. Ibáñez circular, 8 Oct. 1929.

106. Chile. Fomento (1929). Oficios con Antecedentes, v. 328, no. 3, Luis Schmidt, no. 403, 19 Mar. 1929. Basic studies of Chilean labor in this period are, Jorge I. Barría Seron, *El movimiento obrero en Chile: síntesis histórico-social* (Santiago: Ediciones de la Universidad Técnica del Estado, 1971); Peter De Shazo, *Urban Workers and Labor Unions In Chile, 1902-1927* (Madison:

University of Wisconsin Press, 1983); and Arthur L. Stickell, "Migration and Mining: Labor in Northern Chile, 1880-1930," (Ph.D. diss., Bloomington, University of Indiana, 1979).

107. Chile. Fomento (1929), v. 328, no. 3. Oficios, "Reglamento para contratos de Obras Públicas"; RG 59: 825.00-General Conditions/18, Julius G. Lay, Chargé d'Affaires, no. 379G, Report on General Conditions Prevailing in Chile, 1 Dec. 1929-31 Jan. 1930.

108. Chile. Diputados. *Boletín de sesiones ordinarios*, Dip. Toro, 30 June 1930, 687.

109. Intendant reports in Chile. Interior, v. 7628 and Governor reports in v. 7633 (1930).

110. Chile. Interior (1930), v. 7632. Governor of Tocopilla, 31 Mar. 1929.

111. Jorge Rojas Flores, Alfonso Murua Olguin, Gonzalo Rojas Flores, *La historia de los obreros de la construcción* (Santiago: Programa de Economía del Trabajo, 1993), 34. They do not cite any source for this information. I disagree with the interpretation that workers had more power than they realized. For this alternative view, see Jackie Roddick, "The Failure of Populism in Chile: Labour Movement and Politics before World War II," *Boletín de estudios latinoamericanos*, 31 (Dec. 1981), especially pages 83-88.

112. Camara de Comercio de Chile. Memoria (1932), 21 and RG 59: 825.00 /658 Culbertson, no. 883, 11 June 1931.

113. *New York Times*, 6 June 1932.

114. Carlos Humud Tleel, *El sector público chileno entre 1830 y 1930* (Santiago: Universidad de Chile, 1969), 180.

115. Klubock, op. cit., 1:116.

116. Karin Alejandra Rosemblatt, "Gendered Compromises: Political Cultures, Socialist Politics, and the State in Chile, 1920-1950" (Ph.D. diss., University of Wisconsin, 1996), 30-52.

117. Alejandra Brito Peña, "Del rancho al conventillo: Transformaciones en la identidad popular-femenina (Santiago, Chile, 1850-1920)," *Voces femeninas y construcción de identidad*; Alejandra Brito Peña, ed. and et al. (Buenos Aires: Consejo Latinoamericano de Ciencias Sociales, CLACSO, 1995), 13-59; and Alvaro Góngora Escobar, *La prostitución en Santiago, 1813-1931: visión de las elites*, vol. 8, *Colección Sociedad y Cultura* (Santiago: Dirección de Bibliotecas, Archivos y Museos, 1994), 231-32.

118. Lucia Santa Cruz et al., *Tres ensayos sobre la mujer chilena, Siglos XVIII-XIX-XX* (Santiago: Editorial Universitaria, 1978).

119. Asunción Lavrin, "Women, Feminism and Social Change in Argentina, Chile, and Uruguay, 1890-1940," in Donna Guy, Mary Karasch, and Asunción Lavrin, *Engendering Latin America*, vol. 3 (Lincoln: University of Nebraska Press, 1995), 97-114.

120. Elizabeth Quay Hutchinson, "Working Women of Santiago: Gender and Social Transformation in Urban Chile, 1887-1927" (Ph.D. diss., University of California Berkeley, 1995), 13, 64-76.

121. Chile. Dirección Estadística, 1930 census.

122. Felix Gilbert, *The End of the European Era: 1890 to the Present* (New York: W.W. Norton and Co., 1970), 26-27.

123. In a famous work, John Johnson called them "middle sectors," and argued that they played a reformist and democratic role in Chilean public life. The portrait I draw in this work differs sharply, both in its characterizations and interpretation of the middle class. John Johnson, *Political Change in Latin America: The Emergence of the Middle Sectors* (Stanford: Stanford University Press, 1958), 66-67.

124. See, for example, middle-class lobbying on the shoe industry. Chile. Hacienda. Ministerios (1931). Min. de Fomento, no. 628, 2 Dec. 1930.

125. Frederick M. Nunn, *The Military in Chilean History: essays on civil-military relations, 1810-1973* (Albuquerque: University of New Mexico Press, 1976), 154.

126. George McBride, *Chile: Land and Society* (New York: American Geographical Society, 1936, reprinted Octagon Books, 1971), 230.

127. Gibbs, MS 11,470, v. 30, 21 Jan. 1931.

128. RG 151: Bureau of Foreign and Domestic Commerce, Commercial Attaches: Santiago, Ackerman, Special Report no. 9, 6 Jan. 1931.

129. BOLSA, B11/5, 1930, W.C. Maycock to Chairman, 9 Apr. 1930.

130. Paul T. Ellsworth, *Chile: An Economy in Transition* (New York: The MacMillan Company, 1945), 11.

131. RG 151: Commerce Dept., 640 (Chile 1921-48), Assistant Vice President, National City Bank, NY, to Secretary of State, 2 Mar. 1929.

132. RG 165, War Dept., MID 2347-=0-35/1, Wooten, no. 376, 19 Jan. 1930; and RG 59: 825.00-General Conditions/21, Culbertson, no. 6168, 10 Oct. 1930, General Conditions.

133. RG 59: 825.51/423, Stimson memorandum, 13 Aug. 1931.

134. RG 165: War Dept., MID 2347-90-30/9, Wooten, no. 1043, 12 Aug. 1931.

135. Chile. Interior (1931), v. 7881. Informe de la Situación Económica-agrícola de la region austral; Fomento (1930). Oficios con Antecedentes., v. 479, no. 5, Emiliano Bustos, no. 838, 15 Apr. 1930; and RG 151: Bureau of Foreign and Domestic Commerce, Commercial Attaches: Santiago, Randall, Special Report no. 7, 16 Sept. 1931.

136. Daniel Armanet, *El crédito bancario y el valor de la moneda* (Santiago: Editorial Nascimento, 1938), 45.

137. Chile. Fomento (1931). Oficios v. 594, no. 2, memo no. 243, 11 Feb. 1931.

138. Silas Smith Millar, *El comercio ante la crisis económica* (Santiago: n.p., 1932), 1.

139. FO 371-14216 (A8336/817/9), Chilton, 10 Dec. 1930; RG 59: 625.003 /129, Don Jay Berry, 20 Nov. 1930; and RG 151: Bureau of Foreign and Domestic Commerce, Commercial Attaches: Santiago, Randall, Special Report no. 7, 16 Sept. 1931.

140. FO 371-15081 (A3005/3005/9), Sir Henry Chilton, annual report, 11 May 1931.

141. Ellsworth, op. cit.

142. RG 84: 600. (Valparaiso, 1931), Don Jay Berry, "Review of Commerce and Industries for the Quarter ending July 30, 1931," *Boletín Oficial de la Bolsa de Corredores de Valparaiso*, 3:66, 27 Feb. 1930, and 4:95, 9 Apr. 1931.

143. Fernando Pinto Lagarrigue, *Crónica política del siglo XX: desde Errázuriz Echaurren hasta Alessandri Palma* (Santiago: Editorial Orbe, 1972), 167.

144. Chile. Interior (1931), v. 7912. Copia de Orden Confidencial.

145. *La Nación* (Santiago), 28 noviembre 1928; FO 371-15077, A13/13/9 and 371-14216, A6241/2158/9; *New York Times* (New York), 6 June 1932; *El Mercurio* (Santiago), 24 Sept. 1930; RG 59: 825.00/583, Culbertson, no. 597, 26 Sept. 1930, 825.00/591; Camden L. McLain, Consul Concepción, report, 1 Oct. 1930; RG 165: War Dept., MID 2657-0-137/2, Wooten, no. 718, 28 Nov. 1930, and MID 2563-72/3, Wooten, no. 1290, 5 Apr. 1932; RG 84: 800 (Concepción), McLain to Culbertson, 24 Sept. 1930; and Robert Alexander, *Arturo Alessandri: A Biography* (New Brunswick, NJ: Rutgers University Latin American Institute, University Microfilms International, 1977), 2:523-24.

146. FO 371-13475, A7930/1336/9, and FO 371-15077, A300/13/9; and Pinto Lagarrigue, *Crónica política*, 172-74.

147. United States, Department of State, *Papers Relating to the Foreign Relations of the United States, 1931* (Wash, DC: Government Printing Office, 1946), 1:901-906; RG 59: 825.00/662. Culbertson telegrams, 11-26 July 1931; Pinto Lagarrigue, *Crónica política*, 177-78; and Víctor Contreras Guzmán,

Bitácora de la dictadura: administración Ibáñez, 1928-1931 (Santiago: Imprenta Cultura, 1942), 165.

148. *La Nación* (Santiago), 24 julio 1931.

149. RG 59: 825/00/562, Culbertson, no. 543, 14 Aug. 1930; France-MAE, Chili, v. 8, 14 Aug. 1930; and Sáez, *Recuerdos*, 2:119.

150. *El Diario Ilustrado* (Santiago), 22 July 1931.

151. Vial Correa, *Historia de Chile (1893-1973): la dictadura de Ibáñez (1925-1931)*, 538.

152. FO 371-15077 (A 5117/13/9), Sir H. Chilton to Mr. A. Henderson, 31 July 1931, and France-MAE, Chili, v. 8, 28 July 1931. These accounts indicate that the street fighting was a good deal bloodier than any Chilean historian has admitted.

153. U.S. State Dept., *Papers Relating*, 1:904-905, 825.00/662, Culbertson telegrams, 11-26 July 1931.

154. RG 59: 825.00/672, Culbertson, no. 915, 24 July 1931, no. 919, 31 July 1931; RG 59: 325.2522/2, Culbertson, no. 918, 29 July 1931; Culbertson Papers, Library of Congress, cont. 98, "Ventures in Time and Space," v. 2, chap. xvi, 11; FO 371-15077 (A 5117/13/9), Sir H. Chilton to Mr. A. Henderson, 31 July 1931; France-MAE, Chili, v. 8, 28 July 1931; Pinto Lagarrigue, *Crónica política*, 177-78; and RG 165: MID 2657-0-96/31, Wooten, no. 1012, 22 July 1931.

155. Alexander de Conde, *Herbert Hoover's Latin American Policy* (Stanford: Stanford University Press, 1951), 90; and Council of Foreign Relations, *The United States in World Affairs, 1931*, 53.

156. Ziebura, *World Economy and World Politics*, 15.

157. Charles P. Kindleberger's conclusion in, *The World in Depression, 1929-1939* (London: Allen Lane, 1973). For an excellent overview of Latin America in the Crash and immediately thereafter, see the articles in Rosemary Thorp, ed., *Latin America in the 1930s: The Role of the Periphery in World Crisis* (New York: St. Martin's Press, 1984), especially the lead articles by Thorp, Carlos F. Díaz Alejandro, and the concluding one by Kindleberger.

Fig. 1. President-elect Herbert Hoover and President Carlos Ibáñez del Campo, Feb. 1929. Hoover visited Latin America after winning election in Nov. and before his inauguration. He praised Ibáñez as a modernizing leader in Latin America. Library of Congress.

Fig. 2. U.S. Embassy, Santiago. Seated center front, Ambassador William S. Culbertson was proud of the role he played in protecting U.S. business interests during the upheavals of 1931-32. Seated far right front, U.S. Military Attache, Colonel Harold Wooten reported on Chilean military intrigue and social conflict. Picture taken just before Culbertson left Chile. Library of Congress.

2
Provisional Presidents

"Is this a socialist republic of the Chilean workers
or of the Chilean debtors?"

Hoy, August 1932

W hen Ibáñez fell, he left a political vacuum and an economic
disaster. During the rest of 1931 and all of 1932, the nation
endured the most rapid turnover of chief executives in its history. No
sooner had Ibáñez left, than a jockeying for office and power began
among remnants of his government and the Parliamentary Regime. At
first, it seemed that the old party bosses would be able to restore the
status quo ante 1924. Their candidate, Esteban Montero, the honest
lawyer who had helped reveal the state of Ibáñez' finances, won an
election and began a restoration of party-based government under the
1925 Constitution. Their victory was short lived. By early 1932, Montero was ousted in a coup. There followed a series of governments, each
backed by the military, which finally collapsed in complete disorder
after a few months. Another election was held and the old lion of
Tarapacá, Arturo Alessandri, won and served as president until 1938.

Throughout 1931 and 1932, the economy spiraled downward. Data
from these years is difficult to translate into contemporary terms. There
is no debate, however, over the character of the disaster. The loss of 80
percent of all export income left the nation distraught and the government destitute. The government had relied on trade-based levies, the
nitrate export duty, and import tariffs. The economic bottom probably
was not reached until late 1932 or early 1933, that is, not until after the
Alessandri administration began. Thus, each chief executive in this
interim between Ibáñez and Alessandri tried to confront, alleviate, or
arrest a depression that continued to worsen.

In general, the complexity and brevity of this period of provisional presidents has discouraged any sustained analysis. The provisional presidents were quite forgettable: Montero, the well-meaning but naive professor of law, and Carlos Dávila, the righteous journalist. Only Marmaduke Grove, the fire-breathing demagogue, seems to merit sustained attention. But something was occurring beneath the presidency, the revolving juntas, and the many party intrigues. At the political level, a revival of the multi-party system demonstrated that it could not address, often could not even articulate, the crisis. At an economic level, no ideology, let alone a coherent set of policies, prevailed. So, the year 1931 led to a series of improvisations. These did not alter the impact of the depression—they could not do so—but once improvisations were codified into law, they would shape all future possibilities. In many respects, this chaotic time established the terms of politics into the following decades. Many of the laws of the period, often passed by executive decree, remained in force until the fall of President Salvador Allende in 1973.

To make some sense of the disorder, it must be remembered that the political party system had a life of its own. The largest parties, the Conservatives, the Liberals, and the Radicals had, in the nineteenth century, represented an evolving social structure. The Conservatives represented elite interests in land and finance, especially near the capital, and support for close ties between Church and state. The Liberals also represented the elite but wanted a more secular state and often represented wealth made in the export-oriented provinces. The Radicals had become the dissident party of the middle class, a splinter group of the Liberals. Time had reduced the importance of differences between the Liberals and Conservatives; the Constitution of 1925 codified a separation of Church and state. The electoral and legislative rules encouraged political entrepreneurs of every social background and ideology to start their own parties. Parties multiplied within each social class and personal loyalties could be distributed among several of them. One could, thus, find Ibañistas scattered among Liberals, Radicals, and some who called themselves Socialists. A good part of the narrative that will follow involves attempts by temporary chief executives to cobble together some kind of coalition. One of their central problems was that parties could not deliver supporters. Another was that no one could imagine how to forge a new party or movement sufficiently strong to control the presidency and the legislature.

In this setting, the armed forces and, in particular, the army functioned as a sort of party. Each provisional president had either to confront the armed forces or to recruit them. They were a bastion of Ibañistas, therefore distrusted by party leaders. They had the capacity to disrupt, even overthrow, a government, as Montero discovered. But they alone could not govern. As the armed forces backed one leader and then another, a major part of the elite and the middle class began to fear social breakdown or even revolution.

Beyond the issues of party and political allegiances were those of economic administration. The U.S. corporations lobbied against government initiatives. These regulated prices, altered labor relations, raised taxes, and imposed nationalist ordinances on everything from the purchasing supplies to repatriating profits. The crisis was forcing each administration into improvisations that undercut free trade and economic orthodoxy. The Great Depression finished what World War I had begun. It put an end to nineteenth-century capitalism, also called *economic liberalism*. This was not a change that foreign investors readily accepted. Issues of "economic diplomacy" appeared which pitted foreign interests against the Chilean governments and so helped, in our contemporary terminology, to destabilize each administration. The issues involved such fundamental elements of the economy as currency controls, import licenses, and the supply of fuel. The ways in which economic orthodoxy, or at least the attempt to restore it, broke down and how that altered relations between the Chilean governments and foreign investors comprise one of the central concerns of this narrative. The quarrels between governments and foreign interests go to the heart of several issues involving economic development and dependence.

A final factor was the wave of misery that gripped Chile. In October 1931, the bishop of the nitrate province of Tarapacá claimed there were at least 10 thousand unemployed in Iquique alone and most had been out of a job for a year:

> More than one hasn't a peso in his pocket; more than one walks away the time, lolling and waiting through the endless hours of worry without consolation; and each has taken all his goods and utensils to the pawnbroker, from the marriage bed to the last chair, from the wedding ring to the last keepsake, from the watch to the last suit.[1]

In 1931, officials estimated that the unemployed numbered between 80 thousand and 125 thousand (of an active population of 1.2 million).

The government provided those who remained in the mining areas one meal a day. When rations ran out, they were reduced to what they could find. Some even ate grass.[2] The loss of the mining zones as a market and the inability to finance crucial imports shut down much of the nation's industry, putting 25 thousand out of work. In the south, a drought and the loss of markets cost 30 thousand jobs. People were starving.[3] In December 1931, the major copper companies cut Chilean production 25 percent.[4] By June 1932, close to a quarter of a million Chileans were unemployed.[5] Six months later, the number reached about 325 thousand or 10 percent of the total population and over one-third of the work force.[6]

Officials were frightened. The Intendant of rural Talca reported, in June 1932, on the daily arrival of workmen at the office, pleading for work, or at least a piece of bread, for themselves and their children. "Starving and in rags," they seemed dangerous "not because of some political movement but because of the unbearable weight of their destitution and suffering." He told his superior, "Honorable Minister, these people are capable of anything before dying of hunger."[7]

Montero's Administration

Ibáñez' legacy created problems for each of the presidents until Alessandri was elected in 1932. The public anger against the "dictator" and his supporters did not abate for more than a year. The very presence of officials appointed by Ibáñez and of the Congress "elected" during his administration morally compromised each of his successors.[8] Ibañistas remained in the armed forces, and political intrigues engulfed the officer class throughout the early 1930s. While a new presidential election was scheduled to replace Ibáñez, no congressional election was called.

The man of the hour was Juan Esteban Montero Rodríguez. Recall that he, as Minister of the Interior, along with the Minister of Finance, Pedro Blanquier Teylletche, had undermined Ibáñez by ending censorship and revealing the government's sorry financial state. He became the first provisional president, having been recruited as Minister of the Interior again when Ibáñez left. Montero belonged to those middle-class groups seeking political participation in the 1920s. He was educated at the English elementary and the Catholic high school in Valparaiso. He received a law degree from the University of Southern California, and was successful in an unassuming way. He was a Radical, a member of the Party's directorate and belonged to the Rotary Club. His reputation came from being an admired Professor of Law at the University. Santiago's political circles were still small in 1931. Once the election was scheduled, he came under intense upper- and middle-class pressure to run. He first feigned reluctance but, after garnering a crucial endorsement of the Union of Professional Associations, he began his campaign on August 18, 1931.[9] The Radical, Conservative, and Liberal parties all backed him.

Montero's administration had three phases: the first while he was provisional president in late July and early August, 1931 (see Table 2.1); a second when his elected administration was first in office, from December 1931 until March 1932; and the third, brief era when he shifted economic policies and tried to ward off total disaster and a coup. In the first, it was his cabinet that acted while he ran for office. Its leaders were Manuel Trucco Franzani, whom Montero had made Minister of Interior and who, therefore, became provisional president (or vice-president) in Montero's absence and Pedro Blanquier, who served as Minister of Finance. Trucco Franzani carried out many of the policies that weakened Montero's position after the election. In the second period, Montero became embroiled in a series of quarrels with the U.S. Embassy and U.S. corporations, quarrels that further undermined his public acceptance. In the third, from March to early June 1932, he demonstrated that, while he was learning on the job and beginning to break with economic orthodoxy, he remained a political naif.

When Montero began, he wanted to undo policies of the "dictatorship." He supported economic orthodoxy, that is, he wanted a balanced budget, to preserve the gold standard of the peso, and have the market decide the winners and losers.[10] The administration guessed revenues would be 275 million, and expenditures 437 million, pesos. The government forced employees to take pay cuts of up to 30 percent in the form of "loans" to the government, a decision that would generate a military uprising. Congress, with only one dissent, went along.[11] The basic direction of policy remained unchanged during the presidential campaign when Trucco was provisional president. Montero inherited a bureaucratic structure and an officer corps in the armed forces full of Ibañistas. No means existed to replace these people. Montero or Trucco would have had to go through a Congress that was fearful of executive initiative and that included party hacks that were backing Montero's

Table 2.1: Chronology of the Provisional Presidents, 1931-1932

Date	Event
July 26, 1931	Ibáñez flees for Argentina.
July 27, 1931	Juan Esteban Montero Rodríguez becomes provisional president.
Aug. 9, 1931	Montero begins presidential campaign.
Aug. 20, 1931	Montero resigns provisional presidency to campaign; his Minister of Interior, Manuel Trucco Franzani becomes provisional president.
Sept. 1-9, 1931	Naval mutiny occurs.
Oct. 4, 1931	Montero is elected president, defeats Alessandri.
Dec. 4, 1931- June 4, 1932	Montero serves as president. Montero is overthrown by coup.
June 4-16, 1932	Grove-led "Socialist Republic" in effect.
June 16-July 8, 1932	Juntas are led by Carlos Dávila.
July 8-Sept. 13, 1932	Dávila is provisional president.
Sept. 13-Oct. 2, 1932	Junta led by General Bartolomé Blanche.

campaign. He might have shifted government resources to build a following for himself, but there was not much room to maneuver. The entire executive branch, aside from the military and national police, had 24,600 employees in December 1931: 14.7 thousand were teachers, there were only 3.6 thousand working throughout the country in the crucial Ministry of Interior (which oversaw provincial administration), only two thousand in Finance (which managed all taxes), and fewer than a one thousand in Public Welfare that included the small public medical program; the presidency had 12 employees.[12] Avoiding any greater deficit became an administrative obsession. Blanquier insisted that the government was too large and cut employees throughout 1931.

The policies of the provisional presidents exhausted the government's financial resources and undercut its ability to confront the crisis. So much gold flowed out of the Central Bank so quickly that the government could not provide credit to anyone.[13] It openly refused to help the hacendados at a time of rising real interest rates, falling prices, and declining property values. Blanquier responded to this crisis by reducing Ibañista-granted subsidies to agriculture and refusing to provide any new assistance.[14] When it was discovered that only a third of all debtors to the State Mortgage Bank were meeting their payments, the government seriously considered massive foreclosures. That would have meant not only ruining a substantial portion of the landed rich but destroying real estate developers as well; the latter had become the major debtors to the State Mortgage Bank.[15] By December 1931, the State Mortgage Bank and the private mortgage institutions of Santiago were facing insolvency.[16] The massive foreclosures were never carried out but policies of the provisional president seriously wounded the elite.

While Montero, Trucco, and Blanquier intended a return to classical economic attitudes, the relation of their policies to economic doctrines is not so simple. The crisis rolled at them with such force that they were forced to increase the government's economic role. At the end of July, the government approved four new laws. It allowed the Central Bank new discount facilities, broadening the kinds of paper that could be used as securities against loans. This measure allowed the domestic credit structure to persist. A second measure had the bank buy 21.4 million pesos in COSACh bonds, rescuing what remained of the nitrate sector for the moment. The third changed the structure of all the debts of the municipalities, the state railways, and the State Mortgage Bank. They were required to pay all foreign debts in pesos, deposited with the central government. The central government then used these funds on its own expenditures and broadened the foreign debt suspension begun by Ibáñez. The law had the effect of widening the economic differences between Santiago and other cities, for the government continued spending on the capital as provincial centers became unable to borrow.

The fourth and most important change established a Currency Exchange Control Commission [Comisión de Control de Operaciones de Cambio]. Styled on a similar commission in Germany, it was charged with preventing the outflow of gold and hard currency. Officials hoped it would preserve the value of the peso.[17] Instead, it invented or rewrote the rules governing access to gold and hard currency, and these changes broadly affected the market for most commerce. Under Montero and the other provisional presidents, the Currency Exchange Commission became the most powerful economic institution in the government.

Given its importance, it is worthwhile to stop and look at the Commission's authority which broadened as hard currency disappeared, that is, well into 1932 and even after Montero was driven from office. It had six members, half chosen by the president and half by the Central Bank, which actually handled all moneys.[18] It supervised all the currency rules related to foreign trade. All exporters were required to sell the Bank their bills of exchange (that is, checks drawn in hard currency) at a fixed rate. The flow of funds from foreign bank branches to their home countries was also regulated. The difference between the sums foreigners wanted to repatriate and the amounts they were allowed to send home created "blocked currencies." These blocked amounts included everything from unpaid imports to bank accounts denominated in U.S. dollars or British pounds. The currency exchange rules, codified in April 1932 as Law no. 5107, imposed heavy penalties, up to 10 thousand pesos, for any violation. The basic task of the Currency Exchange Commission was to issue and supervise all licenses to use gold or foreign currency. It immediately favored national over foreign firms, and new trade, especially the purchase of fuels and government supplies, over the settlement of debts.

Currency controls created a black market called, in the 1930s, a *curb market*. Santiago businessmen learned to manipulate the new rules, and by the end of November 1931, the black market rate for the U.S. dollar was 13 pesos against the legal rate of 8.2. Those with a stock of imported goods saw their peso value increase by 25 to 50 percent in three months.[19] Such gains were short-lived since supplies could not be renewed. Importers, facing long waits for Commission-approved exchange, closed their firms. Domestic industrialists, farmers, and cattlemen were now freed of foreign competition, albeit in a much-reduced market.

The results of currency control in Chile were the same as in other nations in the 1930s. (Currency commissions became common in Europe as well as Latin America.) Hard currency and gold continued to leave the country. When it began its operations in August 1931, the Currency Exchange Commission had 53 million pesos worth of foreign currency. By January 1932, it was down to 15 million pesos, a little more than US$1.0 million at the official rate.[20] The gold standard was suspended in June 1932. Its failure to preserve the gold peso did not interrupt the Commission's operations. It had become a center of favoritism. Among others, the British felt the impact of its bite. When the British went off the gold standard before Chile did, the Commission switched to calculating its reserves in U.S. dollars.[21] Instead of gaining from a cheaper currency, the British saw their cash assets reduced in paper value by 20 percent, a change that accelerated their departure from Chile.[22] As we shall see, the Currency Commission's operation also affected U.S. interests and caused considerable conflict between Chilean administrations and the U.S. government.

A final change under the Montero-Trucco provisional presidencies must be mentioned, the creation of the prohibitive tariff. This was also justified by the hard-currency shortage. Ibáñez had begun some protective policies when, in September 1931, the government raised tariffs to new heights. The Society for Industrial Development submitted a list of goods to be reclassified and the government approved it, raising all duties an average of 41 percent and covering 70 percent of all imports.[23] The Chileans believed they had little choice: the United States had imposed the Smoot-Hawley Tariff and was raising copper duties; Britain had the new Import Duties bill and was moving toward an imperial preference system.[24] Greater self-sufficiency seemed the only future. And so, provisional administrations, devoted to a nineteenth-century definition of capitalism and to reversing the actions of the "dictator," accelerated two trends Ibáñez had begun: the promotion of domestic manufactures as replacements for imports, and a cooperation between private sector associations and the government that contemporary scholars call *corporatism*.

At the heart of this last idea is the view that government (or, in the theoretical sense, "the state") creates society and must preserve, by whatever means, a sense of social order and hierarchy. As specialists note, the idea of a corporatist state is very old in western history and was revived in Europe in the 1920s.[25] Corporatist thinking underlay fascism, but Mussolini and Hitler's governments were only two forms of the corporatist state. Alternative forms of corporatism existed within elected governments, even European liberal democracies, and persisted in Latin America and elsewhere well after World War II.[26] The core of the new corporatist state was a set of understandings between private, organized interests (guilds, business and professional associations, sometimes even unions) and the state in which the former could at least veto any policy that altered their place in the social order.

Montero could not have intended an extension of Ibañismo as his legacy. He built his campaign for president around the fact that he was a nice, honest man—he was not Ibáñez and he was not Alessandri. The professional guilds championed him as the only man who "can save us from the danger of Alessandri."[27] For awhile, these qualities were a welcome respite from the 1920s.

In addition to his public prestige and broad support within the upper and middle classes, Montero had several other advantages in the campaign. The Ibañistas were discredited and remained quiet after the election. The labor-based left began to mobilize but was ideologically fragmented and uncertain of its goals: should it spend its energies reviving labor organizations or should it concentrate on mobilizing for elections, or even a revolution? The Anarchists kept their distance from the Communists, and the Communists split in 1930-31 into Trotskyists, led by Senator Manuel Hidalgo, and Communists (Stalinists) with Elías Lafertte at their helm.[28] In Santiago, there was middle-class dissent from the government's policies. Associations of the white-collar unemployed, hit by the government's contraction, formed the Radical Socialist Party and demanded that Congress be dissolved and that the government stop inflation and revive a public works program. For a short time, the Chilean Student Federation at the university turned leftward.[29] In February, 1932, a number of non-Communist associations, most of whose leaders were in their twenties, gathered into the Socialist Party.[30] None of these factions had a viable national candidate.

Montero's only real opponent was Arturo Alessandri, and, in many ways, it was Alessandri that became the central issue in this contest. He was widely detested by the elite and the professionals as the man who had unleashed passions in the 1920s that he could not control—the man who paved the way for Ibáñez. He had, like Montero, proclaimed an unwillingness to become the next president. But his friends made a show of calling upon him, and he felt that he could not refuse. These friends, scattered among Liberals and Radicals, had to join Alessandri in a coalition that included some Trotskyists. A hostile press called the former president, the candidate of the left.[31]

Alessandri had little money and a weak program. His proposals either repeated Montero's policies or seemed irrelevant. He wanted to cut government, something Montero and Trucco were already doing. Alessandri demanded an end to paying on the foreign debt; Montero had already suspended debt payments.[32] For the moment, the debt was not an issue in public life. Alessandri demanded the end of COSACh, the nitrate combine, but the nitrate plants had closed and the former president was unable to explain how abolishing COSACh would reopen them.

The decisive event of the campaign was a naval mutiny.[33] On September 1, petty officers led rebellions in Coquimbo, a northern port, and Talcahuano, the port for southern Concepción. The mutineers controlled enough ships to threaten any port but their early actions were limited to making demands. Their first was for a restoration of pay. When they were better organized, they also demanded a public works program to be financed by forced loans from the rich. They also thought the rural poor should receive land by subdividing haciendas.

This was a radical moment in Chilean social history. The government decided the Communists were in charge, a conclusion reinforced when the Communists began organizing labor support for the mutiny in Santiago, Valparaiso, and Concepción.[34] Sections of all three cities shut down. Class warfare seemed imminent. Efforts to negotiate a settlement ended when Minister of Finance Blanquier refused any concessions. Fearing an attack on Valparaiso and the spread of social rebellion, the cabinet authorized the air force to bomb the fleet.[35] The intensity of the government's panic is revealed in a request to the United States to send help in the form of warships, non-poisonous gas, and bombs.[36] On September 6, the air force quickly subdued the fleet at Coquimbo by dropping bombs near the ships and strafing them. Only one man was killed. But at Concepción, unemployed workers joined the mutineers; the air force strafed and the army machine-gunned the crowd. The Communists later claimed that hundreds were killed—the government admitted 80 dead—before the ships surrendered on September 9.[37]

The election took place three weeks later. The public was in no mood for demagogues. Alessandri's base of support dissolved. Montero won handily and was inaugurated in early December. Unfortunately, Montero failed to see that he still needed to build support for his programs as well as for himself. Government had been steadily losing respect during the campaign. Every social stratum had suffered economic reverses and seen little in the way of official help. The elite had lost many of its financial resources. The middle class had lost jobs in the government and suffered massive salary cuts to keep those few jobs that remained. The military now endured a reaction to its previous support for Ibáñez; the navy went through a humiliating series of courts-martial.[38] Montero's sense of public relations was so poor that the government canceled veterans pensions for the War of the Pacific (1879-83).[39]

Table 2.2: Cost of Living, 1929-1932
(Index 1913=100)

Date	Wholesale Prices	Imported Goods	Industrial Goods	Cost of Living
Jan. 1929	191	207		102
Jan. 1930	181	205	201	101
Jan. 1931	149	178	182	103
June 1931	150	220	187	99
Dec. 1931	150	220	187	99
Mar. 1932	166	204	204	104

Source: Raúl Simon report of May 1932, in United States State Department, Record Group 59: 825.51/545, Culbertson no. 1173, 6 June 1932.

Given the character of the crisis, perhaps no government could have won much public support. Export markets were still in decline. Miners and their families lived by the thousands in Santiago's warehouses.[40] One of the most serious accusations against the government was that it was doing nothing to control inflation. Prices in the capital were rising in late 1931 by 20-25 percent a month.[41] Prices had fallen in 1930 and earlier in 1931 and the overall cost of living in March 1932 was only two points above that of 1929 (see Table 2.2). But wages were not recovering. As the crisis deepened, the government began to abandon economic orthodoxy. It decreed a rent reduction of 20 percent and froze electric and tramway rates. It also created a Price Control Commission whose members included two cabinet ministers and members from Santiago's chamber of commerce as well as from the professional guilds. This Commission could fix the price of "goods of prime necessity" (food, clothing, medicine, heat and transportation) and could even seize goods in order to assure their availability.[42]

Montero's labor policies alienated businessmen and the elite without rallying working-class support. Price controls drew little praise from unions. Hacendados demanded that the president set aside labor laws that applied to rural workers. He refused to rescind the code but he did not enforce it either.[43] The president appealed to a renascent labor movement; he also intensified police spying on unions and political parties in the capital.[44] In addition, he tried some imaginative ideas that Ibáñez had considered in the waning days of his government. Titles to land in the southern provinces were handed out to some unemployed, turning them into "colonists." But the government could not even provide settlers with tools or seed. He promoted gold panning. One of his bureaucratic initiatives was to create a gold-mining service to find deposits and help the unemployed work them.[45] Several thousand men went into the hills where they worked without salary, selling their nuggets to the service at a set price. The Mining Fund lacked the means to operate all of its locations; some of them shut down in the midst of crisis.[46] Despite some success, no one with influence took the program seriously. When the gold program was first announced in Congress, one observer noted, "it provoked cynical laughter."[47] Every subsequent administration until the late 1930s would expand this program and it would keep tens of thousands from starving.

The government's seeming indifference to the general welfare encouraged political desperadoes. On Christmas Day in Copiapó, young Communists, thinking they could provoke a general revolution, attacked a military post; fighting lasted two days and cost the lives of five police and five workers.[48] One demoralizing event followed another. Government funds ran so short that, in early 1932, it stopped payment on the meal tickets for the unemployed in the north. In April 1932, the peso had fallen to 55 against the U.S. dollar; dollars had become unavailable at the official rate of 16 to one. A bank panic led to violence and martial law in Santiago.[49]

As conditions worsened, foreign governments began to react. The United States and British embassies reflected the opinions of foreign interests resident in Santiago, who were closely tied to the Chilean elite. They had welcomed Montero as an alternative to Alessandri and granted him a grace period, but feared social turmoil. In early 1932, they publicly put aside the foreign debt issue. They said nothing about rising tariffs, since their own were so high. But they did begin to protest the obvious preferences of the Currency Exchange Commission for Chilean interests over foreign ones. These early protests involved few threats. France was the only nation that cut off Chilean nitrate imports in response to Commission decisions.[50]

Nonetheless, it was under Montero, that the actions of foreign embassies, in support of and often in league with foreign companies, began to destabilize the government. Much of this "economic diplomacy," which in this period might better be called "economic confrontations," involved access to hard currency and centered on the Currency Exchange Commission. The government intervened in the currency market to supply itself with essentials. Its rules soon went beyond this to cover rewriting "entitlements" in foreign trade. Those who were hurt by these new rules included foreign corporations and they organized against them. Unfortunately, many who either did benefit or might have benefitted from the Commission's decisions did not rally to Montero's defense.[51] His enemies multiplied as his public defenders dwindled.

An example of the impact of the new rules was the government's fight with the oil companies. The Currency Exchange Commission reduced the supply of dollars and pounds to Shell-Mexico and West India Oil (the Standard Oil subsidiary), who responded by cutting back imports. Montero tried to avoid a public fight. As stop-gap measures, the government promoted burning such nationally produced fuels as coal and creosol.[52] It also tried to swap Chilean nitrate for oil from the Soviet Union, but the companies refused to process it.[53] Instead, in March 1932, they raised gas prices 25 percent and triggered demonstrations by Santiago's bus and taxi drivers. At one point, car owners circled La Moneda in protest. Montero and his Ministers of Development, Finance, and the Interior met with the oil company executives and told them that they were turning the country over to communists. But the executives refused to import more gas until paid for past deliveries in hard currency. Montero then threatened to confiscate their assets. The companies called his bluff. So, the government lost the battle and to make scarce supplies go further, instituted a pricing system in which the companies charged private cars more than buses and taxis.[54]

Montero had no alternative. The companies had stopped Ibáñez' efforts to create a state oil monopoly. Now, they successfully lobbied the State Department and the British Foreign Office to stop Montero's revival of the idea.[55] Nationalization of the petroleum industry was a popular idea even among the upper classes, drawing strong support, for example, from the National Mining Society [Sociedad Nacional de Minería].[56] The companies saw any threat of nationalization as a regional one. In justifying its stance in Chile, Standard Oil told the State Department that it had US$150 million invested in Latin America.[57] Despite Montero's acquiescence, the problem did not go away.[58] In May 1932, the companies again complained they were not being given enough hard currency. The Minister of Development announced the country would have to reduce its gasoline and oil consumption by 50 percent. As it was, most service stations in Santiago were sold out by nine o'clock every morning. To forestall another price increase, the government reduced gasoline taxes 81 percent.[59] Montero's helplessness could not have been more evident.

Clashes between foreign companies, particularly those of the United States, and the government increased as Montero became desperate. When the Singer Sewing Machine Company tried to export five thousand unsalable sewing machines, the government imposed a fine that kept them in the country.[60] When the telephone and electric companies tried to raise rates, the government canceled the rate-hike provisions in their contracts.[61] The U.S.-owned Chilean Electric Company [Compañia Chilena de Electricidad] became a losing proposition.[62] At the time that it codified the currency exchange law, the government also imposed an "unemployment tax" on capital gains. The government charged domestic firms 5 to 6 percent; foreign firms paid 8 percent.[63] The management of foreign mining companies awoke one morning to discover a new measure that required them to return to Chile a set percentage of their sales, in hard currency, and then to sell this money to the Central Bank at an unfavorable exchange rate.[64]

The attitude that prevailed within the government was summarized in a meeting between U.S. Embassy officials and the Exchange Commission. When one executive complained that West India Oil was running in the red, a commissioner replied, "It's a big company and can stand the loss."[65]

Currency policies also affected U.S. citizens. Under Law 5107 (the exchange act), the government ended the illusion of convertibility. It allowed banks and pension funds to pay off foreign currency accounts at 20 percent of their face value. The U.S. Embassy in Santiago was soon inundated with protests from employees and former employees of U.S. companies, many complaining they had accepted lower interest rates for years in order to have the security of dollar accounts.[66] Foreign contractors, who had once accepted government bonds denominated in gold or hard currency, were now paid in depreciated paper pesos.[67]

By the end of April 1932, the U.S. Embassy and the Montero administration were at a critical juncture. In this situation, Montero had little leverage; there was no alternative trading nation. So, Montero promised Ambassador William Culbertson that he would remedy the many currency issues, even as his administration tightened control of the economy. It was a promise the president could not keep.

Clashes between the government and the foreign sector not only reflected the depression's impact but a changing attitude within the administration. By March 1932, the proliferation of government interventions was mocking all pretensions to economic orthodoxy. Near the end of the Montero administration, it seemed to be moving—without any clear guide—toward some form of corporatism. Proposals suggested some public-private partnership in which private associations drew up plans for government policies and received state credit and subsidies to expand market activities. The overall intent was to transfer income from foreign firms to the government and the domestic credit sector. Had anyone cared to notice it, most of these proposals had been drafted by the Ibáñez bureaucracy before the "dictator" fell. Montero could not implement them because they had been designed for an export economy that no longer existed. The Ibañistas who remained in his government hated him and the elite parties that had put him in office.

By April 1932, it was obvious Montero would not survive. His policies against censorship and in favor of basic liberties emboldened his opponents. Alessandristas and Ibañistas began a press campaign against him a few weeks after his inauguration.[68] A remnant of the Ibañistas openly maneuvered to attack. The president still had the nominal support of the Radicals and a reform section of the Liberals, but the professional and aristocratic elements that had elected him felt little stake in his survival. His opponents reopened the political campaign. The basic issues were the persistence of an non elected Congress and the nitrate combine of COSACh. Defense of each of these institutions brought the president nothing, but he was afraid that the end of either of them would make matters worse.

Montero believed that if he disbanded Congress, a new legislature would move to the left—not to the Communists, but rather to the Radicals, Democrats, and others proposing more distributive measures. The term *socialist* was used loosely in the early 1930s to describe any government measure aimed at rescuing existing sectors. Montero's own Radical Party, at its convention in December 1931, declared that capitalism was bankrupt, that the government should seize the "major means of production" and that the party was now the workers' ally in the class struggle.[69] Arturo Alessandri proclaimed that "state socialism" was the future of republican governments.[70] Congress held by-elections as members left or died. These revealed the public's antipathy to economic orthodoxy and Congress responded by fracturing into small parties and factions. Without patronage, no government could command much loyalty. Each partisan group tried to find the policies to build a broader social base. The president, therefore, defended a Congress that had no commitment to him; he gradually lost the ability to pass legislation.

COSACh became a political albatross. Both the firm's supporters and critics misunderstood what was happening. Montero knew nothing about the nitrate industry. His ministers and the firm's Guggenheim-appointed managers told him the industry would fail if the firm collapsed. Montero's opponents claimed, inaccurately, that the combine had caused the nitrate collapse. COSACh had been created to consolidate Chile's and the Guggenheim's roles in an international nitrate cartel. The cartel's failure left it without much reason for being but with the combined debts of all the companies that it had absorbed. The government preserved COSACh because it did not know what else to do.[71] Montero missed the symbolic importance of the issue. By spending scarce resources on the firm, he became, in the public view, a stooge of the Guggenheims, and of their agent in Santiago, Cappelan Smith. This link became stronger after April 1932, when Alessandri won a by-election to the Senate representing the nitrate zone and made denunciation of COSACh his campaign theme.[72] The issue that had not worked in the election of 1931 now drew blood.

The president limped toward political disaster, having offended foreign interests, having failed his allies, and having almost nothing to offer either the middle class or the working class. The political spectrum was too fragmented, the institutional bases too weak, to assemble a response to the nation's problems. Montero's attempts had, however, underlined what would not work. The rhetoric of economic nationalism had grown stronger. The days of oligarchic liberalism, of a belief in the magic power of the market and of the beneficence of foreign trade, were over.

Government by Coup

As left-wing students held street demonstrations within hearing of La Moneda, Montero reflected on the rumors about his opponents. He knew that the Alessandristas, the Ibañistas, and the New Public Action [Nueva Acción Pública or NAP] headed by Eugenio Matte Hurtado, were plotting against him.[73] Interestingly, all of these groups included Santiago professionals who were Freemasons. Montero did not know who was working with whom, or what kind of action anyone was planning. As it turned out, neither did the conspirators.

The rumors placed Carlos Dávila Espinoza at the center of most plots. He was a journalist and had served as Ibáñez' ambassador to Washington. He had returned to edit a news weekly, *Hoy*, which, along with the Alessandri-sponsored newspaper, *Crónica*, delivered a constant barrage of anti-Montero opinion. Dávila was believed to be gathering the Ibañistas into a civilian faction that could act with a like-minded group in the army. The same rumors also mentioned Marmaduke Grove and Eugenio Matte.[74] One conspiracy came to light when Dávila split with other Ibañistas over possible government policies. He and Arturo Merino Benítez, head of the air force, were arrested. Loyal troops and the carabineros occupied the area around La Moneda.[75]

Around this time, Montero made several mistakes. He called together many of the leaders from the Parliamentary Regime to discuss a way out of the legislative impasse, the imposition of martial law, and the likelihood of a coup.[76] Of all people, he approached his nemesis, Arturo Alessandri, and offered his son, Jorge, a chance to form a cabinet. Montero was broadcasting his desperation and vulnerability. When the younger Alessandri refused the offer, Montero appointed him head of the State Mortgage Bank. Then, he appointed Marmaduke Grove as head of the air force—a fatal decision.[77]

Dávila was released on a legal technicality and went into hiding, from which he issued pronouncements. Socialism would arrive peacefully. There would be no Bastille, no march on Rome, he said. An executive committee would simply seize the means of production and begin planning for a different future.[78] Montero, even when he invoked martial law, did not impose a repressive regime. Opponents were free to circulate leaflets and even clandestine newspapers and news magazines.[79] Elías Lafertte, the leader of the Communist Party, reports in his memoirs how easy it was to escape police surveillance.[80] The greatest impediment to Dávila's conspiracy was his fellow conspirators. There were too many egos in a still fragile movement.

In May 1932, the few remaining nitrate plants closed. Those workers fortunate enough to have a public works job earned three pesos a day—the skimpiest lunch cost a peso and a half. The government remained in a quandary.

With Dávila in hiding, Grove decided to act, mobilizing the troops at El Bosque, the air force base, on June 3. Montero immediately tried to remove him; but Grove refused to resign or leave El Bosque, and the coup was on.[81] Army leaders viewed Grove as an Ibañista because of the 1924 coup, and they refused to attack El Bosque. Montero again turned to Alessandri. The former president was sent to negotiate with Grove; but he made a minimal effort. Grove later claimed that, as Alessandri left, he told his old companion in exile, "Don't hesitate, Colonel." Alessandri always denied making this comment; but he never argued in defense of Montero's government.[82]

Major sections of the public were shocked and disappointed. As rumor of an attempted coup spread, professional men and some small landowners began arming a "White Guard" to support Montero.[83] Medical students, lawyers, and other professionals circulated leaflets in support of the government, claiming they would strike if it fell. Grove raised the ante and flew thirty planes over La Moneda. On the first pass, civilians who had rallied in the plaza to support the government fled to side streets. On the second pass, the plaza emptied.[84] A disgusted British official believed that a competent "machine-gun company" could have put an end to the coup by shooting down a couple of planes.[85] Montero was unwilling to fight. Early in the evening of June 4, the president asked Grove to La Moneda and handed over the government.

A junta was formed with General Arturo Puga Osorio, Montero's Minister of Interior, as provisional head of state. The actual government was a committee that included Grove, Dávila, and Matte Hurtado (head of the NAP). From the outset, it was Grove, as Minister of Defense, who took action. A personality conflict developed between Grove and Dávila, who considered the air force colonel too provocative and likely to alienate the United States. Within a few days, Dávila was marginalized within the government and, on June 12, was forced out of the junta. Matte Hurtado sided openly with Grove and his NAP used this period to recruit party support in the capital. Grove's bravado had won him respect within the government and he was determined to keep the initiative. He ordered the army to occupy the streets of the capital and declared a three-day bank holiday. He then gave a series of broadcasts, almost instituting government by radio, in which he dissolved Congress, increased the range of products under price control, and promised to collectivize agriculture. The government planned to seize all major industries, including the mines and called an assembly to draft another constitution.[86] Grove loved center stage. In his first public address, he favorably contrasted his proposals with those of the "deluded Jesus Christ."[87] It was also Grove who coined the left-wing phrase that would haunt populist politics for the next two decades when he called for a regime to provide each ordinary man, "bread, a roof, and an overcoat" [pan, techo, y abrigo].

His political support was ridiculously narrow. Its core was in the air force, which had only 1.2 thousand men (300 of them officers). By comparison, there were 18 thousand troops in the army and 13 thousand carabineros.[88] None of the other military leaders lent him public support. Army and navy officers quickly began debating in private whether they should follow government orders.[89] His chief civilian support consisted of the NAP and a very loose-knit collection of five or six other "socialist" parties, each with a handful of middle-class members.[90] (This claque included the young Oscar Schnake Vergara, who would play a major role in left-wing politics in the late 1930s and 1940s.)

The government issued, "A Program for Immediate Economic Action," justifying the coup. The lengthy statement claimed that Chile was "an economic colony" in which, "everything has been systematically handed over to foreigners." The crisis was the result of economic liberalism, foreign borrowing, and the actions of foreign commercial houses. A new government's top priorities must be, "feeding the people, clothing the people, and housing the people."[91] In an interview, Grove, who assumed an executive posture within the junta, argued that he had saved the nation from communism.[92] In fact, he was so desperate for support, he courted both the Stalinists and the Trotskyists. Each wanted more government posts than he was willing to provide. The Communists never became part of the government, but their leader, Lafertte, was regularly invited to government councils.[93] Another Grove pronouncement gave this government its name, the Socialist Republic. Political life became a series of street demonstrations and ad hoc rallies, of secret meetings within the government and conspiratorial movements outside it. At rallies of the unemployed, government defenders said Chile was in "the hour of social conquest," which called for a rejection of all bourgeois leaders and reformers.[94] Grove's major support came from a labor movement that was regenerating its ranks, but neither the General Confederation of Labor [CGT] nor the Chilean Labor Federation [FOCh] were in the government.[95] At many of the rallies workers demanded firearms.[96]

The government ruled by decree. Within the capital, it seized the assets of major businesses and foreign firms. Short of even day-to-day cash, Grove sent the police into jewelry stores, confiscating gold.[97] The oil companies retaliated by stopping imports of gasoline, which brought transportation to a near halt. Foreign banks cut off all credit for trade.[98]

While the elite and most of the middle class could do nothing about the coup, they did react. From the very first they rejected Grove and socialism.[99] Not one of the professional guilds supported the government. The lawyers went on strike, the courts in Santiago stopped functioning, and the head of the Supreme Court resigned. Businessmen in Valparaiso openly condemned the coup.[100] The White Guard, formed to protect Montero's administration, continued meeting in secret and became the nucleus of an anti-left, paramilitary organization. Provincial elements found it easy to mobilize government opponents. As early as June 6, a counter-revolutionary movement began in the south. Army and naval garrisons in Concepción and Talcahuano mutinied.

In a little less than two weeks, the government unraveled from within. Grove forced Dávila out. Merino Benítez had been recruited as Undersecretary of Aviation; he now resigned. The military kept its distance.[101] The Ibañistas in the bureaucracy knew this was not the regime they had wanted. Dávila easily recruited army officers to overthrow the junta. Grove had promised to die before surrendering La Moneda. But on June 16, when the army invaded the presidential palace, he negotiated for his life and was taken, swearing at what he considered a military betrayal, to Valparaiso. Along with Matte Hurtado and some 20 others, he spent the next year imprisoned on Juan Fernández Island.[102] Laborers rose in support, but too late. Dozens died in a strike at Braden and in strikes and riots in Santiago, Valparaiso, San Antonio, Concepción, and Temuco. The aftermath, which included extensive use of martial law, was far more brutal than when Ibáñez fell.[103] The "Socialist Republic" was over.

The contest for power within the government was resolved; the army had become the arbiter of disputes. Even so, Dávila formed his first cabinet entirely of civilian Ibañistas. There would be, for the next few months and especially before mid-July, more conflicts and disputes, each of them consolidating the authority of the army within the government and of Dávila as chief executive.

Dávila supported state intervention and wanted to combine "socialism" with protection of industry. In other words, he wanted a state-led development—a "revolution" from the top down. He intended to nationalize key sectors without alienating the United States. He was a great admirer of the U.S. and he feared the power of its corporations in Chile. His socialism excluded labor. As his Minister of the Interior, he chose Juan Antonio Ríos, a member of the southern, conservative wing of the Radical Party. Ríos, once an Alessandrista who became tied to Ibáñez, banned the Communists and suppressed the CGT and the FOCh. The junta prohibited saying or writing anything that threatened "the social or political order of the State."[104] In his first public statement, Dávila proclaimed, on June 17, that the government was "in the hands of civilians because this is the firm decision of the Armed Forces. . . . Socialism is not disorder but control: it is not carried out by improvisations but by planning; it does not mobilize the masses in order to launch them into a ruinous violence but seeks to guide them and to assure them justice and well-being."[105]

The army could not supply a sufficient base for government, and Dávila had to cobble additional support from various factions. An ad hoc quality characterized his entire administration, with careerism as its defining characteristic. For example, he recruited some Alessandristas into the ministries but forced Alessandri into the Spanish Embassy, accusing him of subversion.[106] The old lion was caged! Dávila tried to buy middle class support, creating five thousand new jobs in three months; he also lavished money on the military.[107] His most complex task was to appropriate Ibañismo without Ibáñez. The former head of state, recognizing that his supporters had seized office, decided to return. But Dávila no longer wanted his former patron; Ibáñez was forced to stay on his farm.[108] On July 8, Dávila, with the Army's blessing, dissolved the junta and became provisional president.[109]

Dávila's feelings about the United States were not reciprocated by American interests. He became fond of the United States while serving as Ibáñez's ambassador to Washington. Despite his attitudes, the U.S. corporations, the State Department, and the U.S. Embassy in Chile never liked him. They saw him as dangerous and immediately began to weaken his administration.

In the United States, Hoover was president; his Secretary of State Henry Stimson set harsh, even humiliating conditions for recognition. Other governments—Argentina, Britain, most of western Europe, and Central America—waited to see what would happen between the United States and Chile.[110] The U.S. position was stated by Stimson in instructions to the Santiago Embassy in mid-July. Another round of "economic diplomacy" had begun and this time American interests had far more leverage. Dávila was told that if the Chilean government wanted recognition, it had to promise no confiscation of foreign property and to treat foreign firms with the same consideration given domestic companies.[111] Dávila tried to comply. No threats were made against the nitrate or copper companies; the idea of an oil monopoly was shelved; talk of nationalizing the electric, tramway, and telephone companies ceased; and the Central Bank, seized by Grove, was returned to its former status. Although Chile could not pay its foreign debt, it did not repudiate the obligations.[112] Dávila even allowed copper interests a say in official appointments affecting their sector.[113]

The United States was still unhappy and refused recognition even after Austria, Bolivia, Costa Rica, Cuba, Mexico, Peru, and Uruguay had established relations with the new government. At one point, U.S. Ambassador Culbertson asked a Chilean official why there was still talk of socialism and was assured that this rhetoric was for domestic consumption only. The Chilean, according to Embassy notes, explained, "that a Chilean speaking before a crowd in the street might make the most absurd statements but that when that same Chilean was put in a position where he would be responsible for his actions, he would adopt a totally different attitude."[114] In dealing with the United States, the issues that beset Dávila were the same that had plagued Montero. Like Montero, Dávila hoped COSACh would revive the nitrate trade. Efforts to establish a new international fertilizer cartel fell apart in August, and COSACh averted liquidation only by borrowing from the Chilean government.[115] The firm was in a hopeless situation: its overhead to produce and ship a metric ton of salitre was US$44. That same ton sold for US$32 on the open market.[116] Officials under Dávila considered nationalizing the nitrate sector, renouncing COSACh's debts, and running the industry at cost as a means of reviving employment.[117] But Dávila was unwilling to take such a chance. Instead, he tried to barter nitrate for wheat from the United States, an effort the State Department blocked, and fuel from Russia, which the oil companies prevented.[118] Fuel remained scarce. Like Ibáñez and Montero, Dávila threatened nationalist measures. Unlike Montero, he tried rationing. But when the Currency Exchange Commission was unable to pay for past deliveries, the oil companies again cut off imports. Chile literally ran out of gas.

Problems of finance and exchange pitted the administration against foreign banks. The foreign debt issue was moot. The State Department ordered U.S. bond companies and other representatives of creditors to stop lobbying it on the subject.[119] The U.S. and British governments did press Dávila on the issue of "blocked currencies." They demanded that Chile spend some hard currency on paying foreign pensioners living abroad and on honoring obligations for unpaid imports.[120] The State Department created a legal precedent out of its strategy for pressuring the Chilean government for repayment of pensions owed U.S. citizens.[121] In the end, Dávila could not reconcile the demands of the U.S. government and corporations with the needs of his government.

In so many ways, the journalist, ambassador, and former Ibañista typified the muddled middle class. Dávila loved the romance of political conspiracy and making broad promises; he had little idea of how to organize an administration. At a time of fiscal insolvency, he believed that a government-directed recovery was possible. He spoke in favor of a balanced budget. He wanted to enlarge the public sector with state industries *and* promote private enterprise. He thought that well-trained bureaucrats, "technical experts," who saw "in capital a social function and not an instrument of exploitation" would carry out his plans.[122]

Dávila's basic proposal was to spend 190 million pesos in new expenditures: 50 million in public works and the rest on increased credit for mining, agriculture, and manufacturing. The proposal anticipated the collection of 100 of the 150 million owed in back taxes and payments in arrears on purchases of public lands. The rest would be covered by new taxes and loans.[123] In late June, his government raised the income tax rates on the rich, that is, on salaries above 50 thousand pesos; the highest rate on two million pesos reached 25 percent.[124] The land tax remained unchanged at 6 percent.[125] But taxes were not due for another year; moreover, the government neither had an enforcement mechanism to assure payment, nor the means to collect back taxes on short notice.

In practice, his program emphasized extending credit to established sectors. The chief beneficiaries of his administration were the landed rich. Under two finance ministers, both log rollers for the Liberals and one of them a heavily indebted hacendado, the government printed 170 million pesos to rejuvenate the public works program and then 190 million to bail out the Central Bank and state credit agencies.[126] All mortgages were extended. Indebted landowners were allowed to consolidate their debts and reduce payments 50 percent, and their interest rates fell below the discount rate of the Central Bank.[127] These policies, in the words of one minister, permitted, "the distressed debtors . . . to work with a lesser burden and [so] restore the economic power of the country."[128] Dávila's own magazine, *Hoy*, asked, "Is this a socialist republic of the Chilean workers or the Chilean debtors?"[129] Inflation intensified, driven now by monetary policy. Between the time of the coup and the last of the provisional presidents, the money supply more than doubled, with the government directing the Central Bank to use funds to roll over bad loans in real estate, agriculture, and commerce (see Table 2.3 below). As inflationary expectations built, speculation in commodities went wild.[130] Between October 1931 and December 1932, wholesale prices rose 138 percent.[131] The purchasing power of wages registered an 18 percent drop.[132]

Despite the debt relief, the upper class hated Dávila. He was a social upstart, a former Ibañista, a man out of place who had been imposed on the country by an increasingly detested army. The turmoil and uncertainty led some sections of the upper class to recruit portions of the middle class into paramilitary organizations, which often had support from foreign corporations. Paramilitarism and the threat of general violence were, along with the collapse of exports and high rates of inflation, part of the legacy of the Crash. It is said that the 1930s

Table 2.3: Money Supply, 1932-1934

Date	Money in Millions
May 20, 1932	342
June 23, 1932	487
Dec. 25, 1932	810
June 12, 1933	883
Oct. 13, 1933	850
May 4, 1934	941
June 6, 1934	876

Source: United States State Department, Record Group 59: 825.5151/214, Scotten no. 159, 1 Aug. 1934.

represented a return to civilian rule; it is not as frequently mentioned that many civilians had taken up arms. In a pattern that is explained in Chapter 5, under Dávila these ad hoc units formed the Republican Militia.[133] This was also when the Naci movement began from the nucleus that met in Santiago in April 1932. The government was losing its monopoly of force. Military officers, who were largely middle class, reluctantly backed the government despite their dislike of Dávila's "socialist" proclamations. Dávila rewarded them and the carabineros with salary increases, rapid promotions, and higher living allowances for quarters and subsistence.[134] One leftist pamphlet labeled the administration a military committee with Dávila at its head.[135] It would have been slightly more accurate to call it a collection of military officers, lawyers, and log rollers in search of popular policies.

Labor, the last social class, began to mobilize, triggering a variety of government responses. Dávila mouthed populist expressions but he could not recruit labor leaders into his government. First, such a move would alienate the military. Second, the leaders generally hated him for overthrowing Grove. Some small, socialist factions got minor government jobs; but most of the left remained under surveillance or in exile.[136] Like Ibáñez, Dávila wanted a captive labor movement. Unlike Ibáñez, he failed to create a new structure to control the labor organizations. The government apparently expected popular support to materialize out of self-interest. It decreed the eight-hour day for urban workers, although employers could demand a 48 hour week. Labor courts, established in the 1920s, became active and generally sided with employees against foreign companies.[137] The gold-panning program was intensified and broadened but employed only six thousand Chileans.[138]

Dávila's treated labor inconsistently: workers were allowed to assemble at times, repressed at others. As a precaution, he expanded the state's police powers and improved the government's network of informers. The government censored the labor press and sanctioned wiretaps.[139] Confused and intimidated, labor leaders were unsure how to proceed. When a labor faction called for a strike or demonstration, no one knew what might happen.[140] On one occasion, for example, a dozen Communists were released from jail just as other Communists were being arrested and exiled to remote islands.[141] Labor's gravest threat to Dávila's administration was that Grove might return and act as the catalyst for a general uprising. The government made sure Grove remained on Juan Fernández Island.

Lacking a political base and a congress, the government relied on decrees and the armed forces. The decrees seemed more and more removed from reality. As an illustration, Dávila's administration created a new General Price Commission, adding dozens of articles to the list of controlled prices, and giving the Commission power to expropriate whole factories and to order goods produced at a set price. General Bartolomé Blanche, an Ibáñista, was put in charge.[142] But the government's monetary policies were feeding inflation, and the combination of price controls and more money simply drove more goods into the black market. No foreign currency was available at the official rate, and the black market rate was five times as great.[143] No one of importance was ever prosecuted under the complex currency statutes. To cover its own desperate currency needs, the government relied upon U.S. mining companies, who obeyed the tax and the monetary measures each administration improvised.[144]

By September 1932, Dávila was an executive without a political base. The British chargé claimed this was not a government but, "a collection of inexperienced individuals masquerading as such."[145] The major powers looked upon his government as dangerously incompetent and out of control. He assured U.S. companies, but they kept their distance. After pressing for one final set of assurances on currency rules, the State Department instructed Ambassador Culbertson, on September 10, to recognize Dávila's administration. Culbertson decided to wait a few days. Dávila had helped the rich and they rejected him. He provided public works and both the middle class and labor resented the inflationary results. And all the time, unemployment remained high. The government had no new institutions to show for its efforts. It had built neither a new party, nor established new connections between state and public. The impact of inflation, the worsening economy, and the spread of paramilitarism factionalized the military—the very force propping up the government. His government had issued more than six hundred decree-laws, often in such haste that the provisions from one edict contradicted those of another.[146] On September 13, Dávila was overthrown.[147] When officers in the air force quarreled with some in the army, Dávila's government was the chief casualty. The army removed him and he fled to the United States.[148]

Army officers turned to General Bartolomé Blanche, who became the next provisional president. The Ibáñistas were back. Blanche called for a new presidential election and the release of most political prisoners—Grove was a notable exception.[149] Public hostility exploded. Elements in the army knew it was time to return to the barracks. Responding to professional sentiment in Antofagasta, the head of the division there, General Pedro Vignola, refused to recognize the Blanche government. Blanche dispatched a general to remove him, the citizens in Antofagasta rallied to Vignola's defense, and the army faced an uprising in the north and demonstrations in almost all major cities. In the south, the Republican Militia displayed its arms. As military officers met at La Moneda to receive his decision, Blanche resigned. The officers were jeered by a large crowd.[150] The military gave in to the civilian demand that the President of the Supreme Court, Abraham Oyanedel, be appointed provisional president. Following his installation, he called immediately for a new presidential election.[151]

* * *

Montero and the provisional presidents had set the stage for the leftward tilt of public life. As Chile moved away from economic orthodoxy, its political class had little idea how to proceed. There was no clear link between policies and public support for government. The bases of patronage, built over the decades of an export-based economy, disappeared; and no party, faction, or leader knew how to build new structures of politics and administration. Montero failed at reviving the civilian regime that had preceded Ibáñez. The coup against him set other efforts at reconstruction in motion, all of them hampered by the lack of money and legitimacy. As each failed, it left detritus in the form of decree-laws, inflation, and public demoralization. Grove proved that the Chilean left was not prepared to take power; Dávila, that inflationary policies were no way out of the depression. Finally, the military divided and lost all capacity to impose another chief executive.

All the executives after Ibáñez antagonized foreign interests. This marked a change with the past but did little to reduce Chile's dependency. Chilean nationalists became bolder as the collapse of trade ruined established links between foreign and domestic capital; but U.S. interests still ran the mines and utilities and supplied essential imports. Chilean presidents could threaten; but foreign corporations could retaliate with crippling blows. After Dávila's government collapsed, U.S. Ambassador Culbertson concluded that all foreign interests remained secure. The British minister in Santiago agreed.[152]

The governments after Ibáñez were hobbled from one month to the next, when even small amounts of hard cash and fuel made a difference. One of Dávila's finance ministers begged the foreign banks in Santiago for 150 million pesos to "tide over the government." They turned him down.[153] The oil companies could choke Santiago to a standstill any time they chose. All the provisional presidents but Grove were so afraid of the Guggenheims that they bailed out the debt-ridden COSACh with scarce funds. When Dávila threatened a takeover of the firm, its manager, G.B. Whelpley, told his subordinates to let the government know he would answer such a move by dumping nitrate on the market and cutting off Chile's shipping.[154]

A final legacy of this interregnum created a situation ripe for political desperadoes. Small factions within the military and among the elite and the middle class saw the government as up for grabs. A mentality supporting putsches was taking root, undoubtedly drawing inspiration from events elsewhere in Latin America and Europe. University students conspired to return Grove to office by force in 1932.[155] Paramilitarism blossomed. Civility was disappearing from public life.

There appeared, in the capital, the specter of mob rule. When Grove was removed, the unemployed rioted in several cities. In the capital, tramway cars were destroyed and demonstrators, attempting to seize an arms depot, were driven back with machine-gun fire. Forty-seven were killed.[156]

One by one, the nation's institutional structures either disappeared, became irrelevant (one hears little from the Church in the crisis), or splintered into factions. The question that faced Chile in 1932 was whether it was possible to construct a governing coalition. The received opinion was no.

Endnotes

For abbreviations used in notes, see Endnotes, Chapter 1.

1. Chile. Diputados, *Boletín de Sesiones Estraordinarios*, 2 Nov. 1931, 750; Elguín quotes letter printed in *El Imparcial*, 27 Oct. 1931, written by Bishop of Tarapacá, Carlos Labb.

2. *La Hora* (Temuco), 17 Dec. 1931.

3. RG 151: Commerce Dept., Bureau of Foreign and Domestic Commerce, Commercial Attaches: Santiago, Harold M. Randall, Special Report no. 11, 7 Oct. 1931, quoting different Chilean officials.

4. Chile. Relaciones Exteriores v. 93 (1931), Oscar Blanco Vial to Sant., 1 Dec. 1931; and Ignacio Aliaga Ibar, *La economía de Chile y la industria del cobre (algunas reflexiones sobre la post-guerra)* (Santiago: Universidad de Chile, published dissertation, 1946), 202-203.

5. RG 59: 825.00-Revs/117, Culbertson, no. 1178, 15 June 1932.

6. RG 59: 825.504/97, Bowman, 14 Dec. 1932.

7. Chile. Trabajo (1932), Oficios, v. 24, no. 1, Gmo. Donoso Grez, Intendencia de Talca, no. 10, 2 June 1932.

8. RG 165: MID 2657-0-96/33, Wooten, no. 1021, 28 July 1931.

9. FO 371-15077 (A 5117/13/9), Sir H. Chilton to Mr. A. Henderson, 31 July 1931.

10. Chile. Relaciones Exteriores v. 79 (1932), *New York Herald Tribune*, 5 June 1932.

11. *The Times*, London, 13 Aug. 1931; RG 59: 825.0177/4, Wooten, no. 1075, 28 Aug. 1931; and Chile. Diputados, *Boletín de sesiones ordinarios*, Hector Alvarez, 5 Aug. 1931, 125.

12. Chile. Interior, v. 8119 (1932), Contraloría General, 10 Dec. 1931.

13. RG 59: 825.515/32, Culbertson, no. 1144, 20 Apr. 1932, enclosed statement of Central Bank.

14. Chile. Fomento (1931), Oficios v. 594, no. 2, memo no. 243, 11 Feb. 1931. The extent of the crisis is clear in, Chile. Interior, v. 7881 (1931), *Informe de la situación económica-agrícola de la regiona austral*; and RG 59: 825.50/23 Bowman, 27 Feb. 1932, enclosure, no. 1, Agriculture in Chile, 12 Apr. 1932. By early 1932, short-term interest rates stood at 10 percent and property values fell to 4 billion. The cost of producing grains and livestock exceeded returns on many estates by about 6 percent.

15. Chile. Hacienda, Antecedentes de Oficios v. 3 (1931), Min. de Hacienda, no. 804, 17 Dec. 1931. On Alessandri's comments, see RG 59: 825.00/741, Chile-American Association, Confidential Report no. 5, May 1932.

16. Chile. Hacienda, Antecedentes de Oficios, v. 3 (1931), Min. de Hacienda, no. 804, 17 Dec. 1931.

17. FO 371-15077 (A 5117/13/9), Sir H. Chilton to Mr. A. Henderson, 31 July 1931.

18. RG 59: 825.5151/23, Stimson memo, 9 Nov. 1931; and FO 371-15079 (A5275 /544/9), Chilton, 4 Aug. 1931.

19. RG 165: MID 2515-0-10/6, Wooten, no. 11559, 5 Nov. 1931; and RG 59: 825.5151/23, Thomas B. Bowman, American Consul General, 7 Dec. 1931.

20. RG 59: 825.5151/34, Culbertson, no. 1109, 1 Mar. 1932, enclosure Comisión de Control de Operaciones de Cambio a Culbertson, 26 Feb. 1932: reply to Culbertson's letter.

21. BOLSA, B12/1, 1931, W.C. Maycock to Ch., 6 Nov. 1931. On the misguided defense of gold, see Albert O. Hirschman, *Journeys Toward Progress: Studies of Economic Policy-Making in Latin America* (New York: The Twentieth Century Fund, 1963), 179.

22. Gibbs, L64.22, Ms. 16,882/33, London, 22 Dec. 1931.

23. RG 151: Bureau of Foreign and Domestic Commerce, Commercial Attaches: Santiago, Randall, Special Report no. 7, 16 Sept. 1931.

24. A.J.P. Taylor, *English History* (New York: Oxford University Press, 1965), 330.

25. Charles S. Maier, *Recasting Bourgeois Europe: stabilization in France, Germany and Italy in the decade after World War I* (Princeton: Princeton University Press, 1975).

26. Another key work on Europe is, Andrew Cox and Noel D. Sullivan, eds., *The Corporatist State: Corporatism and the State Tradition* (Brookfield, VT: Gower Publishing Co., 1988); major studies on Latin America, include Fredrick B. Pike and Thomas Stritch, eds., *The New Corporatism; socio-political structures in the Iberian World* (Notre Dame: University of Notre Dame Press, 1974); and Alfred C. Stepan, *The State and Society: Peru in Comparative Perspective* (Princeton: Princeton University Press, 1978), especially his introduction. There is also the prolific, Howard J. Wiarda, *Corporatism and Comparative Politics: the other great "ism"* (New York: M.E. Sharpe, 1997); Howard J. Wiarda, *Corporatism and National Development in Latin America* (Boulder: Westview Press, 1981); and Howard J. Wiarda and Harvey F. Klein, eds., *Latin American Politics and Development*, 4th ed. (Boulder: Westview Press, 1996).

27. Alessandri, *Recuerdos de Gobierno*, 2:439-40.

28. Robert J. Alexander, *Trotskyism in Latin America* (Stanford: Hoover Institution Press, 1973), 91-94.

29. *La Hora* (Temuco), 19 Dec. 1931; RG 59: 825.00/683, Wooten, no. 1033, 6 Aug. 1931; and RG 59: 825.00-Gen cond./27, Culbertson, no. 1075, 12 Jan. 1932.

30. RG 59: 825.00/722, Culbertson, no. 1126, 21 Mar. 1932; and Paul Drake, *Socialism and Populism in Chile, 1932-1952* (Chicago: University of Illinois Press, 1978), 70.

31. RG 59: 825.00/697, enclosure 2, clippings, *El Mercurio*, 22 Sept. 1931.

32. RG 59: 825.00/702, Culbertson, no. 983, 7 Oct. 1931, *El Mercurio*, Montero's platform, 27 Aug. 1931.

33. The account is based on British Foreign Office and U.S. State and War Department reports. See especially FO 371-15078 (A5884/13/9), FO 371-15078 (A6725/13/9), H. Chilton, 6 Oct. 1931; RG 59: 825.00-Revolutions/25, Culbertson tel., 5 Sept. 1931, and Culbertson tel., 6 Sept. 1931; 825.00-Revolutions/42, Culbertson, no. 958, 9 Sept. 1931, report of Commander Ernest L. Gunther, naval attaché; and RG 165: MID 2657-0-96/39, Wooten, no. 1093, 11 Sept. 1931. There are two informative articles on the subject: William F. Sater, "The Abortive Kronstadt: The Chilean Naval Mutiny," *Hispanic American Historical Review* 60:2 (May 1980), 239-268; and Philip Somervell, "Naval Affairs in Chilean Politics, 1910-1932," *Journal of Latin American Studies* 16:2 (Nov. 1984), 381-402.

34. The exact relation between the Communist Party and the mutiny itself is a source of disagreement. See Sater, op. cit., 264; and Somervell, op. cit., 400.

35. On the military units and government fears see Carlos Sáez Morales, *Recuerdos de un soldado: el ejército y la política* (Santiago: Biblioteca Ercilla, 1934), 3:40-41; and Sater, op. cit., 247.

36. RG 165, MID 2657-0-96/38, Wooten, no. 1091, 10 Sept. 1931.

37. RG 59: 825.00B/32, Cole, no. 528, Riga, 8 July 1932, quoting an account of Lafertte's address taken from a Russian periodical.

38. Carlos Maldonado Prieto, "Entre reacción civilista y constitucionalismo formal: las fuerzas armadas chilenas en el periodo 1931-1938," *Contribuciones/Programa FLACSO-Chile* no. 55 (Agosto 1988), 38, cites Frederick M. Nunn, *The military in Chilean History: essays on civil-military relations, 1810-1973* (Albuquerque: University of New Mexico Press, 1976), 223-26.

39. Chile. Hacienda (1932), Defensa Nacional to Hacienda, 7 Apr. 1932.

40. RG 59: 825.6374/975, J. memo of telephone conversation, 19 Apr. 1932.

41. FO 371-15078 (A7554/13/9), H. Chilton, 10 Dec. 1931. They were rising in the provinces as well, even in the north where no one had work, see Chile. Hacienda, Antecedentes de Oficios v. 1 (1932), Min. del Interior, 27 Nov. 1931: report from Alcalde de Antofagasta on Oct. 31.

42. RG 165: MID 2515-0-10/7, Wooten, no. 1342, 17 May 1932.

43. Camara de Comercio de Chile, *Memoria* (1932), 21, 24-25.

44. RG 165: MID 1657-0-143/1, Wooten, no. 1271, 15 Mar. 1932; and Sáez, *Recuerdos*, 3:51.

45. Chile. Fomento (1933), Oficios v. 813, no. 1, Min. de Fomento Decreto, no. 284, 20 May 1931; and FO 371-15825 (A4207/86/9), Thompson report, 2 June 1932.

46. Chile. Fomento (1932), Oficios v. 704, no. 3, op. cit.

47. RG 59: 825.51/600, Bowman, 28 Feb. 1933.

48. FO 371-15824 (A210/86/9), Chilton, 29 Dec. 1931; RG 165, MID 2657-0-137/8, Wooten, no. 1199, 30 Dec. 1931; Andrew Barnard, "The Chilean Communist Party: 1922-1947," (Ph.D. diss., University of London, University College, Dec. 1977), 143; and Germán Urzúa V., *La democracia práctica: los gobiernos radicales* (Santiago: Editorial Melquíades for CIEDES, 1987), 79-80.

49. Chile. Fomento (1932), Oficios v. 704, no. 3, Nicolás Marambir, Caja de Crédito Minero to Min., 2 Apr. 1932; and *New York Herald Tribune*, 8 Apr. 1932.

50. Chile. Hacienda, Antecedentes de Oficios v. 2 (1932), Embajada de Chile in Washington, 23 Nov. 1931; and *New York Times*, 22 Nov. 1931.

51. I am using the term *entitlement* in the sense proposed by Amartya Sen, *Poverty and Famines: an Essay on entitlement and deprivation* (Oxford: Oxford University Press, 1981), 45-47. Sen emphasizes the role of law and regulation in creating *rights* to resources.

52. For a list of all laws and decree laws relating to petroleum see Chile. Hacienda, Dirección General de Impuestos Internos, no. 753, 20 Jan. 1934.

53. Hoover Papers, Pres., op. cit., 24-25; and Ryszard Stemplowski, "Chile y las compañías petroleras, 1931-1932. Contribución al estudio del entrelazamiento dominación-dependencia," *Ibero-Amerikanisches Archiv* 4:1 (1978), 11.

54. RG 165: MID 2655-0-64/1, Wooten, no. 1281, 21 Mar. 1932.

55. Hoover Papers, Pres., Box 49, folder on State Department, Latin Affairs, Review of Questions, "Recent Problems in the Protection of American Interests in Chile," 2:24-25.

56. Chile Fomento (1931), Oficios con Antecedentes, v. 601, no. 9, Gandarillas, President of Sociedad Nacional de Minería to Minister, 25 Sept. 1931.

57. RG 59: 825.6363/77, Orme Wilson memo of conversation with Judge Campbell, Attorney for Standard Oil of NY (West India Oil), Nov. 1931; and 825.6363/82, Stimson memo of conversation (on Nov. 23), with Mr. Senior, president of West India Co.; Judge Campbell, representative of Standard Oil Co of NJ; and Edwin C. Wilson, Orme Wilson, Mr. Feis, Mr. Flournoy, and Mr. Stimson of State Dept., 25 Nov. 1931.

58. RG 59: 811.25/75, Norweb, no. 1344, 28 Dec. 1932.

59. RG 151: Bureau of Foreign and Domestic Commerce, Commercial Attaches: Santiago, Randall, Special Reports no. 50, 13 May 1932, and no. 157, 25 May 1932.

60. RG 59: 611.259 Singer Sewing Machine Co./31, memo to E.C. Wilson, 20 Sept. 1932.

61. Hoover Papers, Pres., Box 49, Folder of State Dept., Latin American Affairs, Review of Questions, "Recent Problems in the protection of American Interests in Chile," 2:49-50.

62. Chile. Hacienda, Antecedentes de oficios v. 4 (1932), Miguel Cruchaga, Chile's Ambassador to United States, to Min. de Relaciones Exteriores, report no. 56, 23 Feb. 1932.

63. RG 151: Bureau of Foreign and Domestic Commerce, Commercial Attaches: Santiago, Ackerman, Special Report no. 49, 18 Apr. 1932.

64. Enrique L. Marshall, "Régimen monetario actual en Chile y sus antecedentes históricos," in Humberto Fuenzalida, et al., *Chile: geografía, educación, literatura, legislación, economía, minería* (Buenos Aires: Editorial Losada, S.A., 1946), 247; and Hoover Papers, Pres., Box 49, "Recent Problems," 2:75-76.

65. RG 59: 711.25/75, Norweb, no. 1344, 28 Dec. 1932.

66. RG 59: 325.1143-Howard/16, Culbertson, no. 1331, 7 Dec. 1932. This file contains dozens of cases relating to this problem.

67. FO 371-15820 (2375/2/9), J.H. Thomas, 7 Apr. 1932.

68. Ricardo Donoso, *Alessandri: Agitador y Demoledor* (Mexico: Fondo de Cultura, 1954), 2:75.

69. Luis Palma Zuñiga, *Historia del partido radical* (Santiago: Editorial Andres Bello, 1967), quotes party platform, 174-75. See also Peter G. Snow, *Radicalismo chileno: historia y doctrina del partido radical* (Santiago: Editorial Francisco de Aguirre, 1972), 73-74.

70. RG 59: 825.00-Gen. Cond./41, Culbertson, no. 1162, 18 May 1932; Alessandri's letter to Federation of the Left, in *La Crónica*, 10 May 1932.

71. RG 59: 825.6374/1054, "Report on Companía de Salitre de Chile," Div. of Latin American Affairs, State Dept., 16 Sept. 1932.

72. FO 371-15824 (A2929/86/9), G.H. Thompson, 16 Apr. 1932.

73. Jordi Fuentes and Lia Cortes, *Diccionario político de Chile (1810-1966)* (Santiago: Editorial Orbe, 1967), 351; RG 165: War Dept., MID 2657-0-150/4, Wooten, no. 1369, 15 June 1932; RG 59: 825.504/160, Bowers, no. 4236, 21 Aug. 1942, report by Faust. Drake, op. cit., 72-73; and Luis Alberto Sánchez, *Visto y vivido en Chile: bitacora chilena, 1930-1970* (Lima: Editoriales Unidas, 1975), 31.

74. The U.S. military attaché was one of the best informed men in Santiago. He based his reports on interviews with Chilean officers. See RG 165: MID 2657-0-150/4, Wooten, no. 1369, 15 June 1932. See also Jack Ray Thomas, "Marmaduke Grove: A Political Biography," (Ph.D. diss., Ohio State University, 1962), 41. For an excellent narrative by a Grovista apologist who argues over and over that Grove was not planning any move against the government see Carlos Charlin O., *Del avión rojo a la república socialista* (Santiago: Empresa Editora Nacional Quimantu, Limitada, 1972), chaps. 8 and 9.

75. RG 59: 825.00-Revs/62, Wooten, no. 1300, 8 Apr. 1932, and 825.00/741, Chile-American Association, Confidential Report no. 5, May 1932; and Thomas, "Marmaduke Grove," 180.

76. Sáez, *Recuerdos*, 3:169.

77. Gibbs, L64.22, MS 16,822/35, Valparaiso, 23 May 1932.

78. *La Crónica*, 3 May 1932, Carlos Dávila; Chile. Relaciones Exteriores (1932), enclosure of *Time* article, 16 May 1932. On economic decline, see Chile. Interior, v. 17 [old number] (1932), Prov. 4769, Carabineros, 11 May 1932; and Chile. Diputados, *Boletín de Sesiones Ordinarios*, Dip. Abraham Quevedo, 3 May 1932, 102.

79. Chile. Interior (1932), Prov. 1106, Arriagada Valdivieso, 18 July 1932, one of a series of such reports.

80. Elías Lafertte, *Vida de un comunista* (Santiago: Editorial Austral, 1971), 228-76.

81. RG 59: 825.00-Revs/95, Culbertson, no. 1174, 8 June 1932.

82. Robert J. Alexander, *Arturo Alessandri: A Biography* (New Brunswick, NJ: Rutgers University Latin American Institute, University Microfilms International, 1977), 2:553. Alexander devotes 20 pages to disproving the charge. See also Fidel Araneda Bravo, *Arturo Alessandri Palma* (Santiago: Editorial Nascimento, 1979), 98.

83. *New York Herald Tribune*, 7 June 1932.

84. *New York Times*, 5 June 1932; and *El Mercurio*, 4 Oct. 1932, remembrance of day's events by Carlos Silva Vildósola. See also Sáez, *Recuerdos*, 3:169, 177.

85. FO 371-15825 (A4107/86/9), Thompson, 7 July 1932.

86. *New York Herald Tribune*, 6 June 1932; RG 59: 825.00-Revs/125, Chile-American Association, Monthly Bulletin, Confidential Report no. 6, June 1932; Stemplowski, op. cit., 12; and Urzúa V., op. cit., 94-95.

87. Culbertson Papers, cont. 13 (1925-33), Culbertson to Junia, 15 June 1932.

88. RG 59: 825.00-Revs./128, Stuart Grummon memo, 9 June 1932.

89. RG 165: MID 2657-9-150/4, Wooten, no. 1369, 15 June 1932.

90. Julio César Jobet, *El socialismo chileno a través de sus congresos* (Santiago: Editorial Prensa Latinoamericana, S.A. 1965), mentions six parties including the NAP, but one of them was a fusion of two others, 9-10.

91. Ibid., the entire statement is quoted, 11-16.

92. France-MAE, Chili, v. 8, 16 June 1932; and *New York Times*, 12 June 1932.

93. Lafertte, op. cit., 251-52. See also Alexander, *Trotskyism in Latin America*, 98.

94. See the vivid account of Sáez, *Recuerdos*, 3:188.

95. *La Opinión*, 10 June 1932; RG 59: 825.00B/35, Culbertson, no. 1234, 17 Aug. 1932, enclosure no. 1, Atwood report on Communism, 15 Aug. 1932; Drake, op. cit., 80; and Ricardo Boizard, *Cuatro retratos en profundidad: Ibáñez, Lafertte, Leighton, Walker* (Santiago: El Imparcial, 1950), 141-42.

96. RG 59: 825.00-Revs/85, Culbertson telegram, 13 June 1932.

97. FO 371-15825 (A354/86/9), Thompson telegram, 11 June 1932; and BOLSA, B10/4, 1931-1933, W.C. Maycock to Chairman, Valparaiso, 10 June 1932.

98. RG 59: 825.516/144, Welles memo of conversation with Sir Ronald Lindsay, Brit. Ambassador to Wash., D.C., 11 June 1932; *New York Herald Tribune*, 10 June 1932; and Stemplowski, op. cit., 12.

99. Sater, op. cit., 268, mistakenly argues that no one supported Montero.

100. RG 84:800 (Valparaiso, 1932), Frank A. Henry, 11 June 1932.

101. RG 59: 825.00-Revs/117, Culbertson, no. 1178, 15 June 1932.

102. RG 165, MID 2657-0-137/17, Wooten, no. 1371, June 18, 1932; Culbertson papers, container 101, "Indiscreciones de Morel," typewritten confession of army officer at Grove's interrogation after the invasion of La Moneda, copy given to U.S. Embassy, and "Versión taquigráfica de lo ocurrido antes y después del derrocamiento de la junta de gobierno que creó la República Socialista y de 12 días de duración." Before Grove fell, he shuffled the junta once, between June 13 and June 16.

103. Urzúa V., op. cit., 71; RG 59: 825.00-Revs/138, Culbertson, no. 1181, 22 June 1932; and FO 371-15825 (A4313/86/9), Thompson, 21 June 1932. See also Alexander, *Trotskyism in Latin America*, 98-99.

104. Thomas, "Marmaduke Grove," 214.

105. RG 59: 825.00-Revs/138, Culbertson, no. 1181, 22 June 1932, the translation has been slightly altered for style.

106. RG 59: 825.00-Revs/125, Culbertson telegram, 24 June 1932.

107. RG 59: 825.00/785, Confidential Report no. 10, Oct. 1932.

108. RG 59: 825.00-Revs/125, Culbertson telegram, 24 June 1932; RG 165: MID 2657-0-135/16, Wooten, no. 1390, 9 July 1932, and MID 2657-0-135/17, Wooten, no. 1402, 26 July 1932; Chile. Interior (1932), Prov. 1113, Arriagada Valdivieso, 19 July 1932; and *La Opinión*, 10 July 1932. For a very different view of this incident, see Nunn, op. cit., 213.

109. *La Opinión*, 13 July 1932.

110. On Central America, RG 59: 825.01/144, Eberhardt (San José), 6 Oct. 1932; on Britain and western Europe, FO 371-15826 (A4673/86/9), Mr. P. Mason, Internal FO memo, 22 July 1932, and RG 59: 825.00-Revs/174, Culbertson to Sec. of State, telegram 29 July 1932; and on Brazil, RG 59: 825.01 /64, J.W. memo, 7 July 1932.

111. Quote is from RG 59: 325.22/41, Stimson telegram to Culbertson, 27 July 1932 with original instructions given in, RG 59: 825.00-Revs/158, Stimson to Culbertson telegram, 16 July 1932.

112. RG 59: 825.00-Revs/125, Chile-American Association, Monthly Bulletin, Confidential Report no. 6, June 1932.

113. RG 59: 825.00-Revs/125, Culbertson telegram, 24 June 1932, and 325.11/39, Culbertson telegram, 26 July 1932.

114. RG 59: 825.51/565, Kuhn, Lobe Co., et al., to Secretary of State, 6 Aug. 1932, enclosure, memo of Francis White to Feis, 22 Aug. 1932.

115. RG 59: 662.253, Guggenheim Brothers to President Hoover, 27 July 1931; and 825.6374/1054, Report on Compañía de Salitre de Chile, Div. of Latin American Affairs, Dept. of State, 16 Sept. 1932; 825.6374/997, Culbertson, no. 1205, 20 July 1932, enclosure, cablegram from Medley G.B. Whelpley, Paris, to Nanothree Graham, 10 July 1932; 825.6374 /1010, Swenson, no. 423, 8 Aug. 1932; and 825.516/182, Culbertson, no. 1184, 29 June 1932, conversation with Aureliano Burr, former General Manager of Central Bank.

116. RG 59: 825.6374/992, Culbertson, no. 1185, 29 June 1932.

117. Ibid.,/1009, Sparks, no. 1229, 10 Aug. 1932, enclosure, Medley G.B. Whelpley, NY to Horace R.C. Graham, Santiago, 4 Aug. 1932, telegram V.P. of COSACh to be sent to Hacienda; and 825.00/762. Chile-American Association, Confidential Report no. 8, Aug. 1932.

118. RG 59: 825.6374/1047, Edwin C. Wilson memo, 22 Aug. 1932; FO 371-15830 (A5742/344/9), Thompson, 2 Sept. 1932; and Stemplowski, op. cit., 14.

119. On all the lobbying issues, see RG 59: 825.6363/135, J.H. Senior, Pres., West India Oil, to Edwin C. Wilson, Bureau of Latin American Affairs, 22 July 1932; FO 371-15822 (A5802/2/9), Thompson, 25 Aug. 1932; and *Diario Oficial*, 5 Sept. 1932.

120. RG 59: 825.01/105, Scott memo to Wilson and White, 12 Aug. 1932; RG 151: Bureau of Foreign and Domestic Commerce, Commercial Attaches: Santiago, Ackerman, Special Report no. 53, 22 June 1932; and FO 371-15822 (5277/2/9), Thompson, 21 Aug. 1932.

121. RG 59: 825.516/293, Francis White to W.S. Culbertson, 12 Aug. 1932. The entire file is marked "Precedent Case". See also Hoover Papers, Pres., Box 49, Recent Problems, 2:75-76. On British protests, see FO 371-15822 (5277/2/9), Thompson, 21 Aug. 1932.

122. RG 59: 825.00-Gen Cond/43, Culbertson, no. 1186, 29 June 1932, enclosure no. 2, Dávila radio broadcast, 25 June 1932.

123. Ibid. and *La Nación*, 22 June 1932, statement by Minister of Development [Fomento].

124. RG 59: 825.5123/33, Bowman, 29 June 1932.

125. Chile. Hacienda, Antecedentes de Oficios v. 3 (1932), Dirección General de Impuestos Internos al Min. de Hacienda, no. 1177, 16 Feb. 1932.

126. RG 59: 825.00-Revs/220, Culbertson, no. 1272, 28 Sept. 1932; *Hoy*, 23 Sept. 1932; RG 165: MID 2347-0-30/25, Wooten, no. 1418, 17 Aug. 1932; and FO 371-15822 (A5399/2/9), Thompson, 11 Aug. 1932.

127. Chile. Hacienda, Antecedentes de Oficios v. 8 (1932), Caja Nacional de Ahorros, 15 Sept. 1932; and RG 151: Bureau of Foreign and Domestic Commerce, Commercial Attaches: Santiago, Ackerman, Economic and Trade Notes, no. 45, 24 Aug. 1932.

128. RG 151: Bureau of Foreign and Domestic Commerce, Commercial Attaches: Santiago, Ackerman, Economic and Trade Notes, no. 35, 17 Aug. 1932.

129. Cited in RG 151: Bureau of Foreign and Domestic Commerce, Commercial Attaches: Santiago, Ackerman Weekly Report, no. 6, 8 Aug. 1932, translation slightly altered for style.

130. *La Opinión*, 12 Aug. 1932.

131. FO 371/19773 (A8933/73/9), R.C. Michell, Notes on Recent Chilean Monetary Policies, 1st September 1936, 15 Oct. 1936.

132. *Estadística chilena* (Sept. 1937), Trabajo, 528.

133. Two general studies of the Republican Militia are, Maldonado Prieto, *La milicia republicana, 1932-1936. Historia de un ejército civil en Chile* (Santiago: Servicio Universitario Mundial, Comité Nacional-Chile, 1988), and Verónica Valdivia Ortiz de Zarate, "Los civiles en armas: la milicia republicana, 1932-1936," (Santiago: Master's Thesis, Universidad de Santiago de Chile, Departamento de Historia, 1989). Maldonado emphasizes the anti-communist concerns of the Militia; Valdivia gives a broader institutional interpretation similar to the one offered here.

134. RG 165: MID 2657-0-158/2, Wooten, no. 1428, 23 Aug. 1932; and Sáez, *Recuerdos*, 3:213.

135. Chile. Interior (1932), Prov. 1438, Arriagada Valdivieso, 31 Aug. 1932.

136. Ibid., Prov. 1106, Arriagada Valdivieso, 18 July 1932.

137. On eight-hour day, BOLSA, B13, 1932, W.C. Maycock to staff manager, 21 July 1932; and on labor courts, RG 59: 825.504/88, Culbertson, no. 1212, 27 July 1932.

138. Chile. Fomento (1932), Oficios, v. 702, no. 6, memo, Financiamiento Lavaderos de Oro, 25 Aug. 1932. See also RG 59: 825.6341/3, Culbertson, no. 1226, 9 Aug. 1932, enclosure no. 1, report by Camden McLain.

139. Chile. Interior (1932), Rodolfo Michels Cabero, Intendente de Coquimbo, no. 2162, 31 Aug. 1932; *El Mercurio*, 16 Sept. 1932; and Chile. Interior (1932), Prov., no. 1198, Arriagada Valdivieso, 9 Aug. 1932.

5

140. The reports are contained in Chile. Interior (1932), various volumes and are usually signed by Arriagada Valdivieso, General of the Carabineros.

141. Chile. Interior (1932), Prov. 1427, Arriagada Valdivieso, 30 Aug. 1932.

142. FO 371-15827 (A5996/86/9), John Simon, 1 Sept. 1932; RG 165: MID 2515-0-10/8, Wooten, no. 1440, 31 Aug. 1932; and MID 2515-0-10/9, Wooten, no. 1453, 7 Sept. 1932.

143. RG 59: 825.516/227, Culbertson, no. 1240, 23 Aug. 1932.

144. RG 151: Bureau of Foreign and Domestic Commerce, Commercial Attaches: Santiago, Ackerman Special Report no. 21, 11 Nov. 1932.

145. FO 371-15822 (A5993/2/9), Thompson, 31 Aug. 1932.

146. RG 151: Commerce Dept., 601.2: Exchange, Chile (1932), Grosvenor M. Jones, Chief, Finance and Investment Division to Harold Dotterer, Chief, Division of District Office [San Francisco], 30 June 1932; and RG 59: 825.00/793, Chile-American Association, Confidential Report no. 9, Sept. 1932.

147. Hoover Papers, Pres., Box 49, Folder on State Department, Latin American Affairs, Review of Questions, "Revolutions in Latin America," 1:35.

148. RG 165: MID 2657-0-137, Wooten, no. 1488, 26 Oct. 1932.

149. RG 59: 825.00-Gen. Cond./49, Culbertson, no. 1268, 21 Sept. 1932.

150. *La Opinión*, 2 Nov. 1932.

151. Ibid., 3 Nov. 1932.

152. FO 371-15822 (A5993/2/9), Thompson, 31 Aug. 1932.

153. RG 165: MID 2347-0-30/25, Wooten, no. 1418, 17 Aug. 1932.

154. RG 59: 825.6374/1009, Sparks, no. 1229, 10 Aug. 1932, enclosure, Whelpley to Graham, 6.

155. RG 59: 825.00/762. Chile-American Association, Confidential Report, no. 8, Aug. 1932. See also Frank Bonilla and Myron Glazier, *Student Politics in Chile* (New York: Basic Books, 1970), 85.

156. FO 371-15825 (A4313/86/9).

3

Alessandri, Ross, and Domestic Recovery

Even the most optimistic forecasts at this time do
not allow Alessandri more than two years.
Colonel Harold Wooten,
U.S. Military Attache, Santiago
December 1932[1]

Accused of corruption and nepotism, and undoubtedly unscrupulous, but a great orator who may
fittingly be described as the demagogue who has
climbed over to the conservative side of the barri-
cade. Unlikely to complete his six-year term.
Sir R. Michell, British Minister to Santiago,
February 1934[2]

T he second administration of Arturo Alessandri Palma was among
the nation's most important and controversial. Alessandri was a
man who subsequent generations will study in search of the pattern of
Chilean life and the origins of its dilemmas. His successful campaign
for president in 1920 was an emotional turning point in national life, as
he introduced social issues into the race. In October 1932, only a year
after his defeat by Montero, he ran again as a reformer with labor
support. He won, but this time his administration would become known
as the defender of privilege.

His apologists argue that he completed his term of office and handed the presidency over to an elected opponent, the first time that this had happened in Chile in twelve years. He forced the military back into the barracks. The economy recuperated, unemployment disappeared, the mining sector revived, and the national debt was reduced while the government increased its control of key utilities. These were extraordinary achievements to realize during a depression.

His detractors point to a poverty so pervasive that leftists in the labor movement successfully tagged his Minister of Finance, Gustavo Ross, the "minister of hunger." Foreigners remained dominant in essential sectors. Most of all, Alessandri betrayed the people who had supported him: the miners and urban laborers. The lion built himself a comfortable political den among his former enemies; and his policies enriched the hacendados, the financial speculators, and the nouveau-riche industrialists. When workers complained, he suspended civil liberties.

Alessandri took office as the economy approached bottom. Congress no longer controlled the administration but it could veto, harass, and immobilize the executive. Alessandri surprised everyone by simply remaining in office. How his policies are related to his survival is explained below. His administration also surprised U.S. companies by defying them more successfully than any previous Chilean government. Alessandri often promoted economic nationalism, drawing on attitudes that had already developed in the late 1920s and the first year of the Crash. The character of his negotiations and their surprising results are described in Chapter 4. Then, Chapters 5 and 6 will analyze the changes and errors in judgment that brought the Popular Front, his enemies, to the presidency. Alessandri won office with a coalition of progressive parties. His own, Doctrinaire Liberal Party was solidly bureaucratic and in favor of state intervention in the economy. It included logrollers such as José Maza, Ernesto Barros Jarpa, and Armando Jaramillo, all former officials of banking institutions and past or present members of the Senate.[3] Alessandri's electoral alliance included the Radicals, the Radical Socialists, and the Republican Socialists, each with strong views on state involvement in the economy.[4] The Radical Socialists, supposedly the most leftist, campaigned to reduce the carabineros' power; create a unicameral legislature; dissolve COSACh and socialize the nitrate sector; and establish legal rights for illegitimate children.

There were five candidates in the presidential election of 1932. The Communists ran Elías Lafertte and won a minuscule vote. The core of the left vote went to Marmaduke Grove, whose supporters ran his campaign without a party and while he remained in exile on Juan Fernández Island. (He was unaware until the eve of the election, when he landed in Valparaiso, that he was a candidate.) The right split and ran two candidates: a Conservative, Héctor Rodríguez de la Sotta, and a Liberal, Enrique Zañartu Prieto. Zañartu had become famous by expanding the money supply while serving as Dávila's finance minister. In this spectrum, Alessandri was clearly the centrist candidate, and many conservatives abandoned the marginal figures to his right to vote for him. He also drew on his popularity in the north. He won with almost 55 percent of the vote. Lafertte and Grove together garnered almost 19 percent, which meant that the labor-based left had grown since the 1920s.[5]

Once in office, Alessandri's dilemma was structurally comparable to the situation he faced in 1920. The Congress was fragmented into ungovernable factions. There were 30 parties in public life: 10 held 45 seats in the Senate, and 15 (including the 10 in the Senate plus some others) held 142 seats in the lower house. Alessandri's original coalition had a majority in the Senate but was a few votes short in the Chamber of Deputies.[6] During the 1920s, conservative senators had blocked reform, now it seemed conservative Deputies (meaning Liberals, Conservatives, and splinter right factions) were in a position to do the same.

Unemployment and inflation were the two most pressing public problems. The surge in prices—near the end of 1932, shoes went up 75 percent and cloth 14 percent—benefitted native industry. Gold panning and some industrial recovery made only a small dent in the nation's poverty. In many areas, expectations had fallen to a desire to survive. One foreign observer noted many Chileans now aspired to "a horse and oxen standard of life."[7]

The Power to Tax

Alessandri had to choose how to pay for government. Revenues were obviously going to fall short of expenditures. He decided to raise taxes.

The engineer of his fiscal policies was Gustavo Ross Santa María. Ross descended from the Valparaiso elite: his ancestors on his father's side were the successful British merchant families of the nineteenth century; his mother's family came from the colonial elite. He was a distant cousin and close friend of Agustín Edwards. He had trained in the Edwards' bank in Valparaiso then went to Europe; he returned to be elected to the municipality of Valparaiso. But politics held little interest for him and he spent most of his life in London and Paris, where he excelled in playing the currency and stock markets.[8]

Prior to his appointment as finance minister, Ross' only political notoriety came in 1927 when Ibáñez exiled him.[9] In exile, Ross supported Alessandri. His appointment in 1932 did not attract much notice and was seen as an act of gratitude by the president.[10] Its significance became apparent only when Alessandri sent Ross to London and Paris in November 1932, in an unsuccessful effort to gain credit for the government and to postpone demands on debt payments.[11] It astonished political pundits that an unknown would be entrusted with such an important issue. Ross soon demonstrated his authority by centralizing the review of budgetary and fiscal issues in his office. By January 1933, an exasperated U.S. Ambassador Culbertson wrote, "We have today in Chile virtually a dictatorship of Alessandri and Ross."[12]

Ross believed that the world economy was still deteriorating and that the United States was to blame. He looked to Europe for solutions, both strategic and tactical, and thought the future would consist of trade deals brokered by governments. He argued that South America should consider forming a customs union, with Argentina at its center—Argentina was then the major industrial nation of the region—and that this would provide a market sufficient to ride out the crisis.[13] These ideas were quite uncommon in Chile and remarkably imaginative for any Latin American leader of the time.

Ross also took an unusual tack on the deficit. Unlike most of the upper class, he viewed government as a necessity that had already been cut too much. The Alessandri administration had inherited a budget of 703.6 million pesos. As soon as Congress met, it authorized another 233.4 million for public works. The government expected to collect revenues of 514 million. Ross announced in December 1932 that the nation would pay neither the foreign nor the domestic debt. The administration also dissolved COSACh in January 1933, and so eliminated that company's debt from public obligations. But the 1932 budget was still 218 million short, with an even larger deficit predicted for 1933.[14] To cover the shortfall, the government decreed a 50 percent increase in import duties, with luxury goods paying another 33 percent above that. It revived a nitrate export tax. It also raised the sales tax, which functioned as a value-added tax, from .5 to 2.0 percent. This rate was imposed on every level of commerce: on the manufacturer, the wholesaler, the distributor, the retailer, and finally the consumer.[15]

Alessandri and Ross were not finished. Ross also imposed an excess-profits tax of 25 percent on gains over 15 percent.[16] He raised taxes on land, wine, tobacco, stamps, and entertainment. In his address to Congress defending these increases, Alessandri said the new imposts contained the deficit by generating revenues of 165 million pesos.[17] The conservative leadership in Congress claimed that Alessandri's tax policies would soon consume 40 percent of the national income, which it figured at 2.4 billion pesos. Ross claimed that the national income was probably 7.5 to 10 billion and that taxes might still have to double to cover necessary expenditures.[18] He argued that Chile's rates were still lower than France's, a conclusive point given his admiration of that country.[19] This debate reveals that no one knew the economy's size or the impact of the increases. It is probable, based on contemporary estimates, that the conservatives were closer to the truth than Ross.[20] But those same estimates indicate that government made up only 11 percent of the national economy in 1933.[21]

The conservatives allowed Alessandri and Ross to proceed because they were more afraid of another coup than higher taxes. The press discussed the possibility of another Ibañista movement, this time with Ibáñez himself as its leader. Ross told Congress that the executive would answer for higher imposts but would not be responsible for what might happen if administration proposals were not passed.[22] It was the Liberal-left, including some of the president's coalition, that refused to go along with the tax increases. Alessandri had already invoked emergency powers to repress leftists in the labor movement, alienating some of his original coalition. The tax increases cost him support within the Radical Party. He then had to reorder his support in Congress, attracting members of the Liberal and Conservative parties in order to pass legislation.[23] Aside from his respect for Ross' opinions, Alessandri risked raising taxes because of what had happened in his first administration when he responded to the postwar depression by turning the money press. The ensuing inflation fueled popular disgust with the Parliamentary Regime and led the military to stage the coup in September 1924. Alessandri was determined not to replay the past.[24]

The administration stayed the course and Alessandri and Ross never modified their views. Ross even stood up to the U.S. Embassy, which objected to the sales tax increase on the grounds that it would further depress commerce. He argued that the two were unrelated: "The tax is to aid the government and its offices had the duty of demanding it be paid, while price increases benefit private companies which can raise them as they like."[25] The answer was sincere. The following year, an association of wholesalers and industrialists begged the president to cut back the bureaucracy; but Alessandri insisted, as Ross had, that public employees were needed and were entitled to salary increases. Those benefiting from inflation had no grounds for complaint; they had to share their gains.[26] The government refused special concessions even to interests it favored, such as agricultural exporters.[27] It also defied the lobbying by the Republican Militia (a paramilitary organization Alessandri supported), which favored cuts in military spending, and by the U.S.-owned electric company for tax relief.[28]

The sales tax led to a major confrontation, the retailers' strike of 1935, which contributed to the attitude within the middle class that this administration despised ordinary Chileans. Retailers had protested the increase from the time it was imposed in April 1933.[29] But it took them two years to coordinate a movement through the chambers of commerce. In April 1935, a coalition led by the Santiago Chamber of Commerce, met to organize a general strike. To gain compliance, the retailers threatened to boycott all wholesalers who failed to join and to deny support for the Republican Militia, pro-government newspapers, and all parties that supported the tax. The coalition also demanded that the national detective bureau [Servicio de Investigaciones] stop spying on their meetings.[30] The strike, held May 7, closed businesses in Santiago but met with mixed results elsewhere: of 19 other cities, surveyed by the government, only 6 shut down completely.[31] The very next year, the government raised the sales tax from 2 to 5 percent.[32]

Priorities were now clear: the enhancement of government revenues came first, all other needs, second. Alessandri and Ross believed they were rescuing the state from petty interests, including foreign corporations, that threatened to rip it apart. Still, as Table 3.1 demonstrates, the government remained heavily dependent on imposts linked to foreign trade. In 1935, as an example, the combined return from import, consular, and port duties amounted to 40 percent of all government income. Of all the revenue categories, import duties remained the most lucrative, considerably more so than income taxes. The sales tax became a significant revenue source only after it was increased to 5 percent.

The social security tax does not appear in Table 3.1 but it underlines the direction of tax policy. Chile established pensions for some state employees in 1916, and it expanded the system to private wage workers in 1925 and 1931. The beneficiaries received monthly checks, care at state-run medical clinics, and access to a modest public-housing program.[33] Successive governments ratcheted up the fees for both employers and employees, until near the end of the 1930s, the deductions were generally 7 percent of each salary (9 percent in the mining regions). Because the government also provided a contribution, total costs were even greater.[34]

This expensive system provided few real benefits. Although it improved public health care, a good deal of the fund was eroded by inflation. Government manipulation of pensions was another drawback. In some cases, dissident state employees had their benefits canceled.[35] Desperate individuals often cashed in their pensions, and several administrations raided pension funds to cover current accounts. Congress also used the system for political ends, raising the benefits of white-collar faster than those of blue-collar workers.[36]

Alessandri and Ross were accused of levying regressive imposts. This was true, but it was also true of their predecessors and successors as well. Income taxes, perhaps the most equitable form of taxation, amounted to about 12 percent of all government revenues during Alessandri's second term, a figure that compares favorably with other administrations.[37] For all the complaints about the sales tax: subsequent governments kept it and its importance increased during the 1941-43 period, when Alessandri's opponents were in office. Tax policies during, before, and after Alessandri exhibit remarkable continuity into the 1940s. Through tax policy, the government tried to transfer as many costs as possible to foreigners. Land taxes were kept to a minimum. Indirect taxes were simply easier to collect than a massive income surcharge. Tax policies were not used to transfer income from the rich to the poor. Given the characteristics of Chile's tax bureaucracy, no other program may have been possible.

Nor did Alessandri represent a right-wing break with the past in the pattern of his expenditures. Contrary to the general belief, Alessandri was not antimilitary. In his budgets, the military came first, then policing, followed by education and everything else. In 1933, he cut the

Table 3.1: Government Revenues, 1929-1943
(In percent of total revenue)

Year, 19—	29	30	31	32	33	34	35	36	37	38	39	40	41	42	43
Major Revenue Sources (in millions of pesos)															
	1262	1132	783	514	945	1042	1408	1468	1522	1678	2304	2658	2299	2736	2894
Major Revenue Sources (by percent)															
Property															
Income	25	18	23	2	6	4	2	1	1	1	2	1	1	1	2
Services	5	6	7	9	9	8	6	7	7	7	5	6	8	7	7
Taxes															
Import	29	29	26	26	24	34	35	36	37	39	28	25	26	19	20
Income	12	15	15	10	8	9	7	8	10	10	7	9	13	16	17
Sales								10	12	11	8	8	17	19	19
Real Estate	5	5	6	8	5	6	3	4	4	4	3	3	6	4	5
Other*	6	4	8	19	9	12	17	8	5	5	5	4	7	15	7

*Not all revenue sources are listed; therefore, amounts do not add up to 100.

Source: Chile, Contraloría General, Memoria de la Contraloría General correspondiente al año . . . y balance general de la Hacienda Pública. Santiago, 1932-43.

Table 3.2: Government Expenses, 1932-1943
(In percent of total revenue)

Year, 19—	32	33	34	35	36	37	38	39	40	41	42	43
Total Expenditures (in millions of pesos)	900	957	937	1041	1296	1133	1663	1812	2021	2596	2915	3634
Percentages Spent on Major Items												
Development	13	17	13	15	12	16	13	12	6	10	12	8
Education			17	16	17	21	17	16	8	16	16	14
Finance	18	11	6	6	9	8	6	13	8	13	14	15
Health	0	3	4	5	5	7	6	6	3	7	8	8
Interior	13	17	20	20	19	20	17	18	9	16	15	14
carabineros*	9	10	12	12	10	14	10	10	5	9	9	8
Total Military**	15	22	28	28	28	37	27	25	13	27	23	30
Army	8	11	13	13	13	17	12	11	6	11	9	19
Air Force	1	2	3	2	3	4	3	2	1	3	2	2
Navy	6	9	12	13	12	16	12	12	6	13	12	9

*The carabinero budget was under the Ministry of the Interior; but the presented data is in percent of total government budget.
**The presented data represents percent of the total government budget for all branches of the service.

Source: Chile, Contraloría General, *Memorias*, 1932-43.

army's troops to about five thousand men, but thereafter, spending rose in line with revenues.[38] Nor was he indifferent to public needs: the funds spent on education and health compare favorably with predecessors and successors. He spent a higher percentage of government income on infrastructure—projects such as roads, warehouses, and public buildings—than did the Popular Front that came after him.

The Alessandri administration and its immediate predecessors differed most in their style of decision making. Ross seized the initiative and kept it until he left the Ministry of Finance. He took back the authority that Montero and Dávila had given to the Price Commission and the Exchange Control Commission. Departments in the executive branch could no longer lobby Congress directly; they had to submit all proposals to Ross first.[39] Ross refused congressional demands to oversee the budget unless he needed to publicize an objective. In June 1934, opposition deputies demanded to know what he was doing about the foreign debt: Ross told them not to expect an answer. The president had all the authority he needed to deal with the issue unilaterally.[40] By early 1934, Ross could argue credibly that the budget had been balanced, even though this achievement rested on not paying the foreign debt.[41] See Table 3.2 for data pertaining to government expenditures.

Although inflation continued, Alessandri's policies were not inflationary.[42] His first budget reduced the rate of monetary issue below that of wholesale price increases.[43] As Albert Hirschman noted, Alessandri and Ross carried out a deflationary policy that, in any other setting, would have deepened the impact of the Depression.[44] (As Chapter 2 demonstrated, the Dávila administration had dramatically increased the money supply only a few months before Alessandri was inaugurated.) The government's basic dilemma vis à vis the cost of living was that the declining terms of trade, rising import prices, tariff increases, and earlier monetary expansion had set off an inflationary spiral that was difficult to arrest. The price of imports soared 90 percent in the 1932-33 period, then began to decline in 1934. Unfortunately, a second phase of inflation hit in 1935 as producers tried to make up for lost revenue.[45] Overall, however, prices rose only 35 percent during Ross' term as Minister of Finance, a record every subsequent administration would have been happy to equal. See Table 3.3 for data pertaining to cost of living and average wage between 1927 and 1939.

The economic payoffs of the administration's program were substantial. Most importantly, its fiscal policies helped raise real wages. Another striking result was an increase in the value of the peso. It rose 28 percent against hard currencies in 1933. The black-market rate fell from three times the official exchange rate to only double the rate.[46] On this issue, Ross prevailed over the president himself who retained his populist impulses and tended to blame high prices on the concentration of wealth rather than on monetary policy.[47]

Table 3.3: Cost of Living and Average Wage, 1927-1939
(1927 = 100)

Year	Cost of Living	Official Average Wage
1927	100	100
1928	107	100
1929	109	100
1930	107	nd
1931	nd	nd
1932	114	70
1933	141	86
1934	141	127
1935	144	127
1936	156	147
1937	176	178
1938	184	200
1939	182	228

Source: *Estadística chilena*, 1935-1943, sección "Trabajo."

Government Regulation and Industry

As the rate of inflation slowed and a recovery began, the Liberals and Conservatives started to endorse the administration. Ross, after all, was one of their own. They knew the government would not seek redistributive measures. The transformation from a coalition with Radicals to one backed by traditional economic interests was complete in 1934. The president also courted the Republican Militia, whose defense of property could not have been clearer.[48] In August 1935, the French Minister in Santiago reported that the government had lost interest in "the laboring class" and was now concerned solely with "the needs of the capitalists."[49] There is an economic background to this rapprochement between Alessandri and his former opponents.

Much has been written about economic change in Chile during the 1930s, most of it by economic historians and specialists on dependency. The first set of scholars has emphasized the importance of industrialization. The second has argued that the Depression represented a major break with the past by interrupting the power of foreign capitalists. Both have over generalized.

Industry played an important role in the recovery. Studies on industrial development have traced the origins of import substitution to the late nineteenth century, with a major acceleration occurring during World War I.[50] Neither the direction nor the structural characteristics of industry were changed by the Crash, and as common sense dictates, industrial output fell when purchasing power collapsed. But the Crash also eliminated competition from imports, providing near-captive markets for domestic industry. However, this industrial recovery never created a self-sustaining process of profits, investment, and market expansion. It always relied on factors external to Chile. It is not true, as the dependistas have argued, that Chile was breaking with older capitalist patterns.[51]

Ibáñez and the provisional presidents raised tariffs in the hope of reducing the outflow of needed capital. So did Alessandri. Each president also tried to refinance the economy in some way, with Dávila's inflationary policies producing the most immediate results. In order to make sense of what happened after 1932, the rhetoric of the period must be separated from the reality.

The industrialists were quick to exploit any government declaration on economic nationalism. The role of the Society for Industrial Development [SOFOFA] in tariff promotion has already been mentioned, but this does not mean that either government or Chilean industrialists proposed a consistently nationalist agenda. (The left, interestingly, had little to say about industry.) Nor did anyone propose some realignment of mining with manufacturing and agriculture that promised a more dynamic future. Investment rates rose but technology remained primitive. To take one example, bakeries continued to use antiquated methods; inferior yeast; and to produce heavy dough, that cooked in the morning, turned to hard tack by the afternoon.[52]

But industrial opportunities changed with the Depression. Chile offered investors a modernized version of mercantilism—monopoly. The government promised protection to new investors, foreign or domestic: in addition to tariffs, import quotas and exchange regulations favored domestic products. No product was too insignificant: window frames, light bulbs, and porcelain toilet bowls received consideration.[53] A Danish industrialist, before investing in a window factory in 1933, demanded increased tariffs, government-backed loans, and setting aside immigration restrictions; he wanted to bring his own technicians. He achieved all four.[54] Unfortunately in the literature, industrial growth within Chile is often confused with economic nationalism, ignoring the crucial role that foreign investment played in the process.

Bureaucrats were more nationalists than industrialists. Officials replaced trade-derived revenues with internal taxation, and they found themselves competing with the private sector in spending scarce foreign exchange. The government, for example, continued to promote high tariffs on oil and other manufacturing imports during the recovery when industrialists wanted such duties cut.[55] The director of engineering in the Ministry of Development, Exequiel Jiménez Carrasco, demanded that duties foster industry whatever the overall costs to the economy. He supported, for example, an export duty on wool to force producers to sell to domestic textile producers at lower cost. He opposed a request by RCA Victor to import more radio parts on the grounds these could be produced, at somewhat greater cost, in Chile.[56] The Ministry of Development never coordinated industrialization but it had a say in processing industrial regulation and all exemptions.

The overall impression is one of rising clientalism in which tariff policies were traded for political support. Alessandri had focused first on reducing unemployment.[57] Once the warehouses emptied of the unemployed, the government acted on an ad hoc basis. The textile sector was split, for example, between large factories that favored a high tariff on cotton thread because they produced their own, and small plants that favored a reduction in the duty.[58] Alessandri raised the tariff but, for reasons of patronage, he gave a license to the Palestinian family of Yarur (already established in Bolivia) to set up a new spinning factory.[59] No uniform tariff policy, aside from the exchange- and revenue-driven increase of 1933, ever appeared.

Coordination of government policies and industrial growth was at an incipient stage. Supporters and opponents of the administration commonly set up lists of demands based on party support, not on any strategy for manufactures. The kind of special pleading that occurred emerges from the Congress of National Development held at the University of Chile in mid-November, 1934. The meeting's organizer was Pedro Aguirre Cerda, a member of the Radical Party, who had been Alessandri's minister of the interior in the 1920s, briefly served in the Ibáñez government, and was now part of the president's opposition. The Congress of National Development sent the following recommendations in a petition to the government: it wanted more price regulation, better policing to prevent hoarding, tax exemptions on capital goods, elimination of the sales tax, and better schools and housing for fishermen and their families.[60] This potpourri of demands reflects not only a desire to recruit support (and Aguirre Cerda's efforts to stay in the public eye), but also the patron-client attitude that was central to all political expectations.

Most proposals for development, both from within and from outside the government, had a corporatist flavor. Many were called "socialist," but aside from those made by the Communists and Socialists, few recommended public control of any sector. The dominant political parties were only starting to experiment with how regulation would benefit particular sectors and redound to political sponsors. Common political expectations were that government would facilitate production with protection and cheap credit, and prevent price gouging. The lumber industry's proposal in 1933 for the creation of a "consortium" in its sector was typical. A central committee with representatives from the lumber association and the Ministry of Commerce, would supervise production, standardization of products, technical advice for factories, and all loans from the Agricultural Credit Fund.[61]

One can see, in some of these proposals, the first steps toward the exploitation of natural resources that would become profitable a half century later. Government officials and some political figures often fantasized about the coastline and the sums to be made in fishing and tourism. One proposal argued that the fishing industry could meet 25 percent of the nation's protein needs. It would reduce meat imports, create a new canning industry, lead to the development of refrigeration, and so on. The industry did grow, from about three thousand to more than five thousand workers in the early 1930s, but it was always a cottage affair, badly undercapitalized. The number of canneries jumped from two to 12 but these were often shut down for lack of tin. Well into the Alessandri administration, the government did not coordinate policies regarding machinery for the sector.[62]

Tourism seemed an easy way to keep funds in Chile and attract some from abroad, especially from Argentina. The nation had literally hundreds of miles of spotless, white beaches in the north, and a mild climate in the capital and the provinces near Santiago. In 1936, the Society for Tourism and Hotels was established with 52 million pesos; its first venture, with public and private funds, was the glamorous Hotel Carrera in Santiago.[63] But, by the end of the decade, tourism was still a minor activity.

Regulation and the bureaucratization of industry sometimes led to nothing at all. To revive the nitrate zone, the government created a regional planning institution in Antofagasta and established a loan fund of five million pesos. The institute's archive is filled with elaborate schemes for chemical labs, fishing projects, and other new ventures, none of which was ever funded. Most of the money was never committed; the small amounts that were paid out went to established mines.[64]

Attempts at innovation and diversification also had to overcome stereotypes common among bureaucrats and industrialists. A German technician, hired by the government to develop the fishing industry, was told not to expect much of the fishermen. He expressed his surprise when he found them "intelligent, courageous and hard-working."[65] Another example of commercial attitudes is a history of national industry written by Oscar Alvarez Andrews. It won a prize from the Society for Industrial Development. Alvarez explained Chile's economic problems in terms of *race*: the Spaniard gave Chile a sense of gallantry and "a fanatical pride in status"; the Araucanian contributed a love of drink and an avoidance of work. Chileans of all ranks lacked "an industrial sensibility, economic judgment, and a capitalist mentality. This is why [they are] the toy of foreign capitalists." They were unenterprising and avoided technical innovation. "In a word, we have a mentality that is almost anti-capitalist."[66] This work, written during the Crash but published at the height of a stock-market boom, remained a standard text for the next thirty years.

In fact, Chilean industry expanded during the 1930s in a pattern that paralleled changes in the Atlantic economy. Chilean industrialists paid close attention to what was happening in more developed nations.

Germany, England, and the United States were raising tariffs and changing monetary rules. Why should Chile not do the same? The result is unsurprising: industry became financially and geographically more concentrated. The pattern was already clear before the 1930s, especially in consumer goods.[67] Henry Kirsh notes that textiles, beverages, and paper industries remained as concentrated in 1937 as they had been in 1918, albeit clothing opened up to new firms.[68] Industry was located primarily in Santiago. The effect on electricity is a good indicator of what happened (see Graph 3.1, below). In 1929, Santiago consumed 80 percent of the kilowatt hours produced; in 1939, 84 percent.[69]

Industrial development included foreign ownership. National industrialists supported foreign investment so long as it did not undercut their own market positions.[70] There were 17 major U.S. corporations in Chile during the 1930s. Most of them remained dominant in their sectors well into the second half of the century: Anaconda and Kennecott in copper; International Telephone and Telegraph in communications; duPont in chemicals; Grace in shipping and textiles; Bethlehem in steel; Davis in pharmaceuticals; RCA Victor in radio; Otis in elevators; and, of course, American and Foreign Power (the subsidiary of General Electric, already discussed) in electricity.[71] Other non-American, international

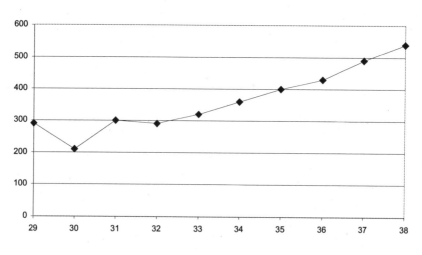

Graph 3.1 Electrical Output, 1929-1938

Source: U.S. State Department, RG 151: Bureau of Foreign and Domestic Commerce, Commercial Attaches, Santiago, Bohan, Special Report no. 16, 5 Jan. 1940.

giants were present, such as Antony Gibbs in merchant activities, Imperial Chemical in chemicals, and Nestlé in sweets and chocolate. The U.S. companies were ascendant.[72]

Industrialization alone could not have pulled Chile out of the Depression. For beneath the rising output was a social fact: a trend already clear in the 1920s continued in the 1930s toward replacing laborers in small shops with those in factories. The number of workers in industry, overall, was falling. In 1925, there were 280 thousand in industry; but this included 198 thousand called "artisan manufactures"—that is, settings with fewer than five workers—and only 82 thousand in factories (five or more); by 1930, the number in small shops dropped to 161 thousand and, in 1935, to 150 thousand; the numbers in factories rose to 96 thousand (1930) and to 100 thousand (1935). An increase of factory workers could not offset a decline of 48 thousand in shops. In 1935, the total industrial labor force was 250 thousand.[73]

The economy remained weak, and many of the problems that had appeared in the 1920s were never quite solved. Total national production did not reach its 1929 level until 1938. A slightly different, and perhaps better, measure is to average the national income (based on contemporary estimates) between 1925 and 1927, that is, once the postwar depression had ended and before Ibáñez launched his deficit-based program. By this measure, Chile recovered from the Depression around 1935.[74] Even so, the effects of the Depression were felt throughout the 1930s. Mining improved; but throughout the decade it never regained pre-Depression levels (see Graph 3.2, above).

The Real Estate Boom

The only activity to undergo a sharp recovery was construction.[75] Here, Alessandri and Ross could take some credit for their policies. The real estate boom, centered in Santiago, was as important to the economy as industrialization. To members of the elite, it may have been more important. The boom was partly the result of changes in the tax code. Anxious to reduce unemployment and spur construction, the government, in December 1933, exempted all new buildings from property taxes for ten years following construction. The exemption remained in force for buildings completed through the end of 1935.[76] The government also gave an income tax exemption on the interest earned on mortgage bonds. The Central Bank was allowed to use these bonds as collateral against loans.[77] Property already provided an important inflationary hedge. In 1934, the peso was worth only 20 percent of its 1913 value, but real estate in the capital had retained almost 70 percent of its value. Its nominal price had risen threefold.[78] In 1934, as a result of Alessandri's policies, a building boom sent Santiago property values soaring above the rate of inflation.

Other factors fed the boom. Foreign firms, unable to repatriate their profits because of the currency laws, poured funds into construction. And migrants continued to flow into Santiago, including elements of the middle class displaced from the entrepôts of the north and from Valparaiso by the export collapse and wealthy Chileans who had been living in Europe. The flood of arrivals and the rent freeze made housing scarce.[79] As a result, speculation bolstered construction late into the decade. It was not until 1938, during a presidential election, that rising costs began to slow the boom. The government responded by funding more public projects.[80] The results are clearly presented in Table 3.4.

Table 3.4: Annual Value of Construction in Ten Largest Cities

Year 19–	Area: 1000 Sq. Meters	Value Millions of Pesos	Costs Pesos/Sq. Meter
31	160	48.3	300
32	206	39.9	193
33	270	69.4	256
34	481	181.1	376
35	515	185.6	360
36	443	175.6	396
37	532	230.5	432
38	543	262.3	482
39	566	278.4	491

Source: United States State Department, Record Group 151: Bureau of Foreign and Domestic Commerce, Commercial Attaches, Santiago, Bohan, Special Report no. 18, 12 Feb. 1940, p. 27.[81]

Agriculture

The weakest element in the government's policy mix was agriculture. The classic study of the countryside in this period is George McBride's, *Chile: Land and Society*. Some of its generalizations have been revised by later scholarship. Nevertheless, it remains a vivid portrait of continuity and change.[82] McBride noticed that the power of the hacendados had been under attack since World War I; but they had survived the challenge. As Thomas Wright has demonstrated, they developed a corporatist ideology that appealed to urban sectors and more sophisticated lobbying techniques in Congress through the National Agricultural Society [Sociedad Nacional de Agricultura or SNA].[83] The SNA, which had formed in the nineteenth century, revamped itself as it reconsidered how hacendados would endure in the modern era. While the style was somewhat new, the combination of law and landed wealth was not. It was a combination that pursued office-holding as a matter of heritage as well as necessity and succeeded relatively well into the 1960s.[84]

Alessandri called for land reform and rural development, ideas popular with all parties to the left of the Liberals. Alessandri, however, had no plan to subdivide haciendas or increase food production, and was unwilling to wage a political fight against the great landowners.[85] In 1935, the total acreage of land held by legal title was 26 percent greater than in 1917, and the number of owners (4,328) had grown over 30 percent. But 246 owners, with more than five thousand hectares each, controlled 52 percent of all the land, a situation almost unchanged from 1917.[86] In practice, each administration from the 1920s to the 1960s had to weigh the prospect of social justice in the countryside against the need to keep urban food prices down.[87] An unvoiced tradeoff resulted: the great estate owners demanded and received continued control of their labor force while unsuccessfully protesting state-administered prices.

As Graph 3.2 shows, agriculture stagnated in the 1930s and was overtaken in economic importance by industry and construction.[88] Government incentives to the rural sector reflected the need to avoid conflict, and with some exceptions, were without focus. Railroad rates remained low, but this subsidized existing arrangements. Credit remained readily available but at relatively high interest rates. The government's one initiative occurred in 1933, when the guano fields in the

Graph 3.2: GDP and Major Sectors
(1929=100)

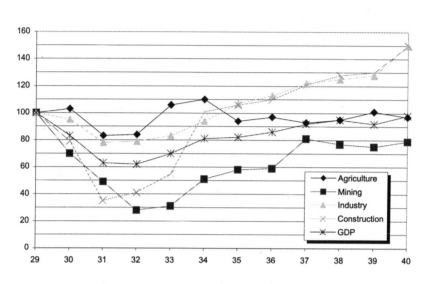

Source: J. Gabriel Palma, "Chile 1914-1935," Palma, J. Gabriel. "Chile 1914-1935: de economía exportadora sustitutiva de importaciones," *Nueva historia: revista de historia de Chile* 2:7 (Jan.-Mar. 1983), 180.

north were appropriated in order to provide farmers with cheaper fertilizer.[89]

The support Dávila had given the hacendados disappeared. No rush of mortgage bonds appeared on the market, and there was no talk of mortgage forgiveness. Mortgage holders got the same tax breaks as urban developers, but land taxes were increased. Export taxes were imposed on apples and other fruit.[90] Agricultural exporters had to sell all bills of exchange to the Central Bank under a decree of the Dávila era that only now was enforced. The hacendado's speculation in export-derived dollars came to an end despite heated protests by both foreign trade and rural associations.[91]

The government's major new policy toward agriculture was the elaboration of price controls, a story that could serve as a textbook illustration of maladministration. In 1929, wheat production was 1.2 million tons; but in 1933 it was only 524 thousand tons, an amount meeting only 75 percent of the nation's needs.[92] Wheat producers in 1932 had avoided domestic price restrictions by exporting. As a result, the government was forced to use hard currency to import wheat, which it then sold at a loss. By 1933, the Alessandri administration shifted gears and ordered an official price increase at home and a restriction on exports. Wheat production rose. However, price supports led to a speculative surge in the commodities' market, which then crashed and left many farmers unpaid, millers afraid to buy, and the government paying above the export price for domestic wheat to keep production from dropping again. The government exported a temporary surplus but, fearing another shortage, it banned the export of wheat, flour, bran, potatoes, beans, and hay in 1936.[93] Food price controls also affected meat supplies. Meat prices soared in 1934 and 1935 as cattlemen used the black market, stopped breeding, and surreptitiously shipped cattle to Argentina. The meat tariff went up and down in response to prices.[94]

In all, Alessandri's agricultural policies were reactive, a scramble to contain the inflation unleashed in 1932 and to avoid the longer-term consequences of agrarian retaliation for restrictive pricing. An article surveying rural production in 1935 noted that agriculture was earning about 3 percent per year on its investment, but mortgage bonds were 7 percent. Farming had become an unwise use of money.[95] By 1937, a modus vivendi was reached between the government and producers that controlled food prices somewhat but failed to create a food supply that met rising urban demand. The results for the future of Chile often have been noted: hacendados were secure in their estates, the rural labor force remained destitute, and there was little incentive to modernize rural production.

* * *

The commonly held view that Alessandri's administration swerved to the right is based on overestimating the extent to which Alessandri himself was ever a leftist in the 1920s. He paid a high price for the mistakes of his first administration and did not repeat them. His tax policy, combined with his opposition to new populist demands, cost him the support of the Radical Party. But he did not abandon all social goals. Rather than abdicating power to the conservatives, Alessandri and Ross developed policies that the Liberal and Conservative parties reluctantly accepted. A quid pro quo gradually developed between the administration and the wealthy. The industrialists and financiers now feared any repetition of coups and the socialist republic far more than they did the president. This conviction became stronger as the left became better organized, and when Alessandri repressed labor, the capitalists applauded. In return, Alessandri and Ross granted very specific favors to capital. Government policies rewarded industry and enriched astute speculators in real estate and currency. None of this broke new economic ground; but it did revive a despondent nation—no small achievement given the Depression's impact. The real basis of Alessandri's authority was that the rich had received a good scare in 1931 and 1932.

Alessandri and Ross carried out the only tax policy possible and, with it, they rebuilt the government's revenue base. They balanced the budget within two years, albeit by not paying the foreign debt, and they eliminated the horror of unemployment through the gold-panning program, a modest revival in public works, and by stimulating construction. The results were conservative: a retrenching by the elite in its established sectors. Yet, it is hard to believe a more egalitarian program might have been effective. It is interesting to compare, with contemporary hindsight, the records of Mexico and Chile. In Mexico, the administration of President Lázaro Cárdenas tried to fulfill the social promises made during the Revolution. But if economic health is measured by per capita gross domestic product (a number obviously unavailable at the time in either country), Chile recovered from the Depression earlier than did Mexico.[96] Such conjectures run counter to the public impressions in each country. It is interesting, as well, that a contemporary survey of Latin America has Chile doing better in the 1930s than such nations as Argentina, Colombia, and Uruguay.[97]

The problems of the Alessandri administration were not the result of failure but relative success. As the next chapter will demonstrate, this success required an unusual defiance of U.S. officials and businessmen. After that, it will be time to look at why Alessandri was unable to turn his economic recovery and more nationalistic attitudes into political continuity.

Endnotes

For abbreviations used in notes, see Endnotes, Chapter 1.

1. RG 165: MID 2657-0-151/8, Wooten, no. 1542, 27 Dec. 1932.

2. FO 371-17508, Sir R. Michell to Sir John Simon, 9 Feb. 1934, List of Leading Personalities in Chile.

3. RG 165: MID 2657-0-151/7, Wooten, no. 1513, 19 Nov. 1932.

4. RG 151: Commerce Dept., Bureau of Foreign and Domestic Commerce, Commercial Attaches: Santiago, Ackerman Weekly Report, no. 23, 6 Dec. 1932.

5. Paul W. Drake, *Socialism and Populism in Chile, 1932-1952* (Chicago: University of Illinois Press, 1978), 99-110.

6. RG 165, US War, MID 2657-0-135/24, Wooten, no. 1476, 5 Oct. 1932; and RG 59: 825.00/799, R. Henry Norweb, no. 1438, 26 Apr. 1933.

7. RG 59: 825.51/600, Bowman, 28 Feb. 1933.

8. Chile, *Hacienda Pública*, May 1938, 872 (campaign biography).

9. Robert J. Alexander, *Arturo Alessandri: A Biography* (New Brunswick, NJ: Rutgers University Latin American Institute, University Microfilms International, 1977), 2:494.

10. RG 151: Bureau of Foreign and Domestic Commerce, Commercial Attaches: Santiago, Ackerman Weekly Report, no. 25, 20 Dec. 1932.

11. *La Nación*, 19 Nov. 1932.

12. RG 59: 825.00/7898, Culbertson, no. 1365, 25 Jan. 1933.

13. *La Nación*, 16 Dec. 1932.

14. On the debt, *La Nación*, 16 Dec. 1932. On other issues, *El Mercurio*, 6 May 1933.

15. RG 165: MID 2657-0-151/21, Wooten, no. 2150, 3 Apr. 1935.

16. BOLSA, B10/4, 1933, W.C. Maycock to Chairman, 9 Feb. 1933.

17. Quoted in RG 59: 825.00-Gen Cond/57, Culbertson, no. 1400, 7 Mar. 1933.

18. RG 59: 825.00-Gen Cond/58, Culbertson, no. 1421, 3 Apr. 1933; and 825.00/800, Wooten, no. 1658, 19 Apr. 1933. See also the arguments of the business press in BOLSA, B10/4, 1933, W.C. Maycock to Chairman, 23 Feb. 1933.

19. Cited in RG 151: 600 (Chile, 1923-48), Ackerman, Special Report no. 28, 21 Dec. 1933.

20. GDP figures from United Nations, *Economic Survey of Latin America, 1949* (New York: UN, 1951), 281; and Universidad de Chile, *Desarrollo económico de Chile, 1940-1956* (Santiago: Universitaria de Chile, 1956), 215. For figures useful in calculating the real size of the economy, see Banco Central de Chile, *Memoria anual, 1955* (Santiago: Banco Central, 1955), 269; RG 151: Bureau of Foreign and Domestic Commerce, Commercial Attaches: Santiago, Ackerman, Special Report no. 32, 11 Nov. 1932; and FO 371-15823 (A8334 /2/9), Pack memo, 20 Nov. 1932.

21. Sebastián Sáez, *La economía política de una crisis: Chile, 1929-1939* (Santiago: CIEPLAN, Notas Técnicas no. 130, May 1989), 8.

22. RG 59: 825.00/797, Chile-American Assoc., Confidential Report no. 15, Mar. 1933.

23. *La Nación*, 6 Jan. 1933.

24. On the relation of inflation to the coup, see especially Carlos Sáez Morales, *Recuerdos de un soldado: el ejército y la política* (Santiago: Biblioteca Ercilla, 1934), 1:71-80.

25. Chile. Hacienda (1933), Antecedentes de Oficios, v. 6 Dirección General de Impuestos Internos, no. 8473, 11 Sept. 1933.

26. Cited in RG 151: 600 (Chile, 1923-48), Bohan, Economic and Trade Note, no. 53, 22 Aug. 1934.

27. Chile. Hacienda (1934), Antecedentes de Oficios, v. 8 Dirección General de Impuestos Internos, no. 7856, 25 July 1934, and Hacienda (1935), Antecedentes de mensajes, Asociación Productores de Manzanas de Chile to Min. de Hacienda, n.d.

28. RG 59: 825.00/800, Wooten, no. 1658, 19 Apr. 1933.

29. *La Opinión*, 30 Aug. 1933.

30. Chile. Interior, v. 8922 (1935), Prov. 5960, enclosure of Camara de Comercio Rancagua list of demands collected by police agent.

31. Chile. Interior v. 8922 (1935), Prov. 5960. Telegrams, 7 May 1935. See also *La Opinión*, 7 May 1935.

32. RG 151: Bureau of Foreign and Domestic Commerce, Commercial Attaches: Santiago, Bohan, Special Report no. 23, 4 Jan. 1936.

33. Adrien Pierre Tixier, "The Development of Social Insurance in Argentina, Brazil, Chile and Uruguay," *International Labour Review* 32 (Nov. 1935), 614.

34. Wilhelm Mann, *Chile, luchando por nuevas formas de vida* (Santiago: Editorial Ercilla, 1935-36), 1:171; and RG 151: Bureau of Foreign and Domestic Commerce, Commercial Attaches: Santiago, Bohan, Economic and Trade Notes, no. 14, 19 July 1938.

35. See comments in Chile. Diputados, *Boletín de sesiones ordinarios* (17 Aug. 1933), 2253.

36. RG 59: 625.111/7, Bowman, 28 Feb. 1933.

37. For more detailed data on taxes, see Chile. Contraloría General, *Memoria de la Contraloría General correspondiente al año . . . y balance general de la Hacienda Pública*, (Santiago), 1932-43. Each volume runs about 140 pages; data used in tables and comments are scattered throughout.

38. RG 165, MID 2008-141/7, Weeks, no. 1791, 18 Oct. 1933.

39. RG 151: Bureau of Foreign and Domestic Commerce, Commercial Attaches: Santiago, Bohan, Economic and Trade Notes, no. 283, 29 May 1934.

40. Ibid., no. 304, 13 June 1934.

41. FO 371-17503 (A557/10/9), Sir R.C. Michell, 2 Jan. 1934.

42. I disagree here with Markos J. Mamalakis, *The Growth and Structure of the Chilean Economy: From Independence to Allende* (New Haven: Yale University Press, 1976), 102.

43. Chile. Hacienda 1934, Antecedentes de Oficios, v. 1, Letter from the president of Banco Central to Min. de Hacienda, 28 Dec. 1933.

44. Albert O. Hirschman, *Journeys Toward Progress: Studies of Economic Policy-Making in Latin America* (New York: The Twentieth Century Fund, 1963), 180-81.

45. *La Opinión*, 31 Oct. 1936.

46. FO 371/19773 (A8933/73/9), R.C. Michell, Notes on Recent Chilean Monetary Problems, 1st September 1936, 15 Oct. 1936; and RG 59: 825.5151/214, Scotten, no. 159, 1 Aug. 1934.

47. *El Mercurio*, 20 Oct. 1937.

48. RG 59: 825.00/808, Culbertson, no. 1498, 12 July 1933. These points are elaborated in chap. 5.

49. France-MAE, Chili, v. 11, 27 Aug. 1935.

50. Oscar Muñoz G., *Crecimiento industrial de Chile, 1914-1965* (Santiago: Universidad de Chile, 1971, 2d ed.), based on (Ph.D. diss., Yale University); Henry W. Kirsch, *Industrial Development in a Traditional Society: The Conflict of Entrepreneurship and Modernization in Chile* (Gainesville: The University Presses of Florida, 1977); Roger Joseph Burbach, "The Chilean Industrial Bourgeoisie and Foreign Capital, 1920-1970," (Ph.D. diss., Indiana University, 1975); Luis M. Ortega, "Change and Crisis in Chile's Economy and Society, 1865-1879," (Ph.D. diss., University of London, 1979); "Acerca de los orígenes de la industrialización chilena, 1860-1879," *Nueva historia*, no. 2 (1981); J. Gabriel Palma, "Chile 1914-1935: de economía exportada

sustitutiva de importaciones," *Nueva historia: revista de historia de Chile* 2:7 (Jan.-Mar. 1983); and "From an Export-led to an Import-substituting Economy: Chile 1914-39," in Rosemary Thorp, ed., *Latin America in the 1930s: The Role of the Periphery in World Crisis* (New York: St. Martin's Press, 1984). For a comparison of the new literature on industry to the dependency view, see Jorge Marshall R., "La nueva interpretación de los orígenes de la industrialización en Chile," Programa Post-Grado de Economía, ILADES (Instituto de Doctrina y Estudios Sociales), Georgetown University, Santiago, Chile, I/10 (Nov. 1988), 1-26.

51. Major authors asserting this include Marcelo Segall, *Desarrollo del capitalismo en Chile: cinco ensayos dialécticos* (Santiago: Editorial Pacífico, 1953); André Gunder Frank, *Capitalism and Underdevelopment in Latin America: Historical Studies of Chile and Brazil* (New York: Monthly Review Press, 1967); and Claudio Véliz, "La mesa de tres patas," *Desarrollo económico* (1967), 3.

52. RG 151: Bureau of Foreign and Domestic Commerce, Commercial Attaches: Santiago, Randall, Economic and Trade Notes, no. 110, 11 Oct. 1935.

53. Chile. Fomento (1939), Oficios, v. 815, no. 3, Min. de Fomento al Presidente de la Comisión de Cambios Internacionales, 4 May 1933, no. 538; RG 59: Frost, no. 876, 22 Feb. 1936, 625.003/180, Dow, 26 July 1937.

54. Chile. Fomento (1933), Oficios, v. 812, no. 2, Exequial Jiménez, Dept. de Industrias Fabriles al Min. de Fomento, 4 Mar. 1933, no. 119.

55. *El Imparcial*, 22 July 1937.

56. Chile. Fomento (1936), Oficios, v. 1164, no. 9, Exequial Jiménez Carrasco, Ingeniero Director, Departmento de Industrias Fabriles, "Informa sobre restricción a la exportación de lanas de la zona central," no. 329, 25 Nov. 1936, and Fomento (1936), Oficios, v. 1159, no. 4, Dept. de Industrias Fabriles, "Propone asimilación para clasificar los elementos no especificados de radioreceptores," no. 200, 2 June 1936. A recent article on Chilean technocrats, claims that there was a basic continuity in bureaucratic nationalism from Ibáñez through the 1930s. See Patricio Silva, "State, Public Technocracy, and Politics in Chile, 1927-1941," *Bulletin of Latin American Research* 13:3 (Sept. 1994).

57. France-MAE, Chili. v. 10, 3 Jan. 1933.

58. Chile. Hacienda (1934), Antecedentes de Oficios, v. 1, Sociedad de Fomento Fabril to Min. de Hacienda, 30 Nov. 1933, no. 136.

59. Burbach, op. cit., 41-42.

60. Chile. Interior (1934), Ruz Gomez Memo: Sociedades 322, 19 Nov. 1934.

61. Chile. Hacienda (1933), Antecedentes de Oficios, v. 3, Asociación de Madereros (Santiago), to Sub-secretario de Comercio, 10 May 1933.

62. Chile. Fomento (1933), Oficios v. 818, no. 6, Exequial Jiménez al Min. de Fomento, 18 July 1933, no. 420; Fomento (1935), Oficios, v. 1035, no. 6, Min. de Fomento al Senado y la Camara de Diputados, no date; and Fomento (1935), Oficios, v. 1035, no. 6, Min. de Fomento al Senado y la Camara de Diputados, n.d.

63. Chile. Fomento (1936), Oficios v. 1163, no. 7, Min. de Fomento no. 796, 16 Sept. 1936.

64. Chile. Fomento (1936), Oficios, v. 1157, no. 2, Instituto de Fomento Minero e Industrial de Antofagasta, Memoria correspondiente al período comprendido de junio a diciembre de 1935.

65. Chile. Interior (1931), v. 7914, memo, Jefatura Sección Pesca.

66. Oscar Alvarez Andrews, *Historia del desarrollo industrial de Chile* (Santiago: La Ilustración, 1936), 18, 19. The extended quote is from page 21.

67. Burbach, op. cit., 32-33.

68. Kirsch, op. cit., 111.

69. RG 151: Bureau of Foreign and Domestic Commerce, Commercial Attaches: Santiago, Bohan, Special Report no. 16, 45 Jan. 1940.

70. Burbach, op. cit., 60-61.

71. Dudley M. Phelps, *Migration of Industry to South America* (Westport, CT: Greenwood Press, 1969, original published 1939), 326-27.

72. Burbach, op. cit., 56.

73. Sergio Ceppi M. de L. et al., *Chile: 100 años de industria (1883-1983)* (Santiago: Sociedad de Fomento Fabril (SOFOFA), 1983), 178.

74. Data for Chile are derived from the national statistics of Sebastián Sáez, op. cit., 8. Sáez also incorporated data from the classic study of Raúl Prebisch, United Nations, *Economic Survey of Latin America, 1949* (New York: United Nations, Economic Commission for Latin America, Department of Economic Affairs, 1951), 272ff.; and four other studies of the GDP. Data for period after 1940 are from ECLA figures as presented in James W. Wilkie and Carlos Alberto Contreras, eds., *Statistical Abstract for Latin America* (Los Angeles: UCLA, Latin American Center Publications, 1993), v. 29, pt. 2, 1290. Specialists will notice my disagreement with Bulmer-Thomas, who, using 1929 as a base year, argues that Chile recovered quickly from the Depression in, Victor Bulmer-Thomas, ed., *Britain and Latin America: A Changing Relationship* (New York: Cambridge University Press, The Royal Institute of International Affairs, 1989), 212.

75. Palma, op. cit., 180, source for Graph 3.2.

76. FO 371/18669 (A2358/446/9), R.C. Michell, 25 Feb. 1935.

77. FO 371/17509 (A7335/5826/9), L.I. Crawford, Manager of Imperial Chemical Industries, 9 Aug. 1934, enclosure.

78. Gustavo Monckeberg, *Análisis del problema de la valorización de Santiago y del pago de las expropriaciones de terrenos por causa de utilidad pública* (Santiago: Editorial Nascimento, 1937), 10.

79. Ibid., 10, 12; and RG 165: MID 2610-66/171, Wooten, 28 Mar. 1933.

80. On this subject, see also Paul T. Ellsworth, *Chile: An Economy in Transition* (New York: The MacMillan Company, 1945), 29.

81. This excellent report reviews the Chilean government's data and corrects a number of errors.

82. George McBride, *Chile: Land and Society* (New York: American Geographical Society, 1936, reprinted Octagon Books, 1971). Important revisions on McBride's work are Arnold J. Bauer, *Chilean Rural Society: From the Spanish Conquest to 1930* (Cambridge: Cambridge University Press, 1975); and the essays by Bauer and Cristóbal Kay in Kenneth Duncan and Ian Rutledge, eds., *Land and Labour in Latin America: Essays on the Development of Agrarian Capitalism in the Nineteenth and Twentieth Centuries* (Cambridge: Cambridge University Press, 1977).

83. Thomas C. Wright, *Landowners and Reform in Chile: The Sociedad Nacional de Agricultura, 1919-1940* (Urbana: University of Illinois Press, 1982).

84. A central thesis of Maurice Zeitlin and Richard Earl Radcliff is that there is no sharp break between an older, land-owning elite and a corporate executive class in Chilean development. See *Landlords and Capitalists: The Dominant Class of Chile* (Princeton: Princeton University Press, 1988), 146-51 for the view that such a change exists as part of modernization, and 161-82 for their evidence that landownership and corporate power are intertwined. On p. 202, referring to the 1960s they say, "the more political offices a man has held, the more likely he is to be from a landed capitalist family."

85. Wright, op. cit., 130-34. For a range of political opinion supporting reform, see interviews in *Hoy*, 20 Oct. 1933.

86. Developed from figures in, Jean Carriere, *Landowners and Politics in Chile: A Study of the "Sociedad Nacional de Agricultura," 1932-1970* (Amsterdam: The Interuniversity Center for Latin American Research and Documentation [CEDLA], Incidentele Publicaties 18, 1980), 30.

87. Brian Loveman, *Struggle in the Countryside: Politics and Rural labor in Chile, 1919-1973* (Bloomington, Indiana: University of Indiana Press, 1976).

88. Graph based upon, Palma, op. cit.

89. RG 59: 825.0141/1, Dow, 24 July 1933, and 825.0141/2, Atwood, 22 Aug. 1933.

90. Chile. Hacienda (1935), Antecedentes de Mensajes, Asociación Productores de Manzanas de Chile to Min. de Hacienda, n.d.

91. Chile. Hacienda (1933), Antecedentes de Oficios, v. 1, Camara Central de Comercio, Valparaiso, 13 Jan. 1933; and Hacienda (1933), Antecedentes de Oficios, v. 5, Comité de Cereales y Leguminosas, Junta Exportación Agrícola al Min. de Agricultura, 16 June 1933.

92. Chile. Hacienda (1934), Antecedentes de Oficios, v. 3, Cámara Central de Comercio, Valparaiso al Min. de Hacienda, no. 419, 19 Apr. 1934, enclosure of letter to President Alessandri, 13 Feb. 1933; and RG 59: 825.00-Gen. Cond./57, Culbertson, no. 1400, 7 Mar. 1933.

93. Chile. Hacienda (1933), Antecedentes de Oficios, v. 5, Comité de Cereales y Leguminosas, Junta Exportación Agricola al Ministro de Agricultura, 16 June 1933; FO 371-17509 (A5731/5731/9), R.C. Michell, memo on wheat situation in Chile, by Vice Consul Haskoll, 15 July 1934; RG 151: Bureau of Foreign and Domestic Commerce, Commercial Attaches: Santiago, Randall, Economic and Trade Notes, no. 400, 12 May 1936; and Wright, op. cit., 116.

94. Chile. Hacienda (1934), Antecedentes de Oficios, v. 4, Superintendencia de Aduanas al Min. de Hacienda, no. 1825, 6 June 1934; RG 59: 625.003/164, Dow, 10 Sept. 1934; and La Opinión, 6 Sept. 1935.

95. La Opinion, 18 Dec. 1935, article by Guillermo Piedrabuena.

96. On this index, Chile reaches 104 in 1935, and Mexico reaches 103 only in 1941. A major factor was the sharp surge in Mexico's population. See note 73 for source of Chilean data. Data for Mexico are derived from Enrique Cárdenas, La industrialización mexicana durante la gran depresión (México: El Colegio de México, 1987), 194-95. Cárdenas, in turn, cites figures from an internal study by the Banco de México. Population figures are from the United Nations, Economic Survey . . . 1949, 408-409.

97. Bulmer-Thomas, op. cit. Of course, I am not in agreement with the basis of calculating recovery used in this estimate, see earlier note.

Fig. 3. President Arturo Alessandri Palma (with his dog) and Minister of Hacienda, Gustavo Ross Santa María, inspect construction site in Santiago, during mid-1930s. Ross, referred to by labor-left as the "Minister of Hunger," is in the forefront. Chile. Archivo Nacional.

Fig. 4. President Arturo Alessandri Palma and a labor delegation in his first term of office, early 1920s. Workers did their best to present themselves socially safe. The suit, tie, and Panama floater—their Sunday best—comprised a labor uniform in their rallies from the first decade of the century into the 1930s. Earl Chapin May, *2000 Miles through Chile: The Land of More or Less* (New York: The Century Company, 1924).

4

Foreign Corporations and Economic Nationalism

> I must confess that all the "economics" I ever learned from the pages of John Mill and the other authorities does not help to follow the course of events in Chile. Either the standard authorities are wrong or the State is endeavoring to do impossibilities.
>
> Manager in Valparaiso, Bank of London and South America, April 1937[1]

The demands of domestic recovery generated contradictory pressures on Alessandri's administration and led it into conflict with the United States. In trying to respond to these pressures, Alessandri at first infuriated U.S. interests; but they gradually accepted his administration as the best of a bad situation.

Governments in Europe were more accommodating, and Alessandri and his finance minister, Gustavo Ross, saw them as counterweights to the United States. Ross, just as he had done on domestic issues, centralized a good deal of the negotiations with other governments and foreign companies in his office. The Europeans had less at risk than the Americans. And, Alessandri, unlike the provisional presidents, had a new bargaining position with the United States based on the rise of compensation trade agreements. This now obscure practice was central to commerce in the Atlantic economies in the 1930s; by 1937, there were 170 such agreements in the world.[2] Essentially, these bilateral-trade agreements instituted special understandings between two countries that did not apply to trade with a third nation. Europe promoted compensation trade as a means of overcoming shortages of gold and hard currency; and Latin American governments eagerly accepted them. Chile's agreement with France was the first of this kind of trade agreement in the entire region.

As the 1930s evolved, it seemed that Germany and Japan might use compensation trade to displace the United States as Chile's dominant trading partner. But a close look at the quarrels between U.S. interests and the Chilean government indicates that U.S. interests never lost their strategic position within the country. Even at the height of the compensation era, the government itself remained highly dependent on U.S. enterprises. Disastrously for the Alessandri administration, a government that negotiated well with foreign interests was tarnished by the process. The conflicts over oil, utilities, and the foreign debt hurt it in key elections then and in historical narratives since.

Compensation Trade

Because they required constant government monitoring, compensation trade agreements meant the final breakdown of liberal trade rules. Each of the two partners to an agreement set up an account in the other nation's currency (usually in its central bank). To use Chile's first agreement as an example, an importer of French goods in Chile paid for them in pesos at the Central Bank in Santiago, which then notified the Compensation Office of the Chamber of Commerce in Paris. The Parisian agency then paid the exporter in francs at the rate agreed upon between the two nations. Each importer had to have prior permission from his own government to make the transaction. Ideally a country could buy from its partner the same amount as it sold to the partner and accounts would balance at the end of fiscal year. Trading firms were assured of price stability while each country avoided a run on its gold or hard currency reserves. In practice, governments set up multiple accounts under each agreement, with different rates of exchange for different purposes, or even more complicatedly, with different requirements for the import license for each account.[3]

In this way, they acquired the ability to alter economic rights related to foreign trade. In a nation such a Chile, which had grown through trade, this affected all commercial life. Compensation trade influenced the size and payment schedules for foreign debts, as well as profit margins and domestic prices. It not only set the terms of currency exchange between two nations, it shaped what kind of market remained within each country for those not party to the agreement. Provisions in the agreement between Chile and France were repeated in agreements made between Chile and other nations. An important subsidiary issue was the repayment of "blocked currencies," those obligations Chileans could not pay for lack of foreign currency. Other issues included Chile's debts abroad and the repatriation of profits by foreign firms. In the case of the French agreement, Chile had to run a trade surplus to pay off old bills it owed that country. Claiming to help Chile, France priced its compensation franc at a rate considerably below that of the international market, thus reducing the relative cost of French goods.[4]

Although reviving world trade, compensation agreements changed trading patterns. France had originally proposed an agreement in 1931; but the turnover in Chilean governments prevented any ratification until just before Alessandri's election.[5] France had always run a trade deficit with Chile, but once the agreement took force, Chile paid old debts and accumulated unused francs in Paris—it became the creditor, at no interest. Reactions within Chile varied according to economic sectors. Seeing power flow to bureaucrats, domestic bankers and the National Agricultural Society denounced the entire process. Mining corporations, even those with heavy foreign ownership, loved the fact that they could sell stock-piled ore. The French bought Chilean nitrate so cheaply that they resold it for a profit in the rest of Europe.[6]

By the end of 1934, Chile had agreements with Germany as well as Austria, Belgium, Czechoslovakia, Denmark, Holland, Italy, Portugal, Spain, Sweden, and Switzerland. All included the provision for clearing frozen currencies.[7] While the French were important innovators in compensation agreements, it was Germany, with its aski mark (the name of its compensation currency) that became its past master, and as we shall see, Chile's major trading partner in Europe. Trade understandings with Argentina and Brazil on many goods functioned as compensation systems but without a treaty.[8]

Britain and the United States routinely protested the practice of compensation trade. The British feared a further erosion of their already weakened trade position.[9] At one point, the Chilean government told British importing houses to import from France.[10] The U.S. State Department attacked all bilateral agreements. It argued that because the United States did not discriminate against Chilean goods and was a major market for nitrates, it was unfair that the French, Germans and others were using compensation agreements to "clear" their frozen currencies, while those of U.S. creditors remained blocked. Moreover, the Europeans were selling their goods at exchange rates considerably below the market rate, and they were using the Currency Exchange Commission to force importers in Chile to buy their goods.[11] The Chilean government's reply to the United States was that the agreements were a necessity; losing compensation trade would cost Chile the major part of its mining revenues. Chile, offering equal treatment, was willing to sign a compensation agreement with the United States similar to, or even more favorable than, that signed with any other country.[12]

The United States refused the offer on the grounds that all bilateral trade was inefficient and deflected commerce from normal prices and channels. U.S. officials ignored or played down the Chilean perspective as much as possible. As one ambassador put it, Chile had no right to operate markets "at a discount."[13] Arguments over compensation lasted until the practice ended in World War II. In 1937, Chile sent Undersecretary of Commerce Desiderio García to Washington to negotiate a new commercial treaty. In anticipation of the meeting, State Department officers drew up a brief for Sumner Welles, Undersecretary for Latin American Affairs, that warned against any acceptance of bilateralism.[14]

U.S. officials saw no reason to facilitate compensation agreements that diverted trade to Europe and Japan. The amounts at stake seemed substantial. By the late 1930s, Great Britain was still the major investor in Latin America but its interests were concentrated in Argentina and Brazil. Argentina, Brazil, Paraguay, and Uruguay made up US$3.25 billion of the US$4.5 billion Britain had invested in all Latin America. By 1939, its holdings in Chile stood at about US$300 million. Total U.S. investments in the region stood at about US$4.0 billion but were much more widely distributed: Argentina, Brazil, Chile, Cuba, and Mexico each contained between US$500 and US$750 million dollars.[15] One of the issues constantly raised in the State Department memoranda about any move toward nationalization or defiance of U.S. corporate goals in Chile was the impact such behavior would have on U.S. interests in the rest of the region. There were about 1.6 thousand U.S. citizens resident in Chile. Total U. S. investment was estimated at US$1 billion in 1929. By 1934, the value of these investments had fallen to about US$680 million (and fell again to about US$600 million by 1939), with US$410 million in corporate direct investments and another

US$270 million in portfolio.[16] (The largest corporate holdings are listed in Table 4.1, below).

One complaint about Chile by the United States was untrue. The currency exchange rates in compensation agreements were generally *not* below market, a fact illustrated in Table 4.2, which compares the dollar export rate in Chile with rates for compensation currencies. (The Japanese invented a currency called the *dollar* for compensation trade.) From these figures, one could make a good case for an open-currency market. Chileans were paying more pesos for goods exchanged in compensation trade than they were for dollar-priced goods. Without compensation agreements, however, trade would have been substantially reduced and the currency values would have been different. There

Table 4.1: U.S. Corporate Investments in Chile, 1929-1932

Activity	Corporation	Millions, US$s
Electricity	Chilean Electric Light & Power Co., subsidiary of American & Foreign Power Co.	190.6
Copper	Anaconda Kennecott, including Guggenheims' interest	214.0 168.9
Nitrates	Guggenheims	141.0
Telephones	Chile Telephone, subsidiary, International Telephone & Telegraph	60.0
Steel	Bethlehem Steel (El Tofo) U.S. Steel	13.0 2.5
Shipping	W.R. Grace (textiles)	8.0
Banking	Grace National Bank National City Bank	15.0 3.1
Telegraph	All America Cable	1.0
Automobiles	Ford	1.0
Railroad	J.P. Morgan, share of Transandine Railroad	unknown
Oil	West India Oil, subsidiary, Standard Oil of New Jersey	unknown

Sources: Hoover Papers, Pres., Box 49, Review of Questions. "Recent Problems in the Protection of American Interests in Chile," 2:68-69; see also FO 371-17508, memo of A.J. Pack, 8 May 1934.

Table 4.2: Compensation Currency Values, 1935

Currency	Equivalent Pesos per US$	Compared to Open-Market Value of US$
US$, export draft	24.37	
Mark, compensation	20.05	17.8% less
Swiss Franc, comp.	26.02	6.8% more
French Franc, comp.	26.19	7.5% more
Florin, comp.	26.41	8.4% more
Lira, comp.	26.85	10.2% more
Koruna, comp.	26.92	10.5% more
Japanese dollar	26.92	26.1% more

Source: RG 151: Commerce, Bureau of Foreign and Domestic Commerce, Commercial Attaches: Santiago, Bohan, Economic and Trade Notes no. 230, 9 Jan. 1936.

is one notable exception to the general rule. In the case of Germany—the most astute nation using compensation trade—the aski mark rate was less than other exchange rates; in 1938-39, it was as much as 33 percent below open-market value.[17]

U.S. officials oversimplified the impact of compensation trade. Some of the major supporters of Chile's European agreements were the U.S. copper companies and nitrate interests. The nitrate market needed France to survive, so the Guggenheims urged the State Department not to protest compensation too strenuously.[18] Other U.S. enterprises in Chile stopped protesting compensation after 1934, and turned a deaf ear in 1937 when Secretary of State Cordell Hull came to Santiago to preach in favor of a multinational lowering of tariffs.[19]

During Alessandri's administration, Chilean imports shifted away from the United States to compensation countries. Aside from a sharp decline in the volume and value of trade, no pattern of change in the 1930s was common to all Latin America. Considering Chile's experience, two elements in regional trade are somewhat surprising. The region suffered a loss of its share of world markets in the Crash (from 8.6 to 7.2 percent); but had recovered its position by 1937.[20] Chile did not do so. British trade with Latin America dropped 51 percent between 1929 and 1937; but in the latter year, Great Britain replaced the United States in terms of the total value of trade with the region. Britain's relative position in terms of Argentina's imports was actually better in 1937 than it had been in 1929. Chile was much more like Brazil, where British trade declined in value and percentages after 1929 and Germany's percentage of trade improved dramatically.[21]

Germany was the primary beneficiary of compensation trade with Chile; in 1938, Chile's trade with Germany surpassed that of Great Britain and rivaled that of the United States. In 1929, Germany had accounted for 15 percent of Chile's imports (249 million pesos) and 11 percent of exports (251 million). In 1936, German imports made up 28 percent (close to 90 million pesos) of Chile's trade while exports, still at 11 percent, now accounted for only 70 million pesos. Just before World War II, its share of Chile's imports remained at about 25 percent, running far ahead of Britain's 10.5 percent. Japan also improved its small-market share: Japanese compensation exports to Chile (mostly textiles) were five times greater in 1934 than 1933 and, just before the war, they climbed to over 3 percent of the total.[22] A U.S. Commerce Department official complained bitterly in late 1934 that the Japanese were copying American fabrics at "40 percent below market."[23] But as Table 4.3 shows, the U.S. predominance in Chile's trade was never in jeopardy: between 1936 and 1939, the U.S. took 22 percent of Chile's exports and sold over 30 percent of all Chilean imports.

Compensation agreements never worked smoothly. The Europeans always wanted a trade balance in their favor, while Chileans continued to prefer U.S. goods when they were available.[24] Chile also had little leverage in Europe. France, for example, assigned preferential treatment to U.S. apple imports over Chilean ones because it was trying to win a greater share of the U.S. wine quota.[25] A sharp upswing in mineral sales through compensation came after 1936, as Europe prepared for war.[26] Compensation trade began to level off, however, as surpluses accumulated in the advanced industrial nations. The onset of World War II then ended the trade.

The Fight with U.S. Interests

Compensation trade and the breakdown of liberal economic rules forced a realignment of foreign interests within Chile. As Germany's trade prospects improved, those of Britain shrank. British officials saw what was happening as part of a pattern in Latin America and rationalized that their country was not losing much. The British Minister in Santiago thought Germany and Japan, "rashly rushing into" a situation of "doubtful profit."[27] One legacy of Britain's earlier success remained: Chileans, who were descended from nineteenth-century merchant adventurers and who became strong supporters of the Chilean right, backed Alessandri against populist pressures to his left.[28]

Table 4.3: Chile's Foreign Trade with Major Partners, 1928-1939

Year	1928-30	1932	1936	1939
Exports Average				
Total	1853	290	562	671
USA	636	76	109	204
Britain	398	91	92	82
Germany	196	39	54	56
Japan	17	0	8	11
Imports Average				
Total	1405	213	346	410
USA	454	51	88	167
Britain	237	27	45	34
Germany	707	100	99	93
Japan	11	1	9	15

Source: Chile, *Sinópsis estadística*, (1933-40).

During the Alessandri administration, Chile's most important foreign issues involved the United States. In almost every case, these issues originated before Alessandri took office. The major change was that compensation agreements and currency controls politicized markets for almost every trade item. The Chilean government used this fact to extract more revenue from key U.S. companies. Chilean officials, however, never deployed their power to reduce the country's vulnerability to U.S. decisions. In dealing with the United States, Alessandri and Ross learned to wave the nationalist banner. But this was a dangerous strategy.

Chile had pushed for a new trade agreement with the United States when the old one expired in the late 1920s; but the effort had stalled. The United States demonstrated a lack of interest. Little or nothing was offered the Chileans and much was demanded from them.[29] Although the United States railed against compensation agreements, it offered Chile no attractive options.[30] Once President Franklin D. Roosevelt was inaugurated, Secretary of State Hull acknowledged that U.S. tariffs had hurt world trade. Even so, the Roosevelt administration efforts at reciprocity, with emphasis on Chilean mineral exports to the United States, were blocked by domestic lobbies in Washington. Trade talks, therefore, focused on temporary issues and generated a series of ad hoc solutions, especially concerning conflicts involving currency exchange rules.

Alessandri and Ross modified the entire currency exchange market, solidifying what had been a series of improvisations into a new set of economic rights. In 1933, Ross drove some hard bargains with the United States; for example, he cleared many of the blocked dollar accounts at a rate very favorable to Chile.[31] Commercial banks acquired the exclusive right to buy most export drafts (denominated primarily in dollars or gold pesos). The major exception involved the mining companies, which exchanged dollars under special rules (explained in the previous chapter). Beyond the banks, there was a small army of brokers in the "curb market." No one bothered these black marketers, and, near the end of the Alessandri administration, the Supreme Court ruled that their operations were "extra-legal" but not illegal.[32] From 1933 until 1937, there were three markets: a government-run market, offering the most favorable rate to importers (the cheapest dollars); a bank-managed export draft market, selling dollars to government-approved businesses; and an open-currency market—the curb market—with the highest price for a dollar. The curb rate was two to three times the official rate.[33]

Obviously, access to the cheapest dollars offered the highest profits and that access depended upon influence with the Currency Exchange Commission or the finance minister. A firm's ability to use the various decrees, statutes, and trading practices was often essential to survival.[34] Even favored importers, however, rarely received all their exchange at an official rate; they would receive part from the government, but would have to purchase the rest in another market. The supply of exchange improved as trade revived, but it was always short of demand and conflicts over it raged into the 1940s and beyond.

Table 4.4: Government-Controlled Hard Currency, 1933-1934

Year Available	1933	1934
Amount Available in Millions of Gold Pesos		
Official Rate	23.7	13.2
Compensation	11.9	5.5
Currencies for Past Obligations Compensation	10.6	5.7
Currencies for New Trade Export Drafts	156.4	109.4
Total	204.6	143.8
Imports Paid Abroad	30.7	15.8
Total Available	235.3	159.6
Percentages Allocated by Exchange Commission		
Government Ministries	41.9	59.4
Government Materials	24.4	4.5
Articles of "Prime Necessity"	26.9	31.4
Drugs	3.0	3.9
All Other	3.8	0.8

Source: U.S. State Department, Record Group 59: 825.5151/214, Scotten no. 159, 1 Aug. 1934.

An increase in the value of the peso was an unanticipated complication of compensation trade. Chileans used the improved purchasing power to buy U.S. cars and radios. An American car that cost ten thousand pesos in 1929, cost 65 thousand in 1932, and 33 thousand in 1934. In 1935, the U.S. dominated Chile's car market and sold two thousand cars—a quarter of them came in parts and were assembled in Santiago—worth 7 million pesos. (In 1929, U.S. companies had sold 10 thousand cars.)[35] Radio imports jumped every year; three major U.S. companies, led by RCA Victor held 60 percent of the market.[36] In an attempt to control the outflow of dollars, Ross imposed quotas on U.S. cars and radios, in 1935. When that was not enough, he demanded that importers purchase German radios through the compensation agreement.[37] General Motors, the National City Bank, and the U.S. Embassy in Santiago sharply protested his decisions. The ban on cars and radios was lifted after a month. A few months later, Ross raised tariffs on them instead.[38] In 1936, the cycle was repeated: another surge in imports led to a new restriction on cars, radios, and other "luxuries."[39]

Higher tariffs and compensation trade attracted foreign manufacturers, who built plants in Chile. In 1937, RCA announced the construction of a radio factory in Santiago.[40] In other words, foreign companies adjusted to nationalist policies and acquired positions within the restricted domestic market. No Chilean leader of the time objected to this trend.

The major conflicts between Chile and the United States, of course, involved minerals. The government and the U.S. nitrate and copper companies often clashed. The companies did not want to weaken the government too much because they needed it to sell their Chilean ores in Europe's cartel markets. In dealing with the U.S. State Department, the companies alternately demanded help with some issues and told the Department to back off on others. No single set of rules ever governed any mining sector, in part because of conflict among the mining companies. The first dispute concerned COSACh. This corporation claimed to have a billion pesos in assets, but it lost 110 million in 1931 alone. Keeping it afloat was bleeding the government.[41] Existing stockpiles of nitrate exceeded a year's normal production. The Guggenheim's technological wonder, the Pedro de Valdivia plant, which had cost US$32 million to build, began operation in April 1931, but was forced to close in October 1932. It remained closed until August 1934.[42] The Guggenheims, the British and Chilean stockholders, and a major British creditor, the Anglo-South American Bank, continuously tried to shift even more of COSACh's obligations to the government. Their efforts were hampered by the round robin of provisional presidents in 1931.[43] One of their major goals was to trade a fifty-fifty split in non-existent profits in return for more government subsidies.[44] While the issue of COSACh seemed unimportant in the 1931 presidential election, public feeling had hardened against the firm by 1932.[45]

Still, Alessandri shocked U.S. interests when he dissolved the firm by decree on January 3, 1933. The president hated the corporation, considering it a legacy from Ibáñez. (In his memoirs, he blamed COSACh, calling it the "primordial cause," for Chile's crisis.)[46] He was also motivated by a belief that abolishing the corporation would revive employment in the nitrate sector. The assets and debts of COSACh were assigned to the nitrate factory owners who had joined it, and the nitrate export tax, the mainstay of government revenues for almost fifty years, was revived. Obligations to COSACh bondholders were canceled.[47] The U.S. Embassy was already upset over the government's behavior toward the U.S.-owned electric company (see below). The Commercial Attache wrote Washington that Alessandri was "developing an extremely national psychosis [sic]."[48] Ross, speaking before the Chamber of Deputies, said that the national interest preceded all other considerations and that the government would reclaim all public nitrate deposits ceded to COSACh.[49] Alessandri argued it was all a matter of common sense. He told a UPI reporter that no one should be allowed to take profits out of Chile at a time of hardship; "large foreign businesses" had to make some sacrifices. Nor should the government carry out policies that might increase inflation or unemployment. "I have no complaint against the Americans, but it appears that they are antagonistic toward me because of the methods I have adopted."[50]

The United States was not alone, the governments of Britain, Germany, and Spain also protested the end of COSACh. The government action ruined the Anglo-South American Bank, the second largest British bank in Chile and one of the largest in Latin America.[51] U.S. Ambassador Culbertson took the decision personally, claiming Alessandri had misled him: the president had promised that no unilateral actions would be taken against American firms. Chile was refusing to honor its obligations, recklessly endangering "good relations."[52]

Alessandri took the offensive and asked for a meeting with Culbertson. He proceeded to rake over every Chilean grievance with the United States since the nineteenth century, concluding his harangue with the Guggenheims' underhandedness in abetting Ibáñez. The two men argued about the firm's legality, and Alessandri pointed out that his administration might be overthrown if the decree was rescinded. In Culbertson's view, the president was obtuse and "full of the ghosts of the past."[53] The ambassador believed that Alessandri was acting like the Peruvian populist President Sánchez Cerro, who broadened his popularity by attacking his predecessor, the autocratic ruler of the 1920s, Augusto Leguía. The ambassador openly defended the Guggenheims and said he saw nothing illegal in what Ibáñez had done. Years later, Culbertson would publicly boast of his role in arguing the cause of U.S. businessmen in Chile. But on this issue, he lost.[54]

On its own terms, the government took over the nitrate industry. A committee of liquidators reorganized the sector and reassigned the COSACh debt to the Guggenheims and the original British factory owners.[55] The committee created a state export monopoly to make certain that the government had a voice in any profit distribution and in negotiating cartel arrangements. The new Nitrate and Iodine Sales Corporation bought all domestic production of nitrate and its by-product, iodine, and handled sales abroad. Ross, while still serving as finance minister, became its very well-paid president.[56]

The reorganization was successful despite the government's inexperience. When Ross first took over at the Ministry of Finance, he wrote the firm of Antony Gibbs and Sons for advice, admitting he knew nothing about the trade. An internal memo of the firm's London office remarks on his extraordinary ignorance, especially of the iodine market. So the firm tutored him, emphasizing how the commodity cartels worked.[57] Ross was an apt pupil; no more complaints about his naivete appear in foreign archives by April 1933. In addition, the government had some luck. Nitrate demand improved, helped by the compensation agreements and by a working truce within the nitrate cartel.

The informal cartel operated like others, but with the curious provision that the Guggenheims had to negotiate as if they were a Chilean firm. As earlier explained, the organization of COSACh was closely tied to their cartel strategy. After COSACh was abolished, the Guggenheims remained the principal salitre producers and so continued as the chief Chilean negotiators in setting market shares with Europe's CIA. They used their clout not only in Europe but in the United States, where they kept a minority share in the market for salitre.[58] As seen in Table 4.5, the Guggenheims improved their position as the market revived. Their firm, Anglo-Chilean, produced granulated nitrate; the old British factories produced crystals.

No formal cartel existed after 1931. Serious attempts at negotiating an agreement were made at Ostend in August 1933 and Frankfort in July 1935.[59] The fear of an all-out trade war, the Guggenheim's influence in Washington, and Chile's cheap labor and ore explain the gradual revival. The price stabilized at a low US$22 per metric ton (it had been US$62 in 1929). Alessandri was right, the end of COSACh increased employment from a low of 8.3 thousand (down from 58 thousand in 1929) to around 20 thousand in 1936. It hovered around that figure into the first stages of World War II.[60]

Table 4.5: Nitrate Production through the 1930S

Year 19–	Number of Factories	Granules	Crystals	Total Metric Tons
33-34	13	199,140	333,037	534,176
34-35	20	608,567	525,496	1,134,034
35-36	21	675,738	543,023	1,218,406
36-37	22	719,569	583,619	1,303,188
37-38	19	806,835	617,454	1,424,289
38-39	18	869,765	557,724	1,427,489

Source: Chile, Interior, v. 10202 (1940) Min. de Hacienda, Superintendencia del Salitre.

The Guggenheims never liked Alessandri but, near the end of 1936, they stopped lobbying the U.S. Embassy for help. By then, they, like the copper companies, were far more concerned with the movement that threatened to replace him. Anaconda and Kennecott (in which the Guggenheims still had an interest) now controlled Chile's most valuable mineral export, copper. In 1935, that mineral represented 45 percent of all exports, nitrate, 31 percent. Ninety-five percent of all production was in the hands of these two firms, which owned three mines: Anaconda controlled the open-pit mines Chuquicamata and Potrerillos in the north, and Kennecott ran El Teniente, the tunnel mine at Rancagua, about a hundred miles south of the capital.[61] The struggle between the government and foreign investors revolved around the now familiar issues of cartels and currency rules.

A standard work on copper traces eight distinct attempts at price collusion between 1870 to 1945.[62] The most significant collusion, the Copper Exporters, Inc., included the U.S. copper giants, their Latin American subsidiaries, and European firms with mines in Rhodesia and the Belgian Congo. It controlled about 85 percent of world production from 1926 to 1931 and sent the price soaring to US$0.19 a pound in 1929. It fell apart when the price dropped to US$0.05 in the Crash.[63]

Alessandri took office just as the copper cartel dissolved. Copper supplies were at an all time high, and U.S. tariffs forced Chilean producers to rely entirely on the European market.[64] Anaconda's mines had a break-even point at a price of US$0.09 to 0.095, just about the world average. The company operated at 10 to 20 percent of capacity.

Kennecott, with a break-even point of US$0.7 to 0.075, ran at 50 percent capacity.[65] Chilean officials had several complaints against U.S. management: foreign control of the mines prevented barter trade; mining company accounts made the mines look unprofitable and so reduced their tax liability; and 163 U.S. administrators were earning more than nine thousand Chileans working in the mines.[66] (They overlooked the fact that the same firms were cutting their U.S. production even more severely than in Chile.)[67]

Prices and exports improved as a new copper cartel formed in 1935, and soon controlled 45 percent of world output. Kennecott and Anaconda were both members, although the United States had ceased exporting its copper.[68] The market's improvement was due not to the cartel but the rearmament programs in Britain, France, Germany, and Japan.[69] Trade volume and prices soared in 1937.[70] The rebound led Chilean legislators to propose an export tax, a measure defeated by skillful company lobbying. The companies argued that the tax would reduce Chile's competitiveness and might even lead to a cut in its cartel share of the European market.[71]

The copper companies lost in the fight over currency rules, which required them to buy pesos from the government. As soon as he took office, Gustavo Ross insisted that the copper- and iron-mining companies spend at least 38 percent of their earnings buying pesos.[72] For each dollar, the companies received 16.50 pesos. The government sold the dollars to importers for 19 pesos or more. By 1937, the mining companies were getting 19 pesos for a dollar, and the government was selling the dollars for 25 pesos each.[73] The currency exchange requirement became the government's major source of hard currency. As Table 4.6 demonstrates, income tax brought the government US$11.58 million between 1934 and 1938; the currency requirement raked in US$14.05 million.[74] Legislation creating the system said it was to last two years and four months; with some modifications, it endured until 1955.[75]

In the late 1930s, the copper companies spent US$48.35 million in Chile, some 44 percent of all their earnings. They feared any change in currency rules far more than an increase in taxes or threat of nationalization. As the U.S. Embassy in Santiago or the U.S. State Department complained about compensation trade or the foreign debt, Chileans answered that any increased demand for hard currency from their government would mean an immediate increase in the currency requirements of the copper companies.[76] This reply toned down U.S. rhetoric.

The striking characteristic of Alessandri's dealings with the United States is that he could not avoid public conflict over the very issues that had plagued his recent predecessors. Alessandri was accused by the left of selling out to foreign investors. In fact, his administration's quarrels involve many of the same names that appeared in earlier conflicts: the Grace shipping lines, International Telephone and Telegraph, Chilean Electric, and the foreign oil companies. His administration did not oppose foreign investment in general or U. S. influence in particular. Well-to-do attorneys and engineers who sat on the boards of subsidiary firms run by William R. Grace, British American Tobacco, and Nestlé were among his supporters.[78] Still, his administration had to juggle pressures from the domestic economy with those of foreign corporations. The political costs of trying to accommodate both were high.

The story of South American Frutera Company is a good example of the conflicts taking place and the use of governmental authority by Chilean capitalists. By the 1920s, Chilean entrepreneurs dreamed of selling fruit to northern, winter markets; but they lacked commercial access and shipping. Apples seemed a possibility: cheap to produce, easily stored and shipped, and with a ready market; and after apples, Chilean trade promoters fantasized about pears, grapes, and so on. A trade did develop as Grace brought bananas into Chile and took Chilean produce northward. In 1933, Chilean fruit exporters formed the South American Frutera Company so they could negotiate as a unit with Grace over control of markets abroad as well as within Chile.

William R. Grace, an Irish immigrant in Peru, made his fortune during the guano boom. In the late 1860s, he transferred his base of operations to New York. The firm became a major merchant operation along the west coast of Central and South America. In its second generation, it undertook the development of Grace Pan American Airways and diversified into sugar plantations, chemicals, textiles, and paper production.[79] In the 1930s, Grace expanded in Chile by investing in textiles and sugar refining; but international trade and shipping remained the core of its business. In 1934, Grace moved to take over Frutera's successful operations by cutting Frutera's access to refrigerated shipping. With the United Fruit Company, Grace dumped bananas on the market in Valparaiso to force Frutera to give up its import activities. It also used its contacts among New York importers to ban Frutera-supplied fruit to that city. When Frutera cried foul, Grace offered to rescue the company by buying 51 percent of its shares.[80]

Frutera struck back the only way it could, through its influence in Santiago. It got the Currency Exchange Commission to grant it exclusive currency permits. When Grace went to pay for its imports, it was

Table 4.6: Copper Companies and Amounts Returned to Chile,
1934-1938
(In millions of US$s)

Year 19—	Total Earnings	In Pesos	Income Tax Revenue	Materials Purchased	Total US$s
Anaconda					
34	3.62	0.99	0.06	0.49	1.55
35	5.59	0.97	0.09	0.67	1.73
36	4.62	1.18	0.13	0.78	2.09
37	14.81	3.45	0.26	2.80	6.51
38	12.16	4.24	1.26	2.24	7.76
Totals	40.84	20.84	1.82	6.99	19.65
Kennecott					
34	15.06	4.88	0.48	3.01	8.58
35	18.46	4.46	2.28	2.33	7.98
36	16.46	3.64	1.48	1.60	6.72
37	38.61	6.75	1.39	3.26	11.41
38	26.94	7.95	4.72	2.67	15.35
Totals	115.55	27.69	9.76	12.89	49.85
Both Companies				Total US$s Returned	% Earnings Returned
34	18.68	5.87	0.54	9.93	53
35	24.05	5.43	2.37	9.71	40
36	21.10	4.82	1.61	8.81	42
37	53.42	10.20	1.65	17.92	34
38	38.10	12.19	5.98	23.11	59
Totals	156.39	48.35	11.58	69.50	44

Source: U.S. State Department, Record Group 59: 825.6352/80, Memo to Welles, 14 Feb. 1939; data is based on information collected directly from the companies.[77]

denied dollars. The Commission also demanded that all bananas coming from Ecuador be shipped by Frutera on the South American Steamship Line, run by the Edwards' clan. It gave the two Chilean firms exclusive permission to ship flour on the return voyage. Grace lobbied the U.S. State Department for help. The Chilean Foreign Office was blunt in its reply. It did not matter that the Commission's decision exceeded its legal authority, because the government could not allow Frutera's influential owners to be driven into bankruptcy. Grace's tactics had captured over 50 percent of the banana market in three months.[81] The conflict was resolved through a quota arrangement with Grace using Chilean-owned subsidiaries in the fruit trade.[82] In short, Chilean businessmen needed their government's direct help in negotiating market shares with foreign firms. Although the public rhetoric was highly nationalistic, the goal for the Chileans was to keep from being driven out of the market altogether.

Oil was another key issue involving economic diplomacy. Alessandri faced two fuel shortages: one when he entered office and another as the congressional elections of 1937 approached. In both instances, the national reserve dwindled until the supply could be counted in days.[83] The oil companies refused to refine any crude oil from the Soviet Union, which Chile was able to obtain in a swap for copper or nitrate.[84] Gasoline had become a political necessity. The left used the price and scarcity of fuel to build support among urban consumers, especially among taxi and bus drivers who were a major labor faction in Santiago.[85] In October 1934, Alessandri responded to this perennial problem by using the law Montero had passed to create the Chilean Oil Company, COPEC [Compañía de Petroleos de Chile]. COPEC began selling gasoline in early 1935. The two foreign oil companies retaliated with a price war. Alessandri then threatened to use the currency rules to hurt the foreign firms. Near the end of 1936, COPEC and the oil companies resolved the confrontation with a tripartite division of the market for gas, kerosene, and other products.[86]

The oil issue illustrates the difficulty of holding together any domestic coalition in the face of foreign trade pressures. Conservatives within the administration strongly disagreed with Alessandri's tactics. Ross opposed Alessandri's push for a state-run energy company, seeing it as a move by the Ministry of Development to encroach on his turf. He told the Santiago managers of the oil companies to lobby the U.S. and British embassies for help. During the shortage of 1937, Ross urged the companies to stop importing fuel in order to weaken the role of the economic nationalists in the administration.[87] The chambers of commerce in Valparaiso and Santiago, the automobile dealers, and the owners of taxi and bus companies also opposed any move toward a state-controlled oil market because they feared a new form of state economic power.[88] The final arrangement owed, in other words, a good deal to Alessandri's manipulative skills, and it operated in the face of strong opposition from domestic capital.

By creating COPEC, Alessandri brought Chile in line with a pattern seen throughout Latin America. Argentina had created its state oil firm in 1922. Bolivia nationalized Standard Oil of New Jersey's holdings in 1937, and Mexico nationalized its foreign oil firms the following year.[89] One of the elements in the rise of economic nationalism in Latin America, a factor difficult to gauge in terms of its impact, is that it was an international phenomenon. Becoming more nationalistic gave a political leader a broader cachet. In any event, given the date of COPEC's origin, Alessandri was more nationalistic than most Latin American leaders in his time.

The divisions within the government, however, limited COPEC's economic role to participation in the national market, pushing oil exploration in Magallanes and subsidizing coal production. Eventually, the combination of policies would alter Chile's fuel situation. The government spent 15 million pesos on unsuccessful oil exploration by 1938. Coal output rose sharply until 1935, when technological bottlenecks and exhausted seams ended expansion.[90] It required a change of administration to enlarge COPEC's purposes and force the foreign companies out of the national market.[91]

Another controversy in economic diplomacy involved electricity, and its centerpiece was the Chilean Electric Light and Power Company, Ltd. Successive incarnations of Chilean Electric had signed five contracts with various political authorities from 1897 to 1931; none of the agreements lasted. The company supplied power to Santiago and Valparaiso. Subsidiaries ran the tramway systems in these two cities and supplied power to the province of Aconcagua (where El Teniente was located). In all, Chilean Electric controlled 85 percent of the nation's electricity. One Chilean government after another had demanded that the company invest in electricity while refusing to grant rate increases to offset inflation. The British owners seemed happy to sell out to the American and Foreign Power Company in 1930.

The 1931 understanding between Ibáñez and the General Electric subsidiary became the basis of all subsequent conflicts. As mentioned in Chapter 1, Ibáñez had approved the sale to American interests only after he received concessions from the company, such as increased investment in electric power and favorable rates for municipalities and industry. The agreement between Ibáñez and the new owners included a provision that the government could buy the company. Nonetheless, in return for a US$2 million dollar loan, Ibáñez set aside this provision for 90 years and fixed the company's rates in gold pesos. Alessandri campaigned against the "gold clause" in the election of 1932 and ended it by decree as soon as he took office.[92]

Chilean Electric had a complex corporate structure: it was controlled by the South American Power Company, a subsidiary of the American and Foreign Power Company of New York, in turn, run by General Electric. Curtis E. Calder was president of South American Power and American and Foreign Power. In 1932, American and Foreign Power had to suspend dividends on stock and new bonds it had issued for Chilean Electric. From that point on, Calder was preoccupied with generating some hard-to-find profits to pay Chilean Electric's bond obligations. The company's effective rates for electricity collapsed with the paper peso. Chile's insolvent municipalities never paid their electric bills while continuing to draw power. The tramway subsidiaries charged fares set in the 1920s.[93] When the company threatened massive layoffs, Alessandri proclaimed, "Foreign companies in Chile that worked full time when returns were good must understand that they cannot consider discharging their Chilean employees now that times are bad!" The threat worked. In March 1933 the company came to the bargaining table. Negotiations between the administration and Chilean Electric concluded with a 30 percent increase in electric rates.[94]

No further controversy ensued until Chilean Electric ran afoul of currency regulations. The company was obtaining dollars on the black market.[95] In October 1935, two of the company's employees were arrested for violating the currency exchange laws. Chilean Electric was accused of exchange violations amounting to 193 million pesos (about US$7.5 million worth). Gustavo Ross ordered these charges but his motives are unclear because he had not used these laws against any other firm.[96] He apparently saw an opportunity to burnish his nationalist credentials. Although he was not running for Congress in 1936, he was looking for ways to enhance his visibility for the 1938 presidential race.

The electric executives refused bail. Charged under the decree-laws of the Dávila administration, their defense rested on claiming these edicts illegal. The legal proceedings began in late October. In November, Curtis Calder arrived in Santiago to begin negotiations with Ross. Reaching a tentative agreement, they formulated the first version of the famous Calder-Ross Agreements on November 26. On December 7, the Supreme Court upheld the constitutionality of the decree-laws involved; on December 11, a judge sentenced the two employees and eight brokers to jail for 21 days and fined Chilean Electric 128 million pesos (a little over US$5 million).

Calder had returned to New York to promote his settlement with Ross—which included paying the fines—to the board of American and Foreign Power. Calder's New York board reluctantly approved the agreement that merged Chilean Electric, its subsidiaries, and some smaller electric companies into one firm. The reorganized company would have eleven members on its board of directors, seven would be Chilean and would include the president of the Republic and high-level banking officials as well as heads of Chambers of Commerce.[97] The new company would spend 20 percent of its gross income on capital improvements.

In mid-December, Alessandri sent the Calder-Ross Agreement to Congress as a project of law, that is, a legislative proposal. The Radical Party, with some support from small parties on the left and the right, immediately labeled it a sell out and demanded an end to all foreign control of electricity.[98] The Chamber of Deputies rewrote the agreement, including a provision that would gradually reduce the stock position of the U.S. owners. A shocked Calder, in a letter printed in all major Chilean newspapers, called the changes outrageous. Alessandri, frightened by the congressional uprising and infuriated by Calder's reaction, referred to Chilean Electric as a bunch of gangsters and threatened to have its entire management arrested.[99]

Ross' maneuvers unleashed the nationalist furies in time for the 1936 elections. Before leaving for Europe in February 1936, he came to a private understanding with Chilean Electric about how the agreement would be implemented. When he returned, he publicly sided with Alessandri, who now supported the changes made by the Chamber of Deputies. Calder, angry at Ross' behavior, published the "secret clauses" governing implementation. And, Ross retaliated with a threat to renew the court case over currency violations.[100]

Another round of negotiations ensued between the company's Santiago managers and Ross, resulting in Chilean Electric agreeing to hire a Chilean as company president. The company's vice-president, its chief administrator, would be from the United States. The preferred shareholders (South American Power) became first in line for dividends. Ultimately, U.S. interests had to write down their common share value to 30 million pesos (US$1.5 million) from the 6 million British pounds (about US$29.2 million) they had paid for the company in the first place.[101] By any standard of profit and loss, they had taken a bath.

The public perception, however, cost the government substantial prestige. The charge of sell out stuck since the company's management continued in New York hands. Alessandri and Ross had created something novel for Chile, a state-run utility that could gradually enhance its role in the national economy. This was the beginning of state-run firms, but the left saw it as less than half a loaf and never credited these two men with any innovation; and the right saw little to compliment. In his memoirs, Alessandri ignores the entire issue.[102]

The same pattern developed around the foreign debt: the government reduced the nation's obligations, but lost political face. Ross correctly saw the debt as an iceberg, largely buried, which any recovery would have to sail past. Like most of Latin America, Chile's debt suspension left it unable to borrow on the New York market. Ross' greatest achievement was to chart the legal path to re-establish Chile's credit abroad on terms the nation could actually pay. In the end, he was seen by much of the nation as a stooge of foreign interests and a freebooter besides.

Until the Alessandri administration, the U.S. and British governments knew there was little point in bringing up the debt issue. They did insist that each administration promise to resume payments at some unspecified time. Through 1931 and 1932, the State Department received an avalanche of letters from creditor institutions and individual bondholders, demanding that it do more to collect what they were owed.[103]

Chileans of all political backgrounds resented the debt. Many had followed U.S. Senator Hyram Johnson's investigations into foreign bond issues. They felt that Johnson's Senate committee had proved extensive corruption on the part of U. S. bankers. Understandably, Chileans began to deny any responsibility for the debt.[104] Agustín Edwards, publisher of *El Mercurio*, former ambassador to London, and scion of Chile's richest family, demanded that the amount owed be reduced to the market price of outstanding bonds in December 1931—a write-down of 84 percent.[105] Chilean congressmen saw no reason why Chile should pay when the United States was doing little to collect debts owed by Germany, and when other Latin American nations were not paying their obligations.[106] Communist José Vega summarized the left point of view by quoting Lenin, who once told Russia's creditors to collect the debt from the Czar because the workers did not owe a cent.[107]

In his electoral campaigns of 1931 and 1932, Alessandri insisted that the New York bankers had sustained Ibáñez' illegal regime and had no one but themselves to blame for the unpaid loans. After his election, he told United Press International that he and others had warned the bankers, "They did not listen to me. The catastrophe we foresaw came to pass and no one has a right today to blame us if we have suspended payment, because we cannot make payment."[108]

Through 1933, bankers and officials in Washington, New York, and London agreed not to press the Chileans for repayment. The U.S. Embassy in Santiago believed that Chile's outflow of wealth, caused by the Crash, had stopped only in late 1932 and that the balance of payments was barely positive in 1933, despite the debt suspension. The Chilean government was still insolvent. Collecting funds from municipalities on their foreign obligations, it had spent the funds on its own debts.[109] In mid-1934, the Embassy estimated that Chile's debt before 1931 amounted to US$243 million, and that Ibáñez had contracted another US$31 million in short-term obligations in the final months of his administration.[110] A significant element in the debt negotiations was the replacement of Culbertson with a new ambassador, Hal Sevier, a Democrat from Texas, devoted to the bottle. Sevier was not as aggressive as Culbertson had been in representing U.S. interests.[111]

Hard bargaining over the debt began in late 1933. Some short-term notes came due and foreign banks wanted them converted into long-term bonds. Instead of dealing with the various foreign obligations in a piecemeal fashion, Ross proposed an across-the-board debt reduction of 75 percent. The U.S. Embassy described the plan as settlement "on a bankruptcy basis."[112]

In January 1935, the legislature passed the Ross plan, as Law No. 5580. Its basic and original feature was to link Chile's payments to its export earnings, that is, its ability to pay. Government income from nitrate, iodine, and copper would be used to pay off the bonds, with half going to interest and half to principal, which was set at the bonds' depressed market price. The law also created a special agency, the Autonomous Chilean Institute for Public Debt Repayment, and it, not the government, would supervise all funds. Any bondholder paid under this plan had to relinquish all claims under the original terms. This last provision was modified in 1938 to reinstate the right to old claims, but Chile never again paid under the original bond stipulations.[113]

The angry creditors objected to this radical change through two of their associations, the British Corporation of Foreign Bondholders in London and the Foreign Bondholders' Protective Council, Inc., in New York.[114] They lobbied their own governments as well as their nations' embassies in Santiago. Even though the president of the New York Protective Council was Reuben Clark, a prominent official of the Latin American section of the U.S. State Department in the 1920s, they received little more than official sympathy.[115]

It was up to Ross to convince foreign creditors that the plan was their best possible option. To win them over, he sent official committees to New York and London. The committee sent to New York failed completely, but the one that went to London succeeded in June 1935, when it convinced the Council of Foreign Bondholders to accept the plan and even gained an endorsement from the Rothschilds. The settlement covered all outstanding obligations, including loans to Chilean municipalities and the debts of the Chilean State Mortgage Bank.[116] The London *Financial News* claimed that "an attitude of fatalistic realism has clearly been the decisive factor. It is only too clear that, at the moment, Chile has little of exportable value other than nitrate and copper."[117] Ross immediately congratulated the British on their reasonable attitude; the major Chilean papers hailed the outcome as a victory.

The U.S. bondholders felt betrayed by the British and still refused to accept the plan. Reuben Clark argued that Law No. 5580 might be acceptable for current payments but was not as a means to clear all debts.[118] Ross took a hard line and, in early 1936, told the bondholders to either accept the new terms or wait forever.[119] During a trip to London in mid-1936, he asked what else could Chile offer but its export earnings? "Is it not obvious that Chile has become business partners with those that lent it money?"[120] On January 15, 1937, he implemented the plan and insisted the matter was closed.[121] Ross resigned his post in March 1937, and began preparing his presidential campaign. Before he left, he made one last effort to win over the New York Protective Council, sending an aide to conduct negotiations. The Chilean administration was now under some pressure since the government knew it was running a current account deficit and wanted to issue new bonds on the New York market.[122] Ross wrote the State Department, prophetically, that persistent refusal to accept Law No. 5580 was going to backfire. Alessandri's opponents in Congress would see the money accumulating and demand that Chile stop paying anything.[123] When it was reworded with a promise to honor the original debt if that ever became possible, the Protective Council accepted the plan—under protest.[124]

Neither side got what it wanted. The bondholders, for all the rewordings, lost heavily. Law No. 5580 reduced the principal to less than US$5. on every US$1 thousand owed on the loans. The interest due was less than one percent stipulated in the original bonds. In addition, the Chilean government used the law to buy back bonds on the open market, wiping out all principal and interest at bargain prices.[125] But the Chilean government, anxious for credit, was cut off for more than a year from the newly formed U.S. Export-Import Bank on the grounds it was not paying enough on its debt.[126] The Chilean government was left with no alternative but to buy everything from weapons to machinery from Italy and Germany under compensation rules.[127]

Ross also lost, despite some favorable notices in the press. The public did not draw up a ledger of gains and losses. It saw a government that paid on the debt rather than investing in public works or spending on the general welfare. Ross' opponents effectively charged that he and his friends had reaped fortunes in bond speculation, buying them up before announcing the plan for debt reduction.[128] No evidence has ever been produced to prove the accusation. Most importantly, the opposition, ranging from the Radicals to the Communists, took a page from Alessandri's campaigns and argued that Chile should not have to pay anything on debts inherited from a dictator.

* * *

Did Alessandri and Ross allow foreigners to dominate the Chilean economy? Did they play the compradores to foreign corporations? The term, originally coined by Paul Baran, refers to native middlemen in a neocolonial situation who benefit from their economic position.[129] The answer must be a qualified yes. The government limited itself to bargaining over foreign control of the domestic economy. On the whole, Ross was a savvy negotiator, and he was the best informed, most cunning strategist Chile had to that date and would have for many decades thereafter. The government still ran small deficits and had little in the way of reserves; private interest rates remained at 7 to 8 percent for preferred borrowers. Debt payments represented less than 8 percent of export earnings even though the nominal value of the debt was two and one-half to five times exports during the Alessandri presidency. From a very negative balance of payments, the Alessandri-Ross team began to run positive trade balances while cutting payments for foreign services; the result was a positive balance of trade (running at about 20-25 percent of all exports) and a pattern of reinvestment that by 1939 had recovered its pre-Crash level.[130] Yet, Ross' achievements did not prevent further encroachments on the Chilean economy by U.S. investors. Its leaders had neither the means nor the will to consider a strategy for greater autonomy. Under Alessandri, for example, the United States completed its influence on the newspaper syndicates when the largest Chilean papers became dependent on the Associated Press and the United Press International for their foreign, and sometimes, their domestic, news. U.S. firms also came to dominate motion pictures and other parts of the entertainment industry.[131]

In fact, throughout the 1930s, foreign companies, especially those from the United States, had the best "voice" in Chilean politics, especially when compared to that of ordinary Chileans. We could say this was part of the asymmetry that existed between the United States and Chile. U.S. companies had a business culture with a well-honed sense of how to press any advantage. They had the legal and political support of their government's staffs in Washington and Santiago. Following Albert Hirschman's terminology, we can also say that Chilean governments were learning to negotiate their goals without forcing an exit by foreign investors.

Alessandri, who never warmed to the United States, was much less concerned with foreign ownership than with the government's capacity to regulate the economy and so reward friends and punish enemies. Proposals on the oil companies and the utilities were means of garnering leverage. Every politician had to posture as a nationalist, and Alessandri succeeded in raising government revenue at foreign expense and influencing foreign corporate behavior. But this was a rearrangement of dependence rather than a series of moves toward autarky, or toward a dynamic industrial policy. A vivid example was the patent law. Originally passed in 1925, it imposed fees on foreigners four times that charged to natives. The fees were increased even further in 1932, 1933, and, most dramatically, in 1935.[132] Foreign corporations, of course, were the most anxious to protect their patents; there were few Chilean inventors. Such a fee structure discouraged corporations from importing inventions from abroad but did little to encourage domestic ingenuity.

Finally, the Alessandri administration represented a last moment of an older, nineteenth-century nationalist sentiment, as the curious episode of Easter Island illustrates. Chile wanted to enter the arms' race of the 1930s. Argentina, Brazil, Chile, Ecuador, Honduras, Nicaragua, and Peru were caught up in naval competition and cutting back imports, imposing new trade restrictions, or reneging on debt payments to pay the bills.[133] Chile was particularly fearful of its traditional rivals, Argentina and Peru. Conservatives, identifying weaponry with strength, fixed on the nineteenth-century idea of building more battleships to protect the fatherland. In early June 1937, the government approached the U.S. naval attache in Santiago with a plan to sell or lease Easter Island to obtain funds for two cruisers. It made similar offers to other countries and stipulated that the highest bidder would get Easter Island and the right to build the ships. Only Japan showed interest. (The Alessandri administration also considered postponing debt payments to acquire the ships.)[134] The United States lobbied Alessandri against pursuing any such deal—arms races were to be limited to the major powers. The idea of selling off or leasing national territory in order to obtain two cruisers would have seemed fantastic to any later administration. Alessandri's government was the last vestige of this kind of nationalistic "conservatism."

In many respects, the most innovative moments of the Alessandri administration in negotiating Chile's place in the world occurred in the first half of his term. After 1936, the administration became less focused, less interested in any confrontation with U.S. interests and more complacent about the direction of the economy. Perhaps recovery was politically enervating. But in its first years, it pioneered a number of changes from the state oil company, COPEC, to the renegotiation of the foreign debt that would allow the country some future room in which to maneuver economically.

But the social base of politics was shifting throughout Alessandri's administration, and as it shifted, Alessandri and Ross' opponents gained the political space to redefine the meaning of nationalism and so altered the significance of what had been accomplished.

Endnotes

For abbreviations used in notes, see Endnotes, Chapter 1.

1. BOLSA, B55, Valparaiso to London, 6 Apr. 1937.

2. RG 59: 611.2531/191, enclosure no. 2, *La Nación* (Santiago), 27 June 1937.

3. Because of the importance of past obligations, the system began with two accounts and became more complex over time, RG 151: Commerce Dept., Bureau of Foreign and Domestic Commerce, Commercial Attaches: Santiago, Bohan, Special Report no. 7, 5 Sept. 1933.

4. Treaty printed in *La Nación*, 12 Nov. 1932; FO 371-16567 (A8829/59/9), Thomson, 22 Nov. 1933. See also Ellsworth, *Chile*, 63, who treats the phenomenon as an economic matter rather than as one involving the political economy of trade; and Hoover Papers, President, Box 49, Review of Questions: "Recent Problems in the Protection of American Interests in Chile," 2:68-69.

5. RG 151: Bureau of Foreign and Domestic Commerce, Commercial Attaches: Santiago, Bohan, Special Report no. 7, 5 Sept. 1933.

6. RG 825.6374/1055, Culbertson, no. 284, 3 Nov. 1932.

7. RG 59: 825.5151/197, Grummon memo, 12 May 1934.

8. Ibid.,/214, Scotten, no. 159, 1 Aug. 1934.

9. RG 59: States, 625.5131/17, Culbertson telegram no. 35, 28 Apr. 1932.

10. FO 371-16567 (A8829/59/9), Thomson, 22 Nov. 1933.

11. RG 151: Bureau of Foreign and Domestic Commerce, Commercial Attaches: Santiago, Bohan, Special Report no. 7, 5 Sept. 1933.

12. RG 59: 825.5151/233, Feis memo, 19 Nov. 1934.

13. Ibid.,/182, Sevier, no. 72, 19 Mar. 1934.

14. RG 59: 611.2531/203, Duggan to Welles, memo, 7 July 1937. See also 611.2531/195, Div. of Latin American Affairs, "Conversations with the Chilean Under Secretary of Commerce," 4 July 1937.

15. League of Nations, Secretariat. Financial Section and Economic Intelligence Service, *The Network of World Trade (A Companion Volume to "Europe's Trade")* (Geneva: League of Nations, 1942), 56.

16. RG 59: 825.00/881, Information Series no. 76, 8 Apr. 1935.

17. RG 151: 600 (Chile 1923-48), Bohan, Economic and Trade Notes, no. 388, 18 June 1938, and Knox, Economic and Trade Notes, no. 239, 8 Mar. 1939.

18. Hoover Papers, Pres., Box 49, Review of Questions. "Recent Problems in the Protection of American Interests in Chile," 2:68-69.

19. RG 59: 825.51/649, Sevier, no. 33, 11 Jan. 1934, enclosure no. 1, memo of 5 Jan. 1934; and RG 59: 825.5151/399, Philip, no. 619, 5 June 1937, enclosure, Frost memo on conversation with Benjamin Cohen, Director of Diplomatic Department of the [Chilean] Foreign Office, 4 June 1937.

20. League of Nations, *World Trade, 1937*, 18.

21. Ibid., 24-27, 70-71.

22. RG 165: MID 2515-H-114/1, Weeks, no. 2021, 17 Oct. 1934; and Chile, *Hacienda pública* (Nov. 1937), 383.

23. RG 59: 625.9417/1, Atwood, 6 Oct. 1934.

24. RG 59: States, 625.5131/20, enclosure no. 1, draft used by Min. of Foreign Affairs for Chile in reply to French Note on Compensation Office, 10 May 1932.

25. RG 59: States, 625.5131/50, Scotten, no. 113, 19 May 1934.

26. Ibid.,/59, Scotten, no. 363, 17 May 1935; and Chile. Diputados, *Boletín de sesiones ordinarios*, Informe comisión, 15 June 1936, 782-85.

27. FO 371-19775 (A2243/410/9), R.C. Michell, annual report, 25 Feb. 1936.

28. FO 371-16569 (A3128/1071/9), Chilton, annual report, 6 Mar. 1933; and FO 371-17503 (A1051/10/9), Mr. Mason memos, 6 Feb. 1934 and 14 Feb. 1934.

29. A fact Ambassador Culbertson openly admitted, RG 59: 711.252/50, Culbertson, no. 984, 9 Oct. 1931.

30. RG 59: States, 611.2531/82, Norweb, no. 1582, 18 Nov. 1933; and RG 151: Bureau of Foreign and Domestic Commerce, Commercial Attaches: Santiago, Randall Special Report no. 19, 24 Nov. 1933.

31. The accounts were cleared at a rate of about half that of compensation nations. RG 59: 625.5131/30, Edwin C. Wilson, 29 Oct. 1932; 825.5151/120, Norweb, no. 1560, 25 Nov. 1933; 625.5131/54, Scotten, no. 133, 27 June 1934; 825.5151/233, Feis memo, 19 Nov. 1934; 625.5131/56, Scotten, no. 244, 14 Dec. 1934; and Culbertson Papers, cont. 14 (1933-34), Medley G.B. Whelpley to Culbertson, 8 Jan. 1934.

32. This winking at the law took a byzantine twist when, as he was leaving office, Alessandri began to allow banks to buy dollars on the black market. RG 151: Commerce, 600 (Chile, 1923-48), Bohan, Economic and Trade Notes, no. 77, 24 Aug. 1938.

33. FO 371-17503 (A1323/10/9), Mr. Mason memo, 14 Feb. 1934.

34. RG 151: 600 (Chile, 1923-48), Bohan, Economic and Trade Notes, no. 77, 24 Aug. 1938; and Bureau of Foreign and Domestic Commerce, Commercial Attaches: Santiago, Knox, Economic and Trade Notes, no. 199, 21 Jan. 1939.

35. RG 151: Bureau of Foreign and Domestic Commerce, Commercial Attaches: Santiago, Bohan Quarterly Automotive Report, 12 July 1934; and FO 371-17508, memo of A.J. Pack, 8 May 1934; *La Nación* 26 May 1936.

36. RG 59: 825.5151/328, John P. Gregg, Special Counsel for RCA Manufacturing Co., International General Electric Co., and American Steel Export Co., to Cordell Hull, 15 June 1936.

37. RG 59: 825.5151/319, Philip, no. 222, 19 May 1936.

38. RG 59: 825.5151/339, Latin American Affairs memo, 20 May 1936, enclosures; and 825.5151/353, Latin American Affairs memo, 30 June 1936.

39. RG 59: 825.5151/360, Philip, no. 361, 10 Oct. 1936; and 825.5151/420, memo of conversation, Desiderio García, Chilean Under Sec. of Commerce, Sergio Huneeus, First Sec. of Chilean Embassy, Carlos Campbell, Commercial Attache of Chilean Embassy, Messrs. Duggan, Heath, Gantenbein, 8 July 1937.

40. Burbach, "The Chilean Industrial Bourgeoisie," 56. See also RG 59: 825.5151/541, Frost, no. 843, 12 Aug. 1939, enclosure, Comisión de Cambios Internacionales to U.S. Embassy, Aug. 1939.

41. BOLSA, B10/4, 1933, W.C. Maycock to Chairman, 3 Jan. 1933.

42. RG 59: 825.6374/1258, Jarvis, no. 73, 31 Jan. 1935.

43. RG 165, MID 2655-0-52/17, Wooten, no. 1463, 21 Sept. 1932; and RG 59: 825.6374/1051, Culbertson, no. 1285, 19 Oct. 1932.

44. FO 371-15828 (A7320/113/9), Mr. Mason, memo, 31 Oct. 1932.

45. BOLSA, B10/4, 1931-1932, Comisión de Tarapacá to José Garrido, 24 Nov. 1932; and Gibbs, L64.22, MS 16,822/36, Valparaiso to Whelpley, 13 Oct. 1932.

46. Arturo Alessandri Palma, *Recuerdos de Gobierno* (Santiago Editorial Nascimento, 1967), 3:28.

47. BOLSA, B10/4, 1933, W.C. Maycock to Chairman, 3 Jan. 1933; RG 165: MID 2655-0-52/22, Wooten, no. 1550, 3 Jan. 1933; and RG 59: 825.6374/1078, Norweb, no. 1354, 7 Jan. 1933.

48. RG 151: Bureau of Foreign and Domestic Commerce, Commercial Attaches: Santiago, Ackerman Weekly Report, no. 28, 10 Jan. 1933.

49. RG 165: MID 2655-0-52/24, Wooten, no. 1572, 18 Jan. 1933.

50. Ibid., enclosure, interview with Alessandri by J.I. Miller of United Press in Santiago, 13 Jan. 1933.

51. RG 59: 611.2531/163 1/2, Office of the Economic Advisor, "Problem presented by Chilean Note of July 20," 11 Aug. 1936.

52. RG 59: 825.6374/1126, Culbertson, no. 1409, 18 Mar. 1933; 825.6374 /1117, Culbertson telegram, 20 Mar. 1933; quote from 825.6374/1129, Culbertson, no. 1411, 22 Mar. 1933.

53. RG 59: 825.6374/1132, Culbertson, no. 1412, 25 Mar. 1933. See also meetings with Ross RG 59: 825.6374/1136, Culbertson, no. 1420, 1 Apr. 1933; and 825.6374/1140, Culbertson, no. 1424, 8 Apr. 1933.

54. RG 59: 825.6374/1136, Culbertson, no. 1420, 1 Apr. 1933; quotes are from 825.6374/1140, Culbertson, no. 1424, 8 Apr. 1933; and 825.6274/1144, Culbertson, no. 1428, 15 Apr. 1933. For the description of the Guggenheim effort to preserve the company, see *La Nación*, 27 Aug. 1933.

55. RG 165: MID 2655-0-52/24, Wooten, no. 1563, 11 Jan. 1933; and Gibbs, L64-22, Ms. 16,822/38, Valparaiso, 31 May 1933.

56. *El Radical* (Valparaiso), 19 Feb. 1936; and Chile, *Hacienda pública* (Aug. 1937), 21.

57. Gibbs, L64.22, MS 16,822/36, Valparaiso, 22 Dec. 1932; and MS 16,822 /37, London, 21 Feb. 1933.

58. RG 59: Chile 825.5374/1265, Dodd, no. 2257, 28 Aug. 1935, enclosure, *Frankfurter Zeitung* (State Dept. trans.), 11 July 1935.

59. RG 59: 825.6374/1188, Straus, no. 181, 18 Aug. 1933, 825.6374/1260, Sydney B. Redecker, American Consul, Frankfurt-am-Main, 6 July 1935; and 825.5374/1265, Dodd, no. 2257, 28 Aug. 1935.

60. Data from Chile, *Anuario estadístico de Chile*, various years.

61. RG 59: 825.6352/46, Dow, no. 161, 17 Oct. 1936.

62. Orris C. Herfindahl, *Copper Costs and Prices, 1870-1957* (Baltimore: Resources for the Future, Inc., and the Johns Hopkins Press, 1959), 70, 92-100, 105, 154, 203-204.

63. On cartel manipulations, see also Alex Skelton, "Copper," in William Yandell Elliott, et al., *International Control in the Non-Ferrous Metals* (New York: The MacMillan Company, 1937), 457.

64. Skelton, op. cit., 511. See also Herfindahl, op. cit., 104.

65. RG 84: 600 (Valparaiso, 1933), Dow to Henry, 30 Oct. 1933.

66. Chile. Fomento (1933), Oficios v. 813, no. 1. Min. de Fomento to Min. de Hacienda, 21 Jan. 1933, confidencial no. 40; and Chile. Hacienda, Antecedentes de Oficio, v. 1 (1933), Comisión de Cambios Internacionales to Min. de Hacienda, 2 Feb. 1933, no. 174 (oficio no. 146).

67. Skelton, op. cit.," 501.

68. Herfindahl, op. cit., 110.

69. RG 59: 625.5131/59, Scotten, no. 363, 17 May 1935; 625.9431/8, Philip, no. 206, 8 May 1936; McClintock memo, enclosure no. 1, RG 151: 601.2 (Chile 1921-38), Knox memo, 5 June 1939.

70. RG 59: 825.6352/49, Philip, no. 559, 13 Apr. 1937.

71. Ibid.,/52, Philip, no. 782, 8 Dec. 1937.

72. Chile. Hacienda, Antecedentes de Oficio, v. 1 (1933), Comisión de Cambios Internacionales to Min. de Hacienda, 2 Feb. 1933, report no. 174 (oficio no. 146).

73. RG 59: 825.6352/51, Dow, no. 124, 28 Oct. 1937.

74. Figures for Table 4.1 from RG 59: 825.6352/80, memo to Welles, 14 Feb. 1939.

75. Ricardo French-Davis, "The Importance of Copper in the Chilean Economy: Two Decades of Historical Background," mimeo from CIEPLAN, 1974; shorter version published in, Ernesto Tironi, ed., *El cobre en el desarrollo nacional* (Santiago: Ediciones Nueva Universidad, CIEPLAN, 1974), 20.

76. See, for example, RG 59: 611.2531/276, Frost, no. 910, 16 Mar. 1938.

77. The information in this table differs from the data in, Markos Mamalakis and Clark Winton Reynolds, *Essays on the Chilean Economy* (Homewood, Il: Richard D. Irwin, Inc., 1965), statistical app., especially 363-79.

78. Roger Joseph Burbach, "The Chilean Industrial Bourgeoisie and Foreign Capital, 1920-1970," (Ph.D. diss., Indiana University, 1975), 62-64.

79. Lawrence A. Clayton, *Grace: W.R. Grace and Co. The Formative Years 1850-1930* (Ottawa, IL: Jameson Books, 1985), chaps. 2-4, 11, 12; C. Alexander G. de Secada, "Armas, guano y comercio marítimo: los intereses de W.R. Grace en el Peru, 1865-1885," *Revista latinoamericana de historia económica y social* [HISLA], (First Semester, 1986), 7:105-106; and Marquis James, *Merchant Adventurer: The Story of W.R. Grace* (Wilmington, Del.: Scholarly Resources, 1993).

80. RG 59: 625.116/15, Scotten, no. 162, 1 Aug. 1934. See also enclosure no. 2, Min. de Relaciones Exterior y Comercio to Cónsul General del Ecuador, 10 July 1934; and 625.116/18, Office of Econ. Advisor, memo, 17 Aug. 1934.

81. RG 59: 625.116.4, R.H. Patchin, vice-president, W.R. Grace and Co., New York, to Sumner Welles, Asst. Sec. of State, 22 June 1934; and 625.116/5, Sevier telegram no. 55, 30 June 1934; 625.116/7, Scotten, no. 136, 3 July 1934.

82. RG 59: 625.1122/10, McNiece, 17 Nov. 1938.

83. Chile. Fomento (1933), Oficios, v. 813, no. 1, Min. de Fomento to Manager, West India Oil Co, 7 Feb. 1933, no. 151; and RG 59: 825.6363/161, Philip, no. 554, 7 Apr. 1937.

84. Chile. Fomento (1933), Oficios v. 813, no. 1. Min. de Fomento to Min. de Hacienda, 21 Jan. 1933, confidencial no. 40.

85. *La Opinión*, 21 Mar. 1937.

86. History of dispute, RG 59: 825.6363/157, Philip, no. 409, 14 Nov. 1936, and 825.6363/4-1945, Sundt, no. 11,988, 19 Apr. 1945; and Alessandri's views, 825.6363/158, Philip, no. 411, 18 Nov. 1936.

87. RG 59: 825.6363/157-159, Philip, no. 409, no. 411, and no. 554.

88. BOLSA, B55, Valparaiso to London, 24 Nov. 1936; *La Nación*, 18, 19 Nov. 1936.

89. Jonathan C. Brown, "Jersey Standard and the Politics of Latin American Oil Production, 1911-1930," John D. Wirth, ed., *Latin American Oil Companies and the Politics of Energy* (Lincoln: University of Nebraska Press, 1985), 41.

90. Chile. Fomento (1939), Oficios, v. 814, no. 2, Min. de Fomento to Min. de Hacienda, 24 Mar. 1933, no. 398: citing note of Comisión Administrativa de Petroleo; BOLSA, B55, Valparaiso to London, 4 Oct. 1938; and Chile, *Hacienda pública* (20 Aug. 1938), 1092.

91. RG 59: 825.6363/175, memo of conversation, 27 Jan. 1939.

92. *Diario Oficial* (Santiago), 12 Mar. 1931; RG 59: 825.6463 Electric Bond and Share Co./33, Culbertson, no. 802, 13 Mar. 1931; Partido Radical, *El Partido Radical ante el "Acuerdo de Caballeros", Ross-Calder Discursos de los Diputados Radicales* (Santiago: Empresa El Imparcial, 1936), 6; and José Miguel Seguel C., *La industria eléctrica ante la legislación chilena* (Santiago: Imprenta de los Talleres Leblanc, 1941), 17.

93. RG 84: Post Records, 610.2 (Valparaiso, 1935), Renwick S. McNiece to Dow, 3 May 1935.

94. RG 59: 825.00/7898, Culbertson, no. 1365, 25 Jan. 1933; and 825.00-Gen Cond/60, Culbertson, no. 1474, 2 June 1933.

95. Partido Radical, *El Partido Radical ante el "Acuerdo de Caballeros"*, 7.

96. On uses of black markets, see RG 59: 825.5151/120, Norweb, no. 1560, 25 Nov. 1933; and Culbertson Papers, cont. 14 (1933-34), Medley G.B. Whelpley to Culbertson, 8 Jan. 1934.

97. *La Opinión*, 29 Nov. 1935; RG 151: Bureau of Foreign and Domestic Comm., Commercial Attaches: Santiago, Bohan, Economic and Trade Notes, no. 210, 17 Dec. 1935; RG 59: 825.6463 Electric Bond and Share Co./120, Philip, no. 287, 10 Aug. 1936; and Seguel C., *La industria eléctrica*, 394.

98. *La Opinión*, 17 Dec. 1935, article by Carlos Keller R.; and Partido Radical, *El Partido Radical ante el "Acuerdo de Caballeros,"* 6-7.

99. RG 59: 825.5151/341, Philip, no. 258, 10 May 1936; and 825.6463 Electric Bond and Share Co./120, Philip, no. 287, 10 Aug. 1936.

100. RG 59: 825.6463 Electric Bond and Share Co./195, State to Bowers, 13 Mar. 1942.

101. The 1930 values were on the gold standard, the 1936 value in dollars was the export draft rate. RG 59: 825.6463-Electric Bond and Share Co./124, Philip, no. 321, 2 Sept. 1936, enclosure no. 2, memo for ambassador. For currency values, *Sinópsis estadística* (1933), 332, and (1940), 594.

102. See chaps. 4 and 5, Alessandri, *Recuerdos de Gobierno*, vol. 3.

103. See for example, RG 59: 611.2531/102, Union State Bank telegram to Hull, 6 Aug. 1934; the file number is filled with telegrams and letters on the issue.

104. RG 165: MID 2347-0-49/1, Wooten, no. 1214, 26 Jan. 1932.

105. FO 371-15820 (A1485/2/9), Chilton, 17 Feb. 1932.

106. FO 371-18665 (A4168/12/9), R.C. Michell, Santiago, 23 Apr. 1935.

107. José Carril Echevarría, *Nuestra deuda externa: suspensión y reanudación de sus servicios* (Ph.D. diss., University of Chile, Imprenta Relampago, 1944), 75.

108. *Washington Post* (Washington), 28 Dec. 1932, interview with UPI.

109. RG 151: Bureau of Foreign and Domestic Comm., Commercial Attaches: Santiago, Bohan Special Report no. 18, 24 Nov. 1933, p. 32; and RG 59: 825.51/649, Sevier, no. 33, 11 Jan. 1934, enclosure no. 1, memo of 5 Jan. 1934.

110. RG 59: 825.5151/214, Sevier, no. 159, 1 Aug. 1934, enclosure no. 1, Heath and Williams report, 30 July 1934.

111. Irwin F. Gellman, *Good Neighbor Diplomacy: United States Policies in Latin America, 1933-1945* (Baltimore: Johns Hopkins University Press, 1979), 72.

112. RG 59: 825.51/683, Sevier, no. 99, 4 May 1934.

113. Edwin Borchard, *State Insolvency and Foreign Bondholders*, vol. 1, *General Principles* (New York: Garland Publishing Inc., 1983 reprint of original New Haven: Yale University Press, 1951), 305; and RG 59: 825.51/710, Scotten, no. 210, 31 Oct. 1934.

114. Borchard, op. cit., 1:193-94, 201; and Gellman, op. cit., 40-41.

115. RG 59: 825.51/701, Scotten, no. 215, 24 Oct. 1934. See also 825.51710, Scotten, no. 220, 31 Oct. 1934.

116. RG 59: 825.51. Financial Missions/5, enclosure no. 1, Scotten, no. 292, 6 Feb. 1935; and RG 151: 600 (Chile 1923-48), Randall, Economic and Trade

Notes, no. 397, 12 June 1935. See also *La Nación* and *El Mercurio* (Santiago), 7 June 1935.

117. *Financial News* (London), 7 June 1935.

118. RG 59: 825.51/825, J. Reuben Clark to Gustavo Ross, night cable, 27 Nov. 1935.

119. RG 59: 825.51/844, White letter, 6 Jan. 1936, enclosure, Ross to Clark, 4 Jan. 1936. See also *La Nación* (Santiago), 1 Feb. 1936; and RG 59: 825.51/840, Philip, no. 56, 21 Dec. 1935.

120. *El Mercurio*, 23 May 1936.

121. RG 59: 825.51/923, Clark to Feis, 4 May 1937: Clark writing as the president of Foreign Bondholders Protective Council, Inc.; and 825.51/933 1/2, Duggan memo, 30 June 1937.

122. The law was the Johnson Act of 1934. BOLSA, B55, Valparaiso to London, 16 Mar. 1937; and RG 59: 825.00/979, Philip, no. 520, 10 Mar. 1937.

123. RG 59: 825.51/948, Ross memo, "Chilean Debt Plan," 4 Oct. 1937.

124. Ibid.,/923, Clark to Feis, 4 May 1937: Clark writing as president of Foreign Bondholders Protective Council, Inc. See also seven enclosures in file.

125. RG 825.51/11-2045, Burnes to Senator Hawkes, 20 Nov. 1945, enclosure, Foreign Bondholders Protective Council, 10 Feb. 1944, "To Holders of Chilean Dollar Bonds."

126. RG 59: 825.77/331, [Welles?] to Heath, 19 Oct. 1937.

127. RG 59: 825.248/116, Frost, no. 848, 28 Jan. 1938.

128. Chile. Interior, v. 9248 (1936), no. 202, Servicio de Investigaciones reporting on a leftist rally and speeches by Grove, Hidalgo, and others that stressed this point.

129. Paul A. Baran, *The Political Economy of Growth* (New York: Monthly Review Press, 1967, orig. 1957).

130. Sebastián Sáez, *La economía política de una crisis: Chile, 1929-1939* (Santiago: CIEPLAN, Notas Técnicas no. 130, May 1989), 12, 18, 21, 61.

131. Chile. Hacienda, Antecedentes de oficios, v. 8 (1932), United Press Association, 20 Oct. 1932.

132. RG 59: 825.542/6, Scotten, no. 275, 21 Jan. 1935.

133. RG 59: 825.5151/452 1/2, Welles to Duggan, 27 Dec. 1937.

134. RG 59: 711.2514/1, Philip telegram, 7 June 1937; and 825.014/57, Naval Intelligence, 101-100, 8 June 1937.

Fig. 5. Cartoon by prominent illustrator "Coke" from magazine *Zig-Zag*, 1932. Caricatures of Chilean chief execututves caught up in round-robin coups of elections, 1931-32. Translation: "A Question of Gills" [a play on words, *agallas* means *gall* as well as *gill*].The larger swallows the smaller fish. United States. National Archives.

Alessandri's Strategies and Social Mobilization

> The trouble was not so much the existence of
> feudal landowners who commanded and of the
> landless who obeyed. It was that the land system
> gave its "caste to the nation" and permeated the
> whole social structure of the country with the psy-
> chology of Master and Servant.
>
> Carlos Dávila, 1936[1]

Seigniorial attitudes originating in the colonial era remained a part of the Chilean political system well into the twentieth century. Political leaders, in the 1930s, tended not to emphasize democracy as much as the issues of social order or social justice. In the code of the era, social order clearly invoked patriarchal values and social hierarchy; the conservatives, from a number of parties, who used this phrase relied on the metaphor that a well-run nation was like a large family. Sections of the middle class and urban labor spoke of social justice, they demanded inclusion in politics (an expansion of the suffrage) and improvements in laboring rights and public welfare. Exactly how either of these competing attitudes would be implemented was unclear. A generation before, the elite and the middle class in politics had debated the social question, that is, the fate of the poor and the threat of rebellion. The discussion now had moved beyond that formulation and into a number of related questions. Who should be allowed to vote? What kind of benefits were really needed? Such questions were often buried in a party system built on patronage and clientalism.[2] This narrative emphasizes the relation of politics to the distribution of economic rights, and how various interests voiced their positions and attempted to alter the system as a whole.

Public rhetoric was still affected by the breakdown of the Parliamentary Regime and the crisis of 1931. Ibáñez, by building support with new public works and by increasing the size and salaries of the military and the bureaucracy, had combined the rhetoric of social order and political reform. By repressing Anarchists and Communists, he reassured capitalists even as the job market expanded. But the economic base of this strategy disappeared in the Crash. What could any government offer the public in 1931 or thereafter?

At the very moment of economic collapse, the change in regime opened the market of public expression. The state lost its autocratic control of the press, of public assembly, and private organizations. Unions, guilds, and professional associations—in conventions, publications aimed at "the masses," and in orchestrated demonstrations—demanded more public programs, the division of haciendas into small farms to help the unemployed, and the domestic appropriation of income that foreigners were taking out of Chile.

Alessandri, like the provisional presidents before him, searched for a new basis of patronage and for the means to control popular mobilization. If he tried to placate popular anger, he faced capital flight and the prospect of class warfare. If he repressed popular mobilization, he would have to rely on the military and the national police—still the bulwarks of Ibañismo. He succeeded in preserving administrative continuity by postponing the problem of political organization. He did not know how to incorporate the mass of the population into an active citizenry (no one else did either), and at a time of economic hardship, he was loath to try.

By labeling some demands as *communist* and appropriating other demands as its own, the Alessandri administration thought it had a means to select the direction of social change. If aspects of the Ibáñez government had been labeled Alessandrismo without Alessandri, the first years of Alessandri's second term could very easily be called Ibañismo without Ibáñez. Alessandri considered himself the patron of labor and allowed some unions to increase their membership, but labor could not organize freely. The army broke any threatening strikes. Through at least the first half of his administration, Alessandri made repeated use of emergency powers and suspended civil rights. Political opponents were harassed, dismissed from the bureaucracy or the armed forces without redress, summarily arrested and imprisoned, and occasionally tortured.

The threats to Alessandri's goals came from the right as well as the left. This was a period of militarism and paramilitarism. Ibáñez and other military figures remained in the wings. The *Nacis* [Nazis] mobilized, certain that the civilian government would fail. The Republican Militia became a formidable presence; Alessandri backed it as a counter to the army.

Alessandri did not see government primarily in capitalist terms; rather he saw business as a necessary support to the state. In late 1933, the Conservative and Liberal parties began to support some of his proposals; that they relied upon someone they had despised a decade earlier was a sign of how limited their options had become. Domestic capital (in finance, mining, land, real estate, and industry) was unable to generate a ruling coalition, a shortcoming that its parties reflected rather than caused. The Chilean elite made few appeals to either the middle or laboring classes. Stunned by the direction of events and angry at the loss of its political predominance, it concentrated on preventing any initiatives that weakened it further. An economic recovery that began in late 1935 made the right even less interested in those below. The Alessandri administration, in league with the right, won a majority in the congressional contest of 1937 but with a narrow social base. From that point until the presidential election of 1938, the right undercut Alessandri's efforts to broaden his coalition. Then, it overreached and ran Gustavo Ross Santa María for president.

The political changes that began with the Crash continued into Alessandri's term. The disaffected, in the early 1930s, organized in the public space created by the government's administrative weaknesses, the competition among parties, the legacy of labor radicalism, and widespread destitution. Social radicals, found in unions and many political parties, employed Marxist and anarchist rhetoric and pinned their hopes for a better life on labor militancy and the surge of anger in the middle class. In 1936, segments of the labor movement and the middle class generated a new political coalition, the Popular Front, supporting many of the demands first articulated in 1931-32. But the Front had its weaknesses. Brian Loveman has pointed out that it opposed helping rural labor. Paul Drake noted years ago that political alignments were far from clear before the major railroad strike of 1936. Even after that event, the factions within the Front had a difficult time resolving their differences.[3] The Front's program promised economic growth, a redistribution of political authority and a change in social goals.[4] This was enough. A populace, worn down by the Depression and offended by events preceding the election, voted the Popular Front candidate, Pedro Aguirre Cerda, into the presidency. Chile had moved to Alessandri's left.

Alessandri and the Social Structure

Chile was still a rural nation undergoing the strains of industrial change. The 1930 census listed 4.2 million inhabitants, with about 700 thousand in greater Santiago. Valparaiso, the next largest city, had about 190 thousand. The population had increased an average of 4.5 percent per year in the twentieth century. Officially, slightly more than half of it was considered *rural*, that is, living in towns of less than five thousand.[5]

Robert McCaa's study of the Petorca Valley, a small mining area north of Santiago, indicates that, from the 1890s to 1930, worsening economic conditions left about a third of all women too poor to marry.[6] About a third of all births were illegitimate. The results of the Depression and the erosion of real wages through unemployment and inflation are not hard to guess. In a 1935 survey of a one thousand poor Chilean families carried out by the League of Nations, it was found that most never ate meat or fruit and subsisted instead on soups made of vegetables, flour, and potatoes.[7] Another study found that about a quarter of the population (200 thousand families) was poorly housed or without a residence. An apartment in public housing built in the 1930s cost 20 thousand pesos, well beyond the average worker's means; most workers paid 35-150 pesos per month rent. In the cities, they continued living in tenements [*conventillos*], some three stories high, that had been built in and since the 1890s. Government inspectors visited 2.8 thousand of these buildings in 1935 and found 1.9 thousand unhealthy and another 225 uninhabitable, although full of people; only 211 were described as *clean*.[8] By the 1930s, the people had begun to marry more often, at a younger age, and to have fewer children.[9]

A small nucleus of landowners and men, who controlled mining, real estate, banking, and industry, occupied the upper echelons of society. They belonged to the Club Hípico, a racecourse with a pool and tennis courts, and to the Club de la Unión, the men's society where they discussed news and stock quotes each morning. They could golf at two elite courses. In 1930, it cost upper-class families ten thousand pesos (about US$1.2 thousand) per year to rent a home in Santiago and have the servants, car, and club memberships required to maintain their status. By 1936, the cost of a rented house in a well-to-do neighborhood had dropped to only 2.6 thousand pesos (around US$135).[10] Rather than buy kitchen appliances, elite women preferred maids, who, after all, were cheaper.[11] One foreign observer noted that status lines were "very closely drawn," and the elite heavily intermarried.[12]

Chile's social structure originated in its countryside. A land survey in 1927-28 found that, of 57 million cultivable acres, 32 million were held in 599 estates. Fifty million acres were pasture, only 4 percent of the land was farmed intensively. Official data in 1935 stated that 1.2 thousand estates contained almost 67 percent of the land while 59,922, representing 58 percent of all owners, held only 1 percent. The average small farm had under 5 hectares, or 12 acres.[13] Another estimate claimed that of the half million who worked the land, 340 thousand were landless. The average agricultural wage was half that earned in the mines or urban industries.[14] U.S. Ambassador Culbertson, a man devoid of social radicalism, wrote, "The laborer on the Chilean fundo is little more than a serf."[15] These conditions, underlined by George McBride in his classic essay of the countryside in the 1930s, were the basis of all social distinction.[16]

At the bottom of society was the *roto*, the broken one, illiterate or barely literate, and kept by the landowners' rules from exercising any civic opportunities. The landlords' power seemed limitless. Dismissals were arbitrary and without effective appeal.[17] Rural workers could be fired for reading a newspaper. Even Catholic periodicals were not allowed because landlords feared, as one observer put it, that "communist propaganda would follow."[18] Traditional landlord contempt for rural laborers was reinforced in the 1930s by the squeeze between the controlled price of food and the rising costs of production, especially the high cost of credit.[19] Conditions were so bad that men conscripted into the army often preferred remaining to returning home; the army provided three meals a day, clothing, and some remedial education. The governor of Yungay, in his 1936 report, said his province had no industries, no labor organizations, roads were poor, electric service limited to one small town, and there was little contact among people. The most notable social development of the past year had been the formation of a soccer club.[20] One woman, interviewed about her childhood in the 1920s and 1930s, remarked that her family lived in the patron's house, "I was almost nude, with the few rags of the poor. They had us as captives, we could not go out or anything." To leave this situation, she literally had to "escape" when the patron was not looking.[21] In a tour of rural estates in the Central Valley, a U.S. military attache said that few homes were heated; pneumonia, tuberculosis and other bronchial ailments were common. Despite temperatures below freezing, many of the rotos he saw wore only sandals, "tied around their feet with leather straps." Aside from the racking coughs, he was appalled by the extent of sexual diseases, and "a large number of blind and crippled people." He concluded, "The laboring classes live under conditions that would soon kill the average American."[22]

While working conditions were changing in response to the market and technological innovations, divisions of labor, even the terms employed, owed a good deal to the late colonial era.[23] The labor core consisted of 58 thousand *inquilinos*, workers who traded their labor for a plot of land and a small house. Some 14 percent of them were women. About 19 thousand of them were craft workers (blacksmiths, carpenters, and the like) or they were foremen. The Chilean hacienda (called a *fundo* in the native literature) could draw upon an army of rural poor, 119 thousand by official count although the actual number was probably larger, to serve as casual laborers at plantings and harvests.[24] In addition, wives and children were expected to "volunteer" their labor in the big house or during animal round-ups or harvests. Since men were usually away working on the large estate, it was up to women to grow the family's food as well as raise the children. Male abandonment of rural families is a common theme in the social literature. There was little chance to act on any social anger.[25] Carabineros acted as hirelings of the *patrón*; a worker who tried to organize a protest was lucky to escape with a beating. Deaths at the hands of the carabineros were reported in Congress. One worker was killed for stealing a sack of beans.

The structure and attitudes of the countryside influenced the rest of society, as Dávila noted in the comment opening this chapter. Education, for example, remained bound to the class system. The best schools were private and located in Santiago and Valparaiso; often they had been founded and were run by immigrants or the Church. The public school system was also concentrated in major cities and was chronically under funded. Schools were often in rented buildings and in gross disrepair. According to the census data, literacy rates in Chile were behind those of Argentina but far ahead of Cuba, Colombia, and Peru. The Teachers Union argued that the official literacy rate (61 percent) was an exaggeration. In the union's estimation, less than half of the school-age population of 900 thousand ever attended school, and only half of the students entering the first grade went on to the second. These deficiencies were not corrected later in life. There were 42 adult night schools in the entire country.[26] Generally, only the well-to-do could attend the university. One writer described the entering class of the medical school as "hand picked" by university administrators.[27]

Table 5.1: Chilean Salary Structure in the 1930S

Monthly Salary in Pesos	Number	Percent
Up to 500	27,673	36
501-1,000	12,373	26
1,001-1,500	3,350	7
1,501-2,000	1,539	3
2,001-3,000	1,360	3
Above 3,000	1,313	3
Total	47,605	98

Source: Department of State, Record Group 59, 825.5041/10, Faust, no. 159, 13 Oct. 1936.

Differences in social background and education, underlined by a racist heritage, created a sharp division in wages. In reports on the copper industry in 1936, U.S. officials noted that white-collar technicians and administrators averaged 1.4 thousand pesos a month (the top tier of about 10 percent earned three thousand pesos a month) while a miner earned 20 pesos a day (by then, around US$1) or 500 pesos for a 25 workday month. The income disparity between workers and their supervisors started at 50 percent in the mines and rose to 100 percent in the mechanical shops. The official "essential wage" [salario mínimo], that is the government's estimate of how much it cost a family of four to live in Santiago, was 8 to 9 pesos per day. Non-official and pro-labor commentators, however, claimed that the minimum daily cost for a family was about 14 pesos, which would mean that an average family needed approximately 450 pesos per month to survive. Only the best wages could cover this minimum. Locomotive engineers earned 23 pesos a day; nitrate miners, 17 a day; coal miners, 15 a day; textile workers, 7-12; and inquilinos about 5 pesos a day.[28] Attempting to gauge what wages would buy over this turbulent period involves a good deal of statistical manipulation; but one sincere effort, limited to Santiago's industrial workers, found their real wages unchanged from World War I into the mid-1920s, then falling 21 percent in the Depression and not recovering their 1920s level until the late 1950s.[29] During the worst of the depression, government relief for an unemployed man with a family was as little as 30 pesos a month; a family with five children was expected to survive on 70 pesos a month.[30] There were around 47 thousand white-collar workers, the beleaguered middle class. A break down of its salary structure helps explain Chilean politics in the 1930s (see Table 5.1).

The distinction between men's and women's salaries was sharp. The 38 thousand men earned an average of 835 pesos per month, while the 9.5 thousand women averaged 287 per month; only 7 women in the country earned more than 2.5 thousand pesos a month. The gender-based disparity among government employees was not quite as bad. But only 1 percent of all government employees earned three thousand pesos or more.[31]

According to government surveys, the general purchasing power of all laborers rose under Alessandri. Table 5.2 compares salary levels with basic expenditures. Putting aside the issue of rural labor, workers appear to be regaining ground in mid-decade. Of course, particular labor sectors often fell below the average. The data is not completely reliable. Although Chilean officials collected data on more subjects than most Latin American bureaucracies, their surveys were fairly simple and often poorly administered. A leftist paper compared its findings with those of the government and claimed that salaries were about two-thirds of what the government believed. For example, the government claimed medical workers earned at least 150 pesos per month, but the paper found that in a Santiago hospital workers earned only 100 pesos per month plus a breakfast of coffee and rolls and a lunch of soup with some meat; nurses earned 300 pesos, considerably less than the government-listed salary for that occupation.[32] At the end of the decade, Socialists disputed the government's figures on the real wage and said they reflected only one-third of the inflation that had taken place.[33]

Table 5.2: Labor Income and Cost of Living, 1928-1937

Year	Average Monthly Income	Average Monthly Expenses				
		Food	Housing	Clothing	Other	All
1928	179.5	71.8	35.9	44.9	26.9	179.5
% income		40	20	25	15	100
1929	179.5	85.9	35.5	45.2	27.6	193.9
% income		48	20	25	15	*108
1932	126.2	82.6	37.4	60.3	28.0	208.5
% income		65	30	48	22	165
1934	188.0	106.6	44.5	78.0	35.5	264.7
% income		57	24	41	19	140
1936	264.5	122.9	48.4	84.8	33.2	289.4
% income		46	18	32	13	109
1937	319.5	147.1	553.4	85.7	35.2	321.5
% income		46	17	27	11	99

*As the Interior Department reckoned expenses, this number exceeds what the workers earned.

Source: Chile, Interior, v. 10203 (1940), Comisariato General de Subsistencias y Precios, Departamento Técnico.

Alessandri knew that his government had to reach urban labor and an impoverished middle class but funds were short. The bureaucracy was underpaid, frequently condescending towards the under class, and often corrupt. In the administration's first two years, unemployment funds often ran out, closing down the rationing programs and leaving providers unpaid. When funds were available, local officials frequently demanded kickbacks for their political parties from the merchants who supplied the programs.[34] These programmatic shortcomings provided political ammunition to an ever more militant, and sometimes violent, set of labor organizations, paramilitary movements, and middle-class associations that are discussed below.

A central policy problem was the unemployed, who had been dumped into empty warehouses. When Alessandri was inaugurated, the warehouses in the nitrate ports of Santiago and Valparaiso were full. The Intendant of Antofagasta called it a "situation without remedy." Thousands of men and their families languished in rags and filth, waiting for their next meal.[35] About one-third of the port of Antofagasta was on rations. Unpaid for weeks, restaurateurs and store owners refused to maintain the soup kitchens; the workers responded by threatening to sack the downtown. The Intendant telegraphed Santiago, "They say they would rather die fighting than starve in their homes."[36] The unemployed remained warehoused in some cities until 1935-36; by then, a paper referred to the shelters in Santiago as "nothing more than slaughterhouses of children."[37] This was hardly what Alessandri had wanted. On entering office, he tried to send the unemployed from Santiago into the countryside. Those who went in the middle of 1933 found no work, and they walked back to the warehouses in the capital. A more permanent solution was to colonize unsettled territory. Ibáñez had started a colonization scheme in 1929, which required only 5 percent down on a property; fewer than 500 farms were colonized before 1932. Montero tried handing out land titles for free, but few even had the means to work the land they received.[38] Colonization programs, including those under Alessandri, seldom helped; it cost over 30 thousand pesos to get a farm started.[39]

It was under Alessandri that the gold-panning program flourished. By January 1933, the gold diggings employed 34 thousand men: 11.6 thousand in mines run by the government; 7.1 thousand on public lands; and 15.2 thousand on their own. Most of the output came from state mines. Only a quarter of the men received any public subsidies, and these cost less per man than the rationing program in Santiago.[40]

For a short while, gold was the country's major export. There were gold sites throughout the country, although the *norte chico* near Coquimbo, the central valley surrounding Santiago, and a zone near Concepción, in the south, were the most important. The gold panners sold their ore to the Directorate of Gold Panning [Jefatura de Lavaderos de Oro]. The Directorate sent the gold to the Central Bank, which sold it, and turned the hard currency gained over to the Exchange Commission while supplying the Directorate with the peso credits to keep the system going.[41] The credits often ran short. There were bureaucratic disputes over jurisdiction, with the Ministry of Labor wanting to run everything. The mining concessionaires who recruited many of the workers often cheated them. Promises of tools and rations made by the government to men starting out went unfulfilled. Most miners found themselves living in shacks or improvised buildings in the middle of nowhere. They spent their days panning in the mountains without proper shoes or warm clothing. A fair number of miners became ill and returned to the capital; but most stayed. They could earn an average of 6 pesos a day, which accorded them some dignity, although company stores quickly took most of the earnings.[42] From 1933 until 1936, gold panning produced around 2 million grams a year. Then production jumped to 3.1 million grams in 1937, its peak year, and declined thereafter until 1941 when it fell to less than .7 million grams and then continued to fall further.[43]

Gold panning, industrial production, and urban construction gradually reduced the number of unemployed. Official figures, although suspect, demonstrate a rapid decline in the mid-1930s.

Table 5.3: Government Unemployment Figures, 1933-1936

	1933	1934	1935	1936
January	262,455	116,298	24,715	13,375
June	178,885	40,527	17,768	13,306
December	132,642	38,309	13,601	15,701

Source: Chile, Interior, v. 9498 (1937) Servicio de Cesantía. *Memoria anual, 1936.* Santiago: Jan. 1937.

Sources concur that prolonged unemployment was disappearing and that mass poverty remained.[44] Government expenditures on rations for the unemployed declined from 56 million pesos in 1932 to only 4.5 million in 1936. The changed circumstances were particularly evident when officials began denying rations to those reluctant to work.[45] Wages remained so low and employment so irregular, that an observer in Santiago said, in 1935, that people floated around "half-starved."[46] Much of the bitterness of the 1930s stems not just from the ruin that followed the Crash but from the humiliations of poverty and the callousness of officials charged with alleviating public misery. This anger would be channeled into politics, where it extended the boundaries of social participation and changed the public vocabulary. The number of voters was growing, the number of parties was large, and government patronage was inadequate to satisfy more than a fraction of those who were now making demands.

Political Parties

The political system had revived its multiparty tradition and a constant jockeying for patronage. In 1930, Chile had 460 thousand registered voters, 175 thousand of them in Valparaiso and Santiago.[47] Creating a populist bloc required carrying these two cities plus the 80 thousand voters in the northern nitrate provinces and southern Concepción. The right counted on winning one-third of the urban vote and carrying the rural provinces by more than 80 percent. In 1932, Alessandri won in the major cities and the mining towns and he succeeded in undercutting conservative strength in the rural zones. Unfortunately for the president's fortunes, personal loyalties counted more than ideology in Congress, and proportional representation gave leaders of small parties a disproportionate leverage in any coalition. Young lawyers and other professionals knew that their political chances improved by forming new associations rather than toiling in the ranks of already established parties, especially when the older parties were run by snobbish landowners and financiers. Soon after the fall of Ibáñez, there were 28 registered parties; by the time of Alessandri's second term, there were 30.[48] Alessandri won with an electoral coalition similar to the one that elected him in 1920. It was organized and run by the Doctrinaire Liberals (his own party) and included the Radicals. Once in office, an empty treasury left him unable to placate his original supporters.

The Radical Party was internally divided, and presented the most complex element in his winning coalition. It had a conservative wing, dominated by southerners and headed by Juan Antonio Ríos, and a set of urban social firebrands, led by Gabriel González Videla.[49] In addition to being disappointed in its spoils, the Radical Party worried about its electoral position within the middle class and segments of urban labor. It was under pressure from the left by Communists and Socialists and from the right by the Nacis and the Republican Militia. Alessandri's proposal to raise taxes cost him one faction of the Radicals; the declaration of emergency powers cost him another. But about half the party still backed him until June 1933, when the polarizing impact of new taxes and high rates of unemployment drove all the Radicals into the opposition. The Party called for a rapid mobilization of labor to help the "dispossessed."[50]

The antagonisms were not all on the Radical's side. Alessandri had his own resentments, especially toward Radicals who had collaborated with Ibáñez. Some had suffered exile as he had, but others, such as Juan Antonio Ríos, had decided that Ibáñez offered "Alessandrismo without Alessandri" and a government job as well.[51] To the president, they were traitors. Even so, the president worked with the right but always hoped to win back the Radicals. Well into the second year of the presidential term, the conservatives complained that they lacked much influence within the administration.[52]

The smaller parties in Alessandri's coalition—the Radical Socialists, the Social and Democratic Republicans, and the Democrats—proposed massive increases in public education, the revival of public works, the state takeover of "inefficient" industries, the creation of provincial assemblies, and women's suffrage.[53] Alessandri had promised some kind of socialism, but he had neither the means nor the will to carry out such measures. By late 1934, he was also afraid of offending the Conservative and Liberal Parties and losing votes for his budgets.

To the left of the Radicals and various Republicans and Democrats were the Socialists and two factions of Communists, all competing for labor support. A variety of Socialist parties regrouped and formed a national party on April 17, 1933; their initial proclamation expressed concern for labor and the middle class. The Communists were divided between the Trotskyists, led by Manuel Hidalgo, and the Stalinists, led by Elías Lafertte and Carlos Contreras Labarca.[54]

Although the Communists claimed international support and had a continental headquarters in Montevideo, they received little help from abroad.[55] When Moscow dispatched an Austrian agent to start simultaneous uprisings in Chile *and* Peru in 1935, he only succeeded in getting a fair number of party members arrested.[56] The Communists were also without a clear strategy. Stalin's orders were to avoid "petty intellectuals" and coalitions with other parties—directions that left the party without a means to influence electoral politics.[57] In 1932, they drew only three thousand votes. One reason was that many workers did not register to vote because the mandatory identity card cost 5 pesos.[58] The Communists' behavior in the naval mutiny and the Christmas uprising had also revealed a putsch mentality. Successive governments had intensified police surveillance of all dissident groups, and by 1933 the carabineros could report that they knew the whereabouts of almost all Communist *cells*, having broken the party code.[59] Efforts to rebuild the FOCh, the umbrella association of labor unions that had given the Communists so much visibility in the 1920s, were undercut by unemployment and low wages.[60]

No single party or organization was able to generate a decisive grass-roots movement. Instead, young hustlers in splinter parties, labor syndicates, paramilitary units, and consumer organizations tried to capture enough support to win themselves a public presence. The rhetoric of reform and revolution overlapped, creating an amorphous radicalism. Party names were confusing: Radicals, Radical-Socialists, Social-Republicans, Democrats, Democratic-Socialists, and Socialists all won seats in the 1937 congressional election.[61]

Aside from persecuting the Communists, Alessandri tried to weaken the positions of the two personalities who could most easily unify an opposition: Carlos Ibáñez and Marmaduke Grove. The political careers of the three were closely intertwined. Grove and Ibáñez had been instrumental in the coup of 1924. Grove and Alessandri, while in exile, had conspired against Ibáñez. Ibañistas, Alessandri, and Grove had worked separately and with one another to destroy Montero. To the end of his life, Alessandri blamed Ibáñez and the police attack on his home in 1929 for the early death of his wife.[62] Alessandri hated this man more than anyone else. The president recognized that either Ibáñez or Grove might organize another attempt against the government. Ibáñez returned in late 1932. He still had support among military officers; and Ibañistas existed in most of the political parties.[63] Throughout the 1930s, Grove was the most admired figure on the left. Grove's radicalism had cost him the support of the military, but his turn at the helm of government was seen by many laborers as their only real moment in history. He could draw a crowd and incite tumult almost at will.

Alessandri also mistrusted the armed forces.[64] One of his first acts was to forcibly retire six generals, and he never hesitated to dismiss an officer at any sign of insubordination. In the first few months of his administration, he kept the Santiago army units on indefinite field maneuvers, dismissed many colonels, and imposed a new oath on the entire armed forces. No soldier could join any party or association that might be construed as *outside* his professional duties. Troop strength was cut to levels below the early 1920s.[65] But the problem did not disappear easily. Alessandri's greatest fear was revived in February 1936, when junior officers, all of them Ibañistas, tried a putsch.[66]

Alessandri convinced a frightened Congress in April 1933 to give him "extraordinary powers," that is, the right to suspend civil liberties and carry out summary arrests and imprisonment. Ibáñez was sent into exile, Ibañistas and Grovistas were arrested and placed in isolated provincial zones, and several Socialists, notably Oscar Schnake, were told to leave the capital. Former president Montero could not resist commenting that the air of conspiracy in the capital was similar to when he was president, with one exception, "don Arturo Alessandri is not plotting against the government this time."[67]

Police reports fed the president's paranoia. In July 1933, investigators intercepted a letter from Ibáñez to Grove complaining about life in exile. The police appended a report claiming they were certain the air corps would join in a Grove-led coup and that all opponents would be killed.[68] In January 1934, Alessandri had his powers renewed, but the public was growing tired of the panic.

In 1933, Eugenio Matte Hurtado, Senator for Santiago, head of the socialist New Public Action or NAP and one of Grove's allies during his "Socialist Republic," unexpectedly died. Grove ran for Matte's seat in a special election. It was just the theater he wanted. He referred to himself as, "the trumpeter of a great approaching battle, a Social Revolution! . . . I am going to the struggle as the representative of a party, the Socialist Party, which is not a political party but a revolutionary organization of combat, which stands upon the fundamental principles of Marxism."[69] To the shock of the administration, he won. The Radical Party, angry with Alessandri, had supported his candidacy. But Alessandri could still call upon loyalists who elected his son, Fernando, to the Senate seat for Tarapacá and Antofagasta, the left-wing mining provinces. The Communist candidate in that election, Elías Lafertte, was easily defeated.[70]

Paramilitary Organizations

Electoral contests and political parties were only part of the political spectrum. The new and dangerous element in public life was the rise of paramilitary organizations. A number were formed in Latin America in the aftermath of World War I and were modeled on Mussolini's tactics and, in the 1930s, on Hitler's Nazis as well. On the one hand, such organizations represented a generalized assault on liberal values; on the other, they were a new means to executive power. Paramilitary units could control the streets and generate a space for their views. They could also create a "crisis," a threat to bring down the government and install their leader—a prospect with special appeal to young men, tired of waiting for change.

In Chile, the rise of the Republican Militia was a crucial and ominous development. Its origins lay in the events of 1931-32, but its antecedents, like those of paramilitary units in other Latin American countries, were in the urban rifle clubs of the wealthy and in the rural tradition of arming hired hands to maintain security. In spontaneous class confrontations before World War I, the rifle clubs were active in repressing labor strikes.[71] Alessandri's political campaign in 1920 had also provoked a paramilitary response from the right.[72] The first upper-class militia formed in Santiago in 1924-26, in response to the coup and the massive strikes of that period. General Carlos Sáez Morales notes in his memoirs that, when President Figueroa was elected, elite youths formed armed units in response to rumors of a coup.[73] It disbanded under Ibáñez. But the rich regrouped and rearmed after the Naval Mutiny in September 1931. Units of the civil guard, sometimes called the White Guard, were mobilized and helped the carabineros patrol the capital. The guard consisted of young volunteers, armed by the government. Its first action was to force left-wing students from control of the university.[74] A second, crucial mobilization took place after the Communist uprising at Copiapó in December 1931; once again, there was close cooperation between the carabineros and the White Guard in that city.[75] At both times, foreign businessmen, most of them Americans or British, established armed neighborhood patrols.[76] Some of these improvised units expanded while Montero was in office. The left also flirted with paramilitarism. Matte's NAP, for example, had armed groups, and the Communists openly demanded guns from Grove.[77] Finally, during Dávila's administration, a set of former army officers, with financing from the rich (Gustavo Ross was a major contributor) and foreign corporations, created the Republican Militia.

The group drew support from rural areas surrounding the capital and consisted of hacendado employees and of young men from the *gente bien* [the upper-middle class]. Its membership list indicates that substantial numbers of the Radical Party, especially in the conservative south, joined the organization.[78] Led by Julio Schwartzenberg and Eulogio Sánchez Errázuriz, the guard had nearly two thousand members by the end of Dávila's administration and continued to meet and train even after Alessandri's election. In early 1933, its headquarters were moved to Santiago and, although still training in secret, its existence was publicly known. Its members, wearing blue overalls with a blue cap and a leather belt, numbered between 10 and 15 thousand by May 1933.

The militia claimed to be nonpartisan but its earliest declaration reveals a fear of labor, at least partly arising from the absence of a dependable army to control it.[79] Its followers were told not to forget June 4, the date marking the birth of the Socialist Republic, when the "urban trash reigned in the streets."[80] Unlike most paramilitary groups, the militia declared itself an arm of constitutional rule and swore to defend "the system of republican democratic government" and "to fight by any means against tyranny, whether communistic, civil or military."[81] Alessandri supported the organization as a counter force to the army and the leftists; he helped arm it. He, along with Ross and many in the cabinet, attended a massive militia parade held in the capital on May 7, 1933.[82]

All of the leftist parties opposed the militia. Although the Radical's executive committee had endorsed the militia when the party was still aligned with Alessandri, anti-militia sentiment built after the party broke with the president. By 1933, Radicals in Santiago openly denounced it, while those in the south often joined.[83] To its opponents, the militia was the "white terror," an armed attempt to stop any further social change.[84] Its style of dress, social origins, and theatrics made its fascist inspiration plain. One deputy called it the armed might of the rich against the poor and a source of illegal government contracts for Alessandri's friends.[85] Another claimed that the president had turned his back on the people and now saw them as *dirt*; he recommended the workers arm themselves.[86]

By the time of a second major parade in September 1933, the militia claimed 50 thousand members.[87] At its peak, its arms included 16 thousand Mausers and bayonets, three thousand Lueger pistols, 750 machine guns, 15 aircraft, and 5 tanks improvised from tractors. It had a general staff consisting of a number of former army generals, a wide variety of services covering everything from propaganda to transport, and an organizational structure that divided the provinces of Chile into six distinct groups of forces. It drilled in battalion strength, with the battalions divided into two companies of about 80 men each.[88] At the second parade, Alessandri told the militia that he and its members had a common bond to uphold the constitution and fight against military governments and communism: "I shall see to it that the red banner disappears from our streets and towns and never returns."[89]

However, once he cowed the army, Alessandri abandoned the militia. Because many of its members expected to be paid for their weekend drilling, maintaining the militia was expensive. Ross diverted government funds to help it grow, the rich and major foreign corporations made voluntary contributions.[90] Such improvised revenues could not sustain a large organization, and the militia began "assessing" some firms, demanding 30 thousand pesos, for example, from the National City Bank.[91] By 1934, the militia's membership fell to 25 thousand as people saw that no pay would be forthcoming. Another negative for Alessandri appeared as army officers confronted the militia at parades, and a minister of defense had to be fired for denouncing it.[92] The militia, at its height, had friendly ties with the carabineros and the navy.[93] Once the Ibáñez corp of officers had been thinned from the army, it made little sense for the president to continue antagonizing the nation's soldiers.[94]

Finally, the political costs became too high. Once the militia was well established, its posturing drew violence. Members were accused but never convicted of political murder.[95] At one parade, a sympathetic carabinero opened fire on an army officer. In April 1934, bombs went off near the homes of Commander-in-chief Julio Schwartzenberg and of other prominent militia leaders. They threatened reprisals and had to be publicly warned by Alessandri to desist.[96] The militia held its last major rally in October 1934. The following July, 600 of its officers met in Santiago and announced they were going on "vacation." There were signs of some partisan quarrels within the organization.[97] In 1936, Schwartzenberg and the militia's general council declared it disbanded. Its members still had ten thousand rifles which were never collected.[98]

The militia's existence, along with the formation of the Nacis discussed below, encouraged other movements and associations to think of arming. Juan Antonio Ríos, who had been a militia supporter, decided to create an Ibañista force. Among political entrepreneurs, armed groups were a means of recruiting young men of good family.[99] There was at least the possibility that the militia might inspire class warfare. A good section of the urban working class and the lower-middle class came to hate it at the same time that they considered forming their own paramilitary organizations. The metal workers, a major Santiago union, started recruiting support for an armed organization.[100] Before the 1930s ended, the Socialists and the Communists had paramilitary columns.

The second major paramilitary movement that grew out of the tumult of 1931-32 was that of the Nacis. Modeling themselves on Hitler's movement, they initially abstained from party politics and claimed to represent an autochthonous, "organic" tradition of nationalism.[101] They decried democracy, moral degeneracy, and unchecked individualism.[102] Their small group (they started with fewer than a dozen members) initially overlapped with that of the militia. Their party's formal name was the National Socialist Movement of Chile [MNS, Movimiento Nacional Socialista de Chile]. Little has been written about them.[103] Eventually, the party ran candidates for office, but it never hid its hostility to republican government or its desire to overthrow the system.

The Nacis were extremely popular in Chiloë, the German-Chilean colony in the south, where about five thousand young men belonged.[104] There, the German-Chileans had been allowed to live on their own terms, a testament to the Chilean regard for European cultures. Chiloë was founded in the 1840s, yet residents of the area still spoke German at home and in their schools. In the 1930s, their community leaders fell in love with the Nazis. Portraits of Hitler and Goebbels were put up in local public schools. German-Chileans who objected to Nazi propaganda were beaten up, had their homes set on fire, and were blacklisted by the community.[105] Their rhetoric about their devotion to Chilean values aside, the Nacis drew upon German nationalism as an important element in their growth. A group of young German-Chileans in Santiago comprised the Naci nucleus in the capital. In all, the Nacis numbered between 20 and 30 thousand members in 1934.

The Nacis' nastiness came out in street fights, staged acts of political terror, and intimidating mass rallies. The Naci Assault Troops [Tropas Nacistas de Asalto] appeared in 1933 and provoked fights with leftists as a means of driving left-wing speakers and newspaper peddlers from the streets of Valparaiso and Santiago.[106] But many Conservatives considered them civilized. I can find no anti-Naci remarks by Ross, for example, until the Nacis attacked him. The Naci board of directors had a patina of respectability; all but two were professional men.[107] An English foreign official traveling in the south remarked, "But with all their Nazi mentality, they are a satisfactory people to do business with. They are straight, they pay their bills and are generally trustworthy."[108]

The Naci ideology was based on the leader-principle [*führerprinzip*]: the state is the embodiment of the leader who has the strength of will to carry through a spiritual regeneration of the nation. In its earliest credo, the Party declared, "The leader is the only one responsible for the political, economic, social, and spiritual orientation of the MNS. As a result, he exercises absolute and unique command over the Movement."[109]

The leader who wrote these lines was Jorge González von Marées, a lawyer of partial German descent and of humble circumstances. He began his career as a reformer and taught laborers in Santiago's night school, rising to an appointment by President Montero as mayor of Ñuñoz, a suburb of Santiago. The coup of 1932 cost him his job. He publicly abhorred violence and class conflict.[110] In one pamphlet, González von Marées elaborated his ideas on everything from music to political heroes. He liked Beethoven, did not read poetry very much, was not interested in flowers, and found Napoleon "the most exciting figure in world history"; but his "idol was Portales." (Diego Portales was the conservative leader who re-established many colonial practices in the Constitution of 1833.) On his thirty-second birthday (April 5, 1932), he founded the Nacis and referred to the major parties as robber gangs, and the social laws as forms of embezzlement; government was organized thievery. He professed a desire to create a "national soul," to defend "liberty" and "family, home, and country." For him, fighting Communism was not enough for Communism was only "a reaction to a corrupt regime." He said some 80 percent of his followers were "working class." He promised that the Nacis would create another form of a market economy in which government would no longer serve the rich. Rather, "money would be at the service of the State," which in turn "would be a mother to all her children."[111] Private property would be universal. The Church, while remaining outside of politics, would regain its "ancient customs."[112]

As this indicates, the Nacis exploited the same social issues as other movements. They argued that labor was the basis of all value. They favored a program to construct public housing. They opposed foreign corporations and domestic oligopolies and demanded the break-up of large estates into small farms. They always portrayed the government as corrupt.[113] Their major apologist, Carlos Keller R., emphasized the Naci themes of nationalism and sacrifice. In Keller's eyes, a government by Nacis would be "syndicalist," organizing economic activities by guilds [*gremios*], which in turn would be connected to a series of government ministries run by a prime minister.[114] Aside from its obvious debts to European corporatism, the roots of this vision can be found in the anarcho-syndicalist movement earlier in the century.

In the Naci view, foreign capital and the Jews were one and the same; much of their anti-Jewish venom was directed at the Guggenheims.[115] Jews were not a major social issue in Chile, but the Nacis did their best to make them one. A key figure in the party warmed up one rally by denouncing the Jews who killed Christ and were now scattered over the face of the earth, "like an octopus that extends its tentacles over humanity in its desire for vengeance and which now controls everything by means of its vast fortunes." González von Marées added, "the Jews want everyone to believe that the doctrines of Karl Marx are anti-capitalist, but this is untrue, because the major servants of capitalism are Marxists and political liberals."[116]

Alessandri, unlike his conservative allies, saw the Nacis as a threat and kept them cornered. He had the police spy on their meetings and break up their rallies, which forced them indoors and into settings allowing only small audiences. He told the Republican Militia that his support was conditional on the group's exclusion of all Nacis. As a result, instead of forming an alliance, the two organizations competed for the same followers.[117]

The Nacis, nonetheless, claimed their share of public space and undermined the government's authority within the middle class. Naci hotheads eventually overstepped the generous bounds they had been allowed by the Chilean political class. In November 1936, Nacis riding on a train at Rancagua opened fire on a crowd demonstrating against them. Alessandri demanded and Congress passed a Law for the Internal Security of the State in January 1937, which prohibited political parties from using force to achieve their objectives.[118]

Until the formation of the Popular Front, the struggle between Alessandri and his opponents was not primarily a party struggle. It was more of a street fight, a fact that helps explain Alessandri's willingness to ignore the Constitution. The president's "extraordinary powers" ended in mid-1934. Until then, his administration used them with enthusiasm. Censorship was extended in every direction, shutting down even satirical magazines. Editors of newspapers and magazines were sometimes deported or suffered internal exile, by being sent to some frontier zone, and the authorities sacked a number of presses.[119] The government also ignored congressional immunity, harassing and even arresting dissident legislators.[120] Even without special authority, the government regularly denied opponents the right of assembly. Police raids, without warrants, were common. Police also acted under secret orders from the Ministry of Interior, and military officials in the provinces harassed dissidents without authorization.[121]

The president was dealing with more than parties and paramilitary groups. While opposition parties and paramilitary organizations could be repressed or coopted, a more general dissent was building. It grew from the sense that the government was indifferent to the fate of ordinary people and it manifested itself in a multiplicity of strikes and demonstrations.

Social Radicalism, Labor, and the Middle Class

In 1936, a wide variety of labor associations and the left-wing parties were instrumental in creating the Chilean Labor Confederation or CTCh [Confederación de Trabajadores de Chile]. Soon thereafter, the Communists and Socialists, the CTCh, and the Radical Party created the Popular Front.[122] These institutional developments were the result of an ongoing struggle by labor and the middle class for expanded political and economic rights.

Historians of labor in Latin America have emphasized that, prior to the 1930s, labor movements were often divided and lacked a radical consciousness. They were more influenced by anarchist or anarcho-syndicalist attitudes than by Marxism. They also note that radical sentiments were not limited to an industrial proletariat and that Latin American labor movements often developed in response to the characteristics of a nation's export economy.[123] Chile's labor movement was divided along a number of lines, ideologically among Communists, Socialists, and left reformers in the Radical Party and other organizations, and socially by specific sectors and crafts. It was also weakened in the Depression by the collapse of the mineral export sectors.

Given these weaknesses and the legacy of repression under Ibáñez, how did the Popular Front win the presidency by 1938? There were three reasons for the development of the Popular Front. The first was the revival of urban social radicalism involving labor and the middle class; the second, the response of political parties and the government to this phenomenon; and the third, the part played by organizations outside of unions and political parties in the transformation of political norms. Each of these reasons involved the middle class, and an understanding of middle class objectives and behavior is central to explaining the successes and shortcomings of the Popular Front.[124]

Making sense of what happened requires putting aside the Popular Front mythology that emphasizes the labor movement alone.[125] Instead, a labor minority acquired some economic rights in the 1930s but lacked an established role in politics. Labor was institutionalized by the end of the 1930s and thus, was part of the public arena. Laborers, within and without unions, carried out strikes and supported substantial political change. But labor was not "incorporated" in any manner similar to the political roles allowed associations of capital such as the Agricultural Society, the Society for Industrial Development, or the professional guilds to lobby government directly.

The labor movement required a good deal of the decade to regroup from the repression of Ibáñez; its mobilization coincided with and influenced the rise of the Popular Front. But labor, alone, could not have created a coalition of parties capable of winning the presidency. On the contrary, the movement to create the Popular Front also changed the prospects of labor mobilizing. It was only in November 1936 that leftist construction unions held their first congress in Santiago. At their second congress, a year later, they created an umbrella organization, the National Industrial Federation of Construction [Federación Industrial Nación de la Construcción], which formed in league with the already existing Popular Front.[126] What is more, labor's mobilization owed a good deal to middle-class radicalism. As the CTCh formed, the central instrument in putting it together (December 25 to 27, 1936) was the Union Front [Frente Sindical], which included such already established national unions as the Teachers Union and the Labor Organization of Chilean Employees, both obviously middle-class associations whose leaders already belonged to the Socialist and Radical Parties.[127] The national labor front grew out of ongoing networks of Santiago's party leaders, labor militants, and middle-class professionals. Had a labor left been the driving force in creating the Front, the 1930s would have been a very different decade in its outcomes.

In order to explain the Popular Front and the relation of the Front to the left, the history of 1930s radicalism has to broaden to include the middle class. Because it was too small to achieve its goals, the middle class aided and abetted labor's resurgence. In alliance with labor radicals and as leaders of reformist and left-wing parties, members of the middle class could demand benefits for both labor and themselves. Certain collective goods, improvements in public education, for example, were easily proposed as forms of national development. But there were also important differences between the rank and file of Chilean laborers and the urban middle class, and as we shall see in the 1940s, whenever these differences became too pronounced—the unionization of rural laborers is one case—labor's interests were sacrificed by the government to maintain middle-class support.

Developing this argument requires considering the ideas of several theorists of modern behavior. The first is Amartya Sen, who emphasizes the role of "entitlements" in any economic system, the rules by which goods and services are produced, transferred, and traded. In a study of the cause of famines, Sen drew a crucial distinction between "food *availability* and that of *direct entitlement* to food" [his emphasis] and found that most people starved because of a lack of entitlement not a shortage of food.[128] In many respects, the tactical alliances that developed between elements of the middle class and the labor movement in Chile during the 1930s were based on the common purpose of redefining existing entitlements. Both the middle class and labor thought that government could channel income from the elite and foreign companies into public works and social spending. This was the heart of their populist alliance.

Labor unions always have a dual character: on the one hand, they argue on behalf of workers in general since they are appealing for public support; but, on the other, their primary objective within a capitalist system is to form a cartel over the supply of labor in a strategic zone or economic sector. As Mancur Olson, the second theorist who is guiding this analysis, notes, their chief means of doing this is to demand through strikes and other actions that employers not negotiate freely with the unemployed.[129] Since they cannot change the system as a whole, they demand special consideration within it. This point seems especially relevant in Chile where a large, impoverished work force languished in the countryside. In the 1930s, one of the entitlements being contested, and a key element in the pursuit of any others, was who would be allowed to form associations in order to make legal demands on the government and employers. What is often missed in discussions of "the labor movement," is that many of the most successful new associations were based on white-collar work. A rapidly expanding minority of labor organized in this decade. At the height of the Ibáñez dictatorship, almost 38 thousand workers and professionals had been recognized as belonging to state-sanctioned labor syndicates. That number reached over 54 thousand in 1932 and rose steadily thereafter (data presented in Graph 5.1).

Graph 5.1: Membership in Legal Unions, 1929-1948
Worker and Professional Syndicates

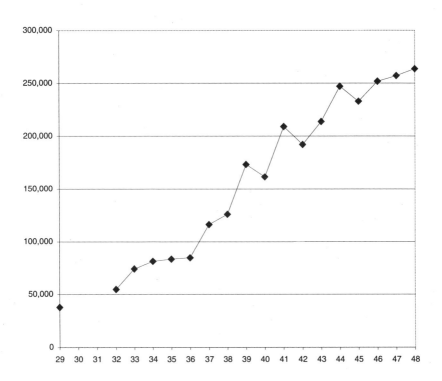

Source: *Anuario estadístico*, 1955.

The labor movement of the 1930s was far more extensive geographically and economically than a decade earlier. New organizations assumed that labor and the middle class were legitimate clients of the state and demanded public works programs, effective labor contracts with guarantees against arbitrary dismissal, shorter work days, better wages, and the right to organize as well as paid vacations and protection against company unions, piece work, and subcontracting by employers.[130] An illustrative example appears in the recent literature on women. The Chilean suffrage movement, like those in the rest of Latin America, dated from early twentieth century; Asunción Lavrin makes the case that Chile, after Argentina and Uruguay, was one of the most progressive societies in discussing women's rights in South America.[131] In 1934, women gained the right to vote in municipal elections the following year. Fresh on that victory, thirty women met at the University of Chile law school and formed the Movement for the Emancipation of Chilean Women [MEMCh or Movimiento Pro-Emancipación de las Mujeres de Chile]. The dominant figures were the crusading lawyer, Elena Caffarena de Jiles, and the Communist journalist, Marta Vergara. They soon issued their own publications, demanding equal pay for equal work and raising such issues as divorce, domestic violence, birth control, and abortion—all scandalous topics at the time.[132]

The economic recovery at mid-decade generated, to use the phrase of a third theorist, Manuel Castells, a fight for "collective consumption" that linked disparate groups.[133] This fight ranged over wages and prices, especially the cost of food and rent. Most importantly, it led to a period of cooperation, particularly in Santiago, between the middle class and the labor movement as both demanded an end to the meat tariff and consumer protections against inflation.

In particular, the middle class could lend its aura of gentility to demonstrations demanding social justice. In the relatively small space of downtown Santiago, even modest gatherings could upset government officials. In January 1937, when workers at a public works project greeted him with raised fists, the president told them, "You are a bunch ingrates. You get excellent wages and still want to start strikes."[134] Of course, Alessandri knew he could not cater only to capital and devoted a good deal of his energy to keeping the middle class and labor in separate camps.[135] Chilean comments on the middle class emphasize its parvenu attitudes, its subservience to superiors, its resentments of the elite, and its lack of confidence in its own goals.[136] Even if true, such fears are understandable. This was a class that owned little, was heavily dependent on either government employment or the fortunes of the export economy and did not control any decisive political institution. Around the time of World War I, it organized associations in professions beyond the traditionally prestigious areas of law and medicine. It gained political ground under Alessandri and Ibáñez, and at the end of the 1920s, it had some welfare benefits and a social security program. But its economic condition remained precarious.[137] The middle class suffered massive unemployment in the Crash and was battered by inflation: teachers, a classic middle-class profession, earned an entry-level salary 458 pesos in 1925 (the equivalent of 2,572 British pence); by 1933, they earned only 398 pesos (393 British pence).[138]

The middle class, which participated in almost all political organizations, had the core of its interests and hopes in the Radical Party. The Radicals' behavior in first supporting Alessandri, then turning against him, and then being courted by the administration before a final break in 1936, reflected middle-class anxieties. The middle class was attracted to the promise of jobs but repulsed by any thought of higher taxes. Its members were active in the Republican Militia, the Nacis, and the NAP [New Action Party] that supported the Socialist Republic in 1932, and AGECh, the Guild Association of Chilean Employees [Agrupación de Gremial de Empleados de Chile], formed in February 1932. Employee organizations among bank clerks, teachers, and the unemployed were militantly in favor of a minimum wage, public job security, and basic health care and life insurance for all.[139] In mid-1933, the unemployed white-collar workers formed a United Front [Frente Unico de Empleados Cesantes de Chile].[140]

Status anxieties played a role in middle-class behavior. Many middle-class organizations, fearing internal conflicts and trouble with the police, dared not take any political stance.[141] They hoped to lobby the government for help without provoking political retaliation. The traditional professions paid from modest to well, but many members or would-be members of the middle class were in the retail trade, which spanned every stratum from the poorest peddler to the merchant houses. In 1936, at a time when Valparaiso was still devastated by the depression, there was a retailer for every 70 people in the city, one for every 50 if you counted the street vendors. The city had over 1.2 thousand grocery stores.[142] In other words, a good part of the middle class avoided conflict or never identified with any social struggle.

But part of it did. Conditions created by the Depression drove part of the urban middle class into a loose-knit association with labor.[143] This intermingling of classes, in demonstrations, in party rallies, and elections was a radicalizing experience. Government contained some of the most outraged elements of the middle class. Teachers and the National Agricultural Society saw each other as class enemies. Labor inspectors and labor courts often expressed resentment of foreign corporations; both frequently complained in public of government indifference to social laws.[144] Government physicians denounced inadequate public health care. In 1934, when doctors blamed government inaction for the spread of typhus in the central valley, the government arrested many under anti-communist laws.[145]

Middle-class organizations often sounded like labor syndicates. In August 1933, Santiago white-collar organizations joined in a city-wide conference of labor associations to demand a minimum wage, the six-hour day, help for the unemployed, and the strict enforcement of all social legislation.[146] But the issue that most drew the middle class and labor together was inflation. In Santiago and Valparaiso, the "public" denounced rising food and gas prices, increases in public transportation, the meat tariff, the sales tax, and the widespread foreclosures caused by the Depression. With the support of these organizations, voicing these demands became safe for politicians.

Vilifying Gustavo Ross and foreign corporations became popular. Ross was vulnerable on the electric company deal and on the foreign debt payments. Radicals and the left parties described both as sellouts, and Ross lacked the skill or even the interest to reverse this judgment.[147] When the Braden Copper Company, the subsidiary of Kennecott that ran El Teniente, was caught underpaying its taxes, the Communist Deputy José Vega claimed congressmen knew that "they were the simple administrators of foreign companies." He added, "these imperialists no longer send us Colonels, nor Captains General, nor Viceroys . . . but these powerful enterprises make decisions about the economy and political life of each South American nation."[148] This kind of rhetoric had become broadly acceptable. By the mid-1930s, the attitude that Chile was a neocolonial appendage of U.S. capital was widespread.

Teachers were an essential link between working-class and middle-class radicalism. Although teachers were most often members of the Radical Party, they also figured prominently among the Communists, the Socialist parties, and the AGECh. They had their own professional associations, dating from 1915, and they were also found in the membership of the Republican Militia and the Nacis. They were the first middle-class group to confront the Alessandri administration.

In November 1932, a teacher earned about 500 pesos a month—at the very bottom of the *empleado* class and often less than a skilled laborer in the mines and railroads. All public school teachers, many of them women, were under the administration of the Minister of Education. When teachers demanded a 100 percent wage increase, the government promised to study the problem. The inaction led to a series of strikes and, in Santiago and Valparaiso, the striking teachers tried to get the tramway and railway workers to join them. At the height of the effort, teachers held their first national convention, in Concepción on January 18-19, 1933. When they marched with red banners and singing the International, the government reacted by banning all their meetings. Police persecution forced them into clandestine gatherings in boarding houses and union halls. The Minister of Education fired 78 teachers who had organized the convention and, within a few days, went through the ranks of declared delegates and dismissed another 120.[149] The Radical Party denounced the action, and the teachers became economic martyrs. Far from backing away, the government continued its harassment, demanding loyalty from students in the normal schools, insisting provincial teachers stay out of politics, and urging the Church hierarchy to police its schools for any "subversion."[150]

The conduct of various parties in the 1930s had as much to do with the middle class as it did with labor. Leaders of the Radical Party stayed with a program that could attract both; they demanded more public works, greater investment in social services and education, and higher taxes on foreign enterprises. Communists and the Socialists were differentiated by their acceptance or rejection of Moscow's leadership; tactically, however, the major difference was how each viewed the middle class. The Communists were a minority even within the left. But they were tenacious, and could point to the Soviet Union as proof that their ideas were viable. Their major social base in the 1920s had been the FOCh [the labor federation]. They ran its headquarters, but they had never controlled the separate unions that created it. The FOCh, in turn, was limited in strength to a few, important sectors, in particular, construction workers and nitrate miners. But it was weak in other key areas, for example, among the copper miners and the dock workers. These were precisely the sectors that became more important as Chile moved away from the nitrate era and toward an economy based on copper. In a series of key strikes that broke out at El Teniente and the port of San Antonio, where the ore from that mine was exported, the Communists were conspicuously unimportant.[151] Additionally, the Communists made almost no effort to appeal to the middle class and often sounded as though they resented its existence.

The Socialists, with a middle-class leadership, pushed hard on consumer issues. However, in the 1930s, they were in the process of building their labor following. One scholar of the party argues that in the early 1930s, about 75 percent of its members were middle class and 25 percent were working class; by the 1940s, the ratio was 55 to 45 percent.[152] Their greatest asset in appealing to workers was Marmaduke Grove. Although police reports indicate that Socialists were spied on, they do not appear as labor activists. In a meeting of the Socialist Central Committee in October 1934, the party leader, César Godoy, proposed labor "shock brigades" as a means of attacking the government. The record of the discussion indicates that the committee was unsure how the rank and file might react; no one else supported the idea. The Central Committee was divided by suspicion and jealousy; apparently there were too many chiefs for so few followers. The police report on the meeting concluded that all the Party's activities seemed limited "now that the masses don't respond."[153]

Organizations appealing to labor or to the middle class were extremely fluid, in terms of tactics and affiliations. There were more political entrepreneurs than the public arena could absorb. Conflicts over ideology often reflected the intensity of competition for a few positions of authority, as head of a party, a union, or holder of even a minor office. Each leader tried to position himself as a mediator of interests. Groups allied with one another and divided as leaders looked for the opportunity to represent a force that had to be given consideration in the public eye and from the government. The FOCh and the railroad workers had split in the 1920s; now they looked for ways to regroup. The Confederation of Labor had once banned the anarchists; in the early 1930s, they reconsidered and dropped the ban.[154] The FOCh, in the 1920s, had viewed petitioning the government as a pointless exercise; in the 1930s, it tried to become the central clearing house of labor petitions to Alessandri's administration.[155] There were, of course, internal contests: unions divided along partisan lines and around personalities. During the metal workers strike in 1934, leaders continued to debate the goals even after the police had broken its ranks and taken the union fund. The debate ended with one faction, accused of *fochismo*, walking out, and as it did, accusing the other of treason and bourgeois behavior.[156]

In all of this, a public space was opening and strikes, as they had been in the 1920s, were still *the* embodiment of class confrontation. While Communists supported strikes indiscriminately and Socialists supported them most of the time, it is impossible to attribute the strike movement to any given party or organization. The government listed strikes as legal or illegal, and obviously wanted to discredit most of them. The number (see Graph 5.2) of illegal often exceeded the legal strikes. However, it is important to remember two facts in all of this: the government under counted all strikes and often declared a strike illegal if the legal union involved had not followed all the rules governing arbitration. Moreover, the radicalism of this era is easily obscured in the numbers, for the government's statistics deliberately omitted such militant behavior as rent strikes, boycotts, demonstrations, and threats to riot that often accompanied major strikes. Limited as these statistics are, they do indicate a steady rise in militancy through the 1930s and then an explosion in the 1940s.

The countryside was not a site of contestation. The major exception to this rule, Ranquil, is discussed below. Rural unionization was marginalized even within the labor movement. There was only one figure identified with efforts to organize inquilinos in this period: Emilio Zapata, a Trotskyist, who after 1933 was a deputy in Congress. Zapata came from the urban working poor. A self-educated man with a swarthy complexion, he proved to be an honest and hard-working congressman. He thought of Chile as "a semi-Yankee colony." But most of his efforts were limited to the haciendas near the capital.[157] In 1935, Zapata created the National Defense League of Poor Farmers [Liga Nacional de Defensa de Campesinos Pobres].[158] But Zapata was an isolated figure, who suffered ostracism within the labor movement and persecution from the government.

Within the cities, repression proved ineffective.[159] Once it had lost its emergency powers and an urban economic recovery was underway, the Alessandri administration harassed but hesitated to smash labor. Among other reasons, the president did not want to lose all hope of attracting the Radical Party. By 1935, legally recognized unions were forming umbrella organizations, the most notable was the Chilean

Graph 5.2: Number of Workers in Strikes, 1932-1948

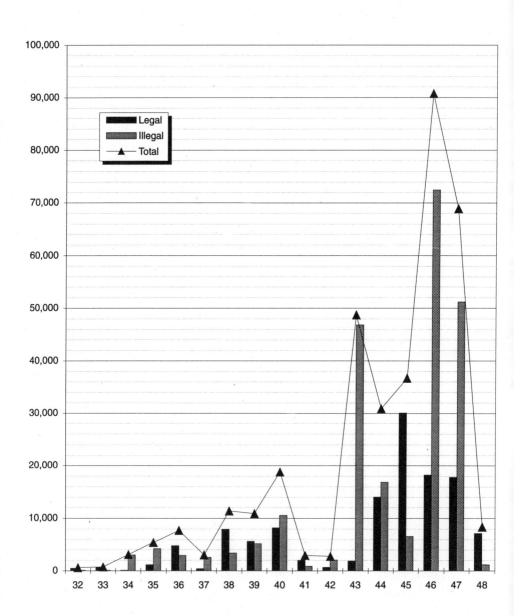

Source: *Anuario estadístico*, 1955.

National Confederation of Syndicates or CNS [Confederación Nacional de Sindicatos de Chile], which started in Valparaiso.

In order to prevent a coalescence of labor and middle-class interests, Alessandri decided to entice the Radicals back into his government in August 1935. Increased government funding gave the president more jobs to offer in return for cooperation. Alessandri's move divided his administration. He alienated the right within his cabinet and Congress. Ross saw it as a blow to his own presidential ambitions. He told the British Ambassador that he would have preferred a dictatorship and "the use of a thick stick." He thought the country was obviously unfit for democracy and concluded, "in order to deal in [the] future with finance I must have control of the streets."[160] Alessandri's courtship also divided the Radicals. The Santiago faction wanted nothing to do with Alessandri, let alone Ross. But in the south, party members were frightened by social changes and wanted a crack down on disorder.[161] To hold the party together, the Radical leadership emphasized the overriding importance of the 1937 congressional election. If the party did not cooperate with Alessandri, it would have too little control over the election registers to prevent electoral disaster.[162] Success in the congressional elections offered the possibility of capturing enough seats in Congress and pressuring Alessandri for enough positions in the cabinet to block Ross' moves toward the presidency.

***

In dealing with the relation of the labor militancy and the middle class, we must recall the observations of Jürgen Habermas on the creation of a "public sphere." Two events dramatized the rising conflict between social radicals and the government—and fueled public outrage at the latter's conduct. Neither event began with the middle class, but in each, a provincial conflict was translated by public reaction, especially in Santiago, into a portrait of official callousness and so directly shaped middle-class sentiment. The first was a rural uprising at Ranquil, an event that seemed removed from any labor association but confirmed the opinion within the Radical Party and leftist circles that Alessandri had abandoned all concern for working Chileans. The second, the railroad strike of 1936, was a catalyst in the formation of the Popular Front and the collapse of Alessandri's attempt to include the Radical Party in his government.

Ranquil is in the southern, frigid zone of the Bío-Bío River; the nearest city, Temuco, is 75 miles away. The uprising stemmed from the colonization program to reduce unemployment. Many of the colonists, who were farming and panning for gold, were displaced nitrate miners. They became embroiled with the owner of a large estate over control of their farms. The landlord prevailed and a southern court, in late June 1934, ordered the national police to remove fifty small holders from the estate. What happened next is unclear. The government claimed that Juan Leiva Tapía, a Peruvian who had worked in the Santiago Communist Party, turned up at Ranquil, recruited one thousand followers, and went on a series of raids. Leiva Tapía's forces, in this version, sacked estate stores, stole gold, and took women hostage. Various accounts agree that the small holders recruited gold miners and railroad workers into their ranks, and that they killed some laborers who refused to join them. The government sent one hundred carabineros with rifles and machine guns to Ranquil. After a gun battle on June 30, Leiva Tapía and at least twenty others, including women and children, were dead.[163] Some reports claimed that the police killed sixty or more.[164] Until the 1960s, this was Chile's largest rural uprising.[165]

The government used it as an excuse to raid the Communist Party headquarters in Santiago, close the left-wing newspaper, *La Opinión*, threaten the Socialists, and carry out widespread arrests.[166] The uprising came as a surprise to nearly everyone—the left included. No union movement or party faction had been organizing the gold panners or any other group in that part of the countryside. In his memoirs, the leader of the Communist Party, Elías Lafertte, is circumspect about the entire episode. Lafertte describes his former assistant and traveling companion, Leiva Tapía, as a young *campesino*, who had helped him flee to Montevideo the previous year. He illustrates Leiva Tapía's militancy and self-importance, by recounting how the firebrand had shouted at one provincial meeting, "I'm here to officially seal the worker-peasant alliance!" Lafertte says nothing about the uprising at Ranquil, however, except to lament his colleague's death.[167] Ranquil had a far greater impact on urban politics than on rural life; the government's behavior linked it to repression of the left. It also aligned the government with landlord power at a time when the middle class was disgusted with the tax privileges and the ostentation of the rural elite.

The railroad strike began in the south-central, agricultural region on February 3, 1936. The heart of the strike was in Talca. The railroad workers were not a confrontational part of the labor movement. Their leader, Juan S. Solís, had been Chile's representative to the International Labor Organization of the League of Nations. There is no hint of militancy in his record. But the workers were facing another surge in the cost of living, compounded by the 5 percent sales tax that had just gone into effect.[168] Despite the government effort to recruit the Radical Party, the specter of a strike that could tie up crop shipments, outrage the hacendados, and leave the cities without enough food, forced Alessandri's hand. The government called the strike "revolutionary," placed the state lines under military control, and immediately arrested Solís.[169] With the carabineros patrolling the lines, the strike began to wither by February 7. Communication among workers was poor. Just as the railroad workers were surrendering, the coal miners and the laborers at the military arsenal near Concepción walked out. The miners demanded a 60 percent wage increase.[170]

Alessandri waited until Congress adjourned on February 7, and that afternoon he declared martial law throughout the south-central zone. He warned that the Communists, as he had once predicted, were at Chile's door. The strike had "the cooperation of evil citizens who have endangered the political and economic rule of the Republic to accomplish their criminal ends." A suspension of civil liberties was necessary in order to avoid national "suicide."[171] To the public in Santiago, all this seemed unreal. Foreign observers noted that paranoia was general among the rich but that labor was not demonstrating or striking in the capital. (Upper-class hysteria had reached the point that people who favored divorce or birth control were being labeled communists.)[172] Having committed the troops, Alessandri could not back away. Congress refused his demand for extraordinary powers. And it refused again, even after Juan Antonio Ríos and a collection of Ibañistas were caught attempting to kidnap the head of the army.[173]

In the meantime, those Radicals who opposed joining the administration and favored creating an electoral alliance with the left won their party over. The Radical Youth called the president a "dictator."[174] In late March and early April, Santiaguinos heard details of the repression; they learned of summary arrests, military beatings, and the incarceration of up to two hundred men in each cell. The victims were as young as fourteen.[175] The Communist Party, influenced by the new Stalinist line, had been calling for a coalition of "anti-fascist" parties to form a Popular Front. Before the railroad strike, most of the Socialist Party was firmly opposed to the idea. They were afraid that the Radicals, whom they saw as "demo-bourgeois and prisoners of fear," would dominate such a coalition.[176] Now, the Socialists dropped all opposition. In April 1936, the parties that would make up the Popular Front backed a common candidate and won a by-election for the Senate. As an indication of how politics would obscure class, the Popular Front candidate was a Radical millionaire and landowner and his opponent a much more humble Democrat backed by the administration. The vote was close, 17 to 16 thousand. The seat represented a conservative zone hit by the strike, the provinces of Bío-Bío and Cautín.[177] Nonetheless, the administration had to face the fact that opposition parties might control the Senate when it reconvened.

Alessandri could not prevent an alignment of parties into opposing coalitions. On May 6, the Socialists, Communists, and Radicals formally constituted the Popular Front. The Conservative, Liberal, and splinter parties supporting the administration began calling for a National Front to oppose it.[178] Alessandri made one more effort to end the Front by appointing two Radicals to his cabinet. The party's directorate was furious and forced the two to resign in October.[179]

In December, the Radical Party Assembly reinforced its commitment to a left alliance based on the examples of France, where, it claimed a Popular Front had destroyed a "pre-fascist" administration, and of Spain, where a Front had "decisively beaten reactionaries." The party also called on the coalition to be an anti-imperialist association inspired by the Chinese struggle against Japan, the Brazilian National Liberation Alliance, and the Cárdenas administration in Mexico.[180] At Christmas, the National Confederation of Syndicates [CNS] also met, regrouped with the FOCh, and formed the Chilean Labor Confederation or CTCh. Center-left unions now had an umbrella organization. The Popular Front would soon incorporate the CTCh.[181]

A contest for Congress was well underway, and beyond it loomed the contest for the presidency in 1938, a contest all sides thought would be decisive.

Endnotes

For abbreviations used in notes, see Endnotes, Chapter 1.

1. Carlos Dávila, "Foreword," in George McBride, *Chile: Land and Society* (New York: American Geographical Society, 1936, reprinted Octagon Books, 1971). I have altered the translation, substituting *servant* for *man* since this was the meaning of the quotation.

2. For a discussion of the relation of labor to the Chilean bureaucracy, see Raúl Atria, "Tensiones políticas y crisis económica: el caso chileno, 1920-1938," *Estudios Sociales* 10:37 (3d trimester, 1983), 195-96.

3. Brian Loveman, *Struggle in the Countryside: Politics and Rural Labor in Chile, 1919-1973* (Bloomington, Indiana: University of Indiana Press, 1976); Loveman, *Chile: the Legacy of Hispanic Capitalism*, 239-44; and Paul W. Drake, *Socialism and Populism in Chile* (Chicago: University of Illinois Press, 1978), chaps. 6 and 7.

4. Drake, op. cit., 180.

5. Chile. Dirección General de Estadística, *Resultados del XX Censo de la Población efectuado el 27 de noviembre de 1930* (Santiago: Imp. Universo, 1931), general data in vol. 1.

6. Robert McCaa, *Marriage and Fertility in Chile: Demographic Turning Points in the Petorca Valley, 1840-1976* (Boulder, Colorado: Westview Press, 1983), 46-47, 68.

7. Cited in RG 59: 825.5018/9, Dow, no. 180, 13 Aug. 1935.

8. Cited in Chile. Diputados, *Boletín de sesiones ordinarios*, Dip. Humberto Mardones, V., Aug. 1935, 1924-25, and RG 59: 825.502/12, Dow, no. 102, 24 July 1935.

9. McCaa, op. cit., 67, 118.

10. Between 1935 and 1940, the export draft rate hovered around 19.3 pesos per U.S. dollar. RG 165: MID 2610-66/120, Wooten, 5 June 1930; and RG 165: MID 2610-66/208, Weeks, 26 Feb. 1936.

11. RG 151: Commerce Dept., Bureau of Foreign and Domestic Commerce, Commercial Attaches, Santiago, Bohan, Special Report, no. 16, 4 Jan. 1940.

12. RG 165: MID 2610-66/208, Weeks, 26 Feb. 1936.

13. Chile. Dirección General de Estadística, *Censo de agricultura, 1935-36* (Santiago: 1938), 125, 248, 268.

14. *La Opinión*, 18 Dec. 1935, article by Guillermo Piedrabuena.

15. RG 59: 825.50/24 Culbertson, no. 1148, 27 Apr. 1932.

16. McBride, op. cit.

17. Brian Loveman, *El campesino chileno le escribe a su excelencia* (Santiago: ICIRA, 1971).

18. RG 59: 825.61/17, Milliken, 6 May 1939.

19. RG 59: 825.50/24 Culbertson, no. 1148, 27 Apr. 1932, enclosure no. 2, "Recommendations to Solve Agriculture Crisis in Chile," McLain, 14 Mar. 1932, citing data in report of Chilean Agricultural Ministry issued Feb. 1932; and *La Opinión*, 18 Dec. 1935, article by Guillermo Piedrabuena.

20. Chile. Interior, v. 8945 (1935), Prov. 11671, Gobernación de Yungay, 7 July 1935.

21. Macarena Mack, Paulina Matta, and Ximena Valdés Subercaseaux, *Los trabajos de las mujeres entre el campo y la ciudad, 1920-1982* (Santiago: CEDEM, Centro de Estudios de la Mujer, 1986), 15. The work consists of a moving series of interviews of working women.

22. RG 165: MID 2008-154/1, Wooten, no. 554, 24 July 1930.

23. Arnold J. Bauer, *Chilean Rural Society*, emphasizes the importance of changing market conditions to changes in rural labor.

24. *Censo de agricultura, 1935-36*, 34, 265, 284, 498; Arnold J. Bauer and Ann Hagerman Johnson, "Land and Labour in rural Chile, 1850-1935," in Kenneth Duncan and Ian Rutledge, eds., *Land and Labour in Latin America*, 83-100; and on the issue of inquilino impoverishment, see also Cristóbal Kay, "The Development of the Chilean *hacienda* system, 1850-1973," in the same volume, 114-15.

25. In addition to Loveman, *El campesino chileno*, see Ximena Valdés Subercaseaux, *Mujer, trabajo, y medio ambiente: los nudos de la modernización agraria* (Santiago: CEDEM, Centro de Estudios para el Desarrollo de la Mujer, 1992), by the 1950s, women had almost disappeared as inquilinos, 32. On the literature of family life, Ximena Valdés Subercaseaux, Loreto Rebolledo G., Angélica Willson A., *Masculino y femenino en la hacienda chilena del siglo XX* (Santiago: FONDART-CEDEM, Fondo de Desarrollo de la Cultura y las Artes, Min. de Educación, and Centro de Estudios para el Desarrollo de la Mujer, 1995), 91-116.

26. Chile. Diputados, *Boletín de Sesiones Extraordinarios*, 23 Nov. 1937, Exposición de la Unión de Profesores de Chile, 104-12.

27. RG 59: 825.42/41, Milliken, no. 23, 6 Apr. 1936, and 825.42/42, Milliken, no. 34, 21 Apr. 1936. See also Amanda Labarca H., "La educación en Chile," in Humberto Fuenzalida et al., *Chile: geografía*, 88.

28. RG 59: 825.6352/46, Dow, no. 161, 16 Oct. 1936, "Copper Industry in Chile," 13; and 825.5041/10, Faust, no. 159, 13 Oct. 1936.

29. Muñoz G., *Crecimiento industrial de Chile*, cuadro V-4, 194.

30. RG 59: 825.504/104, Dow, 6 Feb. 1935.

31. RG 59: 825.5041/10, Faust, op. cit.

32. *La Opinión*, 2 Feb. 1935, and 11 June 1936.

33. Chile. Diputados, *Boletín de sesiones ordinarios*, Dip. Emilio Zapata, 18 July 1939, 1295, and July 1940, Gustavo Rosales G., 1397-98.

34. Chile. Interior, v. 8663 (1934), Partido Demócrata, Iquique, 28 Feb. 1933; Chile. Diputados. *Boletín de sesiones ordinarios*, 29 May 1933, Dip. Martínez Montt reporting on trip to Talcahuano and Concepción, 161.

35. Chile. Interior, v. 8373 (1933), Prov. 541, Int. de Antofagasta, 6 Nov. 1933.

36. Chile. Interior, v. 8663 (1934), Antofagasta telegram, 15 Mar. 1933.

37. *La Opinión*, 26 Feb. 1935.

38. FO 371-15825 (A4207/86/9), Thompson, 2 June 1932.

39. RG 59: 825.52/15, Bowman, 28 Dec. 1932; and 825.52/25 Colonia Agricola Catemu/1, Frost, no. 827, enclosure no. 19, Aug. 1939.

40. RG 59: 825.6341/9, McLain, 23 Jan. 1933.

41. Chile. Fomento (1932), Oficios, v. 702, no. 6, memo, Financiamiento Lavaderos de Oro, 25 Aug. 1932, and Fomento (1939), Oficios, v. 815, no. 3, Jorge L. Bravo, Jefe Lavaderos de Oro al Min. de Fomento, 9 Jan. 1933 [the document was misfiled].

42. Chile. Fomento (1933), Oficios, v. 813, no. 1, Min. de Fomento al Administrator de la Caja de Seguro Obrero, 25 Feb. 1933, no. 257, citing report of Consejo de Defensa Fiscal; Fomento (1939), Oficios v. 815, no. 3, Min. de Fomento al Min. de Hacienda, 17 Apr. 1933, no. 481; Fomento (1933), Oficios, v. 815, no. 3; and Min. de Fomento al Jefatura de Lavaderos de Oro, 17 Apr. 1933, no. 482, cites Min. de Trabajo, Oficio no. 556 of 7 Apr., examples of hiring advertisements in *La Nación* (Santiago), 30 Jan. 1933; and Chile. Diputados, *Boletín de sesiones ordinarios*, Dip. Carlos Alberto Martínez (Socialist), 19 June 1933, 633.

43. *La jefatura de lavaderos de Oro (Su creación, organización administrativa y funcionamiento)* (Santiago: Dirección General de Prisiones, 1943), 60-63.

44. RG 84: Post Records 600 (Valparaiso, 1934), Henry to Dow, 1 Mar. 1934.

45. Chile. Interior, v. 9498 (1937), Servicios de Cesantia. Memoria Anual, 1936, Jan. 1937; and on bureaucratic behavior, see RG 59: 825.00/804, Chile-American Association Confidential Report no. 16, Apr. 1933.

46. FO 371/18669 (A2358/446/9), R.C. Michell, 25 Feb. 1935.

47. Figures from 1930 census.

48. By another count, there were 40. France-MAE, Chili, v. 9, 21 Dept. 1932, Report of M. Lorion, Attache; and RG 165: MID 2657-0-151/7, Wooten, no. 1513, 19 Nov. 1932.

49. Chile. Interior, (1934), Servicios de Investigaciones, Actividades Revolucionarias, 19 June 1934; FO 371-18664 (A7289/11/9), V. Cavendish-Bentinck, 12 Aug. 1935; and Chile. Colección Pedro Aguirre Cerda. v. 47 (1936), Fs. 141. Carlos Schurman R., Dip. Rio Bueno, 19 Aug. 1936.

50. RG 59: 825.00-Gen Cond/61, Culbertson, no. 1493, 3 July 1933.

51. Ricardo Boizard, *Patios Interiores*, 70-72.

52. RG 59: 825.00/845, Sevier, no. 98, 4 May 1934.

53. *La Nación* (Santiago), 3 and 7 Jan. 1933.

54. Julio César Jobet, *El partido socialista de Chile* (Santiago: Editorial Prenso Latinoamerica, S.A., 1971), 1:34-61; and Drake, op. cit., 167-73.

55. RG 59: 825.00B/20, Culbertson, no. 1130, 30 Mar. 1932, report by Norweb on "Communism in Chile"; 825.00B/21, Culbertson, no. 1138, 12 Apr. 1932; and 825.00B/20, Francis White to Culbertson, 6 July 1932, enclosed report, "The Moscow-Directed Communist Movement in Chile."

56. FO 371/18665 (A8420/11/9), V. Cavendish-Bentinck, 4 Sept. 1935; France-MAE, Chili. v. 11, 4 Sept. 1935, enclosure of Attaché Militaire: H-R. de Boyve, 18 Sept. 1935.

57. Manuel Caballero, *Latin America and the Comintern, 1919-1943* (London: Cambridge University Press, 1986), 46, 104-105.

58. FO 371-18664 (A3643/11/9), R.C. Michell, 9 Apr. 1935.

59. Chile. Interior, 8373 (1933), Prov. 427, Jefe de la Zona Norte, Sub-prefecto de Investigaciones.

60. RG 59: 825.00B/20, Culbertson, no. 1130, 30 Mar. 1932, report by Norweb on "Communism in Chile."

61. RG 59: 825.00/975, Philip, no. 507, 17 Feb. 1937.

62. Robert J. Alexander, *Arturo Alessandri: A Biography* (New Brunswick, NJ: Rutgers University Latin American Institute, University Microfilms International, 1977), 2:494ff.

63. Ibid.

64. For a different interpretation, see Frederick M. Nunn, *The military in Chilean History: essays on civil-military relations, 1810-1973* (Albuquerque: University of New Mexico Press, 1976), 175.

65. *Hoy*, 30 Dec. 1932; RG 165: MID 2008-150/21, Wooten, no. 1526, 6 Dec. 1932; MID 2008-150/22, Wooten, no. 1544, 27 Dec. 1932; MID 2008-172/1, Weeks, no. 1715, 11 July 1933; and MID 2008-141/7, Weeks, no. 1791, 18 Oct. 1933.

66. RG 59: 825.00-Revs/242, Philip, no. 126, 2 Mar. 1936.

67. The quote is from RG 59: 825.00/805, Wooten, no. 1661, 29 Apr. 1933. See also 825.00-Gen Cond/63, Norweb, no. 1531, 5 Sept. 1933; and FO 371-17508 (A3028/3028/9), Sir R. Michell to Sir John Simon, 16 Feb. 1934, "Annual Report, 1933."

68. Chile. Interior, v. 8666 (1934), Prov. 6775, Servicio de Investigaciones, 17 July 1933.

69. Cited in RG 59: 825.6374/1236, Chile-America Assoc., General Review Chilean Affairs, Apr. 1934; translation slightly altered for style.

70. RG 59: 825.00/839, Hal Sevier, no. 84, 10 Apr. 1934.

71. Thomas E. Skidmore notes that in 1920, before Alessandri's election was affirmed by a special tribunal, the right unleashed the Ligas Patrióticas on his followers and known anarchists. Skidmore, "Workers and Soldiers: Urban Labor Movements and Elite Responses in Twentieth-Century Latin America," in Virginia Bernard, ed., *Elites, Masses, and Modernization in Latin America, 1850-1930* (Austin: University of Texas Press, 1979), 106.

72. Verónica Valdivia Ortiz de Zárate, *La milicia republicana. Los civiles en armas. 1932-1936* (Santiago: Dirección de Bibliotecas Archivos y Museos. Centro de Investigaciones Diego Barros Arana, 1992), 14. I had written my own account of the militias before encountering Valdivia's excellent work. Hers relies heavily on newspapers, and she had access to the militia's own bulletin.

73. Carlos Sáez Morales, *Recuerdos de un soldado* 2:37-39.

74. RG 59: 825.00-Revs/48, Wooten, no. 1083, 3 Sept. 1931.

75. Valdivia Ortiz de Zárate, op. cit., 19.

76. *New York Times*, 5 June 1932. On civic guard in mutiny, see Sater, "The Abortive Kronstadt," 248.

77. Ricardo Donoso, *Alessandri: Agitador y Demoledor* (Mexico: Fondo de Cultura, 1954), 2:128; Sáez M., op. cit., 3:308-309.

78. See the list in *La Opinión*, 13 Nov. 1932.

79. Chile. Colección Pedro Aguirre Cerda. v. 47 (1936), Fs. 198. Adolfo Oettinger, 9 Oct. 1936; FO 371-17508 (A 3028/3028/9), Sir R. Michell to Sir John Simon, 16 Feb. 1934, "Annual Report, 1933"; RG 165, MID 2008-171/1,

Wooten, no. 1603, 28 Feb. 1933; RG 59: 825.00/803, Culbertson, no. 1453, 10 May 1933; France-MAE, Chili. v. 10, Capt. H. Siméon, Attaché Militaire, 8 May, 1933; Nunn, op. cit., 228-29; and Fernando Pinto Lagarrigue, *Crónica política del siglo XX: desde Errázuriz Echaurren hasta Alessandri Palma* (Santiago: Editorial Orbe, 1972), 226.

80. *Boletín informativo de la milicia republicana*, nos. 5 and 8 (1934), cited in Valdivia Ortiz de Zárate, op. cit., 26.

81. RG 151: Commerce Dept., Bureau of Foreign and Domestic Commerce, Commercial Attaches, Santiago, Ackerman Weekly Report, no. 45, 8 May 1933.

82. RG 165: MID 2008-171/2, Wooten, no. 1667, 8 May 1933.

83. Chile. Colección Pedro Aguirre Cerda. v. 47 (1936), Fs. 198. Adolfo Oettinger, 9 Oct. 1936. Writing from Valdivia Ortiz de Zárate.

84. FO 371-16567, A4010/73/9, Chilton, 10 May 1933; and France-MAE, Chili. v. 10, 2 June 1933.

85. Chile. Interior, v. 8373 (1933), Prov. 517, Carabineros, 22 July 1933.

86. RG 165: MID 2008-171/1, Wooten, no. 1603, 28 Feb. 1933; FO 371-17509 (A5826/5826/9), L.I. Crawford, Manager of Imperial Chemical Industries, 27 Apr. 1934, enclosure of monthly report, France-MAE, Chili, v. 10, 2 June 1933.

87. Membership must also have varied widely over time, see in addition to the notes above, France-MAE, Chili, 18 Oct. 1934; and FO 371-17507, A8470/230/9, R.C. Michell, 16 Oct. 1934.

88. RG 165: MID 2008-171/5, Weeks, no. 1772, 25 Sept. 1933. See also France-MAE, Chili. v. 10, Capt. H. Semeon, Attaché Militaire, 6 Dec. 1933. See also Valdivia Ortiz de Zárate, op. cit., 36, diagram on 37.

89. Quoted in RG 165: MID 2008-171/4, Wooten, no. 1765, 6 Sept. 1932, translation modified for clarity; and France-MAE, Chili. v. 10, 13 Sept. 1933.

90. RG 59: 825.00/848, Sever, no. 105, 15 May 1934.

91. FO 371-16568, A9439/73/9, Thompson, 13 Dec. 1933.

92. RG 165: MID 2008-175/1, Weeks, no. 1830, 20 Dec. 1933.

93. Valdivia Ortiz de Zárate, op. cit., 77, 92.

94. FO 371-17507, A230/230/9, Thompson, 8 Jan. 1934; and RG 165: MID 2008-171/9, Weeks, no. 2062, 20 Dec. 1934.

95. RG 59: 825.00/792, Chile-American Association, Confidential Report no. 13, Jan. 1933.

96. FO 371-17509 (A5826/5826/9), op. cit. and *El Mercurio*, 14 Oct. 1934.

97. FO 371/18664 (A6949/11/9), Cavendish-Bentinck, 29 July 1935.

98. RG 165: MID 2008-171/10, Weeks, no. 2294, 21 July 1936.

99. Chile. Interior, (1934), Servicios de Investigaciones, Actividades Revolucionarias, 19 June 1934.

100. Chile. Interior, (1934), Ruz Gomez memo: Sociedades, no. 129, 9 May 1934.

101. Chile. Interior, v. 9506 (1937), Prov. 12661, Int. de Malleco, 22 Nov. 1937.

102. H.E. Bicheno, "Anti-Parliamentary Themes in Chilean History," *Government and Opposition* 7, no. 3 (Summer 1972), 373; and Mario Sznajder, "A Case of Non-European Fascism: Chilean National Socialism in the 1930s," *Journal of Contemporary History* 28 (1993), 269-70.

103. Aside from the sources in the previous note, there is a study by Michael Potashnik, "Nacismo: National Socialism in Chile, 1932-1938," (Ph.D. diss., University of California Los Angeles, 1974), especially 125-70, which provides a rosy portrait of this movement. Its inaccuracies come from relying heavily on the memoirs of Carlos Keller R., *La eterna crisis chilena* (Santiago: Nascimento, 1931), 146-76. Keller was a Naci intellectual. Another apologia, but important for its extensive use of newspapers and interviews of the era, is by the nephew of González von Marées, Rodrigo Alliende González, *El jefe: la vida de Jorge González von Marées* (Santiago: Ediciones Los Castaños, 1990). The best new work is also sympathetic to the movement, is the already cited Sznajder, "A Case of Non-European Fascism."

104. RG 59: (decimal number missing), Naval Attache's report, 104-400, 28 Aug. 1933.

105. RG 59: 825.42/51, Armour, no. 162, 23 July 1938, enclosure no. 5, interview with William L.F. Horsey, manager United Press, 18 July 1938. Horsey was an Englishman who had just returned from southern Chile.

106. Sznajder, op. cit., 271.

107. RG 165: MID 2657-0-151/16, Weeks, no. 1769, 22 Sept. 1933; Chile. Diputados, *Boletín de sesiones ordinarios*, 4 Sept. 1933, 2278-97.

108. FO 371-20620 (A3136/3136/9), H.H. Cassells, Valparaiso, 15 Mar. 1937.

109. Quoted in Potashnik, "Nacismo: National Socialism in Chile," 70; the declaration was made in July 1932.

110. Chile. Interior, v. 8374 (1933), Prov. 4778, Int. of Ñuble, report of 17 Oct. 1933; and (1934), Ruz Gomez memo: Sociedades, no. 134, 14 May 1934.

111. "Reportaje Conservador, al jefe del nacismo" (Santiago: ca. 1936).

112. Chile. Interior, (1934), Ruz Gomez memo: Sociedades, no. 358, 24 Dec. 1934.

113. Potashnik, "Nacismo," 196, 201; I believe Potashnik overstates the social welfare message of the Nacis. See González von Marées' comments further along in the text. Chile. Interior, v. 8666 (1934), Prov. 6775, memo: Servicio de Investigadores, 3 Sept. 1934.

114. Carlos Keller R., *La locura de Juan Bernales* (Santiago: Editorial Sociedad Amigos del Libro, 1949), 198-99. This novel portrays the movement up to 1938. Alliende González emphasizes this idealism as well in, *El jefe*, 81; he quotes González von Marées' written message to his wife, "In short, being a Naci is honor and sacrifice!"

115. Chile. Interior, (1934), Diego Ruz Gomez memo: Sociedades, no. 365, 31 Dec. 1934.

116. Chile. Interior, (1934), Diego Ruz Gomez memo: Sociedades, no. 358, 24 Dec. 1934.

117. RG 165: MID 2657-0-151/6, op. cit., and FO 371-17508 (A3028/3028/9), Sir R. Michell to Sir John Simon, 16 Feb. 1934, "Annual Report, 1934."

118. Sznajder, op. cit., 272.

119. RG 59: 825.00/858, Chile-American Association, Confidential Report no. 28, July 1934; and 825.6374/1237, Chile-American Association, Inc. Monthly Bulletin, Confidential Report no. 27, June 1934; FO 371-17508, Sir R. Michell to Sir John Simon, 9 Feb. 1934, "List of Leading Personalities in Chile"; *La Opinión*, 26 Jan. 1935 and 15 May 1935; and Chile. Diputados, *Boletín de sesiones ordinarios*, Dip. José Vega, 14 July 1936, 1723.

120. See, for example, what happened to Senator Matte, Chile. Diputados, *Boletín de sesiones ordinarios*, 12 June 1933; and RG 59: 825.00-Gen Cond/66, Hal Sevier, no. 10, 4 Dec. 1933.

121. Chile. Diputados, *Boletín de sesiones ordinarios*, José Vega, 22 July 1936, 1918-19, and Luis Cabrera, Oficio no. 854, 29 July 1936, 2112-13.

122. Alan Angell, *Politics and the Labour Movement in Chile* (London: Oxford University Press for the Royal Institute of International Affairs, 1972), especially chaps. 5 and 6; and Julio Faúndez, *Marxism and Democracy in Chile: From 1932 to the fall of Allende* (New Haven: Yale University Press, 1988), 34-37, 78-79. See also Drake, op. cit., and Jobet, op. cit. For a work on labor alone, see Jorge Rojas Flores, *El sindicalismo y el estado en Chile (1924-1936)* (Santiago: Colección Nuevo Siglo, 1986).

123. Standard surveys of the subject are Moisés Poblete Troncoso and Ben G. Burnett, *The Rise of the Latin American Labor Movement* (New York: Bookman Associates, 1960); Alexander, *Labor Relations in Argentina, Brazil and Chile* (New York: McGraw-Hill Book Co., 1962); Victor Alba, *Politics and the Labor Movement in Latin America* (Stanford: Stanford University Press, 1968); Hobart Spalding Jr., *Organized Labor in Latin America: Studies of*

Workers in Dependent Societies (New York: New York University Press, 1977); Skidmore, op. cit.; and Charles Bergquist, *Labor in Latin America: Comparative Essays on Chile, Argentina, Venezuela, and Colombia* (Stanford: Stanford University Press, 1986).

124. Jaime García Covarrubias, *El partido radical y la clase media: la relación de intereses entre 1888 y 1938* (Santiago: Editorial Andres Bello, 1990), 110-15, argues the Radical Party saw itself as the middle-class movement, especially in its support of literacy; but he does not analyze the other parties and movements that the middle class also supported.

125. Ruth Berins Collier and David Collier, *Shaping the Political Arena: Critical Junctures, the Labor Movement, and Regime Dynamics in Latin America* (Princeton: Princeton University Press, 1991).

126. Rojas Flores, Alfonso Murua Olguin, and Gonzalo Rojas Flores, *La historia de los obreros de la construcción* (Santiago: Programa de Economía del Trabajo, 1993), 47-49.

127. Crisóstomo Pizarro, *La huelga obrera en Chile, 1890-1970* (Santiago: Ediciones Sur, 1971), 110-11, recounts the origins of the CTCH.

128. Amartya Sen, *Poverty and Famines: An Essay on Entitlement and Deprivation* (Oxford: Oxford University Press, 1981), 2; quote on 165.

129. Mancur Olson, *The Rise and Decline of Nations: Economic Growth, Stagflation, and Social Rigidities* (New Haven: Yale University Press, 1982), 201-202.

130. Chile. Fomento (1939), Oficios, v. 814, no. 2, Min. de Fomento al Secretario-Jefe de la Presidencia de la República, 24 Mar. 1933, no. 399, citing petition from Comité Unico de la Construcción (sent 3 Mar. 1933); Chile. Interior, v. 8372 (1933), Prov. 15634, Pliego de Peticiones, 13 Oct. 1933; and *La Nación*, 27 Jan. 1933. See also *La Opinión*, 1933-37, as examples the issues for 19 Jan., 7 Aug., and 11 Nov. 1933; other sources are detailed below in discussing specific strikes and other labor actions.

131. Asunción Lavrin, "Women, Feminism and Social Change in Argentina, Chile, and Uruguay, 1890-1940," in Donna Guy, Mary Karasch, and Asunción Lavrin, *Engendering Latin America*, vol. 3 (Lincoln: University of Nebraska Press, 1995), 15-26.

132. Antezana-Pernet, "Mobilizing Women in the Popular Front Era: Feminism, Class, and Politics in the Movimiento Pro-Emancipación de la Mujer Chilena [MEMCh]," (Ph.D. diss., University of California Irvine, 1996), 63, 128, and 150; and Karin Alejandra Rosemblatt, "Gendered Compromises: Political Cultures, Socialist Politics, and the State in Chile, 1920-1950" (Ph.D. diss., University of Wisconsin, 1996), 160-61.

133. Manuel Castells, *City, Class and Power*, Elizabeth Lebas, trans. (London: MacMillan Press, 1978), 19.

134. Rojas Flores, Murua Olguín, and Rojas Flores, op. cit., 42.

135. I draw this insight from a discussion of game theory, in Kerry C. Schott, *Policy, Power and Order: the Persistence of Economic Problems in Capitalist Societies* (New Haven: Yale University Press, 1984), 159.

136. For example, Mariana Aylwin Oyarzún et al., *Chile en el siglo XX* (Santiago: Emisión, Ltda, 1986), 66.

137. George Strawbridge, *Ibáñez and Alessandri: The Authoritarian Right and Democratic Left in Twentieth-Century Chile* (Buffalo: Special Studies Council on International Studies, State University of New York at Buffalo, Sept. 1971), 33; Chile. Interior, v. 9213 (1936), Prov. 4182, Min. de Salubridad Pública, memorándum sobre el proyecto de Reforma de la Ley de Empleados Particulares.

138. *La Opinión*, 15 Julio 1933.

139. RG 165: MID 2657-0-151/7, Wooten, no. 1513, 19 Nov. 1932; *La Opinión*, 25 Aug. 1933; 1 Aug. 1937.

140. Chile. Interior, (1932), Prov. 1279, Arriagada Valdivieso, 11 Aug. 1932; *La Opinión*, 12 June 1933.

141. *La Opinión*, 2 Mar. 1937.

142. BOLSA, B55, Valparaiso to London, 2 June 1936.

143. *La Opinión*, 25 Aug. 1933.

144. RG 59: 825.504/88, Culbertson, no. 1212, 27 July 1932; 825.00/823, Chile-American Association, Confidential Report no. 19, Nov. 1933; Chile. Fomento (1933), Oficios, v. 814, no. 2, Min. de Fomento al Min. de Trabajo, 10 Mar. 1933, no. 339, reporting complaints of Dirección General de Obras Públicas about labor inspectors; and Chile. Interior, v. 8665 (1934), Prov. 4214, Int. de Tarapacá, 19 Oct. 1933.

145. Chile. Interior, v. 8373 (1933), Prov. 442, Int. de Aconcagua, 10 Aug. 1933.

146. *La Opinión*, 25 Aug. 1933.

147. On the general issue of cost of living and food protests, Chile. Interior, (1934), Memorándum reservado, 21 Dec. 1934, v. 8665 (1934), Prov. 4298, Pamphlet of Communist Party, enclosure, v. 9236 (1936), Prov. 9855, Dirección General Carabineros de Chile, 7 Sept. 1936; and *La Opinión*, 12 Apr. 1937. On other issues, *La Opinión*, 10 Aug. and 17 Dec. 1935, 14 Jan. and 11 June 1936; 21 Mar. and 26 July 1937; RG 59: 825.00/960, Philip, no. 435, 12 Dec. 1936; and 825.51/925, Philip, no. 603, 19 May 1937.

148. Chile. Diputados, *Boletín de sesiones ordinarios*, José Vega, 4 June 1935, 318.

149. RG 59: 825.00-Gen Cond/54, Culbertson, no. 1322, 30 Nov. 1932; RG 165: MID 2657-0-137/23, Wooten, no. 1583, 25 Jan. 1933; and FO 371-17508 (A3028/3028/9), Sir R. Michell to Sir John Simon, 16 Feb. 1934, "Annual Report, 1933."

150. Chile. Interior, v. 9250 (1936), Min. de Educación, Escuela Normal de la Serena, and v. 9248 (1936), no. 174, Liceo de Hombres, Taltal, 30 Mar. 1936; Chile. Diputados, *Boletín de sesiones estraordinarios*, 1 Dec. 1937, Exposición Sindicato de Profesores Particulares, 381-85.

151. Chile. Interior, (1934), Servicios de Investigaciones, Memorándum reservado, 11 Nov. 1934. v. 8945 (1935), Prov. 11908. Int. de Antofagasta, 27 June 1934, v. 8643 (1934), Prov. 16781, Gobernación de San Antonio, and 17 Oct. 1934, v. 9248 (1936), no. 185, Gov. de San Antonio, 16 Mar. 1936; and *La Opinión*, 3 Sept. 1937.

152. Benny Pollack, "Class and Mass in the Chilean Socialist Party," in *Mobilization and Socialist Politics in Chile*, Benny Pollack, ed. (Liverpool: Centre for Latin-American Studies, Monograph Series, no. 9, 1980), 23.

153. Chile. Interior, (1934), Servicios de Investigaciones, Memorándum reservado, 9 Oct. 1934.

154. Chile. Fomento (1939), Oficios v. 815, no. 3, Min. de Fomento al Director General de los Ferrocarriles del Estado, 17 Apr. 1933, Confidencial no. 478, cites report from Min. del Interior; Rojas Flores, *El sindicalismo*, 71; and *La Opinión*, 10 June 1932.

155. Chile. Interior, (1934), Ruz Gomez, 2 Oct. 1934, and Interior, (1934), Ruz Gomez, Memorándum, Sociedades, no. 322, 19 Nov. 1934.

156. Chile. Interior, (1934), Ruz Gomez, Memorándum, Sociedades, no. 123, 3 May 1934.

157. See the excellent description by the conservative Boizard, op. cit., 9; and Chile. Diputados, *Boletín de sesiones ordinarios*, Emilio Zapata, 31 June 1933, 1790-99; and 8 Jan. 1934, 2340. See also Chile. Fomento (1936), Oficios v. 1039, no. 6, Min. de Fomento al President de la Camara de Diputados, no. 694, 30 Sept. 1935; and for secret police records, Chile. Interior, v. 9250 (1936), Oficio no. 96, Dirección de Investigaciones, Identificación y Pasaportes, Marked Confidential, 16 Mar. 1936; quote on colony, *Hoy*, 20 Oct. 1933.

158. Loveman, *Struggle on the Countryside*, 150-64.

159. For a farce about wiretapping, see *La Opinión*, 2 Apr. 1935.

160. FO 371-18664 (A7635/11/9), V. Cavendish-Bentinck telegram, 18 Aug. 1935.

161. Ibid., 12 Aug. 1935.

162. James Petras, *Politics and Social Forces in Chilean Development* (Berkeley: University of California Press, 1969), 121, incorrectly describes the entire setting. See Chile. Interior, v. 9248 (1936), no. 178, and *El Diario Ilustrado*, 5 Apr. 1935.

163. RG 59: 825.00/854, Robert M. Scotten, Counselor at Embassy, no. 140, 7 July 1934; 825.6374/1237, Chile-American Association, Inc. Monthly Bulletin, Confidential Report no. 27, June 1934; and FO 371-175-7 (A6236/239/9), R.C. Michell, 19 July 1934.

164. Chile. Diputados, *Boletín de sesiones ordinarios*, 13 July 1934, 1489ff.

165. Loveman, *Struggle in the Countryside*, 144, calls it the largest between 1919 and 1964. I cannot think of any other uprising on this scale between 1900-19.

166. FO 371-175-7 (A6236/239/9), R.C. Michell, 19 July 1934.

167. Elías Lafertte, *Vida de un comunista* (Santiago: Editorial Austral, 1971), 257-76, quote on 275.

168. RG 59: Chile 825.5045/67, Philip, no. 122, 27 Feb. 1936.

169. RG 59: 825.5045/2, Philip, no. 93, 4 Feb. 1936.

170. Ibid., no. 96, 8 Feb. 1936.

171. *El Mercurio*, 10 Feb. 1936.

172. France-MAE, Chili. v. 11, 21 Feb. 1936; BOLSA, B55, [W.C. Maycock] Valparaiso to London, 11 Feb. 1936. See also reports of 5 Feb. 1936 and B2/15, 1935-1936, W.C. Maycock to Chairman, Valparaiso, 13 Feb. 1936.

173. RG 59: 825.00-Revs/242, Philip, no. 126, 2 Mar. 1936; and 825.00/913, Philip, no. 139, 14 Mar. 1936.

174. *El Radical* (Valparaiso), 19 Feb. 1936, paper of Juventud Radical.

175. Chile. Diputados, *Boletín de sesiones estraordinarios*, 6 Apr. 1936, Dip. Rolando Merino R., 455.

176. Jobet, *El socialismo*, 34.

177. RG 59: 825.00/922, Philip, no. 196, 28 Apr. 1936.

178. RG 59: 825.00/924, Philip, no. 207, 9 May 1936.

179. Ibid., no. 334, 15 Sept. 1936; and 825.00/951, Philip, no. 376, 21 Oct. 1936.

180. *La Opinión*, 22 Dec. 1936.

181. RG 59: 825.504/160, Bowers, no. 4236, 21 Aug. 1942, report by Faust.

6

The 1938 Election and
The Popular Front

There is always a group of Radicals with the government, which I conserve like gold, in spite of the insistent complaints of rightist leaders who fight tenaciously with me to get rid of those Radicals, so that they can have a government which will intervene with blood and fire in the elections. They will never make me fall into such foolishness, but as you will understand, they bother me a great deal.

Arturo Alessandri to Agustín Edwards, 1938[1]

The union has refused all my good offices and overtures. I am convinced that it is headed by foreign agitators (presumably communists). The local union cannot possibly possess sufficient funds to carry on a prolonged strike, which it insists it will do. So it has to have received funds from elsewhere. If it strikes and it becomes necessary to machine gun ten, twenty, or three hundred of them, I shall not vacillate for one moment. If on Sunday at the election [to vote on the strike], a two-thirds majority of the laborers attempt to enter the polling place, I will station police to prevent their entry and there will be no legal strike. If they strike otherwise, they will be disturbing the public order and measures will be taken in accordance with the Law of Internal Security.

Carlos Souper M., Intendant of Antofagasta
(referring to the strike at "Chuquicamata,"
the Anaconda copper mine),
February 1938[2]

The political evolution of twentieth-century Chile is punctuated by a series of key presidential contests in 1920, 1938, 1964, and 1970. Each seemed to be about the enlargement of civil and social rights and economic opportunity, but each also involved an attempt by the privileged to retain economic and institutional prerogatives. Each contained a struggle over ideas, patterns of behavior, and institutions that was, in Gramsci's famous term, *a fight for hegemony*, that is, a conflict over the ruling social norms.[3]

With the exception of 1964, each presidential victor won with a minority coalition and had to face the entrenched hostility of the losers. Since presidential elections did not decide congressional majorities, each winner faced legislatures that blocked his agenda once in office. Each also had to contend with foreign control of the mining sector and a foreign presence in other areas of trade, finance, and manufacturing. The following narrative is about the 1938 election and an analysis of the effort by President Pedro Aguirre Cerda, head of the Popular Front, to turn his victory into a new direction for government. Aguirre Cerda's opponents viewed his victory as an apocalypse. A year after the election, the American travel essayist John Gunther interviewed "Rightists," who, "still talk of it like an unreal nightmare; they can't get over it. Moreover, they admit candidly why they did lose. They lost because they were ignorant of the temper of the country, egotistical, super confident, and greedy."[4] They had tried to buy the election and came close to succeeding.

In the 1938 contest, the electorate polarized and the opponents saw it as zero-sum game. The questions that dominated the election were those of distribution: Would foreign interests continue to run key sectors? Would there be any reform of land holding? Would the working people gain a better wage?

Alessandri had hoped, in 1936, that reincorporating the Radical Party into government and some changes in the patterns of patronage would sustain his agenda. The formation of the Popular Front ended that possibility. He always worked against the Front, and thought even at the last hour that he could recruit a core of Radical support. He reluctantly backed Gustavo Ross Santa María for the presidency, a man he felt was a poor candidate and, though he never publicly admitted it, would make a poor president. His apprehensions aside, he made every effort to help Ross but, in a moment of rage and fear, his administration's actions derailed the electoral train the right had put together. The

Popular Front won the election in reaction to a government massacre, which grew out of a putsch. Alessandri and Ross left the country after Aguirre Cerda won and their absence gave the new president greater public space and helped permit the changes that they had so bitterly opposed.

After the election, capitalists turned on the new government in Congress, in the press, and in foreign embassies. Aguirre Cerda's message was populist not socialist; but, like most populists, he frightened the wealthy.[5] Moreover, the timing seemed wrong. The examples of France and Spain that so inspired the formation of the Popular Front in 1936 had overwhelmingly negative connotations by late 1938.[6] Then an earthquake in the south gave the government a second opportunity to present its goals as a response to an emergency. Aguirre Cerda achieved some of his objectives but the costs of maintaining his coalition escalated with the impact of World War II and the consequences of government deficits. The Popular Front was a socially progressive administration built on naive economic assumptions and it set the stage for the dilemmas of populist administrations that followed.

The Critical Election

There were three major candidates in the 1938 presidential election.[7] Gustavo Ross Santa María reorganized the right around the old Liberal and Conservative parties. Carlos Ibáñez del Campo led a movement dominated by the Nacis [the MNS]. Pedro Aguirre Cerda was the Popular Front candidate, a Radical in alliance with the Socialists, the Communists, and the Chilean Labor Confederation [CTCh]. Ross clearly had the upper hand. With his superior funds and organization, he planned to buy victory. This was a style of vote-getting common until the coup of 1924. The landowners and principal figures of smaller towns would march their dependents to the polling booths, hand them cash, some wine, and a meat pie. During the few days required to count the ballots, they awaited the inevitable victory with a series of banquets.[8] Bribery decided the congressional elections of March 7, 1937, when 80 percent of the 475 thousand registered voters turned out. The right won 206 thousand votes, the reformers and the left, 148.9 thousand votes (40 percent). According to the Popular Front, the Conservative and Liberal parties spent 20 million pesos on that election.[9]

Three days after the congressional contest, Ross resigned as finance minister. He remained a public figure, running some errands for the administration, and he was still the president of the Nitrate and Iodine Sales Corporation.[10] He kept a hand in where it counted, negotiating, for example, with Allen Dulles who came from New York representing clients holding Chilean government bonds. (Dulles gained nothing but came away impressed with Ross.)[11] No mention of Ross' candidacy appeared in the press until March 1937; but he had the support of the right-wing party directorates.[12] The Liberal and Conservative parties held a joint convention in late April 1938, after the right had carried the municipal elections of April 3 with almost 60 percent of the vote.[13] Ross left his supporters to arrange his nomination while he went to Europe. His chief opponent in the Conservative Party withdrew a few days before its convention so that Ross' nomination was more a coronation than a victory. He heard the news while abroad and took his time returning, arriving to the welcome of a crowd of 15 thousand waiting at the airport on June 8, some five months before the presidential election.[14]

Ross and his political handlers knew better than to provoke his opposition in Santiago and Valparaiso. In the campaign, Ross held banquets and indoor rallies in the major cities, venturing outdoors only in the smaller towns. He campaigned in the south and never visited the northern mining provinces. His slogan was, "Order, Work, Production"; his song, "It is Ross we love."[15] The campaign was carefully staged from the rural assemblies of *guasos* [cowboys in elaborate regalia] to the formal dinners in Santiago. Although extremely effective in a private setting, Ross was never at ease in public. He traveled with a bureaucratic regalia that protected him from all personal contact outside of the elite. He was austere in appearance and often spoke of the workers as "human raw material."[16] The French Minister, who liked him, admitted he had "a regrettable character."[17] A sympathetic U.S. Embassy official recorded that Ross was considered an "unscrupulous conservative." His bald pate lent itself to a "death's-head caricature."[18]

Conservative youths found him appalling. A new generation had entered the Conservative Party, drawn from Catholic schools and the Catholic University, where French theologian Jacques Maritain was their guiding light. These young men wanted "social peace" and a government concerned with alleviating mass misery. Many had taken part in the demonstrations that brought down Ibáñez in 1931. In 1937, they formed the Falange, a clique within the Conservative Party, and in 1938, they openly lobbied the party to find another candidate.[19] In a letter circulated to party leaders, future political leaders such as Bernardo Leighton and Eduardo Frei Montalva and the already well-known Manuel Garretón argued that Ross was simply unfit to be president. He hated politics; and he was hated by the people. He was arbitrary, someone who would be a good business manager but unsuited to be president of a democratic nation.[20] In the end, they bit their collective tongue and campaigned on Ross' behalf, explaining that they were "submitting themselves hierarchically," for the well-being of Chile.[21]

The key institutions of civil society endorsed the well-fueled Ross machine. Although the Church was formally neutral, clergymen organized campaign rallies for Ross.[22] The Edwards' newspaper chain and the government press flattered him at every turn. In all, four major dailies backed him: *El Mercurio*, *El Diario Ilustrado*, *La Nación*, and *El Imparcial*.[23] The powerful commercial societies or guilds supported him without reservation. Jaime Larraín García Moreno and Miguel Letelier campaigned for him on behalf of the National Agricultural Society [SNA]; so did Walter Mueller, president of the National Development Corporation [SOFOFA]. Other campaigners included Gaston Goyeneche, president of the National Chamber of Commerce; Juan Mickle, manager of the Confederation of Commerce and Industry; and Victor Muñoz Valdés, secretary general of the Small Business Association.[24] These associations contributed heavily as did wealthy individuals. Ross demanded and received funds from U.S. corporations. U.S. copper companies openly boosted his candidacy. Curtis Calder, the president of American and Foreign Power, who had argued with Ross over the fate of Chilean Electric, kicked in some "commissions." In return, Ross promised to double Santiago's tramway fares the following year. As an official act of good will, the Chilean Electric Company received a rate increase in September.[25] In addition, Alessandri sold quantities of placer gold on the black market for rates of 26 to 34 pesos to the dollar, registered the sales at an official rate of 25 to the dollar, and gave the difference to the Ross campaign.[26]

Ross was widely expected by foreign corporations to be a strong chief executive and even to continue many Alessandri policies they disliked. Nevertheless, two factors put them behind his candidacy: an open fear of the left and confidence that Ross would not endanger the structure of economic relations between the United States and Chile.

U.S. interests, for example, supported Ross even though they assumed that a Ross administration would continue currency restrictions and increase regulations on utilities and mining companies, and probably raise taxes on foreign companies.[27] For its part, the Ross campaign argued against the notion of "imperialism," and said that "foreign capital . . . deserves our respect and gratitude."[28]

On other issues, Ross promised full support for the armed forces and the national police. He planned to decentralize the executive administration, although he did not explain how or why. His economic policies were very specific. He would not raise taxes; government would concentrate on increasing production and rising output would raise revenues. He wanted a balanced budget, low interest rates, an industrial policy that favored firms using Chilean raw materials, and, most interestingly, "a subdivision of land to in order to improve cultivation."[29] He had no social agenda. To Ross, the social issues in this election were simple. If he did not win, "the elements of dissolution" and of "anarchy" would take over.[30] Ross and Alessandri knew that they had little labor support. Alessandri had cut government spending in the campaign year and was unworried about labor's response. He also canceled the legal charters of unions supporting the Popular Front.[31]

Carlos Ibáñez del Campo was the wild card in the election. He had returned from a long exile in 1937, but Ross ignored him while concentrating his attack on the Popular Front. Ibáñez ran as the Naci candidate, but his base of support extended well beyond that small party. He drew followers from the right and the reformist middle class. Much of his financing came from small businessmen and industrialists, Chileans of German descent, and some large landowners.[32] Juan Antonio Ríos helped organize the Ibáñez publicity campaign and convinced some Radical Party members to sign on. Members of the small Democratic Party, once important in the labor movement, also endorsed Ibáñez. Writers interested in social issues, such as Ricardo Latcham, Vicente Huidobro, and Tancredo Pinochet, supported his campaign in the belief that he would create an "organic democracy, which . . . replaces the demagogue with the technician within a system of social responsibility."[33]

The Ibáñez campaign reveals how easily issues were blurred, and how diverse factions could be recruited with populist rhetoric. Through his widespread use of newspapers, he reached a substantial public. He had his own weekly, *Clamor*, and the support of the Naci newspaper,

Trabajo, and of Dávila's still-influential publication, *Hoy*.[34] He promised the industrialists cheap credit and protection of private property; the middle class, social order and better government salaries; and the working man, full employment through government projects. He held successful rallies for white-collar employees, and toured factories recruiting support from labor and management.[35] Many reformers began their careers in the 1920s as Ibañistas, now they treated his campaign with respect. Members of the Front hoped to get Ibáñez to drop his effort and join theirs.[36] When he announced his candidacy, the Socialist Party had to expel his supporters from its ranks. The new U.S. Ambassador, Hofmann Philip concluded in October 1937, "The influence of Sr. Ibáñez cuts through all parties."

Ibáñez and the Nacis argued that two elements had hurt Chile: the oligarchy and foreign corporations. By abandoning the nineteenth-century nationalist programs of Manuel Montt and José Manuel Balmaceda, in favor of selling resources to foreigners, the oligarchy had helped impoverish Chile. The Naci leader, González von Marées, admitted Ibáñez made mistakes in the 1920s, "as a result of his inexperience in government," but blamed subordinates for most of the problems from that era. The campaign emphasized the higher real wages and full employment of the 1920s, omitting any reference to the expansion of the foreign debt.[37] Finally, the campaign demanded a reduction of U.S. influence, although nothing was said about how this would be done, and spoke of developing better ties with Italy and Germany.[38]

Not wanting to appear solely as a Naci candidate, Ibáñez subsumed the role of the MNS in a political organization he called the People's Liberation Alliance [Alianza Popular Libertadora]. His program endorsed democracy, absolute respect for civil rights, election reform, a campaign against corruption, administrative decentralization, better local government, improved budgeting, and reform of the civil service. Like the other two candidates, he never mentioned raising taxes.[39] He also favored some kind of government planning through an economic council and an end to foreign debt payments.[40] He came across not only as the strong man of the 1920s but as someone who had not enriched himself when he was in office.

Aguirre Cerda came from modest circumstances but had married well and had acquired land and social standing. Trained as a school teacher and lawyer, he was also a Freemason. He joined the Radical

Party and was first elected as a deputy representing San Felipe in 1915. His first cabinet post was as Minister of Education and Justice in 1918 under President Luis Sanfuentes. He steered a bill through Congress that made primary schooling compulsory. Under Alessandri, he served as Minister of Interior from 1920 to 1924. When Ibáñez first took office, Aguirre Cerda went into exile and wrote a study of Chilean industry. He returned, however, to take up a budgetary post with the sponsorship of Ibáñez' son-in-law. He knew, of course, that association with the Ibáñez government compromised his political future, and he justified his decision on the grounds that his was a professional not a political job.[41] But the decision to work with Ibáñez, taken on financial and family grounds, probably estranged him from Alessandri. He is not mentioned as being close to Alessandri when the latter returned to Chile.

After Ibáñez was overthrown, Aguirre Cerda practiced law and used his contacts to promote experiments in economic development and to encourage an economic activism among professionals in agriculture, industry, and mining. When most Radicals broke with Alessandri, he followed. By the mid-1930s, he was president of the Radical Party and dean of the School of Industry and Commerce at the University of Chile (later, the School of Economics). He used his university position to hold conferences on economic policy among businessmen and to attack the government.[42] He was also one of the chief promoters of the Chilean Oil Company [COPEC], which he viewed as an instrument to break the duopsony of Shell Mex (of Royal Dutch Shell) and West India Oil (Standard Oil of New Jersey). After the founding of COPEC in 1934, he was its president for a brief period.[43] Aguirre Cerda thus had a multifaceted background, having moved from the struggling middle class into the land-owning gentry. He expressed social concerns but saw their solution entirely in economic terms. Most of the Radicals of his background and connections had always supported Alessandri or Ibáñez and, in 1938, many of them were drawn to Ross.[44] To attract them, he used his work in COPEC and industrial councils as proof of his nationalist credentials, and he attacked Ross as the puppet of foreigners.[45]

Many Popular Front members saw him as too conservative and the Front convention was a raucous affair. The Radicals had 400 of approximately one thousand delegates at the Front's convention; it took them fourteen ballots to recruit a majority and impose him as the candidate.[46] Even then, the leftist parties thought that he lacked popular appeal. On the hustings, Front organizers frequently coupled him with more charismatic speakers, especially Marmaduke Grove. In fact, the campaign revived the slogan of Grove's Socialist Republic, "bread, roof, and overcoat." One could hardly imagine a stranger pairing. Grove was incendiary; he drew crowds but frightened the propertied classes with the language of class warfare. Once, in Osorno, he demanded the crowd strangle a heckler.[47] To everyone's surprise, Aguirre Cerda was a dogged campaigner. He was known to be in poor health but held large rallies in the provincial capitals and, between February and October 1938, tried to visit every *pueblito* in the central valley. This won him respect on the left and increased his popularity.

The Popular Front campaigned on a platform of fairer taxes, economic nationalism, and better administration. Elaborate specifics promised a reduction in indirect taxes, national economic planning, protecting the nation from "imperialist firms," ending monopolies, and agrarian reform to benefit small- and medium-sized farms.[48] As the campaign went along, the member parties buried their differences and built some common enthusiasm for their candidate. For its part, and in keeping with the Comintern strategy, the Communist Party behaved in a circumspect manner during the campaign, supporting the Front ticket while promising to respect property and to oppose fascism.[49] Aguirre Cerda also had the backing of the CTCh, the Chilean Labor Confederation, and picked up crucial support from the teachers.[50] And he had a respectable presence in the daily press; the progressive dailies, *La Hora*, *Claridad*, and *La Opinión* backed him.[51]

There is no hint of social anger in Aguirre Cerda's writings. He saw Chile's problems in Jeffersonian terms. A proper government should help the "productive class" buy small farms, and increase rural output.[52] In the campaign, Aguirre Cerda emphasized state assistance for industry and promised, somehow, to increase the amount of cultivated land to reduce food prices. He promised "scientific taxes." He recognized that the rural population was "vegetating," and talked of the minimum wage for farmhands.[53] The young Conservative, Ricardo Boizard, visited him at his farm early in the Popular Front administration, and concluded, "His views on the social problem were, as I had imagined, that of a good bourgeois who summarizes his philosophy in the need to quiet the poor if he is himself to enjoy tranquillity."[54]

Aguirre Cerda campaigned against "imperialism" without providing any details of a nationalist program. He said that he did not repudiate foreign capital; but it would be necessary to "carefully review the privileges [granted in] other eras," and to "share the wealth that, up to now, they [foreigners] had taken with them."[55] The U.S. Ambassador called his pronouncements "vague" and noted U.S. corporations were "apprehensive."[56] On the eve of the election, Aguirre Cerda told the British Ambassador that Britain should help finance the construction of several electric plants, "which would supply power to new national industries at very low prices until these industries could pay more."[57] He gave little thought during the campaign about how Chile would negotiate with the major powers; he promised to cut Chile's diplomatic corps to a quarter of its size. After the election, he told a southern newspaper he would not attack foreign capital but would establish a scientific institute to promote all kinds of investment. "All new industry will be aided by the State."[58] He told a U.S. journalist:

> We do not want to put the state into industry, but rather to make the government, as in England, an instrument to better the condition of the people. Chile is not ready to nationalize or socialize its great copper and nitrate industries. It lacks the capital for that. We do not intend to use foreign capital as a football. My government will be nationalistic, in the sense that it will defend Chilean interests; but its nationalism will be of the head as well as of the heart. We plan to study carefully the relation of government and industry here. One defect of foreign capital in Chile has been its tendency to build up concentrations of tremendous size. We shall encourage the development of small and medium-sized industries, in which Chilean capital can enter. We do not intend to "Mexicanize" Chile.[59]

In this last comment, Aguirre Cerda addressed the fears of U.S. State Department officials that a conspiracy existed between the government of Lázaro Cárdenas in Mexico and the Popular Front.[60] He tried to address the continuing hardship of the Depression and the provincial resentment of bureaucratic centralization in Santiago. This last issue had been part of the Radical Party's rhetoric since it was formed in the late nineteenth century. Campaigning by train at Laja, he said ministers would be rotated between Santiago and the provinces, forcing them to learn the country's problems. Another crowd heard him promise free school breakfasts and lunches to eliminate children's hunger.[61] In the southern interview, he emphasized education and public hygiene.

Aguirre Cerda's promises were not the Popular Front's central strength, however. Instead, it benefitted from the accumulation of resentments in urban society: the now numerous humiliations of the Depression, the Radicals' disappointment under Alessandri, and military men angry at their dismissals all fed the desire for change.[62] With the CTCh, the Front carefully nurtured political committees in every provincial capital and mining town, which focused people's attention on low wages, unemployment relief, and the legacy of the nitrate collapse.[63] In Santiago, the committees lent support to consumer strikes and public complaints over municipal fees, gas prices and bus fares, and Ross' deals with Chilean Electric.[64] The Front was always considerate of white-collar organizations even of those that refused to join it, for example, its campaigners showed up at the Santiago meetings of the Renters League demanding rent reductions.[65] The campaign also made an issue of the Spanish Civil War. The Republican cause was emotionally popular: Alessandri and close supporters, such as Agustín Edwards, favored Franco.[66] This collection of issues would not have brought about a Front victory, for the coalition's appeal was undercut by Ibáñez. The most reasonable pre-electoral expectation was that Ross would win a plurality, which, in the Chilean tradition, would have led to a vote in Congress that made him chief executive. One confrontation, however, changed the electoral equation: a Naci putsch and the Alessandri government's reaction to it.

The campaign was volatile from the beginning. Socially and ideologically, it intensified a fight that had been building since at least 1936. While they had little chance of winning, the Nacis and their incessant provocations changed the emotional stakes. Their Assault Troops often left blood on the streets. There were dead of both sides in Valparaiso in 1936 when the Assault Troops quarreled with Socialists over the distribution of newspapers.[67] At a confrontation in Rancagua in November 1936, the Nacis killed several people; the local ringleader was sent to jail for 40 days and fined.[68] In the 1938 campaign, the Nacis attacked Ross' campaign with rocks; guns were fired in one incident.[69] Alessandri repressed them in Santiago but he never used the same vigor as he applied to the Communists. This was true even though Naci violence had justified passage of the Law of Internal Security, a law then deployed against working class organizations.

To Alessandri and others in government, the Nacis were, after all, young men of good families, just a little headstrong. The Nacis were taken seriously only near the end of the campaign: after the attack on Ross and after Brazil and Uruguay, in reaction to their Nazi problems and under pressure from the United States, had closed all German language schools.[70]

As it became apparent that the right might buy the election as it had the 1937 congressional contest, resentments and suspicions against the government deepened within the Popular Front and the Ibáñez forces. The tension surrounding the campaign reached one peak when the president gave the opening address to Congress in May 1938. Members of opposition parties openly accused him of rigging the election for Ross. The president of the Radical Party, Gabriel González Videla, asked permission to give an address before Alessandri spoke; when he was turned down, members of the Popular Front began to walk out en masse. Carabineros guarding Alessandri thought they saw a weapon and wrestled a Socialist to the floor. González von Marées then fired his pistol into the air and was set upon by police, who also grabbed González Videla. Deputies ended up in the hospital. The president went on to give his address despite the explosion of a smoke bomb.[71]

Emotions rose even higher. A congressional investigation into the incident kept it alive and colored the rest of the election.[72] Despite all the clamor, only one figure was punished: González von Marées was sentenced to a one-and-one-half years of seclusion. To reduce the prospect of street fighting, the government banned, in June 1938, all outdoor demonstrations in Valparaiso.[73] Aguirre Cerda, feeling the anxiety of his supporters, promised a popular rebellion if the Front was cheated in the election.[74] González von Marées announced the Ibáñez campaign would win "by reason or force [the national motto] . . . and if circumstances require, with a blood bath of those who oppose our high purpose."[75] Rumors of a Naci coup were common by late August.[76]

Unfortunately, they were true. On September 4, Ibáñez held a massive demonstration at the Parque Cousiño.[77] The rally was no longer to build support for the election but to test the size of Naci strength. Satisfied, González von Marées, who had not yet begun serving his sentence, put a simple plan into effect. The next day at noon, the Nacis began their attack. González von Marées coordinated events by radio from the distant suburb of Las Condes. About five dozen Nacis seized the social security building and the administrative center of the university—both within easy view of La Moneda, the presidential palace. They barricaded themselves within, to wait for the army to show up and rescue them from the "crisis" they had created. They expected rebel army units to use the disturbance to overthrow the government. At the social security building, within shouting distance of the presidential palace, they shot a carabinero. At the same moment, a Naci unit blew up two electric pylons on the outskirts of the city.[78] The army did not behave as the Nacis expected. Instead of rescuing the Nacis, the carabineros and army units pinned them inside the buildings. The administration became afraid that as workers left their jobs at nightfall, a stand-off would create a revolutionary situation.[79] To prevent this, the army and police stormed the buildings and the young Nacis, many of them university students, were captured, herded together into the university building, and shot. Sixty-one died.

The ensuing scandal plagued Alessandri for the rest of his life. It is unlikely that he ordered the massacre, but he inexplicably went home when the fight seemed over and, so, created a vacuum of leadership just when leadership was most needed. In any event, no one believed his account.[80] The government had shot the wrong class of people.[81] Then it launched a cover-up, which failed.[82] The reaction of middle-class youths was visceral: the School of Medicine declared a work stoppage, the School of Engineering flew the flag at half mast, and the president of the University Student Federation called the Naci deaths, "the cruelest and most outrageous political act in American history."[83] Eventually, Alessandri's Minister of Interior took the blame and resigned. Years later, conservative youths would still confront Alessandri at public gatherings and call him a murderer.[84]

Ibáñez surrendered to a military barracks once he heard of the attempted coup. He denied all involvement but was never able to explain why his machine gun was found at the university.[85] He was eventually tried and acquitted. González von Marées was caught, tried, and sentenced to twenty years.[86] Soon after his conviction, he said that Ibáñez knew of the plan but got cold feet at the last minute.[87]

The withdrawal of Ibáñez from the campaign was the most important political effect of the uprising. He and González von Marées subsequently endorsed Aguirre Cerda.[88] This realignment of loyalties placed the Popular Front in La Moneda.[89] After Aguirre Cerda won on October 25, Alessandri and Ross exhorted the military to intervene and nullify the election. Throughout his second term, Alessandri had argued for the restoration of civil authority and had dismissed Ibañista officers who threatened constitutional rule. Now, he was upset that the military supported a constitutional transition.[90] Many soldiers identified with elements of the middle and working classes that favored social reform and political continuity.[91] Alessandri and events during the Depression had "created" an armed forces more devoted to the constitution than the president. Ross, seeing that his chance had passed, made an ungracious concession of defeat and left the country.[92] Alessandri left as soon as his term ended. Thereafter, Alessandri always claimed the restoration of constitutional government as one of his greatest achievements, but he never mentioned his behavior in 1938.[93]

Popular Front Promises and Frustration

The inauguration of President Aguirre Cerda began a brief era, lasting until 1952, in which the Radical Party controlled the presidency in alliance with other parties. The government of Aguirre Cerda, the era of the Popular Front, lasted two years and eight months. The changes the Front instituted included the expansion of social welfare measures, the incorporation of a significant part of the work force into labor unions, the creation of a national agency to finance development, and the extension of the franchise. In the euphoria of 1939 and 1940, before the limits of his presidency became clear, it seemed that Aguirre Cerda might redefine the future of Chile to include steps toward socialism.

The era as a whole was shaped by World War II, Chile's dependence on copper, the enlarged role of the state within the economy, the expansion of the middle class, and the persistence of mass poverty. Most of the electorate accepted some form of mixed economy; conflicts centered on the extent and role of government power. By 1950, it was clear that the economy was stagnating with low rates of agricultural and industrial growth and high rates of inflation, often above 20 percent.

His nationalism notwithstanding, Aguirre Cerda's plans required foreign support and cooperation. On the eve of his inauguration, he told foreign representatives what they wanted to hear. To assuage the Vatican, upset by his victory, he promised not to attack the Church.[94] He assured the United States that his program resembled the New Deal, which it did in some ways. He toned down the rhetoric of the campaign and made little mention of the help foreign companies had given Ross.

This did not help him very much with foreign interests, who remained close to the elite and were frightened of his political allies. Some foreigners could barely hide their contempt. The British ambassador described the new president as "an older and much uglier man than I had anticipated, and, besides appearing to be partly Indian, his face seemed to be marked with smallpox scars." The ambassador thought the president was too weak to control the leftists in his coalition.[95]

Aguirre Cerda thought the approach of war gave him leverage in international negotiations. He hinted that Chile might grow economically closer to Germany, if financial aid was not forthcoming from the United States and Britain.[96] In its first exchange of messages with Washington, the Popular Front requested a US$50 million loan from the U.S. Export-Import Bank.[97] This was the opening move to the economic diplomacy between the Chilean Radical presidents and the U.S. government. The outcome of this move would revise the old foreign debt in order to facilitate the Chilean government's new debts with the U.S. government and postwar international agencies it helped create.

Within Chile, as one right-wing congressman put it, 80 percent of the Chilean economy had voted against Aguirre Cerda. The Chilean elite underwent a transition in generation in the 1930s. Those who would control the production of coal, livestock, nitrates, paper, shipping, wine, and domestic banking for the next twenty years were now in control.[98] Their initial response to the Popular Front victory was to reduce their investments in Chile: stock values dropped 16 percent in the first six months of the new government.[99]

The Front's opponents seemed implacable. A genial man, Aguirre Cerda proved to be resilient and even tenacious on issues that he thought would improve living standards. He submitted a wide array of social and economic legislation and even demanded that women be given the vote in national elections. Congress included a formidable array of his opponents. Opposition parties in Congress delayed every bill the administration submitted. Many on the right wanted to end the government by any means available. Three months into Aguirre Cerda's presidency, Alessandri predicted a coup and seemed untroubled at the prospect.[100] However, the right was weakened by post-election recriminations and hostility. Young conservatives split from the Conservative Party, and the Liberals broke into several factions.[101] During the Front, political zealots organized six distinct paramilitary organizations, including one led by former heads of the Republican Militia.[102]

Aguirre Cerda tried to retain the support of the Nacis and Ibáñez. The Nacis were pardoned for their actions on September 5, while the carabinero hierarchy was prosecuted for the massacre (those convicted were later pardoned).[103] González von Marées used the opportunity to rename his followers as the People's Socialist Vanguard [Vanguardia Popular Socialista]; he insisted that this was a new party that bore no resemblance to German Nazis.[104] The president also tried to keep Carlos Ibáñez as an ally; but Ibañistas remained aloof and out of the cabinet. The president, of course, never offered them any major voice in policy.

Nine months into the new administration, Ibáñez and González von Marées tried a coup. Aguirre Cerda, like Alessandri, recognized that the coup of 1924 had made soldiers a dangerous factor in national politics. When officers objected to seeing the Communist flag during a parade, it was Army General Ariosta Herrera who voiced their complaint. Aguirre Cerda removed the flag and, after the parade, forced Herrera into retirement. He joined Ibáñez and González von Marées when they made their move.[105] Workers responded to the threat by gathering 60 thousand strong in the plaza before the presidential palace, demonstrating their support for the Popular Front. It was the last Ibañista conspiracy. Another group of officers were forcibly retired, and Ibáñez was again marginalized and sent into exile.[106] Appraising the damage, one officer claimed that Ibáñez' antics had cost the army 400 officers since 1931.[107] The government later removed González von Marées with a stroke of ingenuity in 1940. A deputy had been murdered, and in the midst of the public outcry, the government used its police powers to commit him to a mental institution; the humiliation ruined his reputation and that of his followers.[108] Herrera was exiled to Mexico.

The president reached out to the left. The Communist, Indalecio Prieto, represented the dying Spanish Republic at Aguirre Cerda's inauguration and received a tumultuous welcome.[109] A leader of the mutiny in 1931 was appointed mayor of Valparaiso, infuriating the naval hierarchy.[110] The Socialists received three cabinet posts; the Communists requested one but were turned down.[111] The president also welcomed the Socialist Militia, a paramilitary force organized during the election and led by Oscar Schnake that claimed 15 thousand members.[112]

The Radical Party and the CTCh remained the core of the government's support, and the new administration was seriously weakened when the Radicals divided over the spoils. Conflicts within the party, most notably the southern versus Santiago factions, had never been resolved and divided the Front administration. In 1940, the Socialists divided as well as they fought for positions in the cabinet, the bureaucracy, and prominence in the legislature.[113] Not surprisingly, the Radicals and Socialists fought one another in very public ways. The president could do little more than keep these quarrels from tearing the Front apart. In poor health, he literally shortened his life fighting for his government.[114]

The Front's central achievement was that it permitted a mobilization from below. Aguirre Cerda's victory created a surge to join legal unions that continued through the next two years; and the proliferation of unions and militant associations changed the social and political landscape.[115] With the government's support, union membership reached 193 thousand by 1942; 122 thousand members were in factories.[116] As an important piece of evidence on the role of the middle class in the Front, the pace of white-collar unionization briefly exceeded blue-collar efforts: 252 industrial and 461 professional syndicates were founded in 1939. State decrees raised wages, with white-collar workers getting increases out of proportion to their numbers.[117] As a result of the change in administration and policies that reduced the level of class hostility, 1939 saw few major strikes. Wages in Santiago rose 8.5 percent while the cost of living rose only 0.3 percent; workers began to catch up with past reversals.[118] At El Teniente, where he had not been allowed during the campaign, Aguirre Cerda made a triumphal visit in 1939. His new Minister of Labor, Antonio Paupin, made a separate trip and was also greeted by a massive turnout. The miners soon ended the company union and formed their own.[119]

Workers organized in some surprising activities: traveling salesmen formed a union, as did midwives; and at the end of 1939, government employees defied a ban on organizing and formed an ad hoc association. In addition to higher salaries, workers viewed unions and the CTCh as vehicles of political protection, providing, among other things, enrollment in social security programs. In order to achieve recognition as a profession, the midwives lobbied for restrictions on who was allowed to practice.[120]

Labor also lobbied the government on pensions, consumer issues, and work-place safety. The government could be intrusive. By law, it could set prices; mediate labor disputes; decree basic wage levels in many sectors; inspect factories and apartments; and arrest, fine, and even imprison those who defied its edicts. But the government's limited resources restricted its efforts outside Santiago and Valparaiso. Enforcement was a major problem. Even when misconduct was investigated,

nothing might be done for years. For example, the Province of Llanqui-
hue, in the far south, had one labor inspector. Workers with complaints
had to convince him to come out to their rural sites; these trips could
take up to three days. It usually took two or three inspections to get a
judgment, and an employer could appeal it to a judge.[121] Government
managers often ignored sanitation regulations and labor rights. The gold
fields, which employed 10 thousand men in 1939-40, provided a
notorious example.[122]

Disparities in income and class remained substantial. Government
workers in the provinces earned 100 pesos a month while division heads
received one thousand pesos. In the private sector, janitors and office
boys earned between 300 and 500 pesos a month, while business
managers were paid five thousand; six thousand; or even twelve thousand per month. Such disparities led to very distinct lifestyles. Renting
the cheapest apartment in an arriviste section of the city cost two to
two-and-one-half times the wages of a maid. Government housing
programs made sharp distinctions between white-collar homes (two
rooms with an indoor toilet) and blue-collar dwellings (one bedroom
each with a communal bathroom for each building).[123]

One interesting phenomenon was the widespread acceptance of the
"family wage" by which male heads of households with children earned
more than bachelors performing the same jobs. Recent scholarship
argues that this development was a conservative, not a progressive trend,
and signaled the persistence of gendered stereotypes that were untrue,
notably the idea that women could depend on men to support them. The
practice of the "family wage" began in the nitrate zone in the 1920s and
spread, thereafter, to the copper mines and other modern centers of
production. The goal was to tie men down with family responsibilities.
Historians critical of the "family wage" note that men often did not use
the additional money to support their families.[124]

The issue of the family wage is part of broader revisionist argument,
the Popular Front did little to advance opportunities for women. The
Communists undermined the feminist agenda of MEMCh in 1940—at
the height of the Popular Front era. Once they had taken over its
leadership, they emphasized class issues over feminist ones. Among
other fears, the labor left worried that women in the labor force would
undercut male wages. In general, the Popular Front leadership said little
about the chauvinistic attitudes among working-class men. Women
were not included in the CTCh. However, they did get the vote at the

municipal level.[125] Although women in working class areas voted for the Popular Front in municipal elections, the Front did nothing about electoral rules that favored the registration of well-to-do women over the working class. The results were predictable: the women's vote supported right-wing candidates; the idea that women were against the progressive change became general among left and reformist parties.[126]

The Front effort to win over urban consumers comprised another approach to labor and the middle class. The General Commissariat on Subsistence and Prices, suspended for three years by Alessandri, was revived and expanded. It controlled food and housing prices and could close any store in violation of its decrees for 30 days.[127] The Commissariat became especially active after war broke out in Europe, when it went beyond setting prices and tried to control the distribution of products. Among its other effects, it created official monopolies for imported goods.[128] The government also financed *people's restaurants*, glorified soup kitchens that served thousands of meals in the capital and other major centers.[129] In addition, the Santiago Renters League obtained a decree that froze rents at their September 1938 level.[130] The Front used broad governmental powers to regulate utilities and urban industry. It rolled back electric rate increases that Alessandri had granted and redefined schools, barracks, and churches as *residential*, entitling them to lower rates.[131] It renewed a 1932 decree-law that allowed the president to intervene in any sector that he thought suffered from overproduction.[132] All of this was ameliorative. Aguirre Cerda and his advisors wanted to reconstruct the economy, to raise output, and to generate growth through cheap credit to industry, cooperatives, and small farmers.[133] The populist urge hit Congress as well: the Chamber of Deputies was awash in proposals for public works and general subsidies. Every chamber of commerce, business society, and consumer cooperative received at least some consideration, a fact that helped increase the organization of civic life in the major cities.

Although the government counted on labor support, it also wanted to control labor mobilization. Like most populists, Aguirre Cerda wanted labor as a client, not a partner in government. Labor leaders tried to march workers to the government's tune. For example, the CTCh opposed a strike in the copper mines in 1939 because it would have hurt the government's efforts to secure loans from the United States.[134] The labor federation did little to help government workers who had grievances. Alessandri's practice of spying on labor rallies was continued.[135]

Over complaints of the Minister of Development, Congress expanded the credit facilities of the Central Bank.[136] Rallies and demonstrations in front of Congress kept up public pressure for action. The most famous, on March 19, 1938, drew 150 thousand people into a parade that lasted six hours.[137] Unions, rural workers, government workers, and rent strikers held rallies. No one mentioned fiscal restraints or discussed inflation.[138]

Aguirre Cerda and all subsequent Radical presidents sacrificed the support of rural labor to expediency. Price controls on food subsidized urban consumption; how were they to be maintained if rural wages rose? Aguirre Cerda never challenged the National Agricultural Society or the southern section of his own party. The minimum wage and social security were not extended to agricultural laborers. In 1939, an observer called the Chilean tenant or inquilino, "little more than a beast of burden, ignorant, uneducated, with an incredibly low standard of living."[139] U.S. Ambassador Norman Armour, no friend of the Chilean worker, visited one estate and found the house built like a fort, with modern conveniences, beautiful gardens, footmen, a French chef, and "an atmosphere of modern feudalism."[140] Most rural strikes, frequently led by Emilio Zapata, occurred on estates near Santiago where they could generate some press coverage.[141] Although they were limited, such strikes were enough to frighten the Socialists, who expelled Zapata when he refused to stop organizing the countryside. One strike effort involved 300 workers on the estates of Jaime Larraín García Moreno, president of the SNA. Larraín convinced the government to stop it.

Urban labor expressed concern but did little for rural workers. There was a small cooperative movement, which included efforts at joining small urban factories with small farmers. The movement was dominated by middle-class reformers who made a series of proposals for transforming the countryside. Under the law, cooperatives could be either consumer or producer associations. Associations of both types advocated the division of large estates into small farms to increase competition and production. One cooperative society envisioned brigades of workers under state supervision during a period of tutelage, learning agricultural skills and new political views.[142] For all the Radical Party's rhetoric about social change, nothing substantial was done. Cooperatives received credit but not enough for sweeping market experiments.

The government's policy leaders had little faith in the rural Chilean, a fact that helps explain why it invested so little in rural education or efforts to help small farmers. The Front's first Minister of Finance, Roberto Waccholtz, said that cooperatives could not change the countryside because of the rural workers' poor character and physique. He argued that a "gradual process of racial rehabilitation" was necessary, views that echoed Gustavo Ross' belief that only massive European immigration could rescue the racial stock of the rural population.[143]

Early in his administration, Aguirre Cerda granted the U.S. historian of Latin America, Frank Tannenbaum, an interview in which the president outlined a program of rural regeneration. The president was free of racist assumptions but took a long view of social change. He wanted to build new community centers or villages and break the power of landowners over rural labor and to develop rural schools and to provide basic amenities. He wanted the state railways to buy crops and cut out profiteering by middle men and hacendados. He also wanted a highway between Santiago and Puerto Montt (virtually the southern end of inhabited Chile) and to line it with housing on each side. All this required granting state credits to small farmers, but no amounts were mentioned. Professor Tannenbaum concluded that the president "is essentially a very conservative person."[144]

The government gave little priority to the president's dream. In March 1939, it established a Peasant Information Institute, an educational agency, and allocated it 150 thousand pesos (then about US$6 thousand) and four employees. In practice, repression remained the central policy; there were several edicts banning all labor organizing in the countryside.[145]

The character of its coalition shaped the government's policies. Within the Radical Party, the rural and southern wing remained hostile to social change. The Front had to court other parties in Congress in order to pass any legislation.[146] The left within the Front was divided between the Socialists and the Communists (the Trotskyists had merged with the Socialists). The two parties regularly fought over control of the Chilean Labor Confederation. In August, the Socialist Bernardo Ibáñez (unrelated to Carlos Ibáñez) won an election for president of the CTCh.[147] The Socialists also won a predominant position in the CTCh directorate, holding 8 of 16 seats (the Communists had 5).[148] Obviously, the left party that controlled the Confederation gained visibility and financial resources within the booming labor movement. Fights over control of the CTCh intensified after 1939 since every party wanted a slice of the patronage it could provide.

The Socialists militantly pressed demands on the government, pushing especially for CTCh-led strikes at U.S. mining firms. As they saw it, they faced one contest with the Radicals in the government and another with the Communists in the CTCh. To their frustration, their opponents often joined forces: the Communists under the leadership of Carlos Contreras Labarca (the aging Lafertte had stepped aside) were unquestioning allies of Aguirre Cerda; and the Radicals often threw their support to the Communists in the labor organization.[149]

When sections of the Communist Party in Santiago quadrupled their membership in 1939, a Socialist faction, based in the Santiago city council and fearing the Communists' success, decided that the Communists had to be expelled from the Front.[150] The removal of the Communists would enhance the Socialists' chances of controlling the expanding purse of the CTCh and bolster their importance to the Front in all future elections. In September, after war had broken out in Europe, Oscar Schnake, head of the Socialist Militia, rival of Marmaduke Grove for party leadership, and the government's delegate to the Americas Conference in Havana, returned from visiting the United States and demanded that the Communists immediately leave the government. He called them a sell-out, a fifth column from Moscow, and an ally of the Nazis for supporting the Nazi-Soviet Non-aggression Pact and for advocating neutrality in the war. They were, Schnake claimed, agents of social conflict rather than social change.[151] The Socialists then threatened to leave the Front. Their pressure worked: they were rewarded with more positions in the government. Aguirre Cerda brought Schnake and his fellow firebrand, Salvador Allende Gossens, into the cabinet. All this maneuvering for position diverted the Front's leadership from confronting the government's major problem (a problem that is still ignored in the historical literature of the period). Who was going to pay to incorporate the working class as a client of the state?

Endnotes

For abbreviations used in notes, see Endnotes, Chapter 1.

1. Quoted in Robert Alexander, *Arturo Alessandri: A Biography* (New Brunswick, NJ: Rutgers University Latin American Institute, University Microfilms International, 1977), 2:748.

2. Interview with U.S. Consul Adams, RG:825.504/109, Adams, 18 Feb. 1938.

3. See Lynne Lawner's introduction in Antonio Gramsci, *Letters from Prison*, Lawner, trans. (New York: Harper and Row, 1973), 42-43.

4. John Gunther, *Inside Latin America* (New York: Harper and Brothers, 1941), 241.

5. The interpretation here has a different focus than that of Drake, which stresses many of the similarities in the campaign promises of the candidates. I agree with Drake that the Popular Front policies decisively benefitted the middle class. See Paul Drake, *Socialism and Populism in Chile* (Chicago: University of Illinois Press, 1978), 175-241.

6. Marta Infante Barros, *Testigos del treinta y ocho* (Santiago: Editorial Andres Bello, 1972), 49.

7. A recent and important exception is Tomás Moulian and Isabel Torres Dujisin, *Discusiones entre honorables: las candidaturas presidenciales de la derecha entre 1938 y 1946* (Santiago: Facultad Latinoamericana de Ciencias Sociales [FLACSO], 1987), an excellent work based on newspapers of the era and especially good on 1938.

8. Ricardo Boizard, *Historia de una derrota: 25 de Octubre de 1938* (Santiago: Editorial Orbe, 1941), 32, 155.

9. RG 59: 825.00/984, Philip, no. 535, 30 Mar. 1937; and BOLSA, B55, Valparaiso to London, 9 Mar. 1937.

10. Chile. *Hacienda Pública*, Aug. 1937, 21; BOLSA, B55, Valparaiso to London, 16 Mar. 1937; and RG 59: 825.00/979, Philip, no. 520, 10 Mar. 1937.

11. On Dulles' visit, RG 59: 825.51/933 1/2, Duggan memo, 30 June 1937; and on letter to State, 825.51/948, Ross' memo "Chilean Debt Plan," 4 Oct. 1937.

12. María Teresa Covarrubias, *1938: La rebelión de los jóvenes* (Santiago: Editorial Aconcagua, 1987), 98.

13. RG 59: 825.00/1001, Philip, no. 658, 14 July 1937, and 825.00/1022, Philip, no. 941, 30 Mar. 1938.

14. RG 59: 825.00/1030, Norman Armour, no. 8, 26 Apr. 1938, 825.00/1045, Chile-American Association, Incorporated, Confidential Report no. 75, June 1938; and *La Opinión*, 13 Feb., 5 and 24 Apr. 1938.

15. Chile. *Hacienda Pública*, 20 Aug. 1938.

16. For examples of rallies, see Chile. Interior, v. 9769 (1938), Prov. 12902, Servicios de Investigación, 29 July 1938. See also Moulian and Torres, op. cit., 121.

17. France-MAE, Chili. v. 11, 12 Mar. 1937, J. de Beausse.

18. RG 59: 825.00/1038, Armour, no. 125, 2 July 1938.

19. Alejandro Silva Bascunan, *Una experiencia social cristiana* (Santiago: Editorial del Pacífico, 1949), 71-82, 89.

20. Covarrubias, op. cit., 111.

21. *El Diario Ilustrado*, 29 Apr. 1938.

22. *La Opinión*, 8 June 1938.

23. Germán Gamonal, *Jorge Alessandri: el hombre, el político* (Santiago: Holanda Comunicaciones, S.A., 1987), 81.

24. *El Diario Ilustrado*, 19 Oct. 1938.

25. RG 59: 825.6463 Elec. Bond and Share Co./133, Armour, no. 249, 10 Sept. 1938, enclosure, memo of conversation with Curtis E. Calder, Santiago, 22 Aug. 1938; and 825.504/121, Armour, no. 309, 15 Oct. 1938.

26. The black market operation is described in RG 59: 825.5151/503, Frost, no. 469, 21 Jan. 1939; and for the extensiveness of Ross' bribery, see Alberto Cabero, *Recuerdos de don Pedro Aguirre Cerda* (Santiago: Imprenta Nascimento, 1948), 183.

27. RG 59: 825.00/1038, Armour, no. 125, 2 July 1938; and 825.00/1051, Armour, no. 230, 27 Aug. 1938.

28. *La Unión* (Valparaiso), 29 June 1938.

29. Luis Ortega Martínez, Carmen Norambuena Carrasco, Julio Pinto Vallejos, and Guillermo Bravo Acevedo, *Corporación de Fomento de la Producción: 50 años de realizaciones, 1939-1989* (Santiago: Corporación de Fomento de la Producción, 1989), 37.

30. Chile. Interior, v. 9769 (1938), Prov. 12902, Servicios de Investigación, 29 July 1938; and Chile. Hacienda, "Exposición sobre el estado de la hacienda pública," (Santiago: Oficina del Presupuesto, Oct. 1938), Min. Francisco Garces Gana; and RG 59: 825.504/121, Armour, no. 309, 15 Oct. 1938.

31. RG 59: 825.00/1077, Armour, no. 309, 15 Oct. 1938.

32. Ibid.,/1032, Armour, no. 52, 18 May 1938.

33. On Ibáñez' return and early campaign, Würth Rojas, *Ibáñez: caudillo enigmático*, 203; on Democrats, Chile. Interior, v. 9505 (1937), Prov. 12658,

Carabineros de Chile, 25 Nov. 1937; and on reformers, *La Opinión*, 19 Aug. 1938.

34. RG 59: 825.00/1010, Philip, no. 739, 29 Oct. 1937.

35. *La Opinión*, 10 June, 20 and 27 Aug. 1938.

36. Andrew Barnard, "The Chilean Communist Party: 1922-1947" (Ph.D. diss., University College, University of London, Dec. 1977), 196.

37. Chile. Interior, v. 9506 (1937), Prov. 12661, Int. de Malleco, 22 Nov. 1937.

38. RG 59: 825.00/1051, Armour, no. 230, 27 Aug. 1938.

39. *La Opinión*, 10 June 1938.

40. RG 59: 825.50 Economic Council/1, Frost, no. 141, 12 May 1938; and 825.00/1051, Armour, no. 230, 27 Aug. 1938.

41. Jordi Fuentes and Lia Cortes, *Diccionario político de Chile (1810-1966)* (Santiago: Editorial Orbe, 1967), 16-17. The importance of his marriage was noted by John Gunther, op.cit., 241. For a fuller portrait of his career, Cabero, op. cit., 50-124; and Luis Palma Zuñiga, *Pedro Aguirre Cerda: maestro, estadísta, gobernante* (Santiago: Editorial Andres Bello, 1963), 11-104.

42. Chile. Colección Pedro Aguirre Cerda, v. 47 (1937), Fs. 363. Octavio Allende E. to A.C.

43. Roger Joseph Burbach, "The Chilean Industrial Bourgeoisie and Foreign Capital, 1920-1970," (Ph.D. diss., Indiana University, 1975), 66-67.

44. See Alessandri's letter to Agustín Edwards in Alexander, op. cit., 2:748.

45. Chile. Interior, v. 2 [old number] (1936), Carabineros de Chile, no. 197, 20 Aug. 1938.

46. Elias Lafertte, *Vida de un comunista* (Santiago: Editorial Austral, 1971), 300-11; Cabero, op. cit., 162; and Gabriel González Videla, *Memorias* (Santiago: Editorial Nacional Gabriel Mistral, 1975), 1:172-73.

47. Chile. Interior, v. 2 [old number] (1936), Carabineros de Chile, no. 197, 20 Aug. 1938.

48. Ortega Martínez et al., op. cit., 39. The summary of the election in this work excludes any mention of Ibáñez.

49. Chile. Diputados, *Boletín de sesiones ordinarias*, Dip. Carlos Contreras Labarca presented Communists' views, 8 June 1937, 395-400.

50. *La Hora* (Santiago), 1 Nov. 1938.

51. Gamonal, op. cit., 81.

52. Pedro Aguirre Cerda, *El problema agrario* (Paris, 1929), 244. See also Pedro Aguirre Cerda, *El problema industrial* (Santiago: Universidad de Chile, 1933).

53. Infante Barros, op. cit., 47 and 104.

54. Ricardo Boizard B., *Patios Interiores* (Santiago: Nascimento, 1948), 23.

55. Marta Infante Barros, op. cit., 104, citing interview in *El Mercurio*, 6 Nov. 1938.

56. RG 59: 825.00/1051, Armour, no. 230, 27 Aug. 1938.

57. FO 371/21437 (A8158/571/9), Leigh-Smith, 23 Oct. 1938.

58. Interview with Charles A. Thomson of Foreign Policy Assoc. with Aguirre Cerda in Oct. 27. This was done for North American Newspaper Alliance, quoted in RG 59: 825.00/1084, Armour, no. 329, 29 Oct. 1938.

59. RG 59: 825.00/1062, Armour, no. 255, 14 Sept. 1938.

60. Chile. Interior, v. 3 [old number], no. 50, Servicios de Investigaciones, 7 Oct. 1938; and Int. de Malleco, 6 Oct. 1938.

61. Chile. Interior, v. 3 [old number], no. 50, Servicios de Investigaciones, 7 Oct. 1938; and Int. de Malleco, 6 Oct. 1938.

62. Frederico C. Gil, *The Political System of Chile* (Boston: Houghton Mifflin Co., 1966), 63.

63. Campaign is described in *La Opinión*, 24 Aug. 1937. See also RG 59: 825.00/1009, Carlos C. Hall, Consul Antofagasta, voluntary report, 23 Sept. 1937.

64. *La Opinión*, 21 Mar. 12 Apr., 28 Oct., and 9 Nov. 1937, and 15 Jan. 1938.

65. Ibid., 2 and 21 Mar. 1937.

66. Ibid., 13 Oct. 1937; and Alexander, op. cit., 2:662.

67. RG 59: 825.00/932, NcNiece, no. 106, 17 June 1936. On fighting between Nacis and Socialists generally, see Alexander, op. cit., 2:678; and Julio César Jobet, *El partido socialista de Chile* (Santiago: Editorial Prenso Latinoamerica, S.A., 1971), 1:38.

68. RG 59: 825.00/984, Philip, no. 535, 30 Mar. 1937.

69. Chile. Interior, v. 2 [old number] (1938), no. 168, Carabineros de Chile, 6 Aug. 1938, and Prov. 14908, Carabineros de Chile, 9 Sept. 1938.

70. RG 59: 825.42/51, Armour, no. 162, 23 July 1938.

71. This sequence is reconstructed from accounts in FO 371-21437 (A4234 /671/9), C. Bentinck, 23 May 1938; RG 59: 825.00/1032, Armour, no. 52, 18 May 1938; 825.00/1036, Armour, no. 83, 6 June 1938, enclosure no. 1, Mr. Dow's report on Incidents in the Chilean Congress on May 21, 1938 (the best account by an eyewitness); and Fernando Pinto Lagarrigue, *Crónica política*

del siglo XX: desde Errázuriz Echaurren hasta Alessandri Palma (Santiago: Editorial Orbe, 1972), 251.

72. Covarrubias, op. cit., 98.

73. Chile. Interior, v. 30 [old number] (1938), Prov. 15357, Int. de Valparaiso, 10 June 1938; and v. 22 [old number] (1938), Prov. 11623, Carabineros de Chile, 5 July 1938.

74. Chile. Diputados, *Boletín de sesiones ordinarios*, Dip. Luis Urrutía Ibáñez, 6 June 1938, 502-503, citing open letter from the candidate.

75. Pinto Lagarrigue, op. cit., 253.

76. FO 371-21437 (A6807/571/9), P. Leigh-Smith, Chargé, 24 Aug. 1938.

77. RG 59: 825.00 Revs/249, Armour, no. 245, 7 Sept. 1938; and Alexander, op. cit., 2:682.

78. RG 59: 825.00 Revs/249, Armour, no. 245, 7 Sept. 1938. See also Sznajder, "A Case of Non-European Fascism," 284-85; Rodrigo Alliende González, *El jefe: la vida de Jorge González von Marées* (Santiago: Ediciones Los Castaños, 1990), 115-43; and Arturo Alessandri Palma, *Recuerdos de gobierno* (Santiago Editorial Nascimento, 1967), 3:186-93.

79. For a repetition of government arguments, see RG 165: MID 2271-0-87/19, Wooten, no. 2583, 14 Sept. 1938; and RG 59: 825.00/1072, Armour, no. 292, 4 Oct. 1938.

80. Alexander, op. cit., 2:690.

81. France-MAE, Chili. v. 12, 21 Sept. 1938; and FO 371-21437 (A7177/571/9), Leigh-Smith, 8 Sept. 1938. See also his report of 12 Sept.

82. RG 59: 825.00/1072, Armour, no. 292, 4 Oct. 1938, enclosure no. 1, transcript of Alessandri's radio address, 30 Sept. 1938, altered slightly for style.

83. Infante Barros, op. cit., 25.

84. Moulian and Torres, op. cit., 244.

85. RG 59: 825.00 Revs/250, Armour, no. 252, 9 Sept. 1938, memo of conversation with Gustavo Ross.

86. France-MAE, Chili, v. 12, 28 Oct. 1938.

87. *El Mercurio*, 30 Mar. 1939; RG 59: 825.00/1137, Armour, no. 602, 5 Apr. 1939, citing news accounts in Naci paper, *Trabajo*, and González von Marées interview in *La Hora*; and Würth, op. cit., 208.

88. RG 59: 825.00/1077, Armour, no. 309, 15 Oct. 1938, on prediction of victory for Ross; and FO 371/21437 (A8158/571/9), Leigh-Smith, 23 Oct. 1938, interview with Aguirre Cerda.

89. An observation made in Moulian and Torres, op. cit., 197; and the central thesis of Infante Barros, op. cit., especially 15-30.

90. FO 371-21437 (A8765/571/9), C. Bentinck, 14 Nov. 1938; and Covarrubias, op. cit., 120.

91. RG 165: MID 2657-0-163/16, Wooten, no. 2620, 26 Oct. 1938.

92. RG 165, MID 2657-0-163/19, Wooten, no. 2639, 15 Nov. 1938; and Frederick M. Nunn, *The Military in Chilean History: essays on civil-military relations, 1810-1973* (Albuquerque: University of New Mexico Press, 1976), 235. See also BOLSA, B55, Valparaiso to London, 2 Nov. 1938.

93. BOLSA, B55, Valparaiso to London, 26 Oct. 1938.

94. FO 371/21437 (A9684/571/9), C. Bentinck, 16 Dec. 1938.

95. Ibid., 21 Dec. 1938.

96. RG 59: 825.51/1034, EA to Welles, 27 Dec. 1938.

97. To fund Chile's credit structure, the money was for the State Mortgage Bank. RG 59: 825.00/1097, Armour, no. 371, 23 Nov. 1938, and 825.51/1033, memo of conversation: Norbert Bogdan, Schroeder and Co., and Spruille Braden, 23 Dec. 1938.

98. Urzúa V., *La democracia práctica*, 138-41.

99. Based on a survey of 18 publicly traded corporations, Chile. Diputados, *Boletín de sesiones ordinarios*, Dip. Sergio Fernández L., 25 July 1939, 1462.

100. RG 59: Chile 825.00/1213, Bowers, no. 512, 14 May 1940; and Alessandri, RG 59: 825.00/1130, Armour, no. 555, 8 Mar. 1939, enclosure no. 1, Armour interview with Alessandri.

101. RG 59: 825.00/1102, Armour, no. 408, 6 Dec. 1938; and Michael Fleet, *The Rise and Fall of Chilean Christian Democracy* (Princeton: Princeton University Press, 1985), 46-48.

102. Urzúa V., op. cit., 151.

103. RG 165: MID 2054-106/81, Wooten, no. 2, 11 Jan. 1939; and MID 2054-106/98, Wooten, no. 17, 12 July 1939.

104. RG 59: 825.00 Revolutions/256, Armour, no. 439, 28 Dec. 1938, enclosure of interview between Mr. and Mrs. Evans Clark of Twentieth Century Fund with González von Marées, 23 Dec.

105. RG 59: 825.00/1097, Armour, no. 371, 23 Nov. 1938, 825.6363/175, memo of Conversation, 27 Jan. 1939; 825.00/1122, Frost, no. 489, 4 Feb. 1939; and FO 371-22736 (A534/156/9), C. Bentinck, 12 Jan. 1939 and 20 Mar. 1939.

106. The account here differs substantially from the views of Nunn, op. cit., 236. See Würth, op. cit., 211; RG 59: 825.00/1159, Trueblood, no. 767, 11 July

1939; 825.00/1168-1169, Frost telegrams 25-26 Aug. 1939; no decimal number, Frost, no. 872, 26 Aug. 1939; RG 165: MID 2657-0-136, Wooten, no. 3068, 26 Aug. 1939; and FO 371/24182 (A3760/51/9), R. Hogge, report on Vanguardia Popular Socialista, 15 July 1940.

107. RG 165: MID 2657-0-136/10, Wooten, no. 3077, 6 Sept. 1939. See also MID 2657-0-136/13, Wooten, no. 2954, 4 Nov. 1939; and MID 2657-0-136/14, Wooten, no. 3140, 16 Feb. 1940.

108. Michael Potashnik, "Nacismo: National Socialism in Chile, 1932-1938," (Ph.D. diss., University of California Los Angeles, 1974), 340, 345; and Arturo Olavarría Bravo, *Chile entre dos Alessandri: Memorias políticas* (Santiago: Editorial Nascimento, 1962), 1:519-28.

109. RG 165: War Dept., MID 2054-106/80, Wooten, no. 1, 21 Dec. 1938.

110. RG 165: MID 2054-106/81, Wooten, no. 2, 11 Jan. 1939.

111. Drake, op. cit., chap. 8. It is often asserted the Communists did not ask for office; but this is not true, see Barnard, op. cit., 235.

112. *La Nación*, 10 Nov. 1938; RG 165, MID 2657-0-163/19, Wooten, no. 2639, 15 Nov. 1938; and MID 2008-171/12, Weeks, no. 2840, 21 Apr. 1939.

113. Alejandro Chélen Rojas, *Trayectoria del socialismo: apuntes para una historia crítica del socialismo chileno* (Buenos Aires: Editorial Astral, 1967), 103; and Benny Pollack and Hernán Rosencranz, *Revolutionary Social Democracy: The Chilean Socialist Party* (London: Frances Pinter, 1986), 19.

114. RG 59: 825.00/1032, Armour, no. 52, 18 May 1938.

115. Ibid.,/1097, Armour, no. 371, 23 Nov. 1938.

116. Alan Angell, *Politics and the Labour Movement in Chile* (London: Oxford University Press for the Royal Institute of International Affairs, 1972), 54.

117. Chile. Interior, v. 10203 (1940), Min. de Trabajo, Comisión Central Mixta de Sueldos y Comisiones Provinciales.

118. Chile. Diputados, *Boletín de sesiones ordinarios*, Dip. Sergio Fernández L., 25 July 1939, 1464, quotes extensively from official data.

119. Thomas Miller Klubock, "Class, Community, and Gender in the Chilean copper Mines: The El Teniente Miners and working class Politics, 1904-1951," 2 vols. (Ph.D. diss., Yale University, 1993), 2:439, 446-47.

120. *La Opinión*, 1 and 25 Aug., and 12 Dec. 1939.

121. Chile. Interior, v. 9994 (1939), no. 11191, Puerto Montt, 4 May 1939.

122. On Zapata, see Chile. Fomento (1939), Oficios, v. 1599, no. 8, Min. de Fomento al Presidente de la Cámara de Diputados, 13 Oct. 1939, Oficio no. 1264; on gold fields in general, see same vol., no. 8, Jorge Parodi Blayfus, Jefe

de Lavaderos de Oro al Min. de Fomento, 19 Oct. 1939, oficio no. 1608; and Chile. Interior, v. 10202 (1940), Min. de Fomento, Lavaderos de Oro.

123. Chile. Interior, v. 10000 (1939), no. 19055, Gobernación San Carlos. See salary scales in, RG 151: Commerce Dept., Bureau of Foreign and Domestic Commerce, Commercial Attaches, Santiago, Minedes McLean, Special Report no. 26, 28 Apr. 1939. On wages, Chile. Diputados, *Boletín de sesiones ordinarias*, Dip. Juan Guerra G., 29 June 1938, 1135, and July 1940, 1397-98; and on housing, RG 59: 825.48-Earthquake 1939/133, McNiece, 27 Mar. 1939.

124. Karin Alejandra Rosemblatt, "Gendered Compromises: Political Cultures, Socialist Politics, and the State in Chile, 1920-1950" (Ph.D. diss., University of Wisconsin, 1996), 138; and Klubock, op. cit., 1:349.

125. Ibid., 186-90, 220-32; and Asunción Lavrin, "Women, Feminism and Social Change in Argentina, Chile, and Uruguay," in Donna Guy, Mary Karasch, and Asunción Lavrin, *Engendering Latin America*, vol. 3 (Lincoln: University of Nebraska Press, 1995), 316-20.

126. Antezana-Pernet, "Mobilizing Women in the Popular Front Era: Feminism, Class, and Politics in the Movimiento Pro-Emancipación de la Mujer Chilena [MEMCh]," (Ph.D. diss., University of California Irvine, 1996), 116-77.

127. RG 151: Bureau of Foreign and Domestic Commerce, Commercial Attaches, Santiago, Know, Special Report no. 6, 7 Oct. 1939.

128. RG 151: Bureau of Foreign and Domestic Commerce, Commercial Attaches, Santiago, Knox, Economic and Trade Notes, no. 93, 27 Oct. 1939, and no. 135, 7 Dec. 1939.

129. Chile. Interior, v. 10203 (1940), Dirección del Servicio de Restaurantes Populares, 28 Dec. 1938, and no. 907, 7 Aug. 1939.

130. There were two major organizations, the National Housing Front [Frente Nacional de la Vivienda] to which Zapata belonged, and the Central Renter's Committee [Junta Central de Arrendatarios], they often coordinated their efforts. *La Opinión*, 26 July 1938, 21 Feb., and 5 and 17 Mar. 1939.

131. RG 151: Bureau of Foreign and Domestic Commerce, Commercial Attaches, Santiago, Knox, Jr., Economic and Trade Notes, no. 292, 21 Apr. 1939.

132. RG 151: Bureau of Foreign and Domestic Commerce, Commercial Attaches, Santiago, Knox, Special Report, no. 12, 17 Nov. 1939.

133. *La Opinión*, 22 Mar. 1939; and Chile. Fomento (1939), Oficios, v. 1594, no. 3, Min. de Fomento al Director Gerente de la Caja Nacional de Ahorros, 19 Apr. 1939, no. 493.

134. Chile. Interior, v. 9996 (1939), no. 14909, Carabineros de Chile, Antofagasta, 3 June 1939.

135. *La Opinión*, 12 Dec. 1939; and Chile. Interior, v. 10206 (1940), no. 19533, Dirección General de Investigaciones e Identificación.

136. Chile. Fomento (1939), Oficios, v. 1599, no. 8, Min. de Fomento al Presidente de la Camara de Diputados, 5 Sept. 1939, no. 1226.

137. *La Opinión*, 19 Mar. 1939.

138. Ibid., and 2 June 1939, for example on Valparaiso. For groups demonstrating, see notes on renters' leagues in *La Opinión*, 16 Nov. and 12 Dec. 1939.

139. RG 59: 825.61/17, Milliken, 6 May 1939.

140. RG 59: 825.00/1139, Armour, no. 606, 5 Apr. 1939.

141. See, for example, Chile. Interior, v. 9991 (1939), no. 14145, Gobernación de Quillota, 23 May 1939.

142. *La Opinión*, 19 Mar. 1939.

143. RG 59: 825.52/25, Frost, no. 858, 23 Aug. 1939.

144. Ibid., memo of conversations between Aguirre Cerda and Frank Tannenbaum.

145. RG 59: 825.61/17, Milliken, 6 May 1939; Chile. Interior, v. 10205 (1940), Carabineros de Chile, Circular no. 4, Santiago, 19 Dec. 1939; and v. 10179 (1940), Municipalidad de Pirque, no. 245, 19 Aug. 1940.

146. RG 59: 825.00/1159, Trueblood, no. 767, 11 July 1939; and *La Opinión*, 7 Sept. 1939.

147. RG 59: 825.504/133, Frost, no. 825, 15 Aug. 1939.

148. *La Opinión*, 24 Oct. 1939.

149. RG 59: 825.00B/56, Armour, no. 568, 14 Mar. 1939.

150. RG 825.00B/61, Frost, no. 869, 24 Aug. 1939, also same file, enclosure no. 1, interview with Martín Bunster, Min. of Education, 3 Aug. 1939. See also Barnard, "The Chilean Communist Party," 230-33.

151. RG 59: 825.00/1122, Frost, no. 489, 4 Feb. 1939; on elán, RG 165: MID 2008-172/3, Wooten, no. 2839, 21 Apr. 1939; and on coup, RG 165: MID 2657-0-136/10, Wooten, no. 3077, 6 Sept. 1939. See also Florencio Duran Bernales, *El Partido Radical* (Santiago: Editorial Nascimento, 1958), 192-93. Drake sees the Socialists integrating themselves within the bureaucracy, op. cit., 237-41.

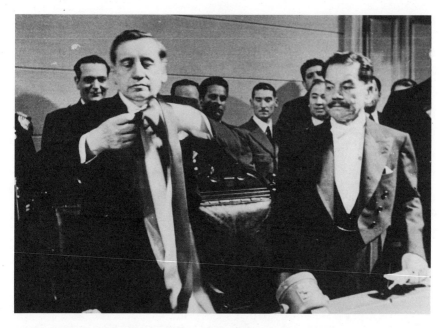

Fig. 6. Inauguration of President Pedro Aguirre Cerda, leader of Popular Front, Dec. 1938. President Arturo Alessandri holds the presidential sash before handing it to Aguirre Cerda. Close comrades in the 1920s, they became bitter enemies in the 1930s. Chile. Archivo Nacional.

Fig. 8. Funeral cortege, President Pedro Aguirre Cerda, Nov. 1941. La Moneda, presidential palace, in background. Chile. Archivo Nacional.

Fig. 7. President Pedro Aguirre Cerda, 1938-41. Official portrait. Chile. Archivo Nacional.

7

The Popular Front and
U.S. Economic Power

> The Government of Chile is confronted with two
> necessities: (1) to increase government revenues
> [...] to permit the Administration [...] to carry out
> its social program; and (2) to obtain more foreign
> exchange to purchase requirements from abroad.
> Unfortunately, the Aguirre Government, as have its
> predecessors, considers that American investment
> interests in Chile are best able to satisfy these
> necessities.
>
> U.S. State Department memo, 30 Jan. 1939[8]

In the late 1930s, a domestic coalition of interests was emerging
within Chile. It would gradually come to support what a later
generation called "development from within." Elements of the coalition
(industrialists, bureaucrats, academics, professional associations, and
labor unions) already imagined how they would gain from the retention
of income derived from exports. Before the outbreak of World War II,
the coalition was still trying to define the elements of economic nationalism. President Aguirre Cerda wanted to industrialize Chile and to
establish government-funded social programs. Chile lacked the capital
to do either. Domestic capitalists, including many new industrialists
who wanted higher tariffs, nonetheless hated his government and
thought its social proposals dangerous. Their allies in Congress bottled
up funding for many of his proposals. The president was left with no
alternative except to seek funding abroad.

Chile's economy and government revenues relied on copper exports.
Negotiations between Chile and the United States over the distribution

of income from this sector traversed the gamut of economic diplomacy: trade agreements, currency controls, the foreign debt, and labor regulations. Chile could derive more income from copper sales, borrow more money from the United States, or see its economy stagnate. Discussions about these possibilities took place in Washington and Santiago among Chilean and U.S. officials and U.S. corporate officers. Often, U.S. officials acted as allies of U.S. corporations, but not always.

The Roosevelt administration was committed to an open world economy, the reduction of tariff and legal barriers to trade and investment, and the end of bilateral agreements. As the war shifted trade patterns, U.S. influence in Latin America intensified and began to alter the region's economies. Even nationalist sentiments in the region, that had hardened during the Depression, could not withstand the weight of U.S. commercial interests.

The U.S. government was also committed to undermining Germany's ties to Latin America. Franklin Delano Roosevelt openly feared the Nazi threat in the region and, by 1939, had married his Good Neighbor policy to a vision of Pan Americanism and the exclusion of Nazis. In August 1940, more than a year before the United States entered the war, the Roosevelt administration created the Office of the Coordinator of Inter-American Affairs [OCIAA] to counter Nazi propaganda in Latin America. Nelson Rockefeller, whose family had oil properties throughout the region, directed the OCIAA and, by war's end, controlled an agency spending US$45 million a year.[2] During a fireside chat in December 1940, Roosevelt warned that ignoring the Nazis in the Americas "is the same dangerous form of wishful thinking which has destroyed the powers of resistance of so many conquered peoples."[3]

Once the war began in Europe in the fall of 1939, the terms of negotiation were dramatically altered—for the worse in Chile's case.[4] If, as Robert Putnam argues, diplomacy involves games on two levels—one international and the other domestic—the war so changed the first level that the second had to adjust.[5] Chile's political system, still adjusting to the realities of the Depression, was plunged into a new international environment over which it had no control.

Before the War

When Aguirre Cerda took office, the world was still in the Depression. Estimates vary about Chile's economy at the end of the 1930s, with some claiming that a recovery began in 1937 followed by a two-year decline, while others insist that the economy either fell in 1938 and rose in 1939, or the reverse. All estimates agree, however, that mining dropped sharply by 1939, while agriculture fluctuated and industry continued to expand.[6] Given the importance of mineral exports, their decline forced the Chilean government to make hard choices.

The Popular Front sought, as had all administrations after 1930, to increase the availability of hard currency, which in 1939 meant gold or U.S. dollars. The nation's shortage of hard currency shaped many of the Popular Front's decisions involving foreign interests and foreign trade. For example, the Front had to decide what to do about compensation trade. In order to improve the balance of hard currency, the Alessandri administration, near its end, had changed the compensation rules: importers had to deposit 20 percent of the purchase price in dollars or gold with the Central Bank in advance of receiving any goods. The government decree amounted to a tax since trading companies had to sell their dollars at 19 pesos each while buying them from the government at 26 pesos. Currency rules that had been designed to extract income from U.S. mining companies now were applied to everyone. Once in office, the Popular Front government made only minor changes in the powers of the Currency Exchange Commission, which continued to extend its authority. In 1939, the Commission demanded that importers stop buying goods from the United States and purchase them instead from compensation countries. It even set quotas for some commodities.[7]

The Alessandri administration's decision to allow banks to deal on the black market, at a price of about 30 pesos to the dollar, was continued by the Popular Front. This led to three money markets: businesses licensed by the Exchange Commission could buy dollars at the cheapest peso price; others, under less stringent conditions but still with a government license, could buy dollars on the export-draft market run through the banks; and everyone else could pay the highest price on the open currency market (originally the black market). In practice, doing business required dealing in all three. Political influence with the Commission and access to the best exchange rate offered the highest profits. Manipulation of the various decrees, statutes, and trading practices was essential to the survival of many firms.[8]

None of this reduced the dollar shortage. In March 1939, the Commission had US$5 million to cover its outlays for the rest of the year; it already owed US$4 million on licensed imports. The government cut private remittances by two-thirds, forced some industries to buy dollars on the open market, reduced funds sent to support Chilean diplomats, and threw all U.S. imports onto the open market. The howl from U.S. merchants in Chile was heard all the way to Washington.[9] At this point, however, the United States had little leverage with the Popular Front for it had not yet offered the government anything for trade concessions.

At the same time and in response to the arms race, Chile's copper sales boomed. Chile became a crucial supplier to the United States. By 1940, of the 354 thousand short tons the United States purchased abroad, 170 thousand came from Chile.[10] In 1941, Chile sold 65 percent of its exported copper to the United States for close to US$150 million.[11] Copper made up 91 percent of all Chilean mineral exports and 56 percent of Chile's total sales abroad. Total returned value to Chile from copper sales rose from US$13 million in 1935 to US$27 million in 1939 and reached US$66 million in 1944. Most of this came in the form of wages, but taxes also accounted for a part. As a result of changes instituted by the Alessandri administration, copper-derived revenues had increased from the equivalent of US$2.8 million in the mid-1930s to US$11 million in 1938. Despite its efforts and for reasons related to the increasing role of the United States government in the copper market, Aguirre Cerda was less successful than Alessandri in milking the copper cow, yet copper company executives painted the Front as dangerous to the industry.[12]

Aguirre Cerda and his Minister of Finance, Roberto Wachholtz, initially demanded that the U.S. oil and copper companies convert 38 percent of their earnings from dollars to pesos at officially controlled rates. The increase in the currency requirement, given the government's manipulation of currency markets, served as an increase in taxation. The demand for a straight percentage meant that, if profits fell, the weight of the requirement could easily plunge the companies into the red. If a company's real operating costs in Chile fell below 38 percent, the government demanded that the company lend it the difference at no interest. The companies lobbied Washington and the Chilean Congress and had the proposal shelved. Two months later, the government asked the copper companies to ease the dollar shortage by selling some of their dollars to other U.S. companies in Chile. The firms refused the request.[13]

Currency requirements posed a greater threat to the copper companies than tax increases or nationalization. Tax increases could be fought by lobbying Congress. The threat of nationalization was remote, for although Chile had more copper reserves than North America and Africa combined, it lacked the engineering expertise to exploit them. The copper companies knew, however, that even their principal congressional allies, the members of the Liberal and Conservative parties, wanted to increase Chile's supply of hard currency. In August 1939, an agreement was struck between the government and the U.S. companies to link any increase in currency requirements to a rise in copper prices; but this worked somewhat against Aguirre Cerda's administration when prices unexpectedly fell.

The government also proposed a smelter at Chañaral, in the northern province of Atacama. Aguirre Cerda and Wachholtz wanted to break the U.S. refiner's hold over small Chilean copper companies. Arrangements made through an international cartel had given U.S. refiners an oligopoly position in Chile. Small Chilean companies had to sell their copper ores at prices fixed by two dominant companies, American Smelting and Refining and Phelps Dodge. Administration efforts to seek alternative refiners in Europe ended when these U.S. interests flexed their muscles within the cartel. The alternative was a smelter in Chile. When Aguirre Cerda proposed it, American Smelting and Phelps Dodge threatened a boycott of Chilean suppliers.[14]

Unfazed, the Popular Front asked the U.S. Export-Import Bank for a loan to build the smelter, saying that even if the U.S. companies carried through with their threat, Chile could still sell the copper to Germany and possibly Japan.[15] The Bank, a government agency founded to promote U.S. exports, already had a relationship with the Chilean government, since it had loaned the Alessandri administration the money to buy railroad equipment in 1938.[16] A new state development agency, CORFO, promised the Bank that it would buy all machinery for the smelter from the United States and projected an annual profit of US$800 thousand/year.

In an unusual show of nationalism, all the major Santiago papers supported the Front's proposal. U.S. copper and smelting interests, however, lobbied the State Department and the Export-Import Bank against the loan. They argued that Chilean competition would close U.S. mines; they feared losing access to silicates in Chilean ores that provided chemicals, necessary for refining copper, unavailable in U.S. ores. (They never mentioned any of this in Chile.) W.R. Grace and Company added its voice to the lobbying against the smelter because of the potential damage to its shipping business. The American Metal Company, Phelps Dodge Refining Corporation, and American Smelting and Refining admitted to the State Department that they had engaged in price fixing with Anaconda and Kennecott and were paying less for Chilean ores than those available in the United States. In October 1939, ignoring the contradiction with their earlier claims, the companies argued that the Chileans lacked the expertise to carry out the project and the smelter would never be profitable.[17] Amazingly, none of this lobbying effort was reported by the Chilean press.

The Popular Front strategy for getting loans for the smelter was to play Nazi Germany against the United States: it sought German financing at the same time it approached the Export-Import Bank. Again, the strength of the U.S. economy interfered. U.S. copper interests used their own contacts in Germany and made a deal with the Norddeutsch Affinerie, the dominant German refining firm. The German firm agreed not to compete with U.S. interests for Chilean ores and, in return, was promised Chilean tin, gold, and copper ores at reduced prices from U.S. companies. The Germans dropped discussions with the Chilean government. The Popular Front did not get its smelter.

The Chileans also hoped to raise copper sales to the United States, but their efforts to reduce U.S. copper tariffs ran into U.S. domestic lobbies led by Michigan and far-western states such as Arizona where massive rallies were held. The pro-tariff interests sent petitions to Washington warning that increasing Chilean copper imports would undercut the domestic sector, wrecking property values in mining states and increasing unemployment.[18] President Roosevelt rarely became involved in Chilean affairs, but this was an exception. He persuaded the U.S. companies not to raise their prices, and, in exchange, retained the tariff. Chileans learned of this in December 1939, and they were told that any deals on imports of onions and beans were off the table as well.[19] The Front's hope was dashed that a sharp increase in copper income would fund its plans for industrialization and social welfare reforms.

In their dealings with the Chilean government, the U.S. copper companies held all the assets. They ran the mines; they owned the technology; they had the basic market information and connections; and their lawyers ran sophisticated lobbies in New York, Washington, and Santiago. They also worked closely with the shipping firms, especially W.R. Grace. In addition to protecting against Chilean government initiatives at refining and diversification, the companies used their leverage in Washington to attack Chilean domestic policies. They insisted that their Chilean costs were rising; they complained of government wage decrees, taxes, and currency regulations. Cry as it might, the Chile Exploration Company, owned by Anaconda, could not hide a 14 percent profit in 1938.[20] The U.S. companies counted on the Chilean right, especially in Congress, where conservatives saw them as allies in the fight against a common enemy, the Popular Front. When copper company executives and State Department officials gathered in Washington to discuss the situation in Chile, Kennecott's president, Earl T. Stannard, told the meeting that he was hoping for an Ibañista uprising. State Department officials asked Stannard not to promote a revolution, and Stannard agreed; but he noted, "nothing could be worse than the present regime."[21] Aguirre Cerda had been in office one month.

No other export offered Chile an alternative to copper. Gold declined in importance, although the Front tripled the state bureaucracy overseeing its production.[22] An attempt to develop borax failed completely.[23] Nitrate production and exports revived in 1937, but then stagnated because of the international surplus.[24]

To make matters worse, a conflict erupted among companies in the United States over the fertilizer market. The nitrate controversy revealed to Chile the rising importance of U.S. regulatory power over trade issues. The struggle began near the end of the Alessandri administration. U.S. fertilizer interests were battling for market shares. One group petitioned the Federal Trade Commission to sue the Chilean Nitrate and Iodine Sales Corporation over its advertising in the United States that claimed salitre had qualities not found in "synthetic" nitrates, such as ammonia. William S. Culbertson, the former Ambassador to Santiago, appeared as counsel for the defense. Nitrate and Iodine Sales managed to get the matter settled out of court by withdrawing all its advertising.[25] Chile was vulnerable because the FTC, like any bureaucracy anxious to publicize its importance, had discovered a target with few U.S. defenders. In 1939, the FTC launched another suit in New York on behalf of farmers who claimed that Nitrate and Iodine Sales was controlling the price of salitre.[26]

Formally, the second FTC action raised the issue of extra-territoriality: did the laws of the United States apply to the actions of a Chilean corporation? Behind the legal maneuvers were two belligerents, the ammonia producers in the United States and the Guggenheims. The former saw Nitrate and Iodine Sales as a Guggenheim entity and used the Federal Trade Commission to harass it. The Guggenheims responded by asking the Chilean government and the U.S. State Department for help.[27] In the end, the Chilean government cut a deal to protect salitre's share of the U.S market, even though the Guggenheims remained the principal importers of the Chilean mineral. Before this arrangement was finally reached, the wrangling among U.S. corporations, the Chilean government, the State Department, and the FTC had gone on for another two years. The delay came as lawyers in the Justice and State Departments fought over the wording of Chile's consent and settlement.[28] In another demonstration of its weakness, Chile protested, to no effect, the construction in Ohio of a new ammonia plant by Allied Chemical.[29]

In 1939, during these quarrels over copper and nitrates, the Aguirre Cerda administration created the Corporation for the Development of Production, hereafter called the Development Corporation [Corporación de Fomento de la Producción, or CORFO], an innovation unique in Latin America at the time. Aguirre Cerda had proposed state economic planning in his campaign, but the administration's efforts to create a planning agency were quickly blocked by the congressional opposition. Then an earthquake, in January 1939, destroyed the region surrounding Concepción, leveling a quarter of that city and almost all of Chillán. Nine smaller centers in southern Chile also suffered massive destruction. Overall, between 12 and 15 thousand people died, about 70 percent of them children. Another 18 thousand were severely injured; 80 thousand were left homeless. Transport, water supplies, and sewage systems broke down; and flour mills, railroad lines, and irrigation systems were destroyed. Property damage was estimated at US$50 million.[30] Aguirre Cerda and Wachholtz saw an opportunity and proposed CORFO, empowering it to raise capital and coordinate spending for reconstruction in the south. The initial proposal, presented 1 February 1939, called for a 100 percent tax increase on certain industries.[31]

The Liberal and Conservative parties made a counter-proposal to CORFO and claimed that disaster relief required no new taxes. In an attempt to undercut the opposition, Wachholtz announced that the agency had already received commitments from the United States for US$80 million in new loans, a lie that boomeranged when the United States denied it. Debate went on for a month as the government redesigned the program, scaling back tax increases.

Every draft of the program, however, relied on foreign loans.[32] On virtually his first day as minister, Wachholtz had told the U.S. Ambassador in Santiago that he expected help from Washington. The United States had helped Brazil and had loaned Alessandri some money, so it should also help the Popular Front: US$10 million a year for the next five years sounded about right. As the cost of rescuing the southern zone mounted, the government suspended all foreign debt payments. To make such a decision while requesting new loans struck one U.S. consul as "rather audacious."[33]

The earthquake also handed the right some political opportunities. Opposition congressmen pointed, with some effect, to the misappropriation and, in some cases, outright theft of relief funds, medicine, and clothing. A thousand bundles of goods from Brazil disappeared and no record was ever kept of supplies that arrived from Japan.[34] Aside from administrative incompetence and even malfeasance, the Front's response to the earthquake underlined its internal divisions. In fact, the administration's original proposal for CORFO split the Front, with Socialists attacking the proposal because it had not been drawn up by the Ministry of Development, which they controlled.[35] The Communists were the only party that supported the government unconditionally; they staged the labor rallies that ultimately pressured Congress into creating CORFO.

CORFO was a major achievement in government planning and capital investment, even though its role in national development took years to formalize. It embodied many of the nationalist aspirations that had begun in the 1920s and had crystallized after the Crash. It established administrative priorities for state investment in infrastructure and targeted sectors. It was not a socially progressive agency. Its initial directorate included Marcial Mora, president of the Central Bank; Santiago Labarca, president of the International Exchange Commission; Juan Antonio Ríos, then president of the State Mortgage Bank; and the heads of the major Chilean guilds: the SNA [agriculture], SNM [mining], and SOFOFA [industry].[36] The central point is that its financial underpinnings cannot be overlooked: how was Chile to realize its nationalist hopes while depending on U.S. government loans?

The War and Domestic Possibilities

Negotiations between Chile and the United States during the war revived issues from the 1930s and altered the bargaining position of

U.S. corporations within Chile. At times, the government and U.S. corporations made deals disliked by Chilean capitalists, that is, the Chilean right; at other times, the right supported the U.S. position in defiance of the Aguirre Cerda administration. A final combination also occurred when Chilean capitalists united with the Chilean government in demanding concessions from U.S. corporations.

For Chile, World War II was a repetition of economic events in World War I. Trade with Germany was cut off by the British navy, and the British blacklisted Chilean firms owned by Germans, by Chileans of German descent, or by Chileans with ties to Germany. Shipping costs doubled. By June 1940, Chilean mineral exports fell to half of their level before the war. The war hit other Chilean sectors hard: Germany had been buying half of Chile's timber, animal, and agricultural exports.[37]

Even before it entered the war, the United States rewrote rules governing its foreign trade to maximize federal control of raw materials, credit, and shipping in the Atlantic economy. The Roosevelt administration saw a chance for economic hegemony. Believing that the war would cost the British their remaining assets in the region, the president hoped to see the United States displace them entirely in Latin America. His administration also tried to undermine Nazi trade with Latin America in order to reduce German political influence in the area. The Germans persistently told the United States they had little interest in Latin America, but they ran a South American spy network from Rio de Janeiro that had agents in Valparaiso. U.S. diplomatic pressure shut down the network in late 1942.[38] In early 1941, as the United States drew closer to the conflict, the Roosevelt administration imposed its own blacklist on Chilean firms with ties to Germany. Once the United States entered the war, Chile also lost its trade with Japan, just at a time when Japanese purchases of Chilean exports were booming.[39]

The Chileans, thrown into a panic by the collapse of trade through late 1939 and 1940, pressured the U.S. mineral companies to return more dollars to the country and keep the mines open. By 1940, Chilean officials and U.S. copper firms controlling Chilean ores assured the State Department that they would cooperate with new regulations in return for increased access to the U.S. market.[40] The copper sector then employed 40 thousand men, nitrates, about 25 thousand. Unlike 1914-16, the onset of World War II did not lead to a surge in mining employment; in fact, as men left the unproductive gold fields, overall employment in mining declined slightly (see Graph 7.1).

Graph 7.1: Employment in Mining, 1934-1943

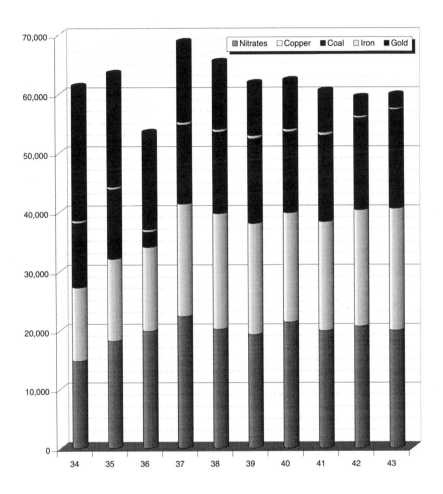

Source: Chile, *Estadística chilena* (Dec. 1943), 691.

The shifting conditions at the end of the 1930s and Chile's inability to broaden its exports to the United States harmed the country's terms of trade, which continued to deteriorate until 1943. This, of course, further reduced the supply of hard currency and hit the government's own revenues.[41] The government's fiscal crisis became so severe that the executive vice-president of CORFO, Guillermo del Pedregal, traveled to Washington in February 1940, to plead for dollars from the Export-Import Bank.[42] The State Department backed his effort which meant it now supported "political" loans to maintain a desired stability, although it never admitted this objective.[43]

Chile's desperation could not have been plainer. In an explanation famous among specialists on Chile, Markos Mamalakis argued that "sectoral clashes," that is, competing demands among Chilean capitalists, were to blame for the country's economic stagnation from the 1940s to the 1960s.[44] What is missing from Mamalakis' interpretation is that Chile's sectoral conflicts were closely tied to its foreign trade and the role of the state in brokering trade-based income. These clashes were fights for position within a dependent economy. It was not only the government but the country as a whole that was short of hard currency and capital.

CORFO became a means of channeling these conflicts. Whatever its rationale, in practice, CORFO became the agency for garnering U.S. loans with which to ameliorate domestic conflicts. The loans allowed the Front to launch a few public works, and very briefly, hold off the ravages of inflation on wages. CORFO's primary domestic goal was clientalistic; it was only secondarily a vehicle of development. (CORFO was also an important training ground in economic planning of every kind.)[45]

Each time the Export-Import Bank turned a CORFO proposal down, it reduced the government's political stability. Unfortunately for the Popular Front, the directorate of the Export-Import Bank did not see itself as a source of foreign stability; it existed to promote U.S. exports. Its primary clients were U.S. businessmen operating abroad. And the Bank was not in any hurry to review Chilean projects. Using its influence with the Bank, the Treasury Department opposed funding "industrial experiments" by foreign governments. Bank officials disliked the nationalist ideology of the Popular Front. After reviewing del Pedregal's request for more than a year, the Bank pledged US$17 million, with the condition that the Bank approve all CORFO projects individually.[46]

Aguirre Cerda did not take this with good grace. In April 1941, U.S. Ambassador Claude G. Bowers reported that the president was "in a rather angry mood" over the loan conditions. He objected to the project reviews and also to a requirement that the money remain in New York until spending was authorized. He asked Bowers if these tough conditions had been set to punish him for allowing Communists in his administration. He explained that there was a Fifth Column in his government, that it was positioned to stage strikes and sabotage operations, but that the government could do nothing without U.S. support. Loans would allow his administration to challenge the Nazis and the Communists "without taking unnecessary chances."[47]

In fact, Aguirre Cerda misunderstood what was happening. The Export-Import Bank was not attacking the left in his coalition; it was imposing the same conditions on more right-wing regimes in Argentina, Brazil, Colombia, and Peru.[48] Like any bureaucracy, it wanted control. As a show of its power, the Bank denied a Chilean request for funds to retool a major nitrate plant in December 1941.[49] The president's assumptions, however, matched a view that was evolving within Chile. Even though the Popular Front had won office with leftist support, the Radicals and the Socialists now saw the Communists as competitors and, therefore, obstacles to their larger goals. They needed to expand the bureaucracy and deliver on their populist promises and were willing to abandon their electoral allies in order to gain the U.S. funds for their projects. They assumed, erroneously, that the United States was as preoccupied with Communists as they were.

Divisions within Chile, of course, weakened the Popular Front's position in negotiating with the United States. Archival records reveal that, if anything, the Popular Front leaders—not least the president himself—were far more preoccupied with how U.S. actions would affect their capacity to maintain office than with how such actions might affect Chile's rate of economic growth. The political needs of the Front leaders was turning them into a new comprador class that dared not be too confrontational with U.S. officials. There was a strong correlation between the role that U.S. corporations would play within Chile and the ongoing economic diplomacy between Chile and the United States. The contests over oil and electricity, which are elaborated below, closely resembled the one already presented over copper. What appeared to be issues tied to particular sectors became contests over foreign loans, taxes, currency rules, and labor regulations.

In an essay on the relation between domestic politics and international relations, Robert Putnam argued that there were at least two levels of negotiation in international bargaining: one level among the negotiators as they represent the interests of their respective states and another as domestic political interests consider whether or not to approve the negotiated outcome:

> At the national level, domestic groups pursue their interests by pressuring the government to adopt favorable policies, and politicians seek power by constructing coalitions among those groups. At the international level, national governments seek to maximize their own ability to satisfy domestic pressure, while minimizing the adverse consequences of foreign developments. Neither of the two games can be ignored by central decision makers [political leaders], so long as their countries remain interdependent, yet sovereign.[50]

The price of losing at either the domestic or international level is high; the threat of such a loss may force a political leader to walk away from the international negotiation (even at the risk of war) and the complications of losing in the national arena include political annihilation. Putnam does not treat the dilemmas of underdeveloped nations as a special case; but I think it is.[51] One factor that Chile illustrates and that has to be considered as both domestic and international in underdeveloped nations: U.S. corporations were present at the international table vis à vis the State Department and at the domestic political table through the Chilean Congress.

Oil company negotiations illustrate the kind of jockeying that took place. On the eve of the war, the technocrats in Chile's Finance Ministry placed a high priority on reducing the nation's bill for imported fuel as a means of saving dollars and raising capital for domestic investment. In January 1939, the Popular Front listed the creation of a state oil monopoly as high on its list of goals. Latin American specialists in the State Department quickly drew a comparison between the Popular Front's rhetoric and the seizure of United States and British oil facilities in Mexico. Chile was not Mexico, and Aguirre Cerda was no Cárdenas. The exact value of foreign oil holdings in Chile is unknown; the companies refused to tell Washington and would not even reveal if they were making money. They clearly wanted to remain in Chile. In the year 1937, they had sold US$8.8 million worth of oil products, 55 percent of the country's total consumption, and were the principal suppliers of fuel to the copper and nitrate plants.

By 1939, COPEC, the Chilean company Alessandri had created, controlled 30 percent of the oil market. The Popular Front government planned to restructure COPEC and monopolize fuel distribution; it promised that foreign companies would be compensated as their resources were taken over.[52] CORFO approached the Export-Import Bank for a loan to finance the take over. The two foreign companies, Shell-

Mex and West India (Standard Oil) feared that a seizure of their equipment within Chile, coming so soon after that in Mexico, would encourage other Latin American nations to do the same.[53]

The foreign companies threatened to pull out of Chile. Aguirre Cerda feared that this would lead to another fuel shortage, and he settled for a US$300 million loan from the companies to the government in return for ending its plans for COPEC's domestic monopoly.[54] Shell-Mex, West India, and COPEC then strengthened their oligopoly by fixing prices and distribution practices, which destroyed all smaller distributors. In 1940, when the Communists pushed for Popular Front support of Mexico in its continuing confrontation with the U.S. and British oil companies, President Aguirre Cerda told them to shut up. Support for Mexico was never raised again.[55]

There was no alternative to relying on foreign fuel. The government tried to create a state-run coal company but was blocked in Congress. The coal mines were decrepit and starved for new investment; output was flat. Many of the older nitrate plants still used domestic coal and, by November 1939, supplies were so low that they had to be rationed in the nitrate zone. State railways were shutting down for lack of coal.[56] In 1940, the coal miners struck. The administration blamed Communist subversives and begged the United States for coal supplies to break the strike.[57] The government's overwhelming dependence on the United States was very evident as it asked for, and received, foreign help in breaking a radical social movement.

There was one Front proposal to nationalize an industry that was implemented, that on electricity and the tramways. It, therefore, merits a more extended discussion involving what nationalization could accomplish in this context. Again, the government's need for dollars shaped the negotiations. Aguirre Cerda's increasing discomfort with the Communists also played a role. Finally, Santiago's need for electric power and public transportation meant that grandstanding against Chilean Electric paid high political dividends. In 1937 and 1938, the Popular Front had repeatedly denounced the Calder-Ross Agreements (discussed in Chapter 5). Chilean Electric lost much of its investment and Calder lost everything he had been promised in the Agreements. The electric company's profits never rose above 3 percent in any year, and they could not be repatriated because of exchange restrictions. It paid no dividends for ten years.[58] Alessandri had promised tax exemptions in return for a government-imposed policy of consolidation that would merge all existing electric facilities in the central axis of Santiago-Valparaiso by 1942. On taking office, Aguirre Cerda continued the consolidation but reneged on any tax exemptions and reversed the rate increase Calder granted Alessandri. Worse still, the municipalities of Santiago and Valparaiso continued using electricity without paying.[59]

Then, the president went further and pushed for nationalization of electricity. The Calder-Ross Agreements included provisions that were unclear. Two required the government to give the company five-years notice of any plan to nationalize electricity and to negotiate the process with the company rather than imposing it unilaterally. Furthermore, the government could not exercise control until compensation was complete. But a third provision allowed the government to take over the company at any time.[60] While the Chilean legislature was never famous for legal consistency, it is hard to explain Chilean Electric's legal sloppiness. Part of all this confusion arose from the many public compromises that went into the Calder-Ross Agreements and which were offset by secret understandings. Of course, once Ross lost the election, these understandings became worthless. The Popular Front planned initially to have CORFO create a series of publicly owned hydroelectric plants. In other words, the Front did not propose purchasing Chilean Electric but intended instead to monopolize all new production so that Chilean Electric would be forced to buy power from the state-run entity.[61]

A subsidiary issue involved the tramways, essential transportation for the working poor in Santiago and Valparaiso. Chile Electric's tramways, run by the Santiago Traction Company, sold 267 million tickets a year: the basic fare was 20 centavos (0.7 of a U.S. cent), unchanged since 1925. The company had stopped all reinvestment; the trams were filthy and falling apart. Motormen earned 20 pesos a day (about 72 U.S. cents).[62] The Socialists and left Radicals, who dominated Santiago politics, insisted that tramway fares remain frozen, whatever the consequences, and that the company's electric profits subsidize transportation. This bloc encouraged new bus companies, a development favored by the middle class.[63]

Curtis Calder was trapped. He knew that he needed a new policy quickly but had little leverage in Chile. Unlike the copper companies, the electric company had not maintained close ties with the legislative right. Calder lobbied Washington and demanded that, in the event of a takeover, the Export-Import Bank cut off credit to Chile until American and Foreign Power, the parent firm, was fully compensated.[64] He estimated the investment at US$80 million.[65]

In the end, Calder's approach to Washington was ineffective. Recognizing that Calder lacked support in the Chilean Congress, the Aguirre Cerda administration moved to nationalize all electricity. The decisive moment came in April and May 1941, when the Santiago Traction Company failed to get a fare increase from the government just as it was hit by a strike. The government ordered the company to raise wages and passed legislation giving the municipality of Santiago control of the line. Then, the president insisted that the electric line and tramway be merged into a single company. All parties in Congress supported the bill, thereby creating Chile's first nationalization. Santiago Traction was so unpopular that U.S. Ambassador Bowers asked Washington to remain neutral in the fight.[66]

The new law altered the company's original contract and the Calder-Ross Agreements. Calder considered the measure illegal but was reduced to quarreling over the price of the company. The government paid nothing for the tramways and used their need for power to push for a nationalization of the electric grid.[67] Calder continued his campaign with the Export-Import Bank. Chilean officials had told him, sotto voce, that the government might take 10 to 20 years to pay for Chilean Electric.[68] The company was in an impossible situation: its workers were mobilized and knew that they had the public's sympathy, and the public blamed the company for run-down trams and power shortages. The Chilean right would gain nothing by defending it. And the company was a losing proposition: its income in 1941 covered only 40 percent of its interest charges and bond obligations.[69] The fight over the utility continued well beyond the Popular Front era, but from this point forward, the government ran the tramways and issued policy on electricity as though it was entitled to administer Chilean Electric. The Radical presidents decreed wage increases and froze rates. By 1943, tramway revenues did not even cover Santiago Traction's payroll.[70]

**

Other Chilean governments had ignored legal niceties in dealing with foreign companies. The Popular Front, however, went much further than any previous administration in referring to popular needs to justify its actions. President Aguirre Cerda summarized this attitude with the comment, "To govern is to educate and improve the public health."

Salvador Allende Gossens, when Minister of Health, prefaced his comments on the nation's poverty and poor health, by saying:

> Chile, like the majority of other South American nations, has lived at the mercy of an economic and cultural colonialism that has obstructed social progress and the development of our natural resources. Moreover, these factors have prevented the people from acquiring a standard of living compatible with a moderately educated and civilized nation. One-hundred-twenty years of independence has been insufficient to instill a civic life within the working class; it has barely been enough for a small percentage, the middle class, to acquire a minimal part of the cultural, technical, and economic advances of humanity.[71]

This important crystallization of nationalist attitudes, however, coincided with the outbreak of a war that would tighten Chile's ties with the United States. By 1938, everyone knew that war was coming; but the Popular Front never calculated its impact on the nation's future. Six months before the war, Front officials were still promoting compensation trade with Germany and Japan. Areas under Nazi control in Europe supplied 50 percent of all Chilean imports. This lack of foresight accentuated the war's impact on Chile. By 1940, the United States was supplying 50 percent of Chile's imports; and by the end of 1941, it was buying two-thirds of Chile's exports.[72]

Chile continued to trade with the United Kingdom, but London, the center of Chile's universe until World War I, had lost interest. British subsidies to steamship lines had ended, and, aside from Shell-Mex, the major British firm remaining in Chile raised sheep in Magallanes.[73] The U.K. kept its Latin American trade at a minimum by using "currency and clearing agreements," a wartime form of compensation trade.[74]

U.S. interests pushed their advantage. They refused to pay higher prices for copper and nitrates.[75] Trade discussions in 1940-41 focused on currency rules, Export-Import loans, and the foreign debt. U.S. protective policies blocked Chile's negotiations for a new trade agreement. Agricultural exports, in particular, were denied access to the U.S. market.[76] At the same time that Chile became more vulnerable to U.S. trade policies, U.S. investors were pouring money into Santiago's factories and businesses. U.S. business interests almost doubled between 1940-43, with the number of firms in Chile increasing from 56 to 96. U.S. investments earned about 10 percent, a rate higher than the average for Latin America and much higher than Chile's rate of economic growth.[77]

As the Aguirre Cerda administration continued to seek loans from the United States to fund its populist policies, the State Department revived the foreign debt issue. Chile had suspended debt payments immediately after the 1939 earthquake but made token payments in 1940. The Amortization Institute, set up by Ross to send money to New York, collected about US$4.5 million that year. It spent US$780 thousand on the debt and sent the rest to CORFO for its projects.[78] The State Department, taking a wild guess based on tax returns, thought that Chile's national income that year was about US$330 million, that the total foreign debt was close US$350 million, and that the internal debt was about US$50 million.[79] Its officials believed Chile could increase its debt payments. The Popular Front, however, hoped to avoid old obligations as it contracted some new ones; it proposed reducing the foreign debt to US$0.15 on the dollar. The State Department was not amused.[80]

For all its talk of economic nationalism, the Front's goals were not matched by a strategic or tactical plan to reduce the country's vulnerability to foreign decisions. At best, it attempted to manipulate the terms of dependence, demanding a greater return (or rent) from the mineral-based economy run by foreigners to fund the demands of its growing public clientele. The war ended Chile's leverage with the United States. Chile could no longer threaten to forge an alliance with the Axis powers. Now, the best it could do was rely on one improvisation after another, hoping in Putnam's game, not to lose too badly on either the domestic or international level.

For its part, the United States knew little and cared less about Chile. It tended to misinterpret what it saw. On the eve of war, Bowers, former U.S. Ambassador to Spain, was sent as Ambassador to Chile. He admitted a stunning ignorance of the country.[81] In his dispatches, he links the Nazi menace to every Chilean development, political or economic. His reports insist democracy is in peril, but he does not recommend any policy to preserve democratic practice. At the same time, his reports argue that Aguirre Cerda should be "dressed down."[82]

A last aspect of U.S. predominance was its impact on popular entertainment and mass information. In the moment, these issues had little monetary weight, but they were already having a profound impact. The everyday images and vocabulary of urban life were being reshaped by imported technology, and the conventions of the commercialized media were following U.S. examples. The dichotomy between the commercial society shaped by North America and the rhetoric of populist nationalism was bound to grow sharper. There were at least 200 thousand radios in the country, reaching about a million people. Another 50 thousand sets were sold each year. In 1940, RCA Victor built a new radio factory in Santiago, dedicated by Aguirre Cerda. The Columbia Broadcasting Company sent programs via short-wave to be rebroadcast in Santiago. Coca Cola set up a new bottling factory, and counted on promoting sales through rebroadcasting its radio programs from Mexico. U.S. companies dominated the movies, with 70 percent of all feature films and almost all the newsreels, and worked closely with government censors in protecting their market position. The Associated Press and the United Press supplied most foreign news and even some domestic information.[83]

If Putnam is right, then these profound changes in mass communications would be another element in Chile's asymmetrical relation with the United States. The U.S. media would represent their national values within the public sphere of Chile. Every aspect of Putnam's *game*, now involved U.S. business interests at both the international and the domestic levels at which it was played.

Endnotes

For abbreviations used in notes, see Endnotes, Chapter 1.

1. RG 59: 825.6363/177, Briggs-Feis memo, 30 Jan. 1939.

2. The major study of U.S. cultural intrusion into Latin America is, J. Manuel Espinosa, *Inter-American Beginnings of U.S. Cultural Diplomacy, 1936-1948* (Washington, D.C.: U.S. Department of State, Bureau of Educational and Cultural Affairs, Historical Studies: no. 2, 1976), 111-83. The data on OCIAA is from Peter Smith, *Talons of the Eagle: Dynamics of U.S.-Latin American Relations* (New York: Oxford University Press, 1996), 83.

3. Russell D. Buhite and David W. Levy, eds., *FDR's Fireside Chats* (Norman: University of Oklahoma Press, 1992), 167-68. On FDR's Latin American policies, see the still basic text, Bryce Wood, *The Making of the Good Neighbor Policy* (New York: W.W. Norton, 1961), especially, 285-361; David G. Haglund, *Latin America and the Transformation of U.S. Strategic Thought, 1936-1940* (Albuquerque: University of New Mexico Press, 1984), especially 180-96; and Frederick B. Pike, *FDR's Good Neighbor Policy: Sixty Years of Generally Gentle Chaos* (Austin: University of Texas Press, 1995), 165-265.

4. Dick Steward, *Trade and Hemisphere: The Good Neighbor Policy and Reciprocal Trade* (Columbia: University of Missouri Press, 1975), 279. See also Lloyd C. Gardner, *Economic Aspects of New Deal Diplomacy* (Madison: University of Wisconsin Press, 1964); David Green, *The Containment of Latin America: a History of the Myths and Realities of the Good Neighbor Policy* (Chicago: Quadrangle Books, 1971); and Robert M. Hathaway, "1933-1945: Economic Diplomacy in a time of Crisis," in William H. Becker and Samuel F. Wells, Jr., eds., *Economics and World Power: An Assessment of American Diplomacy Since 1789* (New York: Columbia University Press, 1984), 286-88.

5. Robert D. Putnam, "Diplomacy and Domestic Politics: the Logic of Two-Level Games," *International Organization* 42:3 (Summer 1988). I am sorry that I encountered this essay only after I had written several drafts of this work.

6. RG 59: 825.52/1408, Bowers, no. 2302, 26 Dec. 1941, enclosure, estimates of engineer Raúl Simon; United Nations, *Economic Survey of Latin America, 1949* (New York: United Nations, 1950), 28; and J. Gabriel Palma, "Chile 1914-1935," 148.

7. RG 151: Commerce Dept., Bureau of Foreign and Domestic Commerce, Commercial Attaches, Santiago, Charles F. Knox, Jr., Economic and Trade Notes, no. 242, 11 Mar. 1939.

8. RG 151: 600 (Chile, 1923-48), Bohan, Economic and Trade Notes, no. 77, 24 Aug. 1938; and Commerce Dept., Bureau of Foreign and Domestic Commerce, Commercial Attaches, Santiago, Knox, Economic and Trade Notes, no. 199, 21 Jan. 1939.

9. RG 59: 825.5151/521, Armour, no. 592, 28 Mar. 1939.

10. United States Tariff Commission, *Latin America as a Source of Strategic and Other Essential Materials*. Report no. 144, 2d Series (Washington: U.S. Tariff Commission, Government Printing Office, 1941), 63; Ignacio Aliaga Ibar, *La economía de Chile y la industria del cobre (algunas reflexiones sobre la post-guerra)* (Santiago: Universidad de Chile, published dissertation, 1946), 195-96; and Raúl Atria, "Tensiones políticas y crisis económica: el caso chileno, 1920-1938," *Estudios Sociales* 10:37 (3d trimester, 1983), 212. This article published by the Corporación de Promoción Universitaria in Santiago, discusses the state, political mobilization, and democracy in Chile.

11. RG 59: 611.2531/694, Heath, no. 2605, 13 Feb. 1942.

12. Ibid.

13. RG 59: 611.2531/276, Frost, no. 910, 16 Mar. 1938.

14. RG 59: 825.6352/72, Frost, no. 518, 20 Feb. 1939, gives account of these efforts in 1938.

15. The key report is Frost, no. 518, op. cit., see also RG 59: 825.6352/74, Economic Affairs memo, 3 Mar. 1939, and 825.6352/101, Bowers, no. 78, 18 Nov. 1939.

16. RG 275: Export-Import Bank, box 2, Case File 174, 24 Feb. 1938: terms of agreement signed by Warren Lee Pierson (president of Export-Import Bank), et al.

17. On lobbying effort, RG 59: 825.6352/61, Pierson to Briggs, 26 Jan. 1939; 825.6352/77, John G. Laylin to Hull, 19 Apr. 1939; 825.6352/84, Frost, no. 782, 18 July 1939; 825.6352/105, Collado memo of telephone conversation with John Laylin, 21 Oct. 1939; and 825.6352/104, Bowers, no. 85, 21 Nov. 1939, memo from John P. Chadwick, American Smelting, Santiago, 13 Oct. 1939.

18. RG 59: 611.2531/580, Petitions to Sec. of State, 32 Nov. 1939; and on Vandenberg, RG 59: State, 611.2531/485, Arthur H. Vandenberg (Sen. Michigan), to Cordell Hull, 9 Nov. 1939.

19. RG 59: 611.2531/9-3040, memo of conversation, Grady and President, 7 Dec. 1939. See also 611.2531/615, Millard D. Brown, Pres. Continental Mills, Inc., Philadelphia to Sec. Hull, 3 Jan. 1940.

20. RG 59: 825.6352/80, memo to Welles, 14 Feb. 1939; and Ibar, op. cit., 271.

21. RG 59: 825.6363/175, memo of conversation, 27 Jan. 1939. The participants were Walter Teagle, Chairman of Board, Standard Oil Co. of New Jersey, E.F. Johnson of the same company and E.T. Stannard; and from the State Department, Messrs Feis, Butler, Sparks, Collado and Livesey. For the details of the proposal were presented in Santiago, see RG 59: 825.5151/505, Armour, no. 474, 25 Jan. 1939.

22. Chile. Interior (1940), v. 10206, no. 15262, Carabineros de Chile, no. 9768, 20 July 1940; and Chile. Diputados, *Boletín de sesiones ordinarios*, 15 July 1941, 1053.

23. RG 59: 825.6374/1335, Dow, no. 28, 8 Mar. 1939; and 825.6374/1343, Armour, no. 610, 11 Apr. 1939.

24. Chile. Hacienda (1940), v. 10202, Superintendencia del Salitre, memo "Actividades de la industria salitrera en el año, 1938-1939," Apr. 1940; and Hacienda (1940), Latorre Izquierdo, no. 596, 3 Sept. 1940.

25. RG 59: 835.6374/1280, W.A. Ayres, Chairman, FTC, to Hull, 26 Mar. 1937; 825.6374/1287, memo of conversation with William T. Kelley, Chief Counsel of the Federal Trade Comm., 27 Mar. 1937; 825.6374/1295, Philip, no. 550, 6 Apr. 1937, enclosure, H.R. Graham, Cia. Salitrera Anglo Chilena to H.E. Hoffman Philip, 5 Apr. 1937; 825.6374/1302, W.A. Ayres, FTC, to Hull, 9 Apr. 1937; 825.6374/1286, /1290, and /1302, memos of conversations, W.S. Culbertson, Counsel for Chilean Nitrate Sales Corp. and the Chilean Nitrate Educational Bureau, Inc. and Messrs Duggan and Gantenbein; and 825.6374 /13/12, United States of America Before Federal Trade Commission, In the Matter of Chilean Nitrate Sales Corporation, a corporation, and Chilean Nitrate Educational Bureau, Inc., a corporation, Docket no. 3089.

26. The case is developed in, RG 59: Chile 825.6374/1344, Armour, no. 632, 18 Apr. 1939; 825.6374/1357, memo of conversation, 12 July 1939, participants Hackworth, Duggan, Sparks, and Whelpley of Guggenheim Bros.; 825.6374 /1362, memo of conversation, Thurman W. Arnold, Asst. Attorney General, Anti-Trust Division, Dept. of Justice, and Guillermo Gazitua, counselor of the Chilean Embassy, Mr. Duggan; and 825.6374/1421, Duggan memo, 26 June 1941.

27. RG 59: 825.6374/1441, Duggan memo, 31 May 1941.

28. RG 59: 825.6374/1415, Duggan memo, 3 July 1941; 825.6374/1448, Duggan memo, 10 Sept. 1941; 825.6374/1432, J.A. Woods, pres. of Chilean Nitrate Sales Corp., NY, to Adolf A. Berle, Asst. Sec. of State, 26 Sept. 1941; 825.6374/1423, Cordell Hull to Francis Biddle, 9 Oct. 1941; and 825.6374/1426, Francis Biddle to Cordell Hull, 14 Oct. 1941.

29. RG 59: 825.6374/1377, Bowers, no. 660, 13 July 1940; memo from Chilean Min. of Hacienda (for Havana Conference); and 825.6374/1430, RA memo, 18 Oct. 1941.

30. For a solid Chilean account, see Chile. Interior. v. 9994 (1939), no. 11198, Min. de Interior, no. 925, 17 Mar. 1939. For firsthand visual reports, RG 59:825.48-Earthquake 1939/53, Armour radio talk, 6 Feb. 1939, talk given on "blue radio network" of NBC under auspices of American Red Cross; 825.48-Earthquake 1939/59, McLain, no. 14, 3 Feb. 1939; and RG 159: MID 2054-106/83, Wooten, no. 4, 10 Feb. 1939. For later survey, 825.48-Earthquake

1939/159, Faust, no. 35, 2 Aug. 1939. Other reports of interest, RG 59: 825.5151/509, McNiece, 9 Feb. 1939; 825.48-Earthquake 1939/81, Frost, no. 506, 15 Feb. 1939. Brian Loveman, *Chile: the Legacy of Hispanic Capitalism* (Oxford: Oxford University Press, 1988, 2d ed.), 247, claims that up to 50 thousand died, a number far higher than that given by any source I could find.

31. The original terms of the proposal are presented in, Luis Ortega Martínez et al., *Corporación de Fomento de la Producción* (Santiago: Corporación de Fomento de la Producción, 1989), 51-52. My account differs from the official history in emphasizing the importance of foreign financing. Ortega M. and others do not mention it.

32. RG 59: 825.48-Earthquake 1939/40, Sparks memo, 31 Jan. 1939; Frost, no. 506, op. cit.; and 825.51/1056, Armour, no. 537, 1 Mar. 1939.

33. RG 59: 825.51/1037, Armour, no. 458, 13 Jan. 1939, enclosure, memo of Frost, 15 Jan. 1939; and 825.5151/509, McNiece, 9 Feb. 1939.

34. France-MAE, Chili. v. 12, 12 Apr. 1939; and BOLSA, B55, Valparaiso to London, 4 July 1939.

35. RG 59: 825.00/1122, Frost, no. 489, 4 Feb. 1939; and 825.48-Earthquake 1939/38, Frost, no. 498, 8 Feb. 1939.

36. Ortega Martínez et al., Op. cit., 62-63.

37. FO 371-22736 (A7612/60/9), C. Bentinck, 26 Oct. 1939; RG 59: 825.50/47 Faust, no. 72, 6 Sept. 1939; 625.6217/16, Flexner, no. 21, 11 Sept. 1939; and on cartels, 825.6374/1375, Bowers, no. 619, 26 June 1940.

38. Haglund, op. cit., 160; and Stanley E. Hilton, *Hitler's Secret War in South America: 1939-1945: German Military Espionage and Allied Counterespionage in Brazil* (Baton Rouge: Louisiana State University Press, 1981), 49, 277.

39. Gardner, op. cit., 126; Steward, op. cit., 26; Irwin F. Gellman, *Good Neighbor Diplomacy: United States Policies in Latin America, 1933-1945* (Baltimore: Johns Hopkins University Press, 1979), 164-65; Lowell T. Young, "Franklin D. Roosevelt and the Expansion of the Monroe Doctrine," *North Dakota Quarterly* (Winter 1974), 23-32; and on Japanese purchases, RG 165: MID 2515-0-20/1, Wooten, no. 3504, 28 Feb. 1941.

40. On copper prices, RG 59: 825.6352/149, memo by HF, 10 Oct. 1940; and 825.5151/638, Eugene P. Thomas, president National Foreign Trade Council, Inc., NY to Welles, 18 July 1941; on smelter, 815.51/1325, Bowers, no. 1338, 10 Apr. 1941, and 825.6352/165, Feis memo of conversation, 6 June 1941; and on labor demands, 825.5045/114, Heath, no. 2719, 2 Mar. 1942.

41. Theodore H. Moran, *Multinational Corporations and the Politics of Dependence, Copper in Chile* (Princeton: Princeton University Press, 1974), 71.

42. RG 59: 611.2517, Bowers, no. 319, 23 Feb. 1940; and 825.51/1247-3/8, Chilean Embassy letter, 12 Aug. 1940.

43. Chile. Hacienda (1940), F. Jorquera, no. 764, 10 June 1940.

44. Markos Mamalakis, "Public Policy and Sectoral Development: A Case Study of Chile, 1940-1958," in Mamalakis and Reynolds, *Essays on the Chilean Economy.* The core of his argument is on 54-82.

45. On this point, see Marcelo José Cavarozzi, "The Government and the Industrial Bourgeoisie in Chile," (Ph.D. diss., University of California Berkeley, 1975), 128ff, and Silva, "State, Public Technocracy, and Politics in Chile," 287-89.

46. Chile. Hacienda (1940), Pedregal, no. 03472, 11 July 1940.

47. RG 59: 825.00/1391, Bowers' letter, 24 Apr. 1941.

48. RG 59: 825.51/1216, Export-Import Directors' Meeting, 7 May 1940; 825.51/1230, Bowers, no. 566, 4 June 1940, memo of conversation with Guillermo Pedregal, 28 May 1940; 825.5151/601, Bowers, no. 884, 15 Oct. 1940; 825.51/1283, Duggan memo, 29 Oct. 1940; and 825.00/1392, Welles' letter to Bowers, 21 May 1941.

49. RG 59: 825.6374/1458, RA memo, 5 Dec. 1941.

50. Putnam, op. cit., 434.

51. Ibid., 430-41. He does not deal with historical change; his examples are drawn from the 1970s and later.

52. RG 59: 825.6363/168, Armour, no. 444, 4 Jan. 1939; 825.6363/175, memo of conversation, 27 Jan. 1939; 825.6363/177, Briggs-Feis memo, 30 Jan. 1939; 825.6363/190, memo of conversation between Welles and Ortega, Ambassador from Chile, 1 June 1939; and Burbach, "Chilean Industrial Bourgeoisie," 77.

53. FO 371/22738 (A3804/353/9), Starling, Petroleum Dept., 26 May 1939, and (A4113/353/9), Starling, 9 June 1939.

54. Chile. Hacienda (1939), F. Jorquera, no. 727, 29 July 1939.

55. FO 371/22738 (A5795/353/9), C. Bentinck, 17 Aug. 1939; and RG 59: Chile 825.00/1210, Bowers, no. 504, 9 May 1940.

56. Chile. Fomento (1939), Oficios v. 1600, no. 9, Min. de Trabajo al Min. de Fomento, 7 Nov. 1939, no. 2225, and same volume, Gerente General de la Corporación de Ventas de Salitre y Yodo al Min. de Fomento, no. 1385.7, 8 Nov. 1939; Chile, *Hacienda Pública* (20 Aug. 1939), 1092; and RG 151: Bureau of Foreign and Domestic Commerce, Commercial Attaches, Santiago, Bohan, Economic and Trade Notes, no. 149, 3 Dec. 1939.

57. RG 59: 825.51/1267, Bowers' telegram, 11 Oct. 1940.

58. RG 59: 825.6463 Electric Bond and Share co./155, Curtis E. Calder to Bonsal, 18 June 1941.

59. RG 59: 825.51-City of Valparaiso/3, McNiece, 18 Mar. 1938; and 825.6463-Electric Bond and Share Co./133, Armour, no. 249, 10 Sept. 1938.

60. Articles 42 and 43, and Article 44 respectively, *La Nación*, 12 Jan. 1936.

61. RG 59: 825.51/1175-1/2, WLP memo to Duggan, 26 Dec. 1939, enclosure, Calder letter to Warren Pierson, pres. Export-Import Bank, 20 Dec. 1939.

62. RG 59: 825.78/18, Bowers, no. 1376, 23 Apr. 1941.

63. RG 59: Chile 825.6463-Elec. Bond and Share Co./134, Armour, no. 734, 17 June 1939; 825.78/15, McNiece, 14 Nov. 1939; and 825.51/1175 1/2, WLP memo to Duggan, 26 Dec. 1939, enclosure, Calder letter to Warren Pierson, president Export-Import Bank, 20 Dec. 1939.

64. RG 59: 825.51/1226, Bowers to Welles, 7 May 1940; and 825.51/1274, Bowers, no. 891, 14 Oct. 1940.

65. RG 59: 825.51/1190, Bowers, no. 319, 23 Feb. 1940, enclosure, Bohen memo of conversation with Pedregal, 23 Feb. 1940.

66. RG 59: 825.6463 Electric Bond and Share Company/164, Bowers to Welles, 22 May 1941. See also 825.6463 Electric Bond and Share Co./148, Bowers, no. 1451, 15 May 1941; and 825.6463 Electric Bond and Share Company/151, Briggs, no. 1494, 29 May 1941.

67. RG 59: 825.6463 Electric Bond and Share Co./155, Bowers, no. 1585, 18 June 1941; 825.6463 Electric Bond and Share Co./172, Bonsal, memo of conversation, 4 Aug. 1941; and 825.6463 Electric Bond and Share Company/180, memo of conversation, 8 Sept. 1941.

68. RG 59: 825.6463 Electric Bond and Share Company/171, Eduardo Salazar, Chilean Electric manager in Santiago, to Calder, 2 Aug. 1941. See also 825.00/1406, Bowers to Welles, 7 Aug. 1941.

69. RG 59: 825.00/1532, Bowers to Welles, 17 Nov. 1941, enclosed memo.

70. RG 59: 825.6463 Electric Bond and Share Co./195, State to Bowers, 13 Mar. 1942; ibid., 202, Bowers, no. 3054, 20 Apr. 1942; ibid., 209, Bowers, no. 3994, 27 July 1942; ibid., 224, Calder to Bonsal, 25 May 1943; and ibid., 228, Heath telegram, 17 Sept. 1943.

71. The president's and Allende's quotes are from Salvador Allende Gossens, *La realidad médico-social chilena (síntesis)* (Santiago: Ministerio de Salubridad, Previsión, y Asisténcia Social, 1939), 5. Allende's work became a classic in the social literature of Chile.

72. RG 151: Bureau of Foreign and Domestic Commerce, Commercial Attaches, Santiago, Charles F. Knox, Jr., Economic and Trade Notes, no. 242, 11

Mar. 1939; and Santiago, Bohan, Economic and Trade Notes, no. 51, 6 Sept. 1939. See also RG 59: 611.2531/676, Chilean Country Commission, 12 July 1940; and 611.2531/694, Heath, no. 2605, 13 Feb. 1942.

73. FO 371-21437 (A3488/534/9), W. Cortes, Board of Trade, 3 May 1938; and FO 371-22738 (A2604/564/9), C. Bentinck, 27 Mar. 1939.

74. Hoover Papers, Reprint Files, *U.S. News and World Report*, 16 Feb. 1940.

75. RG 59: 825.5151/638, Eugene P. Thomas, pres. National Foreign Trade Council, Inc., NY, to Welles, 18 July 1941.

76. See RG 59: 611.2531, 1941-44.

77. J. Fred Rippy, *Globe and Hemisphere: Latin America's Place in the Postwar Foreign Relations of the United States* (Chicago: H. Regnery Co., 1958), 45, 52.

78. RG 59: 825.51/1375, Coit MacLean, Comm. Attaché report, 13 Oct. 1941.

79. RG 59: 825.34/408, memo of Div. of American Republics, 4 Nov. 1941.

80. RG 59: 825.51/1307, memo of conversation with Guillermo del Pedregal and Mr. Collado, 21 Jan. 1941.

81. Claude G. Bowers, *Chile through Embassy Windows: 1939-1953* (New York: Simon and Schuster, 1958), 3.

82. RG 59: 825.00/1416, Bowers' letter to President, 18 Aug. 1941 For Nazi influence in general, see Haglund, *Latin America and the Transformation*, 182.

83. On radio, RG 59: 825.659 Radios/1, Bowers, no. 460, 19 Apr. 1940; and 825.76/51, Bowers, no. 1566, 13 June 1941, enclosure 1, on films, RG 59: 825.4061-Motion Pictures/42, Dow, no. 147, 21 Dec. 1938; and 825.4061-Motion Pictures/55, Joseph H. Hazen, VP, Warner Brothers, 17 Aug. 1939.

Fig. 9. President Pedro Aguirre Cerda and his wife in Talca to tour region devastated by earthquake, 1939. The earthquake motivated Congress to pass Aguirre's economic package. United States. National Archives.

Fig. 10. Chillán, leveled by earthquake, Jan. 1939. United States. National Archives.

8

The War and
Chile's Dilemmas

> What are the characteristics of our national economy? We live by exports that we do not control. . . . A nation that sells 80 and 90 percent of its products to only one country, the sales price of which is fixed by the purchasing nation, runs the risk of perishing with the decline or end of these purchases. Of what use is its independence or the army that defends that independence?
>
> Conservative Senator Eduardo Cruz Coke
> Candidate for president, 1946[1]

World War II changed many aspects of Latin America's development. Its greatest effect was to complete the regional hegemony of the United States. The narrative that follows cannot discuss all of these changes and is focused on how Chilean events during and immediately after the war continue an evolution already clear during the Depression. By the late 1940s, Chile's political and economic arrangements had solidified into patterns that were, for the most part, retained until the coup of 1973. The country was dependent on copper exports, and U.S. corporations controlled those exports. Within that export-based regime, the government and society supported industrial protection and failed to substantially alter the nation's tax base. The growing electorate divided into roughly three equal segments, the right, center, and left; the left included a militant labor movement. Politics focused on issues of distribution but the economy was growing slowly, when it grew at all. This was a situation rife with electoral and economic frustration.

The growth of Chile's economy from 1938 to 1945 barely outpaced the population increase. Chile depended on trade: the value of exports rose 47 percent, outperforming every other economic indicator. Much of the gain in the GDP came from external demand rather than improved productivity. Industrial production rose nearly 30 percent but agriculture, which grew only 9 percent, remained a drag on the economy. Mineral exports rose twice as fast as mining production since ores that had been stockpiled during the Depression were still being consumed early in the war.[2]

By the early 1940s, the political divisions that characterized the country in the late 1960s and early 1970s were already in place. Given the few social improvements, the left concluded that the Popular Front had failed to deliver on its promises: the poor remained poor; foreigners retained economic control; and the rich escaped all efforts at redistribution.[3] The right condemned the Front as responsible for interfering in the marketplace, rewarding inefficiency, and creating a parasitic bureaucracy that grew with each subsequent administration. Neither side looked at how its own behavior was contributing to the trends it bemoaned. Clientalistic practices, continued from an earlier era, were encountering severe limits.

The political system tried to resolve the clientalistic contest by banning the Communists. The ban ended Radical Party presidencies based on center-left coalitions that began with the Popular Front administration of Pedro Aguirre Cerda.[4] The other Radical presidents, Juan Antonio Ríos and Gabriel González Videla, were rivals who governed from 1942 to 1946 and 1946 to 1952, respectively. Ríos came from the right wing of the party and had close ties to Carlos Ibáñez; González Videla was based in the urban vote and often sounded leftist. Once in office, each had to face the contradiction between a state-led pattern of investment to stimulate economic growth and populist demands for better wages, working conditions, and welfare spending. Their failure to resolve this contradiction drove a wedge between the center and left. After 1948, no Radical was ever again a major candidate for the presidency.

The Front Unravels

The Popular Front intervened in the economy in order to build what the private sector could not.[5] State-led investment was already common in Europe and the United States. As mentioned in Chapter 1, Chile had a relatively large state sector for Latin America even before the Depression. The Front had promised a redistributive effort along with major investments. No one represented the confusion about how these two goals were to be reconciled better than President Aguirre Cerda. Even as he was inviting the millionaires of the Radical Party to form a cabinet in 1941, he denounced speculators, investors who lived on dividends, and— without a moment's hesitation from a man who visited his fundo on weekends—absentee landowners.[6] He could say what his government was against but was unclear how it could revive economic performance as inflation began to erode real wages.

Industrial policy remained an improvised set of favors, channeled through a bureaucracy that favored import substitution. Only a few industrial projects were financed, and they stemmed from plans by the engineering profession and the Society for Industrial Development [SOFOFA]. There was, by the late 1930s, a confluence of interests between bureaucrats, devoted to economic planning, and industrialists.[7] The bureaucracy bloomed during the Radical presidencies and new university graduates drew up plans for Chile's future.[8] Congress reviewed these plans, and right-wing legislators, while channeling funds to their supporters, kept projects from moving in any imaginative social directions. Eventually, even the National Agricultural Society [SNA], representing large land-holding interests, endorsed state investment programs.[9] State projects often had little regard for the market. For example, the port of San Antonio was booming because it shipped the copper from El Teniente. Despite its strategic importance, most government programs favored Valparaiso, the declining but traditional center of foreign trade.[10]

Popular sentiment in Chile was unaware of the links between tariffs and industrialization, and focused, when the issue came up at all, on consumer costs. The meat tariff was extremely unpopular in the major cities. The Popular Front was less naive, and, for all its rhetoric, the Aguirre Cerda administration raised tariffs albeit in a piecemeal fashion. High tariffs were imposed on cooking oil, even though the domestic industry used imported materials. Agriculture increasingly relied on imported pesticides; no domestic alternative was ever sought.[11] Although the government claimed it wanted to rationalize tariffs, it never launched a study of the subject nor decreed any over-arching policy. The Popular Front promised an end to political favoritism, but, in practice, tariffs on all goods were negotiable.[12]

Ministries were patronage machines. The Ministry of Development expanded the railroad bureaucracy to reward Front loyalists. Conflicts among ministries (sometimes party-based but more often conflicts between personalities) led to open scandals. Each bureaucratic chieftain wanted to expand his retinue. The State Mortgage Bank and the Central Bank publicly quarreled over who would control credit to mining companies.[13]

Although the Popular Front assisted rural production by maintaining low railroad rates (railroads had always run at a loss) and rural credit at below-market prices, it repressed rural unions. Emilio Zapata, the foremost champion of the rural laborer, lost his congressional seat, and the Agrarian Defense League that he created was smashed.[14] The government provided little new infrastructure, and currency rules and export quotas remained disincentives to agricultural production.[15]

The Front was primarily an urban phenomenon, based on improved wages. As a result of union organizing, strikes, and government decrees, nominal wages skyrocketed. The average wage rose by 70 percent between 1938 and 1941 and 130 percent by 1943. But inflation undercut these gains: real wages between 1938 and 1941 rose 18-40 percent, depending on the sector, and fell thereafter. By comparison, during the Alessandri administration, real wages had risen 70-80 percent, depending on the sector. The gross domestic product per person, rose 10 percent in the first two years of the Front, but then fell in the following three years.[16]

The inflationary erosion of wages continued in the 1940s, an odd parallel to events before 1924 when the elite ran the government. Revenues remained inadequate, depressed by the course of the war, U.S. control of mineral prices, and the poor tax base. The government raised military wages and revived the naval rearmament program.[17] An elaborate credit scheme to help small copper-mining firms treated bonds as legal tender, which fed the inflationary cycle.[18] The Chilean National Airlines [Lineas Aereas Nacionales or LAN] received subsidies covering 60 percent of its costs.[19] Officials at the Central Bank warned Aguirre Cerda in 1940 that subsidies and wage increases were counterproductive and were compounding war-induced price increases. The Front's Finance Minister, Marcial Mora M., dismissed their concerns.[20] By 1943, Chile had a higher rate of inflation than any belligerent in the war and any Latin American nation other than Bolivia.[21] The cost of living compared across cities varied dramatically (see Table 8.1). Santiago, with the most economic opportunities, was the most expensive place to live.

Table 8.1: Cost of Living by Cities, North to South, 1939-1943
(1930=100)

Year	Iquique	Valparaiso	Santiago	Concepción	Osorno
1939	189	200	208	200	201
1940	209	216	241	225	215
1941	222	233	273	256	238
1942	284	315	369	342	302
1943	346	398	430	384	372

Source: Chile, *Estadística chilena* (December 1943), 736.

Other changes during the period of the Front also stand out. Unemployment virtually disappeared in 1941 when only four thousand individuals registered as seeking work. In a work force of 1.7 million, some 190 thousand had paid vacations, a substantial achievement in Latin America in this era. Company stores, famous in the nitrate era, for gauging their employees, now were used by the copper companies to reduce laborers' cost of living, creating a greater degree of job loyalty. In the major copper zone of the north, food prices were three times higher in the town of Calama than they were in the Anaconda-run store at the Chuquicamata mine.[22] The infant mortality rate—an important indicator of misery—fell from 20 to 17 percent. Random medical examinations of blue- and white-collar workers, however, found about one-third suffering from illnesses, the most common being tuberculosis, heart ailments, and syphilis.[23]

The Front had not forgotten the strike of 1936 and tried to reduce wage disparities.[24] It was unsuccessful: there are no recorded improvements in wages or labor rights for women, and the differences between urban and rural labor and that between management and workers remained.[25] In 1940, one nitrate company divided up a bonus of 443 thousand pesos among its small corps of managers while its labor force received a bonus half that size.[26] Official support for the union movement reinforced the distance between white- and blue-collar workers because, in the years of the Front and Ríos presidency, the white-collar workers were the most militant: 20 thousand empleados went on strike in 1940, almost 50 thousand in 1943. The number of white-collar workers rose to about 200 thousand in 1943 and their salaries increased 130 percent between 1938 and 1943.[27] Government regulations and bureaucratic employment helped the middle class outrun inflation until 1948.[28] In many respects, the most notable "labor" achievement of the Radical presidents was its assistance to the middle class.

Table 8.2: Urban and Rural Wages, 1936-1943
(Average daily wages in pesos)

Year	Workers in Urban Industries			Rural Workers	
	Sugar	Cement	Cotton Textiles	Inquilinos	Peones
1937	15.4	18.2	8.6	6.1	3.7
1938	16.6	21.8	10.9	7.6	3.7
1939	17.1	25.0	11.4	9.2	4.5
1940	21.2	29.4	13.6	10.7	7.4
1941	29.9	35.8	17.6	12.3	8.3

Source: Chile, Dirección General de Estadística, *Veinte años de legislación social* (Santiago: 1945), 72, 87.

Chilean wages for manual laborers remained low. Most workers earned less than the equivalent of US$1 per day. A U.S. economist compared wages and productivity in Chile and the United States by studying laborers using the same machinery in both countries. Output per man-hour on Santiago cotton looms, phonograph presses, and other devices was about half that of the United States, but wages were only one-fourth to one-fifth of the U.S. level.[29]

The occupational distribution, according to the 1940 census, was similar to that of ten years before. Industry, for all the attention lavished upon it, employed only four-tenths of one percent more people (16.3 percent in all) than it had in 1930. The major industrial activities had changed little from the early 1920s. The percentage of the labor force in agriculture during the 1930s had declined 2.5 percent, to a total of 35 percent. The most noticeable change was the increase in service-sector employment, from 16.1 to 19.9 percent. Chile was steadily moving toward a Third World situation, with an expansion of the service sector lacking a robust industrial base.[30]

The Front, it must be granted, had little time in which to change anything. It's leaders compounded its problems with the constant fight over spoils. As already mentioned in Chapter 7, before the end of 1941, every member party had attacked the others. Personal conflicts and patronage quarrels drove the Radicals against the Socialists at times, and at others, led them to join the Socialists in attacks on the Communists. Worse, two of the three major parties, the Socialists and the Radicals, divided internally. Factions of the Radicals and all the Socialists, at various points, assailed the Front. Only the Communists remained a united party and unquestioning in their support of the Front.

The Socialists played a major role in the Front's unraveling. Marmaduke Grove still headed the party but Oscar Schnake Vergara, the Minister of Development, played a major role in the party's internal quarrels and its crucial fight with the Communists. Schnake supported nationalist goals, import substitution, and—in an interesting comment on how "nationalism" could be defined in this era—closer ties to the United States. His opponents in the party in late 1939, such as César Godoy and Emilio Zapata, were either expelled outright or were driven into creating a splinter organization. Beginning in September 1939 and culminating in the Sixth Ordinary Congress, December 20-23, 1939, party rifts led to a split and the creation of the Nonconformists, who included five deputies and 10 percent of the Socialist's membership.[31] One of the party's foremost historians claims that bureaucratic infighting among these factions led the Socialists to "near total disintegration."[32] Schnake and his closest allies, Salvador Allende Gossens and Bernardo Ibáñez, were extremely adept. They gained control of the remaining party and of the executive leadership of the CTCh, the labor federation. Schnake's wife became mayor of Santiago. Before they pulled out of the cabinet, the Socialists had been appointed to about a third of the provincial intendancies.[33]

It seemed, in late 1939, that the Socialists might win even more control of the bureaucracy. Allende, a physician and recently installed as the Minister of Health, squared off against Roberto Waccholtz, the Front's first Minister of Finance, over bonuses that Allende wanted to distribute within the Ministry of Health. Waccholtz opposed Allende's gesture and was forced out. With Allende and Schnake in the cabinet, it looked as though the Front would become a two-party coalition of the Radicals and Socialists.

When the cabinet posts were reshuffled in February 1940, Aguirre Cerda skipped over Schnake and the Socialists, turning instead to wealthy Radicals, who formed a "millionaires' cabinet." The Front was moving rightward. The president was not about to rely on young bureaucrats for success. By gaining some support from Liberals and Conservatives in Congress, the Radicals won most government jobs and the battle for bureaucratic control of economic issues.[34] Among the Radicals, the more conservative faction led by Ríos had the advantage. González Videla, the Radical leader of the pro-welfare faction, had become Minister to France.[35]

The Communists were now in a coalition that no longer wanted them. They had won victories such as the admission of Spanish Republican exiles, the unionization of some new sectors, and government acceptance of their political recruiting. They had some public legitimacy, and party membership rose to 25 and 30 thousand.[36] Like the rest of the Front, they did not really expect Chile to move toward socialism, and they did not pressure the Front to seize industries. Opponents of the Front, of course, had always attacked the Communist presence in the government. Now, the Communists' opposition within the Front grew formidable. The Socialists and most Radicals saw them as a liability. Aguirre Cerda knew that they were alienating landowners and industrialists and believed they were hurting his chances of getting U.S. loans (see Chapter 7).

Other issues deepened the wedge between the Communists and the rest of the Front. The Radicals and the Socialists favored the Allies in the war, even though the government remained neutral. The Communists supported the Hitler-Stalin Pact and denounced the Allies as imperialists. The Communist Party was also vocal in its support of Mexico's nationalization of oil (a stance President Aguirre Cerda found particularly embarrassing). Perhaps its most dangerous move, rarely discussed in the literature, was to begin talking of organizing rural laborers just at the moment that Aguirre Cerda was courting the National Rural Society [SNA].[37]

The majoritarian elements of the Socialists and the Radicals were removing dissidents and vulnerable factions, first from their own parties (witness what happened to Zapata), then from the labor federation, and finally, from the Front coalition.[38] The Radicals began their campaign against the Communists in July 1940. Once the anti-Communist campaign was underway, the right joined in. The Liberals and Conservatives, in August 1940, proposed banning them from politics.[39] In response, the Communists called for popular militias to unite with leftist elements in the army, an effort that never succeeded.[40] In December 1940, the jockeying for the congressional elections of March 1941 began. Conservatives in the Chamber of Deputies, with some Radical support, passed an anti-Communist bill. That month, Schnake, in a speech famous on the Chilean left, denounced the Communists as supporters of Hitler and betrayers of the working class. Far from being, as it is often depicted, the start of the campaign against the Communists, Schnake intended it to be the culmination. He delivered his address, and the anti-Communist bill then passed the Senate.[41] All the parties were organizing for the congressional elections in 1941.

Then, another turn in the fight over patronage, ended the anti-Communist crusade. With the bill before him, Aguirre Cerda realized that the removal of the Communists would leave him completely dependent on the Socialists. Having done all he could to promote the Communists' isolation, he now vetoed the bill banning their party, afraid of the Socialists' demand for more official posts. The president also wanted to maintain neutrality while the Socialists demanded that Chile join the Allied war effort. The executive committee of the Popular Front met on January 6, 1941, and decided that the Communists, a crucial margin of support in the next congressional elections, could stay.[42] So it was the Socialists who left in January 1941, and the Front recruited the rump wing of the "Nonconformists"; thus began the "Little Front."[43] The Socialists did not accept this defeat gracefully. The outcome began to deepen some of the party's internal divisions even as the party continued its anti-communist campaign.

In the congressional election, the Communists won almost 12 percent of the vote and the Socialists almost 18 percent, but the Communists won nearly as many congressional seats (15) as did the Socialists (17), and they also won four seats in the Senate.[44] Nevertheless, the Little Front lacked a congressional majority; the Radical Party had not done as well as the president expected. To maintain Socialist support in the legislature, the Little Front let the Socialists keep their government jobs even though the Radicals were demanding retaliation. It was now the Radicals turn to leave and they forced a showdown in April 1941, expelling six members of their party who remained in the cabinet.[45]

Aguirre Cerda's health was failing rapidly as he confronted this crisis. He struggled to maintain Chile's neutrality in the war. The Nazis had invaded the Soviet Union, and now the Communists became ardent supporters of belligerence.[46] Even as the president lay bedridden, the factions within the Radical Party fought over his successor. The president succumbed to tuberculosis in November. The circus of partisan infighting and ministerial appointments and dismissals created a wake of disillusionment.

For an entire generation of leftists and reformers, the Popular Front was the first experience in government. It was on-the-job training in the midst of recession and partisan wrangling. Many of the Front's programs, initiated from various ministries, were more a means of partisan recruitment than a scheme for a government-led economy. Government expansion did not generate any political consensus; each of the three political attitudes had a distinct set of ambitions for the future.

The right took what it could from public programs but never hid its hostility toward the Front.[47] Public rhetoric remained violent; political leaders often had bodyguards and went about armed; there were a few partisan shootouts.[48] One study found that six right-wing paramilitary organizations formed in this period, several with roots in the Republican Militia.[49] These paramilitary units were designed to pressure rather than overthrow the government. It seemed that despite right-wing sentiment within the army officer corps, the right had moved away from thoughts of a coup.[50]

It argued for capitalism but was without a scheme for reviving and diversifying Chile's market economy. Its politics rested not on economics but on cultural fears that the left would level social distinctions and that religious and patriarchal values would be undermined. There is little evidence that Chileans in general supported any form of socialism. Instead, traditional attitudes, religious and social, reinforced conservatism. A religious festival in November 1941 drew 80 thousand and was widely interpreted as a sign of anti-government sentiment. Public reaction to the admission of Jewish refugees forced the Front to halt Jewish immigration.[51] The right made few specific appeals to labor and was completely silent on rural poverty.

Reformers, that is, moderates in the Radical Party, among the Conservative youth, and in other political factions, wanted to extend the suffrage. They rarely discussed how such a change would affect public demands on the government; nor did they spend much time on taxes or capital investment. Like the left, they referred to Chile's economic dependence—indeed, all political factions treated that dependence as a given—but rarely mentioned how to reduce it. In a world at war, the reformers like all other politicians, focused on the truly important, the distribution of offices.

After the Front

The Radical presidents after Aguirre Cerda represented different wings of the party: Juan Antonio Ríos Morales had his base in the south-central agricultural zone and Gabriel González Videla, in the major cities and northern mining areas. Like Aguirre Cerda, each had to placate an aroused public with an inadequate treasury. Like him as well, they were lawyers from the provinces, each with a middle-class following.[52] It was under Ríos that middle-class purchasing power began growing faster than that of urban labor, a trend that González Videla tried to sustain. In favoring the middle class, government intensified changes already developing within the economy. The stimulus of war increased the number of people working in small manufactures or in their own shops by 30 percent, to 117 thousand. White-collar employees in industry grew by 51 percent to 31.1 thousand. By comparison, the industrial labor force grew 29 percent to 241 thousand.[53] But once the war was over, the economy slowed and even stagnated. Public officials and legislators then had to choose between protecting the gains made by the middle class or helping those below it.

As Aguirre Cerda was dying, González Videla, still Minister to France, rushed home only to find that Ríos had lined up the support he needed to win the Radical Party's endorsement. Of the 33 thousand votes cast in the party caucuses, Ríos won by a margin of one thousand. Although many speak of the period after Aguirre Cerda as the Popular Front, the Front no longer existed. The Radicals had sufficient numbers and money to run their own candidate, and this is how they presented Ríos. The Socialists and Communists each had a choice. They could run their own candidates, who were certain to lose, or endorse Ríos. They did the latter and formed a coalition, the "Democratic Alliance," which included the Falangists (formerly the Young Conservatives). Still, this alliance was unlike the Front, the Radicals now dominated the campaign; all the other parties fell into step.[54]

Although Ríos had a well-established reputation as an Ibañista, the right, led by the Conservatives and Liberals, recruited the old caudillo himself as a candidate. A survey of rank-and-file sentiment indicates that the rightist parties from the Liberals to the Falangists divided in their support between the Carlos Ibáñez and Ríos.[55] One of the key factors in the race was Alessandri, who upon returning to Chile and seeing his nemesis resurrected, endorsed Ríos.

In the 1942 election, Ríos won handily, carrying 17 of the 25 provinces and getting 56 percent of the vote. Winning the presidency did not assure the victor a congressional majority; from the beginning of his term, Ríos was struggling to assemble enough votes to pass a budget. The situation was fragile. The shortage of hard currency and wartime shortages rapidly heated inflation. In his first address to Congress, Ríos asked for emergency powers. Congress agreed, and he invoked those powers as often as the legislature permitted. By late 1943, the government was becoming so unpopular that Ríos brought military officers into the cabinet as a symbol of "order."[56] In fact, the president's major opponents were within his own party. The González Videla wing detested him, and he them. By December 1943, nine Radical Deputies were in open defiance of his leadership. Ríos had the political sense to offer González Videla the ambassadorship to Brazil. González Videla left to assume the post.[57]

The jockeying for position and office claimed an important leftist. Marmaduke Grove had divided his own party when he supported Ríos, but the Socialists remained in the government until January 1943, when Grove asked for a party vote of confidence and lost. Salvador Allende became head of the anti-Ríos wing of the Socialists. In 1944, the Grove and Allende factions split into rival parties, with Grove leaving with a minority to form the Authentic Socialist Party, usually called *Grovistas.* (By this time, Godoy's Noncomformists had joined the Communists.) Neither of the Socialist factions had a militant program.[58] Allende's proposals were to improve democracy, to help the working class, and—a sign of the Peruvian Aprista influence on the party—to carry out postwar plans for an "Indo-American continent."[59] Grove counted on the support of Ríos and on the Communists to retain influence, but there is little indication he had any impact on government policy.[60]

Although Ríos ran as an anti-communist, the Communists caused him the least trouble. Their energies were concentrated on getting Chile on the side of the Allied war effort. Party resolutions demanded a military buildup, reforms on public health and job safety, and control of inflation.[61] The party anticipated views that became common in international communism, arguing that the wartime anti-fascist alliance would continue after the conflict and lead to the spread of democracy and class collaboration. It is worthwhile to recall that the Comintern dissolved in June 1943.[62]

Ríos organized seven different cabinets, pushed and pulled by fights over income and spoils; ideological distinctions in this period blurred until they are almost unrecognizable. All the parties on the center or left agreed to a state-led development of a market economy. None proposed any major social programs. It was Ríos who accomplished many of the proposals that had originated in the Popular Front. Specifically, he established the National Electric Company or ENDESA [Empresa Nacional de Electricidad, Sociedad Anónima], with CORFO funding that included U.S. loans. It was built as a seller of power, with Chilean Electric still controlling a major part of the consumer grid and buying from the hydroelectric plants constructed by CORFO and ENDESA. The government sold the power at a loss in order to subsidize industrial and household electrification in the Santiago-Valparaiso zone.[63] Chilean Electric facilities appreciated in value but without any major new investment on its part.[64] The commitment to energy development meant that CORFO had few resources for anything else. By the end of the Radical presidencies, expenditures on energy were taking 46 percent of its budget. Agriculture, by comparison, claimed 13 percent; industry, 11 percent; and mining and housing each, one percent.[65]

The middle class, having increased its income, fearing inflation and further social demands by labor, and acknowledging U.S. hegemony, moved rightward; and the Radicals followed it. At its fifteenth national convention, held in Concepción in January 1944, the Radical Party passed more than one resolution denouncing economic warfare (by which it apparently meant class warfare) at all social levels. It moved away from nationalism, arguing such efforts only increased the cost of living. The party platform envisioned a postwar world in which:

> states recognize their economic interdependence and base their future international organization upon the coordination of the world economy, in such a way that the economy of the Latin American peoples will be coordinated with that of the United States and the economy of the three Americas then coordinated with that of the world.[66]

Middle-class reformers reordered their economic vision. Chile would export raw materials, chiefly to the United States, in exchange for credit and essential imports.[67]

Despite this economic view, Chile was slow to abandon neutrality. Chilean businessmen expected the United States to behave with the same forbearance as Britain had in 1915. They did not protest or interfere in U.S. control of shipping, copper pricing, and Chile's supply of fuel. A small but significant portion of the elite favored the Allies, stemming from family or commercial ties to the United Kingdom. They spoke up, reminding their fellow citizens that this was not 1915 and that Americans had never behaved like the British. Gustavo Ross returned from traveling to the United States and Britain in June 1942, and he declared that the country should do whatever the United States wanted. He called himself a *de Gaullist*, called Petaín a *traitor*, and described Chileans with pro-German sentiment as *the enemy*.[68] Agustín Edwards Ross, editor of *El Mercurio*, was more typical of sentiment within the elite and middle class; he supported neutrality while privately worrying that the United States would eventually retaliate.[69]

Wealthy Chileans saw no reason to get involved in the conflict. Most were not Democrats; much of the upper class viewed Hitler as someone who, whatever his faults, was saving Europe from communism. Some of them expected Germany to defeat the Soviet Union and so settle the war in Europe.[70] Chile was, after all, a country where Ibáñez had styled himself after Mussolini and which had influential, and barely assimilated, immigrant populations from Germany and Italy. In many quarters, pro-Axis sentiment was not seen as an obstacle to good relations with the United States. The Chilean army officer corps favored Germany; German officers had created a new military standard in Chile at the turn of the century. Despite this attitude, the army did not hesitate to ask the United States for equipment.[71]

The Roosevelt administration insisted that Latin American nations, who wanted credit and supplies controlled by the United States, support the Allied effort. As part of that policy, the United States pressured Ríos to break relations with Germany. It controlled the supply of newsprint in order to influence Chilean newspapers, and the amount of radio equipment and the type of programming to shape Chilean broadcasts on the war. The Socialist Party, with Schnake and Allende in the lead, successfully lobbied the State Department for financial help for its newspapers. U.S. presence was so pervasive that elements of Chile's political system began to treat it as just another factor in domestic conflicts.[72]

Ríos knew Chile could not afford to be, along with Argentina, one of only two Latin American nations in defiance of U.S. policy. He never publicly said so and feared the impact on his fragile coalition of siding with the Allies. He tried to sustain neutrality as long as possible. He told U.S. officials that Chile would cooperate in every way with the Allied war effort short of breaking with the Axis. His government, desperate for funds, then raised taxes on the copper mines.[73]

In retaliation for not breaking with the Axis, the United States, in 1942, reduced Chile's supply of imported fuel.[74] In October 1942, Acting Secretary of State Sumner Welles, in an address in Boston, said that Argentina and Chile were permitting German spies to coordinate attacks on Allied shipping. The resulting scandal and humiliation forced Ríos to cancel a trip to Washington. Pressure continued until Ríos finally relented, breaking with the Axis in October 1943. He suffered immediate retaliation at home, with the right denouncing the change in policy.[75] As a precaution, the army retired the most zealous of its pro-German officers.[76]

The U.S. government controlled Chile's foreign trade and the behavior of U.S. companies within Chile. Through its various wartime boards, it controlled the quantity of copper ore being shipped out of the country and the nation's access to international credit. Major U.S. companies in Chile reported directly to Washington rather than to Santiago. Chilean official requests to the State Department for data on these corporations were ignored. There was a basic reason for this behavior, aside from Washington's indifference to Santiago's opinions. As a result of agreements within the wartime boards, companies in Chile such as Kennecott Copper and Bethlehem Steel acquired more supplies at better prices than Chile was receiving.[77]

Chile's wartime experience turned on the "copper agreement," an understanding between Washington's bureaucrats and U.S. copper companies. In it, Chile's copper ore became subject to allocation by the United States War Production Board. In mid-1943, the Board allocated so little to Chile that the country ran short of its own ore.[78] Santiago had the right to review decisions by U.S. officials on Chilean copper, but it never exercised that right. The agreement also forced Chile to accept a below-market price for its copper. In 1943 alone, this difference was worth 55 percent of its exported value.[79]

Chile objected to many U.S. decisions, arguing that wartime policies placed Chile at a disadvantage in trading with the rest of Latin America, that they restricted Chile's growth and prevented efforts at economic diversification.[80] State Department personnel thought that Chilean officials were obtuse. How could they be thinking about diversification and reducing Chile's fuel bill when there was a war going on? The "agreement" remained unchanged.

The same policies affected the nitrate trade. The Chilean nitrate sector was run by the Guggenheims and Du Ponts, who coordinated all decisions with Washington and then reported the results to Santiago. Within Washington, conflicts over nitrates were seen as matters between the Guggenheims, on one side, and Allied Chemical, the Du Ponts, and Shell Oil, on the other.[81] Little attention was paid to Santiago. Chileans worried about a repetition of events after World War I, when the surge in nitrate production during the war flooded the market once the war ended. They asked for and received assurances that, in return for cooperating on wartime quotas and prices (the nitrate price was frozen in March 1942), the United States would work with Chile after the war to prevent a glut.[82] These assurances were ignored. The United States began promoting the use of synthetic nitrates in place of salitre during the war, undercutting Chilean sales to Cuba, for example.[83] Near the end of the conflict, the State Department denied that it had ever promised to help the Chilean nitrate sector survive in the postwar era.[84]

The war sharpened the asymmetries of trade between a large, dynamic economy and an underdeveloped one. Chile had little time and few resources with which to react. Its bureaucratic staff continued to suffer a high political turnover with no person or agency coordinating all trade-related issues. There was no Gustavo Ross in the government. For lack of direction, the government drifted along with whatever policies Washington was initiating.

It was within this setting that problems stemming from the Depression were resurrected. There was still a shortage of fuel, but now Standard Oil used the absence of British competition to increase its market share from 49 percent in 1941 to 79 percent in 1944.[85] Shortages of hard currency continued; the government maintained the currency rules solidified in 1938. The legitimacy of this depression-related innovation became a political article of faith.[86] Chilean officials continued, as much as possible, to ignore the foreign debt inherited from the 1920s, although some token payments were resumed in 1942 and continued until the end of the war.[87] This last attitude, however, was difficult to reconcile with repeated requests for loans from the U.S. Export-Import Bank. By the end of the war, Chile's basic credit line from the Export-Import Bank amounted to US$40 million.

Chile's poor negotiating position with the United States worsened after the conflict. The postwar recession placed the economy in a classic squeeze, and Chile's foreign representatives found themselves arguing with Nelson Rockefeller, who had built his government career by fighting Nazi propaganda in Latin America. In July 1945, as Assistant Secretary of State for Latin America, he drafted a warning to Chile that it should expect "a substantial cut" in U.S. copper purchases. Subsidies for nitrate production would end at the same time. At this time, the State Department and the copper companies lobbied the Export-Import Bank to cut off Chile, arguing that the country was at the limit of its borrowing capacity. The copper firms worried that Chile would cover new loans by raising their taxes.[88] Foreseeing the inevitable, the State Department warned Santiago that, despite these economic reverses, it expected quick suppression of any strikes at the copper mines.[89] All of the Chilean fears concerning the nitrate sector came true.[90] Synthetic nitrate plants built in the United States during the war were sold at a fraction of their construction costs after the war. The plants had a productive capacity 15 times that of Chilean salitre factories, and they quickly flooded the contracting world market. The Chilean sector never recovered.[91] Compensation trade no longer sustained salitre sales in western Europe.[92]

With the mining economy reeling, Chile soon ran out of dollars. The impact on the government was severe. Direct taxes on mining and customs revenues had made up 40 percent of all income between 1938 and 1945, but budgets never balanced. The imbalance grew worse after 1945; by 1950, government spending was 9 percent greater than income. Printing money covered the difference; money was issued to meet the private sector demand for credit as well. Between 1949 and 1952, the total money supply rose 78 percent, well in excess of any increase in the GDP.[93] Inflation and devaluations followed one another in a pattern reminiscent of the nitrate era ,except that the slope of the curves of each phenomenon was now steeper. In 1947, the González Videla administration was forced to curtail all but "essential imports" and cut government salaries.[94]

The Chilean government begged Washington for credit, first from the Export-Import Bank and then from U.S.-dominated international lending agencies, particularly the World Bank. Each request had to be justified along lines acceptable to U.S. officials or to the U.S.-trained technicians who staffed the World Bank and International Monetary Fund. The fate of one loan or another turned on bureaucratic infighting in Washington as much as on the coherence of any Chilean program. A Chilean request in 1946 for money for oil exploration and refining and for creating public housing was turned down, but money was given by the Export-Import Bank for a new steel mill.[95]

All of this was a new dilemma for Chile and had serious consequences for its future. The New Deal and the war were over, and Washington's ideological attitudes were hardening. Chilean leaders still lived in a world shaped by the Depression and wartime promises as the Truman administration prepared for the Cold War. Worse, U.S. economic power in Latin America was now unchallenged. Within the United States, older views about Latin America returned—views that had, only temporarily, been modified to fit the rhetoric of the Roosevelt administration. At best, the Truman administration saw Latin America as a collection of loyal but subordinate allies; Washington's major concerns were in Europe and the Far East.

In a series of conferences (Chapultepec, Mexico City in 1945, Rio de Janeiro in 1947, and Bogota in 1948) the United States insisted on a realignment of Latin American political economies. Latin Americans were told to cooperate militarily in finishing the war, and after 1945, to work against the Soviet Union. At the same time, they were told to rely on less direct aid from the U.S. government and to open their markets to U.S. corporations. On the surface, these agreements were of mutual benefit to all parties. The formal charter of the Organization of American States, passed at the Bogota conference, specified that no state had the right to intervene in the affairs of another and no state could use "coercive measures of [an] economic or political character in order to force the sovereign will of another state."[96] In practice, Washington became hostile to the state-led remedies and economic nationalism that had developed within Latin America during and after the Great Depression. Chile, like the rest of the region, found itself appealing to a hegemonic power that was often indifferent or condescending.[97]

The game of international economic diplomacy became even more one-sided. State Department officials and lending-agency technicians asked hard-edged questions about Chile's ideas on development. To them, many of CORFO's projects defied capitalist logic and threatened the success of foreign, that is U.S., investment.[98] U.S. officials demanded, in 1948, that Chile merge the old foreign debt, at about 20 percent of its face value, into a new loan and that it make regular payments on its consolidated obligations.[99] Seeing the weakened position of the Chilean government, U.S. companies pressed their advantages. Chile wanted to create a state monopoly of copper exports; Kennecott successfully lobbied the Export-Import Bank to make Santiago drop the proposal as a condition for any more loans.[100]

The link between the government's fiscal situation and copper, along with the link between Chile's general economic health and this mineral, became stronger. During the Korean War, the United States once again set a below-market price for Chile's copper. A copper sales corporation created by Chile to market its ore was a fiasco.[101] By the late 1960s, copper supplied more than 80 percent of the country's export income. Anaconda and Kennecott ran the principal mines until they were nationalized in July 1971. Politics in Chile reflected postwar circumstances. A struggle over the distribution of income and political favors was reinterpreted as a battle in the Cold War. This occurred in the midst of the U.S. realignment of its Latin American policies and Chile's deepening dependence on copper and foreign aid.

* * *

What had happened to Chilean economic nationalism and to the calls for socialism? In general, the Radical presidents settled for state economic intervention on behalf of the rich and the middle class. When the demands of these two groups could not be reconciled with even token help to the rest of the population, the Radical Party lost its hold on government.

Year by year, Ríos and González Videla enlarged CORFO, created new state institutions, and strengthened executive control over government and finance. Ríos used "emergency powers" to break strikes and seize control of semi-autonomous credit funds such the Mining Credit Institute and the Industrial Credit Institute of Tarapacá. While he was at it, he also took over the National Air Lines [LAN].[102] Workers were kept from striking, bankers, from pushing up interest rates.

The executive branch in 1943 tried to decree a budget without legislative approval.[103] Such an attempt had caused a civil war in 1891, but now it failed to draw public support and Congress demanded the creation of a Comptroller General [Contraloría General], an agency independent of the presidency that reviewed executive financial conduct. As one conservative historian has pointed out, the innovation was itself unconstitutional.[104] In any event, the parliamentary character of the budgetary process remained, complicated by a new bureaucratic overseer.

The Radical presidents fulfilled some nationalist goals. At great cost, they developed an oil industry, based in the Magallanes fields. They built public housing for a small part of the urban population. Inspired by his experiences in Paris, González Videla took the greatest pride in the beautification of his hometown, La Serena, which became a major government project and a lovely seaside city of vacation villas.[105] The most significant state-led innovation was the electric company, EN-DESA.

In arguing for more loans from the United States in the late 1940s, President González Videla told Washington that the Truman administration's emphasis on free trade was an anachronistic relic. Global developments had created an "economic inter-dependence" in which "the businessman and trader" had to give up thinking of "particular interests" and instead consider "everything else and even the activities of the State itself." Considerations of state survival and of a state-based international economy warranted loaning the Chilean government more money.[106]

In a study of Latin American development policies, Albert Hirschman concluded his section on Chile with the remark that inflation was an alternative to civil war.[107] Hirschman is partially right; civil war was avoided but a conflict took place and only one side was armed. Inflation was redistributing income and wealth. Those who owned property took most of their gains in the form of appreciation. White-collar workers received cost-of-living increases guaranteed by statute beginning in 1942.[108] Those who did not fall into either of these categories were left to founder. Labor began to lose real wages even under the Popular Front. This trend continued after the war as workers' standard of living declined and that of the middle class ceased to improve. Overall, in the 1940s and 1950s, the population grew at a faster rate than the economy. The wage structure remained unchanged, with white-collar employees earning three times the wages of blue-collar workers.[109] Domestic interests fought over shares of the national income. Workers became more militant, with a militancy originating on the shop floor rather than from union leaders. As illustrated in Table 8.3, many strikes were classified as *illegal*, that is, they were not recognized by the state or occurred without undergoing the required arbitration.

Table 8.3: Strikes and Strikers, 1939-1948

Year	Illegal Strikes	No. Workers	Total Strikes	Total Workers
1938	9	3,419	15	11,370
1939	6	5,249	26	10,923
1940	26	10,575	46	18,810
1941	16	890	31	2,293
1942	12	2,069	19	2,740
1943	101	46,832	127	48,729
1944	53	16,849	91	30,888
1945	112	66,612	148	96,736
1946	169	76,475	196	94,737
1947	127	51,169	164	68,986
1948	6	1,203	26	14,344

Source: Moisés Poblete Troncoso, *El derecho del trabajo y la seguridad social en Chile; sus realizaciones, panorama américano, XXV años de legislación social* (Santiago: Editorial Jurídica, 1949), 61-63.

Inflation was once again driving workers into destitution. As early in the inflationary cycle as 1943, the non-militant and anti-leftist carabineros had a hard time feeding and clothing their families despite state subsidies. "Many of them," one observer wrote, "had only cups of tea and bread to consume." Troops were threatening their officers over food.[110] Labor militancy was also fed by dangerous working conditions, and in the foreign mining companies, by racist management. More than 100 thousand work accidents were recorded each year, hundreds of them fatal.[111] In late June 1945, a mining disaster at El Teniente killed 350 men.[112]

From the Popular Front until 1948, the struggle for control of the government and the labor movement reflected the parties search for patronage and the impact of inflation on the rank and file. Party quarrels not only divided the government, they split the CTCh and its many member unions. Public anger over inflation cost the Radical and Socialist parties support in the 1945 municipal elections.[113] By January 1946, the Ríos administration had moved hard to the right and said it would revoke the legal status of any union that went on strike. Ríos became deathly ill that month and everyday tasks of administration fell to the Minister of Interior, Alfredo Duhalde Vásquez, who became vice president. In late January, nitrate workers in Tarapacá struck, demanding wage increases. Duhalde revoked their union charters and sent destroyers to the province's major port of Iquique. In Santiago, on January 28, the Communists, Grove's wing of the Socialists, some left-wing Radicals, and members of the Falange (about eight thousand in all) rallied at the Plaza Bulnes in support of the strike. Duhalde sent a massive police force to stop the rally; the police opened fire, killing six and wounding over seventy. Labor reacted with demonstrations and rolling strikes. One hundred thousand laborers attended the funeral for the victims of the massacre. The government gained labor peace the following month by combining some concessions with repression and by bringing mainstream Socialists into the cabinet, which split the labor movement.[114]

Ríos died of cancer in June 1946, putting an end to Duhalde's administration. A struggle on two fronts now arose. One involving the internecine battle for control of the labor confederation, the CTCh, and the other centered on the next presidential election. On each front, the contending parties failed to confront the causes of Chile's economic problems. The CTCh divided as Socialists and Communists quarreled. To complicate matters even more, the Communists decided to break a pact that all parties had supported; they began to organize rural unions. Their effort continued until rural unionization was banned in 1947 and the Communist Party was smashed.[115]

Given later events, the alignment of parties in the presidential election was astonishing. The right, that is, the Conservative and Liberal parties, split their votes between Eduardo Cruz Coke and Fernando Alessandri (one of Arturo Alessandri's sons). The Socialists divided: Grove's section supported Alessandri while another faction ran Bernardo Ibáñez.[116] González Videla, after obtaining the Radical nomination, assembled an electoral coalition that included the Communists. Pablo Neruda, already a celebrated poet and an icon of the Communists, wrote the lyrics for the campaign song, celebrating the candidate's

Graph 8.1: GDP and Inflation, 1940-1961

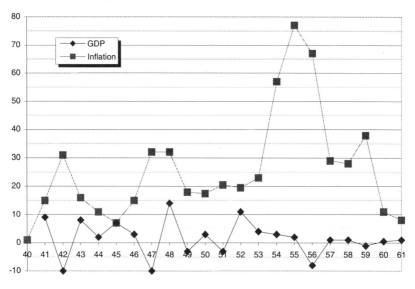

Source: Universidad de Chile, Instituto de Economía, *La economía de Chile*.

populist and redistributive rhetoric. González Videla won, with the Communists providing the margin needed for victory, but found himself without a congressional majority. Worse, soon after he became president, the fight for control of the CTCh came to a head. The confederation split into two groups. Bernardo Ibáñez, its Socialist president (and an ally of Schnake and Allende), used his influence in the government to retain control of the confederation headquarters.[117] The Socialists, however, had played too many bureaucratic games and the Communists swept the confederation election of mid-1947.[118]

These maneuvers proceeded in a nation that presented all the characteristics of "underdevelopment." The meager economic recovery of the late 1930s and the growth of industry in the 1940s masked the damage that the Depression had done. Infant mortality was falling but still high. Most of the population was literate but much of it barely so. Tens of thousands of children were abandoned, growing up on the streets; hundreds of thousands never had an opportunity to attend school. The malnourished rural poor were moving into Santiago, where they formed *poblaciones callampas*, the name given their shantytowns until the early 1970s.[119] In 1947, the economy took a nosedive, with the

GDP dropping 11 percent while inflation soared above 30 percent (see Graph 8.1).[120]

A partisan confrontation followed this inflationary crisis. The standard interpretation, put forward by the government, remained unchallenged into the 1970s. This interpretation suggested that the Communists, following directives from Moscow, had attempted to overthrow the government with a wave of strikes and were stopped.[121] This interpretation ignores the role of inflation. In fact, it was González Videla and the Radicals who decided to force the Communists into a fight for which they were ill prepared and which they lost.[122] Allied against the Communists were the right, that is, the Conservative and Liberal parties, and the leftist wings of the Radical and Socialist parties, who saw a chance to eliminate their competitors in the labor movement. In a critical moment, the United States came to the aid of the anti-communist crusade.

The Communists mistakenly believed they were safe because González Videla was their compatriot. Their role in his campaign had been far more significant than their actions in 1938. They discounted events, in and out of Chile, that signaled they were in peril. Within Chile, González Videla needed to form a congressional majority and the parties he was negotiating with demanded that he remove the Communists from government. The copper companies and the U.S. government demanded that Chile join the Cold War. As late as December 1946, González Videla refused.[123] For their part, the Communists, although cooperating with the government in trying to hold down labor demands in late 1946, became more openly militant by February 1947. They were determined not to back away from the administration's promises to labor (as they believed the Popular Front had done), to extend their own labor base, and to fight against U.S. policies in the region. As Andrew Barnard notes, this was the month that President González Videla returned from an inter-American conference in Rio de Janeiro after having signed provisions on military cooperation with the United States.[124]

In the municipal elections of April 1947, the Conservatives and Communists gained while the Radicals, Liberals, and Socialists lost—the electorate was choosing sides.[125] The Liberals then insisted that the president expel the Communists or lose their support.[126] He gave in and formed a cabinet that included military officers and presented itself as a "technical" government. A hiatus of several months ensued. Bills to ban the Communists were introduced in Congress, while the Radicals pressured reformist labor unions to turn on the Communists in the CTCh.

Strike activity intensified, especially in the copper and coal mining zones. In August 1947, rolling strikes broke out in the coal fields near Concepción, caused by an increase in the official price of bread. The government exacted some wage increases from the coal companies, but the strikes continued. When fuel shortages hit Santiago and Valparaiso, in October, the government protected its urban base by occupying the mines. The miners stayed out, and the Communists tried to help them. The government responded by banning the party, shutting its newspaper, and breaking relations with Czechoslovakia, the Soviet Union, and Yugoslavia. In the strike zone, the army raided homes, killing some miners and carrying off stocks of food. As a final blow, the government banned all fishing in the area. González Videla begged the U.S. government and the copper companies for coal and received some from both.[127] In return, he used arbitration to end strikes in the copper mines and then had the arbiters make no concessions to the unions.[128]

Chile's government was now aligned with the United States. The United States, in turn, saw Latin America primarily in Cold War terms—all requests for aid from any Latin American nation were subjected to the litmus test of anti-communism. Anaconda and Kennecott were lobbying Washington not to cooperate with the Chilean government until it changed its labor policies. From November 1946 until October 1947, the U.S. government cut off all credits to Washington.[129]

The González Videla administration decided not only to remove the Communists from office but from politics, and, while it was at it, to break the labor movement as well. The Communists and leaders of the CTCh in the copper and nitrate mines were arrested and sent to an internment camp in Pisagua. Their families were expelled from company housing. Miners drifted by the hundreds into cities where they encountered black lists.[130] The Communists went underground and were banned, in September 1948, under the famous Law to Defend Democracy. Neruda was stripped of his Senate seat and went into exile to write some of his greatest poetry. In all, about 23 thousand members of the party, or those identified with it, lost suffrage.[131] Eduardo Frei Montalva, then a professor of labor law at the Catholic University, expressed the sentiments of many middle-class reformers when he said that he was happy to see the Communist Party destroyed but sorry that the campaign had become an attack on unions since they were part of "progressive" change.[132]

The repression ended the strike movement but did not stabilize the regime. The government tried to depoliticize the CTCh by rewriting labor laws and banning union association.[133] The tactic succeeded in reducing the Radicals' labor support, narrow as it already was. In 1948, the government had to put down another military plot, once again involving Carlos Ibáñez. It was also hit by white collar strikes, which led Congress to raise bureaucratic wages but not taxes.[134] A cycle of inflation, civil unrest, and government crisis was embedded in the political economy.

Copper prices fell in 1949, sending the administration begging abroad for more funds. González Videla approached Washington with arguments it had heard since Aguirre Cerda: the government needed the loans to maintain political stability and to make up for lost export income; the government also needed to diversify the economy and reduce Chile's dependence on a single mineral; and even, the Communists and the Nazis might still strike a fatal blow if the loans were not supplied. Washington was unimpressed.[135] Some new credits were extended, but the United States kept the Chilean government on a short leash.

In 1952, the electorate retaliated for 14 years of Radical presidents by giving the old putschist Carlos Ibáñez del Campo the presidency. The Socialists split over the actions of party members in Congress in 1948; in 1952, they remained divided. The majority faction supported Salvador Allende Gossens in his first run for the presidency. A substantial minority backed the man the Socialists had once denounced as a dictator.[136] Ibáñez campaigned with a broom in his hand, promising to sweep away the *polítiquería* the Radical Party had generated. By every reasonable measure, his second presidency was a disaster, characterized by even greater corruption and inflation than that of the Radical administrations.

Endnotes

For abbreviations used in notes, see Endnotes, Chapter 1.

1. Address at the University of Concepción, 19 Oct. 1945, quoted in RG 59: 825.50/11-2345, Hunsaker, no. 89, 23 Oct. 1945. The translation is changed slightly for style.

2. United Nations, *Economic Survey of Latin America, 1949*, 281.

3. For the left view, see Bermúdez Miral, *El drama político de Chile*, 88.

4. Tomás Moulian and Isabel Torres Dujisin, *Discusiones entre honorables*, 312.

5. For a glowing estimation of achievements, see Frederick B. Pike, *Chile and the United States, 1880-1962: The Emergence of Chile's Social Crisis and the Challenge to United States Diplomacy* (Notre Dame: University of Notre Dame Press, 1963), 247.

6. Germán Urzúa Valenzuela, *La democracia práctica*, 256.

7. Raúl Atria, "Tensiones políticas y crisis económica," 196.

8. For comments on growth of white-collar positions, see Miral, op. cit., 83, and Marta Vergara, *Decadencia o recuperación*, 131.

9. Ibáñez Santa María, "Los ingenieros, el estado y la política en Chile," 86-97.

10. Chile. Hacienda (1940), Marcial Mora, no. 1234, 30 Nov. 1940.

11. Chile. Fomento (1939), Oficios v. 1594, no. 3, Ezequiel Jiménez Carrasco, Ingeniero Director, Dept. de Industrial Fabriles al Min. de Fomento, 3 May 1939, no. 574; and Oficios, v. 1595, no. 4, Superintendencia de Aduanas al Min. de Fomento, 27 Mar. 1939, no. 1050.

12. See, for example, the inter-agency fight over tea imports, Chile. Hacienda (1939), Wachholtz, no. 1140, 2 Dec. 1939; and Hacienda (1939), Comisión de Cambios Internacionales, no. 36, 21 Dec. 1939.

13. Chile. Fomento (1939), Oficios v. 1600, no. 9, Ferrocarriles del Estado al Min. de Fomento, 14 Aug. 1939, no. 661/550f; Chile. Hacienda (1940), Alfonso, no. 1062, 12 Sept. 1940, and Hacienda (1940), Memoria on Ley, no. 6237, 12 June 1940; and RG 59: 825.00/1450, Bowers, no. 2130, 24 Nov. 1941.

14. On rural unions, Chile. Interior (1940), v. 4 [old number], no. 1834, Min. del Interior, 22 Feb. 1940; (1940), v. 10200, no. 16476, Aguirre Cerda to Sociedades de Agricultura, 20 Mar. 1940; (1940), v. 10201, no. 16705, Min. de Agricultura, 26 Mar. 1940; RG 825.504/4-2745, Bowers, no. 12,034, 27 Apr. 1945, enclosure, Labor and Social Developments in Chile, by Daniel L. Horowitz, 27 Apr. 1945; on Zapata, RG 165: MID 2657-0-136/16, Hill, no. 3206, 7 May 1940; Brian Loveman, *Struggle in the Countryside*, 118, 137, 163; and Jean Carriere, *Landowners and Politics in Chile*, 148.

15. RG 59: 611.2556/19, McLain, no. 8, 18 Jan. 1939, and RG 59: 825.5151 /627, Bowers, no. 1482, 26 May 1941.

16. Chile. Dirección General de Estadística, *Veinte años de legislación social* (Santiago, 1945), 139; Universidad de Chile, Facultad de Ciencias Sociales, Instituto de Economía, *La economía de Chile en el período 1950-1963* (Santiago: Universidad de Chile, 1963), 2:6-9; and Alberto Cabero, *Recuerdos de don Pedro Aguirre Cerda*, 296. Of course, this indicator did not exist at the time; people could only guess at the relation between state policies and economic results.

17. RG 59: 825.34/408, memo of Div. of American Republics, 4 Nov. 1941.

18. Chile. Hacienda (1939), Gustavo Saint-Jean Barros, "Proyecto para el Enriquecimiento de la minería," n.d.

19. RG 59: 825.796/123, Brooks, no. 389, 7 May 1941.

20. Exchange of letters in, Chile. Hacienda (1940), Enrique Ozargun to Hacienda, 13 Dec. 1940 and Marcial Mora, no. 1325, 16 Dec. 1940; and (1940), Marcial Mora to Hacienda, 24 Jan. 1940.

21. Fernando Illanes Benítez, *La economía chilena y el comercio exterior* (Santiago: Imprenta Chile, 1944), 38.

22. Aliaga Ibar, *La economía de Chile*, 259-60.

23. Chile, *Veinte años*, 7, 8, 36, 38, 139, 235; and Universidad de Chile, *La economía de Chile* 2:14.

24. Based on data in, Chile, *Estadística chilena* (Dec. 1943), 683-84.

25. Aguirre Cerda supported but failed to get women's suffrage. Peter G. Snow, *Radicalismo chileno*, 96. On urban-rural dichotomy, see Chile. Interior (1940), v. 10179, Dirección General de Investigaciones e Identificación, memorándum interno, no. 65, 19 June 1940.

26. Chile. Hacienda (1940), Latorre Izquierdo, no. VI/4/51, 19 Jan. 1940.

27. Illanes Benítez, op. cit.

28. Alberto O. Hirschman, *Journeys Toward Progress*, 186; and Pike, op. cit., 273.

29. RG 59: 825.50/80, Bowers, no. 3628, 18 June 1942, enclosed report of Paul T. Ellsworth, p. 50.

30. XI Censo de Población (1940), quoted in Eduardo Ortiz, *La gran depresión y su impacto en Chile, 1929-1933* (Santiago: Vector, 1982), 43; and Sergio Ceppi M. de L., et. al., *Chile, 100 años de industria (1883-1983)* (Santiago: Sociedad de Fomento Fabril, 1983), 196. The structural shortcomings of economic change were pointed out years ago in a now classic essay, Marto A. Ballesteros and Tom E. Davis, "El crecimiento de la producción y el empleo

en sectores básicos de la economía chilena, 1908-1957," *Cuadernos de economía* 2:7 (Sept./Dec. 1965), 6-7.

31. Chélen Rojas, *Trayectoria del socialismo*, 103ff.

32. Julio C. Jobet, *El partido socialista de Chile* 1:53.

33. RG 59: Chile 825.00/1208, Bowers, no. 455, 23 Apr. 1940; RG 165: MID 2657-0-136/16, Hill, no. 3206, 7 May 1940; Paul W. Drake, *Socialism and Populism in Chile*, 237-41; and Julio Faúndez, *Marxism and Democracy in Chile*, 81-85.

34. In addition to Drake and Faúndez, see RG 59: Chile 825.00/1199, Bowers, no. 303, 14 Feb. 1940; RG 165: MID 2657-0-151/25, Wooten, no. 3271, 24 July 1940; Andrew Barnard, "Chilean Communists, Radical Presidents and Chilean Relations with the United States, 1940-1947," *Journal of Latin American Studies* 13:2 (Nov. 1981), 350; and Miral, op. cit., 98.

35. RG 59: 825.00/1199, Bowers, no. 303, 14 Feb. 1940.

36. Barnard, "The Chilean Communist Party," 260.

37. RG 59: Chile 825.00/1210, Bowers, no. 504, 9 May 1940.

38. Loveman, op. cit., 163.

39. RG 59: 825.00/126 1/2, Bowers letter 9 Oct. 1940; on Schnake's attack, see *Diario Ilustrado*, 17 Dec. 1940; RG 59: 825.00-B/97, Bowers, no. 1053, 19 Dec. 1940; RG 165: MID 2054-106/115, Wooten, no. 3414a, 14 December 1940; and Barnard, "Chilean Communists, Radical Presidents," 351.

40. RG 59: 825.00/1238, Bowers, no. 741, 14 Aug. 1940.

41. RG 165: MID 2657-0-151/26, Wooten, no. 3358, 10 Oct. 1940; RG 59: 825.00-B/95, Bowers, no. 1036, 12 Dec. 1940; and 825.00/1287, Bowers, no. 1061, 26 Dec. 1940.

42. RG 59: 825.00/1295, Bowers, no. 1086, 9 Jan. 1941; and RG 59: 825.00/1299, Bowers, no. 1097, 16 Jan. 1941.

43. R 59: 825.00/1316, Bower, no. 1222, 5 Mar. 1941.

44. I differ here from Barnard's view that all this maneuvering hurt the Communists, "The Chilean Communist Party," 251; RG 59: 825.00/1316, Bower, no. 1222, 5 Mar. 1941; 825.00/1509, Bowers, no. 2287, 22 Dec. 1941; and Drake, op. cit., 263.

45. RG 59: 825.00/1338, Bowers, no. 1410, 30 Apr. 1941.

46. RG 59: 825.00-B/129, Bowers, no. 1668, 16 July 1941, enclosure, memo of John B. Faust, which quotes extensively from *El Siglo*; and 825.00/1479, Bowers to Welles, 30 Oct. 1941, *El Mercurio* (Santiago), 5 Sept. 1941.

47. RG 165: MID 2657-0-163/26, Wooten, no. 3185, 8 April 1940; and RG 59: 825.00/1316, Bower, no. 1222, 5 Mar. 1941.

48. Chile. Interior (1940), v. 10205, no. 18429, Carabineros de Chile, Santiago, 10 Aug. 1940; and RG 59: 825.00/1353, Bowers, no. 1464, 22 May 1941.

49. Urzúa V., op. cit., 151.

50. RG 59: 825.00/1385, Bowers, no. 1709, 30 July 1941; and RG 165: MID 2008-172/4, Wooten, no. 3309, 24 Aug. 1940.

51. RG 59: 825.404/24, Bowers, no. 2082, 12 Nov. 1941; RG 59: 825.55/31, McNiece, 16 Aug. 1938; 825.55/37, Dow, no. 27, 4 Mar. 1939; 325.6224, Voight, Hans/1, Armour, no. 685, 17 May 1939; 825.55 J/6, Flexer, no. 88, 5 Dec. 1939; 825.55/J-4, Bowers, no. 197, 9 Dec. 1939; 825.00/1192, Bowers, no. 276, 30 Jan. 1940; Chile. Interior, (1940), v. 10180, Min. de Relaciones Exteriores, 11 Nov. 1940; Potashnik, "Nacismo," 334; and Young, "Jorge González von Marées," 327.

52. Basic biographies are, Luis Palma Zúñiga and Julio Iglesias Meléndez, *Presencia de Juan Antonio Ríos* (Santiago: Editorial Universitaria, 1957); and Gabriel González Videla, *Memorias* (Santiago: Editorial Nacional Gabriel Mistral, 1975), 2 vols. See also Crescente Donoso Letelier, *Alessandri* 2:357; Urzúa V., op. cit., 206-207, 288-90; and the State Department biography on Ríos, RG 59: 825.001, Ríos, Juan Antonio/128, Bowers, no. 4619, 8 Oct. 1942.

53. Ceppi M. de L. et al., op. cit., 194.

54. On the candidates, RG 59: 825.00/1471, Bowers, no. 2173, 1 Dec. 1941; Drake, op. cit., 267-68; Moulian and Torres, op. cit., 160.

55. RG 59: 825.00/1568, Heath, no. 2480, 26 Jan. 1942, report by John P. Faust, Second Secretary.

56. *El Mercurio*, 9 Apr. 1942; RG 59: 825.00/1652, Bowers, no. 3201, 5 May 1942; and Barnard, "The Chilean Communist Party," 305.

57. RG 59: 825.00/1920, Bowers, no. 6815, 19 June 1943; and Pearson, Military Attache report of 2 June 1943. See also Snow, op. cit., 101.

58. Drake, op. cit., 271-75.

59. RG 59: 825.00/1812, Bowers, no. 5577, 28 Jan. 1943.

60. RG 59: 825.00/7-844, Bowers, no. 10,159, 8 July 1944.

61. RG 59: 825.00/1812, Bowers, no. 5577, 28 Jan. 1943. See also Barnard, "The Chilean Communist Party," 276.

62. Caballero, *Latin America and the Comintern, 1919-1943* (London: Cambridge University Press, 1986)op. cit., 137; Johnson, "Chilean Relations with the United States," 356; and Barnard, "The Chilean Communist Party," 328.

63. Zúñiga and Iglesias, op. cit., 121; and González Videla, op, cit., 2:1074-75.

64. There is remarkably little written on electric power in Latin America, but the Chilean pattern seems similar to developments elsewhere. See Marvin S. Fink and staff, *Reports on Electric Power Regulation in Brazil, Chile, Colombia, Costa Rica, and Mexico* (Cambridge, MA: Harvard Law School, 1960), report on "Chile," 1, 10, 26, 32. On government attempts at buy out, see RG 59: 825.6463 Electric Bond and Share Co./195, State to Bowers, 13 March 1942; /202, Bowers, no. 3054, 20 Apr. 1942; /209, Bowers, no. 3994, 27 July 1942, /228, Heath telegram, 17 Sept. 1943. For a view contrary to that presented here, see Zuñiga and Iglesias, op. cit., 121.

65. Luis Ortega Martínez, *Corporación de Fomento de la Producción* (Santiago: Corporación de Fomento de la Producción, 1989), 122.

66. Quoted in, RG 59: 825.00/2089, Green, 27 Jan. 1944.

67. RG 59: 825.00/1718, Bowers, no. 4062, 3 Aug. 1942.

68. RG 59: 825.00/1689, Bowers, no. 3685, 23 June 1942, enclosure, memo of conversation between Ross Santa María and Lyon, 19 June 1942. See also Urzúa V., op. cit., 265.

69. RG 59: 825.911/84, Bowers, no. 3518, 5 June 1942, enclosure, memo of conversation between Edwards and Second Secretary Cecil B. Lyon, 4 June 1942.

70. A point emphasized in, Michael J. Francis, *The Limits of hegemony: United States Relations with Argentina and Chile during World War II* (Notre Dame: University of Notre Dame Press, 1977), 109. The interpretation offered here differs considerably from Francis, who provides little analysis of political differences within Chile.

71. RG 59: 825.00/1650, Bowers, no. 3117, 25 Apr. 1942, Lyon report.

72. RG 59: Chile 825.24/280, Bowers telegram, 13 Jan. 1942; and 825.24/1205, Bowers, no. 6945, 7 July 1943. On Socialists, Schnake and Grove lobbied personally, RG 59: 825.911/107, Duggan memo to Welles, 26 Dec. 1942.

73. Florencio Duran Bernales, *El Partido Radical*, 293.

74. *El Mercurio*, 18 May 1942; RG 59: 825.6363/257, Bowers telegram, 11 September 1942; and 825.6363/276, Bowers to President, 24 Sept. 1942.

75. Welles' statement, RG 59: 825.001 Ríos, Juan Antonio/121A, State telegram, 8 Oct. 1942. Robert J. Alexander makes much of Alessandri's reaction, *Alessandri* vol. 2. On supplies, RG 59: 825.24/611A, Hull telegram, 10 Aug. 1942; 825.24/776, Bowers, no. 5450, 15 Jan. 1943; RG 59: 825.24/1062, Bowers, no. 6505, 17 May 1943; and *El Mercurio*, 9 May 1943.

76. RG 59: 825.24/745-3/5, Philip W. Bonsal memo to Welles, 18 Dec. 1942; 825.20/163, Bowers, no. 6644, 3 June 1943, Report of Military Attache, 3 June 1943; 825.20/195, Bowers, no. 8821, 7 Feb 1944, Report of Col. Johnson, 31 Jan. 1944; and 825.014/118, Bowers, no. 9740, 16 May 1944.

77. RG 59: Chile 825.24/528, Bowers, no. 3661, 22 June 1942.

78. RG 59: 825.00/out of order, Mills report 192, 16 Oct. 1942; *Diario Oficial*, 6 Mar. 1943; and RG 59: 825.23/1129, Bowers telegram, 22 June 1943.

79. Ibar, op. cit., 296; and Duran Bernales, op. cit., 193.

80. RG 59: 825.24/1170, Bowers, no. 6832, 23 June 1943.

81. RG 59: 825.6374/1520, Heath, no. 7662, 25 Sept. 1943, report by Sheldon Mills, "The Chilean Nitrate Problems," 3.

82. RG 59: 825.6374/1540, Edward Browning, Jr., War Production Board, to Philip W. Bonsal, Chief, Division of the American Republics, Dept. of State, 4 Nov. 1943; and 825.6374/6-2244, Bowers to Hull, 22 June 1944.

83. RG 59: 825.6374/1468, Bowers, no. 4051, 1 Aug. 1942, Stephen Mills memo, 1 Aug. 1942; 825.6374/1498, Duggan memo, 23 July 1943.825.6374 /1499, Bowers telegram, 5 Aug. 1943; and 825.6374/1582, J.A. Woods, Pres., Chilean Nitrate Sales Corp. (NY), to Laurence Duggan, 21 Apr. 1944.

84. RG 59: 825.6374/7-2644, James H. Wright memo, 26 July 1944; and 825.51 /10-2144, James H. Wright memo of conversation, 21 Oct. 1944. For obvious reasons, the memo is contained in a separate listing, Strictly Confidential File; 825.6374/1520, Heath, no. 7662, 25 Sept. 1943, report by Sheldon Mills, "The Chilean Nitrate Problem."

85. RG 59: Chile 825.6363/9-1945, Stundt, no. 11,988, 19 Apr. 1945.

86. See González Videla, op. cit., 2:1084.

87. RG 59: 825.51/1520, Duggan memo, 3 Feb. 1944; 825.51/1526, Bowers, no. 4057, enclosure, Dean Acheson to Bowers, 3 May 1944; 825.51/8-2345, Stenger memo, 23 Aug. 1945; 825.51/7-245, Bowers, no. 12,368, 2 July 1945; 825.51/10-2545, British Embassy to Sec. of State, 25 Oct. 1945; 825.51/11-2045, Byrnes to Senator Hawkes, 20 Nov. 1945, enclosure, Foreign Bondholders Protective Council "To Holders of Chileans Dollar Bonds," 10 Feb. 1944; and 825.51/3-1146, Acheson to Senator Cordon, 28 Mar. 1946.

88. RG 59: 825.50/7-1345, Nelson Rockefeller, Asst. Sec. to the Secretary, 13 July 1945; 825.51/9-2045, D.M. Phelps memo, 20 Sept. 1945; and 825.6352/9-1246, memo of conversation, E.T. Stannard, Kennecott, and others, 12 Sept. 1946.

89. RG 59: 825.51/11-646, Spruille Braden, Asst. Sec., to Clayton, 6 Nov. 1946.

90. RG 59: Chile 825.6374/7-1846, Bowers, no. 14,214, 18 July 1946, enclosed correspondence between Stettinius to Fernández.

91. RG 59: Chile 825.6374/7-246, memos of Marcial Mora, Chile's Ambassador to United States, 2, 12 July 1946, and Grew to Mora, 9 Aug. 1946; 825.6374/8-2046, Mora to State, memo, 20 Aug. 1946; and 825.6374/10-1948, memo of conversation, Pedro Alvarez, Chilean Embassy, H.M. Pauley, Dept. of State, 19 Oct. 1948.

92. RG 59: 825.51/3-2147, Vergara to Cady, 21 Mar. 1947, enclosure, Horace R. Graham, Anglo-Chilean Nitrate Corp., NY, to Roberto Vergara, CORFO, NY, 10 Mar. 1947.

93. Universidad de Chile, *La economía de Chile* 2:152-53, 164, 210.

94. RG 59: 825.51/7-2847, Balke to Secretary of State, 28 July 1947; and 825.50 /9547, Bowers, airgram, 5 Sept. 1947.

95. RG 59: 825.51/2-2746, Byrnes telegram to Embassy, Santiago, 27 Feb. 1946; and 825.51/91145, Acheson, telegram to Santiago, 11 Sept. 1946.

96. Articles 15 and 16, quoted in, Harold Molineu, *U.S. Policy toward Latin America: From Regionalism to Globalism* (Boulder: Westview Press, 1990, 2d ed.), 27.

97. On Truman's policies, see Stephen G. Rabe, *Eisenhower and Latin American: the Foreign Policy of Anticommunism* (Chapel Hill: University of North Carolina Press, 1988), 14-25.

98. RG 59: 825.6363/3-2646, memo of conversation of Braden, Wright, Flack, Wells, Brundage, Stenger, Scanlan, Corliss, Piggot, Townsend, 26 Mar. 1946; and 825.51/2-448, memo of conversation of Felix Nieto del Rio, Chilean Ambassador; Roberto Vergara, head of CORFO, NY offices; Paul Daniels, Director of ARA; James Espy, Aching Chief of NWC; James Webb, Jr., JWC; and Edgar Mcginner, Jr., NWC, 4 Feb. 1948.

99. RG 59: 825.51/6-1347, Rogers to Livesey, 13 June 1947, enclosure, Guillermo de Pedregal, President of the Economic and Financial Mission of Chile, to Rogers, 16 May 1947; 825.51/6-1247, James Grafton Rogers, President, Foreign Bondholders Protective Council, Inc., NY, to Frederick Liversey, Adviser, Office of Financial and Development Policy, State, 12 June 1947; and 825.51/1-2948, memo of conversation with Felix Nieto del Rio; Robert Vergara; and Norman Armour, Asst. Sec. of State; Paul C. Daniels, Dir. of ARA; William D. Pawley, James Espy, Acting Chief of NWC, 29 Jan. 1948.

100. RG 59: Chile 825.6352/6-2849, memo of telephone conversation between E.T. Stannard, Pres. Kennecott Copper Corp., Banbridge C. David, NWC, 28 June 1949; and 825.50/6-2049, Aide Memoire, Washington, 20 June 1949.

101. Theodore H. Moran, *Multinational Corporations and the Politics of Dependence: Copper in Chile*, 87-96.

102. RG 59: 825.00/1645, Bowers 2972, 9 Apr. 1942; 825.00/out of order; Mills report 192, 16 Oct. 1942; and *El Mercurio*, 9 Apr. 1942.

103. Urzúa V., op. cit., 258.

104. Crescente Donoso Letelier, "Notas sobre el origen, acatamiento y desgaste del régimen presidencial, 1925-1973," *Historia* (1976), 340.

105. González Videla, op. cit., 2:1133.

106. Quoted in, RG 59: 825.50/8-1148, Bowers, no. 532, 11 Aug. 1948.

107. Hirschman, op. cit., 162.

108. RG 59: 825.504/160, Bowers, no. 4236, 21 Aug. 1942, report by Faust.

109. Instituto de Economía, *La economía de Chile* vol. 2, on GNP, 3-4, on wages, 101.

110. RG 59: 825.105/44, Bowers, no. 7171, 3 Aug. 1943, report of Naval Attache, 3 Aug. 1943.

111. RG 59: 825.504/168, Bowers, no. 5619, 3 Feb. 1943, Strictly Confidential File; and 825.504/2-1543, State Dept. review of "Chilean Labor Difficulties," 15 Feb. 1943, Strictly Confidential File, Chile. *Veinte años*, 7.

112. RG 59: Chile 825.6352/6-2345, Bowers telegram 849, 23 June 1945, records the observations of Deputy Carlos Rosales.

113. On labor disillusionment, RG 825.504/3-2745, Bowers, no. 11,854, 27 Mar. 1945, enclosure, Labor and Social Developments in Chile by Daniel L. Horowitz, 27 Mar. 1945.

114. The best account of events is, Tomás Moulian and Isabel Torres-Dujisin, "Las candidaturas presidenciales de la derecha: 1946," (Santiago: Documente de Trabajo, FLACSO, no. 339, Junio 1987), 23-25. There is a good account of the polarization in Jon V. Kofas, *The Struggle for Legitimacy: Latin American Labor and the United States, 1930-1960* (Tempe: Arizona State University Center for Latin American Studies, 1992), 86. There is an excellent summary of divisions within parties and labor factions in, Barnard, "Chile," in Leslie Bethell and Ian Roxborough, eds., *Latin America between the Second World War and the Cold War, 1944-1948* (Cambridge: Cambridge University Press, 1992), 76. See also Thomas Miller Klubock, "Class, Community, and Gender in the Chilean Copper Mines," 2:611-15.

115. RG 59: 825.504/4-3047, Bowers telegram no. 336, 30 Apr. 1947; Carriere, op. cit., 162; and Alexander, op. cit., 2:860.

116. Moulian and Torres, op. cit., 290; Drake, op. cit., 279-83.

117. The fight for union offices is reported in, RG 59: 825.00/2124, Bowers, no. 9185, 21 Mar. 1944; and Barnard, "The Chilean Communist Party," 340.

See also Bernardino Bravo Lira, *Régimen de gobierno y partidos políticos en Chile, 1924-1973* (Santiago: Editorial Jurídica de Chile, 1978), 143.

118. RG 59: 825.5043/6-2547, W.E.D., no. 15,435, 25 June 1947.

119. Instituto de Economía, *La economía de Chile*, 21-24, based on data from the 1952 census; debate between Bernardo Ibáñez and Senator Cruz Coke in RG 59: 825.50/129, Bowers, no. 7111, 27 July 1943; and Duran Bernales, op. cit., 430.

120. From the study by the Instituto de Economía, *La economía de Chile*.

121. González Videla, op. cit., 1:573-87, 612 ff.; Duran Bernales, op. cit., 477; Pike, op. cit., 264; U.S. Ambassador Claude G.Bowers, *Chile through Embassy Windows*, 166; and Snow, op. cit., 111.

122. I agree substantially with the revisionist work of Barnard, "The Chilean Communist Party," 360-70. My account differs somewhat in detail and emphasis.

123. RG 59: 825.5045/12-2346, Bowers to Spruille Braden, Asst. Sec. of State, 23 Dec. 1946.

124. Barnard, "Chile," 81.

125. Urzúa V., op. cit., 291.

126. In addition to Barnard and Drake, see Snow, op. cit., 111.

127. RG 59: 825.5045/10-947, Bowers telegram no. 783, 9 Oct. 1947; 825.5019/10-1047, Lyon telephone conversation with Spilsbury, Anaconda Copper Co., Washington, 10 Oct. 1947; and González Videla, op. cit., 1:650.
128. Klubock, op. cit., 2:666-67.

129. Jon V. Kofas, "The Politics of Foreign Debt: The IMF, the World Bank and U.S. Foreign Policy in Chile, 1946-1952," *The Journal of Developing Areas* 31 (Winter 1997), 161-62. I discovered this excellent article as this work went to press. Also see, Gaddis Smith, *The Last Years of the Monroe Doctrine, 1945-1993* (New York: Hill and Wang, 1994), 67-68; and Barnard, "Chile," 85-88; David Rock, "War and Postwar Intersections, Latin America and the United States," in David Rock, ed., *Latin America in the 1940s: War and Postwar Transitions* (Berkeley: University of California Press, 1994), 32-34.
130. RG 59: 825.504/2-2448, Trueblood, no. 138, 24 Feb. 1948, enclosure, memo Movement of Communists by James D. Bell, 24 Feb. 1948.

131. Barnard, "The Chilean Communist Party," 373.

132. RG 59: 825.5045/1-3048, Bowers telegram A-52, 30 Jan. 1948.

133. Duran Bernales, op. cit., 413.

134. RG 59: 825.5017/8-1048, Report on "Confederation of Private Employees," 1948; and Hirschman, op. cit., 190.

135. RG 59: Chile 825.6352/42849, Bowers telegram, no. 212, 28 Apr. 1949; and 825.6352/6-2849, memo of telephone conversation E.T. Stannard, Pres. Kennecott Copper Corp., Banbridge C. David, NWC, 28 June 1949.

136. Jobet, *El socialismo*, 66-71.

Fig. 11. Public Buildings, downtown Santiago, 1930s. The new Ministry of Hacienda, 1934. United States. National Archives.

Conclusion

The End of Dependency?

It is now time to reorient efforts to measure efforts
toward success in development by indicators centered on the *quality of life* and on *equality* in the
distribution of goods and services.
                    Fernando Henrique Cardoso, 1981[1]

A long the way of writing this work, the Soviet Union collapsed and
the "left" in Chile, as elsewhere, almost disappeared. Capitalist
rhetoric, couched now as neoliberalism, became the vogue in the media
and in academia. While the left within U.S. academic life had always
been thin, it had a vigorous, even courageous existence in Latin America. It is hard to believe that the author of the above quotation and one
of the founders of "dependency" writing in the 1960s has become
president of Brazil. Even more difficult to believe is that he did so in
opposition to a more left-wing candidate, and that this former dependista now extols the advantages of a less-fettered capitalism—
something he once denounced as unhealthy for Brazil and Latin America. Perhaps Cardoso's journey is only a study in the "fluidity" of all
politically oriented intellectuals; or perhaps it is an announcement that
even those who once professed the need to revolutionize the future have
given up.

Whatever one's take on Brazil's president and his past, this former
radical is not alone. In one country after another in Latin America,
intellectuals, political leaders, and even political parties that once spoke
in terms of "core-periphery" and of dependent development and the
problems of underdevelopment have altered their language. In *Utopia*

Unarmed, Jorge Castañeda noted that throughout most of Latin America the "right and the center" have governed the region in the last two decades and have failed. But the left has not gained from this failure. "Wherever there is a left today, it seems intractably [sic] confronted with a central problem: devising a viable and substantively different alternative to the status quo."[2]

Dependency writing was always indebted to the left. It grew out of a critique of basic capitalist axioms, especially the view that patterns of development in "backward" areas would eventually imitate both the institutions and outcomes of more advanced regions. The assertion that "modernization" would solve Latin America's problems was repeated ad nauseam in U.S. political and economic studies of Latin America in the 1960s. By comparison, dependistas emphasized that the trajectory of change in underdeveloped nations was contingent upon what had already taken place in more advanced, industrialized countries. How the two patterns were related varied according to each author, but all dependistas agreed on two propositions. Underdevelopment and development were global phenomena that occurred not in sequence but simultaneously: "both are linked functionally and, therefore, interact and condition each other mutually."[3] As Theotonio dos Santos put it, "Dependency is a situation in which a certain number of countries have their economy conditioned by the development and expansion of another . . . placing the dependent countries in a backward position exploited by the dominant countries."[4] The second proposition was that the causal links of underdevelopment ran from the "core" to the "periphery," from the capitalist institutions and governments of advanced to underdeveloped nations. Writers disagreed about what could be done, with many insisting that only a break with capitalism through revolution would solve Latin America's problems, and others, such as Cardoso, arguing that some kind of associated development might be possible as a way out of poverty and inequality.[5]

Dependency thinking, of course, had no end of critics—on the right, on the left, and in between. I will not try to summarize these criticisms, for I believe its decline was caused by a sea-change in attitude rather than any intellectual argument. Dependency was more a perspective than a theory; it was undermined by three factors to be explained in the following paragraphs. Dependistas stopped doing much homework. Most of the major names in the literature—Cardoso, Dos Santos, André Gunder Frank, and Osvaldo Sunkel—did relatively little original research, or even research design, in the 1980s. Dependistas within Latin America had a good excuse: they were often persecuted by military regimes. A second problem was that many dependistas came from Sociology and Political Science, not Economics. Some economists worked on key issues related to trade, patterns of industrialization, and income distribution. The United Nations Economic Commission of Latin America inspired by its founder, Raúl Prebisch, altered the kinds of questions asked about Latin American development. However, most dependista assertions could not be easily tested. Attempts to theorize or to operationalize dependista generalizations ran into the headache that they were so broad they could not be quantified into the neat statistical packages that social scientists demanded. A 1978 attempt by Vincent Mahler to develop a "factor analysis" for 13 indicators of "external dependence" was a notable exception to this pattern. It was rarely mentioned by dependistas even though Mahler found that many of their assertions about Latin American development held true for eleven Asian countries.[6] Unfortunately, there were few studies like Mahler's. Dependistas did not want to do that much counting, let alone run regressions, and so tended to fall to the wrong side of the positivist direction that was overtaking the social sciences in the United States and, through U.S. influence, Latin America as well.

The third factor was the course of international events. The defeat of guerrilla movements in the 1970s and 1980s, the collapse of the Sandinista government in 1989, and the severe crisis in Cuba that followed the end of the Soviet Union hurt the plausibility of any left-wing project. These developments coincided with and were influenced by the Debt Crisis of 1982 and its aftermath. At the very moment that financial dependence hit Latin America the hardest, most of the leftists, academic or otherwise, were already on the defensive. The crisis of the Great Depression had led to new political formations, to policies in the 1930s and 1940s that supported Latin America's industrialization and strengthened the possibilities of labor movements and populism. The Debt Crisis of the 1980s undercut the viability of most populist proposals, of state-led efforts at income distribution and social welfare. It was not only the guerrillas that went down but also left-wing bureaucrats, many of them in the middle class, and not a few academics. Those Latin American intellectuals that remained survived in think-tanks that had to appeal to U.S.-dominated aid agencies for funds. Not surprisingly, they left out any mention of Marx or dependency in those applications and learned to frame their work in the dominant "discourse," of capitalist development. An internal consequence of the Debt Crisis was hyperinflation, which ripped Latin America apart in the late 1970s and the 1980s and made the state itself seem bereft. How could anyone believe more government would solve anything?

The decline of dependista perspectives coincided with the rise of the "Chilean model." The military regime of Augusto Pinochet, who gained power through a coup in 1973, survived the Debt Crisis and continued to impose economic policies that stressed an open economy, repressed labor, and reduced social spending. The economy continued to rely on foreign trade and infusions of foreign capital, but government policies encouraged export diversification. Chile moved from a dependence on only copper to also selling small manufactures, timber, seafood, and agricultural products. It increased its list of customers to include Japan and developing nations in the Far East and improved commerce with its neighbors; thereby reducing the concentrated power of U.S. interests. The United States (followed by Brazil and Japan) still supplies 23 percent of Chilean imports, and buys 14 percent of its exports. Japan is now the principal customer, buying 18 percent.[7] The Pinochet regime accumulated substantial monetary reserves, as a cushion against any trade reversal—virtually the only time any government in Chile has succeeded in this task. The distribution of income worsened; but the economy began to grow. From the mid-1980s until the present, growth has averaged 6 to 7 percent, the highest rate the country has seen in 150 years.

The national income per capita had been about average for Latin America in the 1970s and below the regional average for most of the 1980s. Then it began to soar as trade boomed. With a population of almost 14 million, GDP per capita jumped from US$3.7 thousand in 1994 to US$5.1 thousand, in part as a result of a rising exchange rate against the US dollar. This placed it ahead of Brazil but still behind the region's upper tier of nations: Venezuela, Argentina, and Mexico. Still, this amounts to a substantial repositioning of Chile within Latin America; although it is as much of a comment on the economic disasters that have overtaken other Latin American nations as on Chile's success. In the early 1930s, Argentina had a per capita income three times that of Chile. If this pattern continues, Chileans could join the region's wealthiest populations. Infant mortality has fallen dramatically in the last twenty years, and Chileans now live into their seventies.[8]

The country has reduced its debt payments to a manageable level, enjoys a sustained pattern of growth with low levels of inflation, and is realizing an appreciation of its currency against the dollar. In 1989, Pinochet lost a plebiscite and had to step down as president; he remained head of the armed forces. Under the constitution, which he wrote, two Christian Democratic presidents have won office, each as the leader of a multi-party coalition called the Concertación that includes the Christian Democrats and Socialists. Each of Pinochet's successors, Patricio Aylwin and Eduardo Frei Ruiz-Tagle, maintained Pinochet's economic policies while increasing social spending.

In defiance of any dependency perspective, the restoration of elected government and rising per capita income occurred as Chile's reliance on trade increased: from 51 percent in 1987, to 69 percent in 1990, and on to 78 percent in 1994.[9] My purpose here is to review the relation of the research presented in this study to these very sweeping changes in intellectual life and Chilean development. This is, therefore, a very different sort of conclusion than is usually written for monographs. My goals are fairly simple: to demonstrate that history matters and to renew a critique of modernization theory. I will begin with some recent studies that are either critical of dependency attitudes or deny any link between external dependence and internal developments in Latin America in general or Chile in particular. I will then turn to a discussion of what can be rescued of dependista literature, given the current state of our knowledge. I close with some observations on what has happened in Chile, and on how the shock of the long period of the Pinochet dictatorship is still working its way through the society.

The Contemporary Analysis of Latin American Reality

Confidence in government action in both underdeveloped and developed nations has declined. Since World War II a wide variety of distributive efforts in Latin America, from the populism of Peronism in Argentina to the Allende's effort at socialism in Chile, have ended in disaster. In one wealthy nation after another, living standards for working people have stagnated or fallen; no government has combined economic growth with reducing unemployment.[10] Almost all discussion of creating more equitable societies through progressive taxation has ceased. The end of the Cold War has also led to a shift in priorities within the more advanced capitalist economies. A triumphant corporate elite in the United States has become more openly hostile to labor associations and to state-led development. Its views go almost unchallenged in the media, professional policy circles, and various think-tanks. A social Darwinian rhetoric, very reminiscent of the end of the nineteenth century, is used to explain misery within the United States as well as underdevelopment abroad.

The rich possess staggering resources. There are now over 150 billionaires (that is, with wealth of more than a US$1,000 million) in the United States alone, one of whom has more than US$40 billion. Short-term gains through speculative activity, what one recent analyst of corporate behavior calls "value extractions" far exceeds any desire to invest in "value creation."[11] Speculative fever flourished in Chile under Pinochet, leading to a financial bust and depression in the 1982-84 period. When speculators rebuilt their financial engines with infusions of foreign capital, the economy recovered. The richest Chilean has a fortune of US$2.2 billion.[12] By comparison, the current national budget of Chile is US$11 billion; the current total debt, US$25 billion.

There has been a change in thinking as well. Academics writing on Latin America, from the point of view critical of capitalism, have moved away from class analysis and dependency views and toward a preoccupation with cultural nuances and fields that are threatening to develop their own jargon: "postmodern" analyses, "subaltern studies," and "cultural studies."[13] They do not escape pejorative political comments: a critic of their efforts recently referred to "subaltern studies" as "dependency theory in drag."[14] That is not only pejorative but unfair; the rise in such studies indicates a disinterest in some of the older issues of development. The role of the U.S. government and of U.S. corporations in shaping policies within Latin America is being put to one side in order to pursue social and cultural issues.

Those who do tackle issues of underdevelopment or economic instability tend to accept some form of "modernization" as their perspective. They focus on institutional faults or poor economic choices within Latin American nations to explain what has gone wrong. They bash the dependistas, populists, or any scholar that links foreign interests in an economy to adverse domestic consequences. Typifying this attitude, Stephen Haber argued that the New Economic History, that is, the application of econometric models developed in the United States, had not yet reached Latin America and no real scholarly progress could be expected until it did.[15] After a highly inaccurate summary of the dependistas' works, Haber argues that they made major mistakes in relating the past to the present. It is not true, as dependistas believed, that foreign trade decapitalized Latin America through the flow of profits abroad. The dependistas also erred in rejecting any "scientific evaluation" of their theory or theories: "their central tenets were largely inconsistent with the empirical facts. . . . At the heart of the [dependistas'] theory was the notion that the terms of trade of Latin America deteriorated in a secular fashion. Thus, foreign trade underdeveloped Latin America." Contemporary research demonstrates, according to Haber, that for long periods in the nineteenth and twentieth centuries the terms of trade favored Latin America products: "The other major tenet of dependency theory was the existence of a comprador bourgeoisie controlling a weak state that would not and could not act in the national interest."

This is also untrue, Haber claims, since scholars working on the nineteenth century found "national bourgeoisies of considerable political power and developmentalist will."[16] With the exception of refuting some of them, scholars have achieved little in their study of dependista assumptions, opines Haber.

Indeed, both the dependistas and their critics misfocused what was really important in the past. They paid too little attention to *the balance of payments*, and they overlooked the strategic position of foreign capital within underdeveloped nations. The balance of payments includes all commercial flows between two nations, including the repatriation of profits and payments for such services as shipping, banking, and insurance. Recent work on the British empire has emphasized finance, not merely the pattern of industrialization, as a key to understanding why some nations became relatively richer or poorer in the last two centuries. Dependence did not stop growth but it may have enhanced financial vulnerability. Speaking on the influence of British finance in nineteenth-century South American nations, Argentina in particular, Cain and Hopkins remark, "This degree of penetration, direct and indirect, must surely be seen as infringing the sovereignty of the recipients, even as it boosted their incomes."[17] This study adds the observation that the influence of foreign capital can be out of proportion to a mere listing of assets: U.S. capital was an essential element in the operation of the Chilean economy; thus, U.S. interests could destabilize the government if they chose to fight particular policies.

I again note my eclecticism. Dependistas are not the fount of all wisdom nor should anyone automatically reject neoclassical economic propositions. Reflecting on the impact of protectionism in Chile, my narrative indicates that the raising of tariffs in the late 1920s, the Crash itself, and the 1940s comprised a set of ad hoc responses to the continuous shortage of hard currency. They were driven by efforts to recruit political support or, at least, not alienate key elements of the Chilean elite and middle class. Once, however, tariffs protected specific interests, it was very difficult to change them, whether or not they retarded overall growth. Much the same can be said about currency exchange laws. They failed to protect the nation's store of hard currency during the Crash but quickly became the means to arbitrate among interests competing for access to hard currency. These laws also became the means to generate income from the copper-mining firms (and some other foreign enterprises); therefore, they were essential to fiscal stability. A neoclassical approach could find plenty of evidence in each issue for allowing an open market to sort the outcome. However, a market-oriented solution would reopen contests for bureaucratized power and wealth.

Anyone who uses archival documents knows that the past is as disorganized as the present; records do not conform to any theory or set of propositions. Organizing the information in those records involves choosing what is fact and what should be left off the notation. Any theory is useful only as a guide to what may be important. What matters is what happened to people, not what evolves within theory. Theoretical history of any kind tends to lose all personality, to be about no one in particular, and to lose sight of the context in which possibilities unfold. Indeed, both the dependista literature (especially that in Latin America) and the modernization writings tend to downplay any agency at all. Latin Americans as individuals or as cultures often disappear.

There is another problem with an ahistorical faith in theory. Theory dates quickly. No one should be surprised that propositions advanced from a dependency perspective have to be revised or reframed. Every perspective experiences that over time. *Desarrollismo*, as theories of modernization were called in Latin America, has had many of its naive assumptions and over generalizations refuted.

One of the current theoretical explosions in the social sciences has been "rational choice theory," the application of econometric techniques to non-economic subjects, particularly in studying the behavior of political institutions and policy outcomes. Precisely the direction of research that Haber supports. As a result of placing "rational choice theory" under their microscope, Donald Green and Ian Shapiro have invalidated many of its generalizations. They attack its thin empirical foundations on the basis that "rational choice theory has yet to deliver on its promise to advance the empirical study of politics."[18] They find the theory or theories constructed from rational choice assumptions are poorly formulated, ignore alternative explanations, and are often organized in a manner that does not permit falsification.[19] Noting the econometric foundations of rational choice theorizing, they also note that those foundations have been attacked recently with considerable effect.[20] Their comments make an interesting parallel with Haber's critique of dependency thinking. One of their thoughts is germane to theorizing about human behavior:

> One is in possession of an explanation only if one can accurately characterize the causal mechanism involved in producing the relevant regularity; rational choice theorists do not deny this. Too often, however, they fail to appreciate the fact that all such putative characterizations *are conjectures* [my italics]; it is never possible to prove that they are correct. Theorems can be proved, theories cannot.[21]

With this in mind, let us consider the discussion about foreign interests, trade, and Latin American underdevelopment, especially as it pertains to Chile. When the dependistas made their case a generation ago, they over generalized. For example, their views on the terms of trade came largely from the work of Raúl Prebisch, arguing that his findings for the second quarter of the twentieth century applied even to the nineteenth century. While the terms of trade for Latin American products was not always unfavorable, the core of Prebisch's research, drawing on events from the late 1920s until the late 1940s, was correct. Research by a serious numbers cruncher, Angus Maddison, concludes that Latin American terms of trade declined in the Depression; those of Chile fell 46 percent.[22] What was the relation of this change in economic fortune to development? The deteriorating returns from nitrates had several consequences even before the Crash. Political life became increasingly unstable in the mid-1920s as the fiscal base of the government proved inadequate to increasing public demands. One of the central findings of this work was that Chilean dependence on U.S. foreign investment and financial credits was accompanied by policies that expanded the state.

As the Parliamentary Regime collapsed in the 1924-27 period, it seemed that a proto-fascist regime would take its place. Carlos Ibáñez del Campo seized power and rigged his election, yet his promises had a broad audience. To the elite, he promised stability and the repression of a left-wing labor movement; to the middle class, he promised public office and urban improvements; and to a small segment of the work force, he offered some basic reforms and rising wages. To carry out these promises, the state would become stronger, more economically intrusive and socially controlling. Ibáñez was well-liked by foreign, and especially U.S. interests. He had money from New York and London. He worked with the Guggenheims at reorganizing the nitrate industry into the joint venture of COSACh, he worked out a deal with the new U.S. owners of Chilean Electric, and he left the U.S. copper interests in unquestioned control of the major mines. Cooperation with foreign trade interests thus promised new sources of credit to the Chilean state. The state acquired both new means to grow and new models of administration by drawing closer to U.S. interests.

A congruence existed between the need of U.S. interests for new places to invest and sources of minerals and Ibáñez' need for funds to enhance the state's clientalistic projects. U.S. corporations, like the native elite, enjoyed a freedom from any militant labor movement while a rent-seeking coalition (involving not only elite interests but middle-class reformers) developed within the Chilean state. This coalition wanted higher rates of foreign investment, higher levels of state spending, and no higher taxes. Any head of state would have faced a serious crisis in 1929-31, given the nation's dependence on two minerals. But Ibáñez was also caught by the explosion of a global speculative bubble, which as it collapsed left Chile with an unpayable debt as well as massive unemployment.

The course of Chile through the 1930s and early 40s indicates that a sharp deterioration of the terms of trade can "underdevelop" a country. A crisis may hit with a magnitude that requires a decade or more to overcome. The poor terms of trade and the cut off in international lending left the nation with economic and social scars that did not disappear as economic indicators improved. The political system remained fragile, unable to accommodate public pressures without polarization. The debt, inherited from the late 1920s, was not written off until the late 1940s, and continuously affected Chile's access to international credit.

Major differences exist between the account given in this work and the dependista literature. The Crash and its consequences did not reduce Chilean dependence on foreign, and especially U.S. interests, or lead to a more independent path of industrialization. Subsequent events in Chile do not make clear if either of these changes had taken place. During the Crash itself (1929-32), short-lived administrations struck desperate bargains with U.S. interests. As Dávila discovered, by simply refusing to recognize a government the State Department could destabilize it. Chilean schemes proposed to nationalize key sectors of the economy; none of them succeeded in the face of United States and elite opposition. Here was one of the major shortcomings of the dependista literature; it did not look at the structure of the economy in decline. Even as trade and credit flows collapsed, U.S. interests (mining, electricity, fuel, and industry) maintained strategic supremacy. Dependence comes not only from the terms of growth but also from the consequences of speculative implosions. U.S. power within Chile, acquired before the Crash, combined with Chile's persistent shortage of hard currency and the government's continuing need for revenues from trade, meant that Chile during the Crash and Depression remained within a dependent set of economic conditions. The revival of the state under these conditions, from new rules governing currency to the enactment of higher tariffs, was a reordering of clientalistic arrangements within a dependent economy.

Let me now turn to a different critic of dependency: Robert Packenham, who is highly praised by Haber. Packenham has attacked dependency writers tout court, arguing that their enthusiasm for socialism undercut the quality of their research. Like Haber, he insists on classifying errors—the writers he dislikes—into an endless array of categories to attack, rather than appreciating any insights.[23] Although he claims objectivity, his tract is obviously anti-Marxist and against any perspective that assigns a role to foreign interests for Latin American underdevelopment. His accusation against ideologically driven research is silly. Some of the best and truest insights come from political passion. One of the most interesting fields in contemporary history is "gender studies," a broad topic whose origins stem from feminism and a defense of homosexuality. Passion is not peculiar to the left. A new study of the Pinochet regime notes the ideological drive of the foreign-trained "Chicago Boys," the dictator's economic advisers in the late 1970s and early 80s. They were true believers in the worst sense, never questioning the assumptions on which their econometric models were based or the social pain they caused, nor did they ever reflect on the fact that their model became "viable" in Chile as a result of mass murder and torture.[24]

If dependistas blamed the United States for everything, Packenham discounts U.S. behavior as a factor in much of anything, discussing only Brazil as an example of dependent development. There is no acknowledgment that the U.S. government and corporations directly intervened in Latin America and subordinated the region's needs to U.S. objectives at any time. Indeed, one of the most striking elements in Packenham's book is that it is devoid of any historical insight. The research presented in this narrative indicates that from the late 1920s to the end of the 40s, the U.S. government pressured Chilean political leaders on everything from trade relations to issues of internal governance. Other studies show that U.S. behavior in Chile by the late 1940s was part of a set of global objectives.[25] The record of intervention does not end in the 40s. A U.S. Senate investigation revealed U.S. involvement in Chilean elections in the 1960s and 70s, as well as in the events surrounding Salvador Allende's presidency and his overthrow.[26] Packenham mentions none of this: not U.S. strategies for global predominance, not U.S. actions during the Cold War, not U.S. support for Pinochet.

Packenham notes with dismay the spread of dependency thinking in Latin America through the 1960s and 70s. He attributes this, in part, to a psychological dependence, stemming from repeated economic reversals and the need to blame others for their occurrence. He coins what he calls an "irresponsibility corollary" [to a generalization by Albert Hirschman]. This "corollary" consists of a state of denial, a refusal to accept responsibility. "The insistence on failure is accompanied by a refusal to accept responsibility for failure."[27] This section includes a fundamental misreading of Hirschman's sentiments. When coining the term *fracasomania* [disaster-obsession], Hirschman was referring to consequences of economic frustration, not engaging in pop psychology. I cannot recall Hirschman ever dismissing Latin American heartache. As for Packenham's "corollary," individuals who engage in denial exist everywhere, but it is odd that such a variety of cultures, spanning different languages and educational circumstances, would collectively adopt a perspective of "irresponsibility." Why would Brazilians view life in the same economic terms as Mexicans or Chileans? Few political leaders in Latin America have been leftist; why, then, did a nationalist perspective gain such political weight? What was driving centrist and even right-wing leaders to emphasize resistance to foreign domination?

A simple answer to the above questions is that Chileans, and other Latin Americans, were reacting to a pervasive reality. Indeed, Packenham and Haber are wrong in thinking this reaction is somehow focused in the 1960s and 70s. They are mistaken as well in thinking it particularly left-wing. They are fundamentally unacquainted with the range and evolution of ideas in Latin America surrounding political economy. As this narrative points out, Chilean economic nationalism in the late 1920s and early 30s should not be confused with the spread of socialism. Nationalists were members of the major guilds in agriculture (SNA), mining (SNM), and industry (SOFOFA). They were bureaucratic reformers, often with strong backgrounds in law and engineering. The Nacis were economic nationalists. After the Crash, a wide variety of political leaders, including Arturo Alessandri, called themselves "socialist." They, of course, did not want a state-run economy. They wanted the state to play a larger role in managing a market economy. One of the key reasons they promoted greater state regulation was to reduce the social consequences of export-related crises. The same can undoubtedly be said about leaders in other countries, where nationalism was gaining ground: Mexico, Brazil, Argentina had rightists, reformers, and leftists who critiqued the neocolonial role their nations had been assigned in the world. No leftist, Prebisch came out of this milieu.

Chile serves as a good example of how neocolonial problems were integrated into national politics. It was under President Arturo Alessandri (1932-38) and his Finance Minister, Gustavo Ross Santa María, that most of the economic rights and many of the political assumptions of the period down to 1973 were worked out. Their strategy, while never hostile to foreign investment, had to guard against letting opponents seize nationalist ground. The process was contentious: threats of class warfare and of more coups were common. At some point, almost every significant political faction thought of abandoning constitutional government. An economic policy emerged under Alessandri based on minimal payments on the national debt, favoring domestic interests over foreign ones with currency controls, and avoiding any inflationary issue of currency, and it worked. An electoral process was reconstructed. But the electoral contests could not be contained within Alessandri's conservative economic policies. The middle and working classes demanded a further change in distribution, from foreign interests and domestic elites to themselves. All future distributive contests would turn on two axes: foreign versus domestic interests, and foreign and domestic capital against urban populist pressures for government jobs and better wages. In the Popular Front after 1938, the middle class and urban labor gained the right to organize in the work place and compete in the public sphere for income shares. Underlying the expansion of rights within urban society, including fixing the prices of food and rent, was the government decision to ignore and even repress any demands from rural labor.

At every step, what happened within Chile had to be reconciled with the power of foreign corporations and the U.S. government. Key decisions negotiated abroad within international cartels or the offices of the State Department came as a series of shocks that often humiliated Chilean officials and left them uncertain how to respond. As Gilbert Ziebura points out, this was a common problem for governments in the interwar years. Governments were expected to "mediate between two contradictory requirements," somehow strengthening the "position of one's own economy in the international division of labour," while mitigating the impact of the world market "on a nation's internal stability." The government's ability to do this became essential to its legitimacy. In this regard, Gustavo Ross looks fairly good when his record is contrasted with that of later Chilean finance ministers. For Ross succeeded in a field that most Chileans knew little about and that many academics still ignore, "economic foreign policy."[28] As a closing comment on Packenham, the need for political stability was not peculiar to Latin American leaders and they are not alone in wanting to avoid blame when economies go sour.

The evolution of the Chilean state involved, simultaneously, a change in its capacity to negotiate with foreign interests and domestic factions. It was a central mistake of the dependency theorists in the 1960s and 1970s to argue that foreign interests controlled the course or basic direction of national politics. There were, as we have seen, instances when this was true. It was also true that foreign interests sometimes had to accommodate domestic political currents. There are two aspects of economic diplomacy between Chile and the United States that have to be underlined. As Hirschman noted long ago, relations were asymmetrical: U.S. conduct was a crucial element in Chile's survival; but Chile mattered very little to the United States. U.S. economic firms lobbied the Chilean Congress and used whatever they gained from within the

Chilean political system. They also lobbied the State Department, the Export-Import Bank, and other federal agencies when they wanted to pressure the Chilean government. They had strategic as well as economic power. Strategic power—the capacity to cripple an economy —rarely appears in economic history yet it is crucial to the pattern of dependency that evolves. To avoid strategic vulnerability, a dependent state might benefit from inefficient investment. Observe Chile's actions in the late 1930s in regard to fuel and the establishment of a state oil industry through COPEC.

The government was the only entity in Chile that could carry on a foreign economic policy. Domestic capitalists operated on too small a scale. Their influence within the Chilean state was the only counter they had in dealing with a General Motors or W.R. Grace, let alone the copper giants of Anaconda and Kennecott. Even then, the Chileans held a very weak hand. The contradictions Ziebura mentions tended to deepen over time. Attempts to build a more popular government—the expansion of services and the pursuit of a more nationalistic economy—weakened the government's negotiating position vis à vis foreign interests. It was this weakness and obvious vulnerability, I believe, that led government officials of different ideological backgrounds to blame foreign investors for their problems. In the fight for trade-derived income, the elite lost control of the discussion in the 1930s and of the presidency in 1938. However, landowners, financiers, and industrialists could use the legislature to derail presidential initiatives. They quickly turned any government regulation to their advantage. The rising costs of public administration were passed on to the populace in the form of deficit spending and inflation, creating a classic set of populist dilemmas.

Another example of scholarly nearsightedness is a recent anthology by Rudiger Dornbusch and Sebastian Edwards, in which economists attack populist policies that various Latin American governments have pursued since 1960.[29] The central argument running through the cases they present is that populists are mistaken in believing a central government can reactivate a market economy while redistributing income in favor of workers and peasants. Certainly, the populists have made economic mistakes; it would be difficult, however, to prove that those mistakes were any more sweeping or disastrous than non-populist regimes. (How can Dornbusch and Edwards criticize recent economic behavior and not emphasize the role of South American military regimes in the debt crisis of 1982?) Again, it is ahistorical and completely inaccurate to locate populism as a phenomenon after 1960.[30] Most of the attitudes now called populist and many of the dilemmas of redistributive policies were evident well before the 1960s. To overlook the historic origins of such attitudes is, in an important way, to overlook how deeply embedded they are.

The success or failure of "populist" policies must be framed in a larger context—the history of political clientalism. The constituent elements of populism in any particular Latin American nation cannot be explained apart from the evolution of that nation's policies and clienteles. We must also evaluate the distributive efforts of any government against another question: is a poor distribution of income an acceptable outcome of economic policy? If we say no, then what other vehicle, aside from a central government, can address it? An economistic view of populism tends to ignore the fact that all "markets" are politically constructed. New work on the Pinochet years demonstrates the close connection he maintained with financial speculators, letting them influence the policy-making apparatus of the state.[31] While we have a term *populism* to describe the state assignment of economic rights for parts of the middle class and the general labor force, we are still without a term to describe the behavior of rent-seeking elites. An emphasis on the relation between populism and labor, as this work has argued, tends to miss a central problem of populist politics.

There are important lessons in the contrasting experiences of the Alessandri and Aguirre Cerda administrations. While the left painted Alessandri and Ross as lackeys of foreign interests, they were among the most successful Chilean leaders in dealing with foreign powers, especially the United States. Nearly alone among Chilean cabinet ministers in his era, Ross knew how to maneuver in the world of diplomats, international companies, and commodity cartels. He demanded and got foreign companies to pay more taxes and accept greater regulation; foreign creditors accepted, under duress, the terms Ross imposed on foreign debt payments. By contrast, the Aguirre Cerda administration became dependent on what was then a new form of financial vulnerability, loans from the U.S. government.

There was a trade-off between the clientalistic requirements of political stability and the fiscal requirements of containing inflation. Alessandri paid a high price in popularity for his new taxes and the restraints he placed on social programs. Early in his second term, he lost the support of the Radical Party, and with it, any hope of controlling a stable coalition in Congress. The Radical presidents from 1938 until 1952 (Aguirre Cerda, Ríos, and González Videla) were driven by their political base, including the middle class in their own party, to expand public services through deficit spending. This policy triggered a reaction from the elite and eroded real wages through inflation. By the early 1950s, the Radicals had alienated professionals and urban labor. The presidency became the essential arbiter of the political economy, but it could not ameliorate the serious inequities within Chile nor acquire the capital resources with which to reduce its vulnerability to the demands of foreign investors and the U.S. government. World War II, by eliminating Germany as a trading partner and ending the elaborate system of compensation trade, decisively reduced the little leverage Chilean presidents had in the international economy during the 1930s. It was not, as the dependistas had argued, Chile's integration into the world economy that had accentuated its subordination to the United States. It was rather the result of a cycle of two world wars, each of which shifted demand for raw materials in the Atlantic economy as it narrowed Chile's options in negotiating for credit and gaining access to markets abroad.

The aftermath of each world war had a similar pattern: a decline in export earnings; the enhancement of U.S. economic power; a crisis of Chilean government funding, which was addressed by deficit spending; and a social confrontation as members of the middle class and of the general labor force fought to preserve real incomes. This fight was waged on many levels, not only those involving political parties or labor associations. The left has always argued that the Popular Front brought labor into the government; this is true only in a rhetorical sense as workers had little direct say in public policy. The Radical presidencies did bring labor into the public sphere. This changed all policy calculations.

This alteration in sensibilities was a decisive cultural as well as political consequence of the long depression. From that point forward, the fight over income shares would not be limited to elite sectors or the Chilean elite against foreign interests. There was only one way to reduce the number of contestants in this struggle: ban them; force them to *exit*, in Hirschman's terms. This was the outcome of the 1948 attack on labor and the Communists. As I will argue in the second section of this conclusion, it was also the outcome of the crisis in the early 1970s.

Before turning to contemporary Chile, there is one last example of academic thinking that should be discussed. This example involves those who analyze politics without reference to an economic setting. Reflection on the catastrophic breakdown of the early 1970s understandably dominates recent historical studies in Chile. A generation of young scholars, influenced by the writings of the Italian political theorist, Giovanni Sartori, and led in Chile by Tomás Moulian, has come to blame the inherent frailties of a multi-party system for the coup of 1973 and the era of military rule. Sartori argues that parties represent the capacity of a society to actually control the state. In his view, the number of parties in a nation indicates, "the extent to which political power is fragmented or non-fragmented, dispersed or concentrated;" the greater the number of parties, "the greater the complexity and probably the intricacy of the system." Referring to the Weimar Republic and Allende's presidency in Chile, Sartori creates a vision of multi-party doom. Such a system, when it includes the Communists (in his jargon, the Communists are an "anti-system" party) will become "centrifugal" and fly apart.[32] Moulian has elaborated the significance of Sartori's thesis for Chile in a number of writings, many of which have interesting political details. A cottage industry has developed at the Santiago branch of FLACSO [Facultad Latinoamericana de Ciencias Sociales] tracing the background of the largest political parties.[33]

Like so much of political science writing, the theory seems to explain the past without ever looking at how people actually behaved. When read closely, however, none of Sartori's observations seem self-evident. Is it really the case that more parties create greater complexity? Is the political system of the United States, therefore, less intricate than that of 1970s' Chile? It is true, as Sartori and Moulian emphasize, that a larger number of parties creates a greater number of mathematical possibilities in terms of formal alliances and outcomes; but this is far from being the only kind of political complexity. To stay in the 1930s, for example, the politics of Mexico (coalescing around a one-party state) and those of Brazil (where power was moving into the hands of the national executive but where parties were banned between 1937 and 1945) seem every bit as complex as those of Chile. Among the political elements such a party-centered view ignores are national size, the evolution of regional loyalties, race, and ethnicity.

Sartori's other assertions also ring false. It does not seem obvious that the Communists were anti-system either in the late 1930s or the 1970s. A case can be made that they were perhaps too willing to be part of a system that contained elements (parties and economic interests) that wanted to destroy them. In so far as the 1960s and 70s are concerned, there is another problem in this abstracted explanation. The Chilean government was not the only one displaced by military rule. The Brazilian civilian government, with very different political rules, was overthrown in 1964; that of Uruguay, with a well-established two-party system (the most viable in Sartori's view) fell into the hands of the military even before that of Chile. By the end of the 1970s, only two South American governments, those of Colombia and Venezuela, were not dominated by their militaries. Nor is there any avoiding the dismal role of the U.S. government in supporting militarism and attacking Latin American popular movements throughout the 1970s and 80s.[34] There were centrifugal factors causing Latin American civilian regimes to fly apart, but they involved more than a consideration of party systems and political rules. The fact is that the history of Chile in the 1930s and the 1970s, and the histories of other Latin American nations, demonstrate a sad disregard to public civility and constitutional law. When political fights can actually decide not only income shares but the arrangement of social hierarchies, such fights become nasty. In his most recent work, a moving analysis of contemporary Chile, Moulian seems to set aside Sartori's influence to concentrate on the social and cultural factors that are shaping the period after Pinochet. I find myself in much more agreement with this last work, a point to elaborate in the next section.[35]

The era of the Great Depression was in Chile, as elsewhere in the Atlantic economy, a period of stunning idealism in the midst of misery. Working class, as well as middle class, Chileans were aware of events in France, Germany, Mexico, Peru, Spain, the Soviet Union, and the United States. The Front itself took part of its imagery from France and Spain and part from the Peruvian populist party, the Apristas. The Chilean public now included unions, consumer groups, and professional associations, all of them demanding a greater measure of social justice. With the exception of a few key unions, most of these organizations were small, a few hundred or a couple of thousand in number; none was well-financed; they appeared and disappeared rapidly. This was how an impoverished population built its social units. Organizers of labor demands and consumer protests demonstrated tenacity and courage. A generation before, nitrate miners at Iquique, demanding better wages and recognition of their right to organize, had been cut down by machine-gun fire. One is reminded of the faith that existed in much of the Americas and western Europe in this era that labor would be the vehicle by which society was transformed, even redeemed. The working poor of Chile marched, carried out strikes and boycotts, and did whatever they could to link political participation to a decent life. There was repression, but it is important to remember that, outside of Cuba and before the coup of 1973, Chile had created the most formidable Marxist left in all of Latin America. It was not the working class or the Communists who tore down constitutional liberties in the 1930s, the 40s, or the 70s.

The combination of an economy rebuilt upon copper exports, closely tied to the United States, and politics that turned on the brokerage of benefits from a centralized government ended in a catastrophic breakdown in the early 1970s. This third crisis of the Chilean political economy is too large a topic to be summarized here. Rather, I wish to compare the analysis offered in this work to interpretive currents developed from other perspectives, not only to underline the importance of the 1930s and early 40s—the long depression—as a formative experience in Chilean history, but to contrast an analysis that integrates the international and national elements of political economy with any explanation that privileges politics over economics or vice versa.

Another Stage of Dependence?

Returning to the issues that were raised at the beginning of this study, how are we to reformulate the problems of dependence and underdevelopment? While many of the political features of an underdeveloped nation are generated from within its society or societies, we must reassert the importance of systemic capitalist crises as decisive moments in the politics of such nations. A country such as Chile passes not only from one stage of underdevelopment to another but it also configures its political life to complement new forms of dependence. The Great Depression, by altering Chile's export economy, changed the resources available to different political factions within Chile. To analyze how these changes occurred and what they meant, we must return to an age-old issue in Latin American history, the evolution of political clienteles, and combine a history of such clienteles with the insights on the characteristics of economic diplomacy.[36]

At the broadest levels of interaction, the changing structure of international trade has an immediate impact on the viability of government budgets and national credit structures. As a crises works its way through the political economy, some voices are amplified and some diminished. Within Chile in the 1930s, it is clear that the elite's political position was eroded, but its economic position remained surprisingly intact. How was it that a political system accommodated its renewed dependence on the United States and the persistence of a grotesquely skewed distribution of income and wealth with an enlarged public sphere?

A generation ago, John Johnson argued that the "middle sectors" were altering the political map of Latin America. He pointed to many of the features my study of the Great Depression has analyzed—the creation of more industry, the rise of economic nationalism, and the growing importance of political parties—as obvious changes in the region since the 1920s. Chile was one of his examples. He argued that, "A sense of social obligation and the need to pay off political debts have combined to induce the middle sectors to support advanced labor and welfare legislation in favor of the industrial working groups."[37] Johnson did not frame his arguments in dependency terms, either then or later, nor did he pay too much attention to clientalistic traditions.

In contrast, this study has argued that it was the middle class, within a widening public sphere, that decisively altered Chilean politics. It repositioned itself, strategically and institutionally, within the state and so made its behavior the decisive element in political stability. By the late 1920s, it was openly espousing economic nationalism as its first priority and social reform as a secondary concern. It did so in and out of government, in various parties and social organizations, in protest groups and public forums. The middle class believed economic nationalism would promote white-collar opportunities in both the private and public sectors. It was literate, articulate, and relatively successful in pursuing its goals.

When we conjure up the names of political leaders in the long depression, whether on the right or the left (or what passed for the center), we are talking about middle-class individuals, many of them lawyers, who became political entrepreneurs. They wanted government employment and a regulated economy that would ameliorate the worse features of a market economy, not only for labor, but for themselves. They wanted controls on such commodities as urban housing and food. But they did not want to empower the working class, let alone the rural poor. The figure of Pedro Aguirre Cerda represents the middle class well. The portrait of him sitting at his fundo, saying that the people had to be transformed before they could be entrusted with authority summarizes the sensibility of "uplift" that ran through the middle class in the 1930s much as it had through the U.S. progressives a generation before.[38]

This class would become a vehicle of social reform without social transformation, it was also a vehicle of state-led development. Far from addressing the underlying dilemmas, the middle class accepted dependence as part of its price of political inclusion. In many respects, its behavior imitated the national elite, who viewed connections to more developed nations as the key to its own prosperity.

These are broad statements and, even this close to the conclusion, require some illustration. Let me point to the rhetoric of two middle-class lawyers, each of whom became president, a generation apart. González Videla and Eduardo Frei Montalva each tried, in one way or another, to combine the state management of a dependent economy with social reform. There are important differences between the two. González Videla was from the tradition of liberal, secular values that had in the course of the 1920s and 30s come to embrace some Marxist radicalism. Frei came from a Catholic movement that, in the 1930s, tried to instill a social conscience into the party of privilege. But it is not stretching history too much to see Frei as González Videla's political successor, seeking to assemble a multi-class coalition while expanding public spending and calling for loans from the United States to help in efforts at reform. Here, let us focus on them as men who reconsidered the purpose of government during the long depression.

In this regard, we need to reverse the order in which each man is usually considered and present the views of Frei first. In 1939, at the beginning of the Popular Front, Frei published *La política y el espíritu* (Politics and Spirituality). The future president was then an increasingly noticed young man, and the Young Conservatives to which he belonged had just broken with the Conservative Party and were calling themselves Falangists. Although lamenting Chile's tendency to imitate the latest European ideas and fashions, Frei extolled the writings of the French Catholic philosopher, Jacques Maritain. In Frei's interpretation, Maritain's thoughts combined the best of Europe's past, the Middle Ages, with the best of the present, a modern, social sensibility. The medieval era was the pinnacle of Western Civilization, "when human labor counted more than money. A just price and a just wage are truths that no natural law can ignore." The past could not be recreated but the future could generate corporatist organizations of professionals and workers and try to imitate that epoch when there was a "state which, in many respects, was perfect."[39] Lest these views seem too peculiar, a recent study of academic philosophy in Chile argues Frei's work was quite important.[40]

The views of President González Videla emerge, not in his memoirs, but in his supplications to the United States for loans. In the late 1940s, he told Washington that the Truman administration's emphasis on free trade was a relic of a more primitive time. Global developments had created an "economic interdependence" in which "the businessman and trader" had to give up thinking of "particular interests" and instead consider "everything else and even the activities of the State itself."[41] Considerations of state survival and of a state-based international economy justified loaning the Chilean government more money. Each of these men believed that the age of laissez-faire liberalism was over: there was no magic in the marketplace, and social and political stability had to precede innovation. They spoke in terms of cooperation, supervision, and order. Despite the differences in their careers, their views are populist as well as corporatist. Each of them invoked economic nationalism and government regulation as the means to secure a better life for the nation. Neither wanted to displace foreign corporations but viewed the role of chief executive as regulating the market to permit social development as well as growth. Each followed a path of development that enhanced the strategic position of U.S. interests within the country and, when the government's finances failed to expand sufficiently, chose the welfare of his middle-class constituency over the interests of those below it.

The reformers, such as González Videla and Frei, left foreigners and the elite in control of the market economy as they learned to administer a range of social services. Once the middle class gained access to government protection, it lost much its radicalism and resisted attempts at social transformation. Chile was left with low levels of capital investment, a poor distribution of income, and an expensive government with regressive taxation and inadequate revenues. Cycles of heavy state borrowing at home and abroad, and double-digit inflation, characterized the economy into the 1970s. President Salvador Allende mistakenly believed that a presidency built on distributive politics could be converted into an engine of socialism.[42] A state led by an enlarged rent-seeking coalition is as easily brought to reactionary views as to socially progressive ones. In Chile, the middle class became more frightened of radicalism from below than it was of foreign exploitation or elite concentrations of wealth.

This pattern of conflict has been repeated in other countries, although differences in circumstances have yielded different outcomes. In the 1930s, the Mexican middle class gained socially and economically under Lázaro Cárdenas, only to use its enhanced influence to retard any further mobilization of workers and peasants and to support a business-oriented administration under Cárdenas' successor. The middle class in Argentina alternately loved and hated Juan Perón, the classic Latin American populist. Although the Argentine middle class gained access to government positions, it joined the right in 1955 to topple Perón when his government ran out of hard currency and its ability to satisfy popular demands. In each instance, middle-class dissatisfaction intensified as the costs of larger government led to inflation.

No Latin American government has simultaneously improved the national distribution of income while generating higher rates of economic growth. But it is also true that international negotiations cannot be separated from domestic prospects in a trade-based economy. Reviving a social purpose for government will require each Latin American nation to rethink the relation of economic diplomacy to fiscal constraints and popular demands. There is, of course, no set answer to these dilemmas. Steven E. Sanderson emphasizes this point, for the contemporary setting, in his argument against neoliberal destruction of Latin American states. But he also notes that, "Unfortunately, there is no satisfactory base to examine the role of the state in Latin American economies."[43]

After the coup of 1973, the military became the ultimate protector of capitalism in Chile. Augusto Pinochet's dictatorship imposed neoliberal solutions at horrendous social costs. Political parties were banned, popular associations suppressed, unions were attacked and then confined to state-approved activities; leaders of the Allende administration, leftists, and defenders of democracy were tortured, imprisoned in remote penal colonies, sent into exile, or murdered.[44]

The Pinochet dictatorship succeeded in its objectives. It changed the political rules decisively and social interests that were considered important in the 1960s and early 1970s—urban laborers, shanty-town dwellers, and the rural poor—are now largely ignored. For sixteen years, labor and the poor lost most of their voice in the system. Government employment, outside of the military, was cut severely. The government demobilized efforts to redistribute wealth and income. In 1979, the dictatorship enacted a new labor code with a clear bias in favor of employers. By allowing some labor activity, it had an unexpected consequence of beginning a revival of labor resistance.[45] Ironically, state decrees concerning economic policy had a much greater impact on real wages and working conditions than had the market that the dictatorship extolled so often.[46] Shanty-town inhabitants, many of them reduced to destitution, rose up in rebellion by the early 1980s. Pinochet survived by cutting a deal with the old political parties that, frightened of a social uprising, allowed him to remain in office until the 1989 plebiscite.

Since rural misery has played such a major role in stratifying Chilean society, it is sad to note that the countryside has been transformed without altering the fate of the rural poor. The first blow to the hacendado was struck in the late 1960s and early 1970s, as the rural labor force mobilized into parties and unions. On an official level, the government of President Eduardo Frei Montalva (1964-70) passed an agrarian reform law that promised some laborers a chance to have their own farms. At an official level, the competition among parties and ideologies for rural support unleashed the campesino from previous cycles of repression. Rural laborers and Indians seized lands held by estate owners (a pattern of activism paralleling shanty-town land grabs in the cities). President Salvador Allende allowed these grass-roots movements to flourish and by 1973 major tracts of land had changed hands. The second blow came after the coup in 1973 when the military murdered many rural leaders and suppressed rural organizations. It left about 30 percent of land in the hands of *asentados* [land-reform beneficiaries], sold another 30 percent to new landowners, returned about 30 percent to the previous owners, and kept most of the rest in the state sector for forestation and subsequent private sale.[47] Defenders of the Pinochet regime cite this as a progressive outcome. It was nothing of the kind. The asentados were abandoned to a credit market with interest rates in double digits. Estate owners and more prosperous farmers now saw the advantage of mechanization: they would be free of inquilinos who might some day clamor for land reform. The countryside is worked by an unsettled proletariat, which plants and picks the crops that are earning Chile money abroad but which has no labor or land rights. Summarizing a situation that seems right out of the nineteenth century, one expert noted:

> One of the most striking aspects of the contemporary agrarian situation in Chile is the co-existence of a marked process of productive and technological modernization in the countryside and the extreme poverty suffered by thousands of rural families. This contrast reflects the lack of social content in the neoliberal policies applied by the Chicago boys, who were oriented toward the introduction of a "savage capitalism" in the country.[48]

These conclusions are borne out in other studies.[49] The "counter-reform," a one-two punch of repression and "ultraliberal" policies atomized the rural population and left even those with a few bits of land in complete misery: by 1987, 92 percent of the "landowners" that remained had fewer than 20 hectares (49 acres).[50] The outcome also undid the power of landed wealth, in the form of hacendados, and replaced it with more modern kinds of exploitation by corporations and financial groups. Agriculture is no longer protected by the state.

The existence of a rural under class continues to retard wages in any other sector and to lead to a tiered wage structure, with urban skilled workers in one group and the unskilled in another. Recent work by econometricians documents this process in language the Chicago Boys can approve.[51] Chile has had a decade of economic growth and two decades of social misery. The distribution of income by 1989 was among the worst in Latin America.[52] In the early 1940s, the bottom 20 percent of the population received 2.6 percent of the national income; the top 10 percent, 55 percent. By 1971, just before Allende took control, changes in taxation and economic policies had increased the share of the bottom to 4.1 percent and the top to 38 percent. The income share of the bottom 40 percent (or 10 percent of GDP) has not changed since 1940.[53] Now, the top six financial groups control 55 percent of the GDP. Much has been said in the United States about the successful privatization of the social security system, and the way this has boosted stock prices. But paeans to free enterprise do not note that three social security companies control two-thirds of the market, nor that fully 40 percent of the labor force is so poor it cannot make pension payments.[54]

The dictator's policies are praised in U.S. business magazines and economics departments, and so there are some consequences of his regime worth remembering. Chileans gave up their civil rights for sixteen years. Income has risen but only recently. Few note that Santiago, where some five million people now live, is as expensive as middle-sized U.S. cities; a per capita income of five to six thousand dollars does not go very far. Most of the population is well below this level since 20 percent of the population takes 62 percent of the income.[55] As a result of depressions in the mid-1970s and 1882-1984, the wages of most laborers probably reached their early 1970s levels only after the dictatorship had ended—in the early 1990s. For most of the labor force, the last two decades have provided negative experience. There is no substantial evidence that the economy grew faster under the dictator than it had under the troubled administrations of Frei (1964-70) and Allende (1970-73); the highest overall growth rate came with the return of civilian government. Finally, this is not yet some Asian tiger; the overall growth of Chile does not resemble the transformations that had taken place in South Korea or Hong Kong.[56]

Wary of provoking either the armed forces or those who profited from the Pinochet era, the Christian Democratic governments since 1989 have maintained the general economic policies they inherited from the military regime. In some respects, they have endorsed neoliberalism even more than did the dictator; the percentage of the economy devoted to foreign trade has risen sharply in the 1990s.[57] It can be argued that their hands were tied by the Constitution of 1980 that the dictator composed, which left him as head of the army and permitted him crucial appointments to the Senate even after he lost the presidential plebiscite in 1989.

President Patricio Aylwin (1990-94) raised taxes and increased social spending, reducing some of the worst aspects of poverty. His finance minister, Alejandro Foxley, once a sharp critic of neoliberalism, wrote an interesting apologia for the outcome, arguing in effect that this was but the beginning of a restoration of civic society. He stated, "We . . . raised the minimum wage by 36 percent—now the equivalent of U$120 per month—and the family allowance." This reduced the number "living in poverty from 45 percent of the population (at the time the military yielded the government) to 33 percent of the population by 1993."[58]

Defining poverty at below US$120 a month is an interesting comment on attitudes among Chilean technocrats. Since the population is now over 14 million, a third of the nation amounts to 4.7 million—about the size of the entire population in the late 1930s and 40s. The Chile of the Great Depression remains submerged in the nation of the 1990s.

Tomás Moulian, noting that the country no longer looks to its past to guide its future, provides another insight into what the new Chile represents. It has instead become a victim of historical amnesia, an "institutional prison," that pretends current policies grew out of a rational reordering of priorities rather than a reign of terror. Workers, who accepted Pinochet's rules as a temporary strategem to remove the dictator, now find that those labor and political rules are defended as economically necessary to any future. The result is a political system in which a numerical minority has complete predominance and can pass itself off as a majority. Parties have abandoned pre-1973 ideologies.[59] The consumer society replaces a search for social justice within the upper and middle classes. Moulian comments, "The citizenship of the weekend and of the credit card are means of depoliticizing citizens."[60]

The government of President Eduardo Frei Ruiz-Tagle (son of the president in the 1960s) is less socially concerned and has let Aylwin's tax increase lapse. While general social spending has risen, only one percent of the current budget is spent on the social needs of the destitute.[61] Current predictions are that if the economy continues to grow, a declining percentage of the population will live in destitution; but the gulf between the well-to-do and the rest of the population will continue to widen.[62] An elite and middle-class coalition holds together the Concertación, that is, the coalition of Christian Democratic presidents and supporting parties in Congress.

The policies under Pinochet and Christian Democratic presidents have changed Chile enough to challenge a dependency perspective in its fundamental assertions. For the moment, the economy is capitalizing on growth and outperforming the past; Chile has the highest growth rate in the region. There is no doubt that a historic change has occurred. Partly this is a response to changes in the global economy. The United States is still the world's largest economy, but it controls relatively less of the world's trade. Alternative sources of technology and finance have appeared and Chileans have taken advantage of this change. Partly the outcome is a consequence of two internal changes within Chile: the political demobilization of the working poor, which allowed Pinochet to carry out Gustavo Ross' dream of beating capitalism into the nation, and the continuing development of education created a technical class that finally knew its way around issues of trade and finance.

Is the current boom a lull in an otherwise familiar story of an export cycle, based on the interests of a narrow political class? Recent events in the Far East remind us that even Asian tigers can suffer economic catastrophe. Moreover, Chile's export success has come with tremendous ecological costs. Questions are being asked about the obvious deforestation and over fishing; how long can the country exploit nonrenewable resources? The reliance on such resources has reduced industry's participation in the economy from 30 percent in the 1970s to less than 20 percent today.[63] A dynamic industrial base is not evolving from capital gains. This is basically a commercial and service economy riding on a handful of exports. And the pattern of diversification and change is not quite as broad as the model's supporters usually argue. Copper still constitutes about a third of all exports (as recently as 1990, it was 40 percent of all exports); any negative change in that sector would seriously disrupt the economy.

The most important change aside from the decline of the hacendado class, and one not to be minimized, is the reduction in the U.S. role within the Chilean economy. The role of U.S. corporations within the export boom has yet to be studied. But one of the factors that reduced their role in the Chilean economy was Allende's program of nationalization; he nationalized the copper industry. Thus, it was the combination of shocks, of left-wing takeovers, and of right-wing liberalization that altered the structure of dependence. Finally, we must separate issues of dependence from issues of underdevelopment, while the two are related, they are not quite identical. Chile is overcoming some of the worst aspects of underdevelopment, extending longevity, reducing infant mortality, and improving wages over their levels in the last two decades. But what is its economic place in the world economy? Shifts in the center of the world economy have been happening over the last three decades. André Gunder Frank now argues that the rise of the West was simply an interlude between two periods dominated by Asia.[64] I know too little about Asian markets to say much on this subject except that the Asian tigers were always rather small players in global terms and that their current crisis indicates that their growth has not altered their peripheral status.

The Asian Debt Crisis, coming so soon after that of Mexico, indicates that the global system is still being bailed out by the United States and Europe, serving as "lenders of last resort," and demanding, through the International Monetary Fund, that nations obey their rules or suffer an even greater ruin than the crisis itself might cause. In any event, changes in the global system of international finance, with its various foci of power, has not changed Chile's own peripheral role. Chile has little voice in any of these centers.

How would Chile deal with a downturn in copper prices or global trade given its reliance on foreign investment, foreign credit, and foreign trade? This problem would not take the form of a U.S.-led crisis within the world economy, as it did in the Crash. It would stem from the relation of trade to internal speculation within Chile. For all the praise given to higher domestic savings (largely through the privatized social security funds), the country still needs foreign capital and must offer a premium to foreign investors. The fact is that throughout the 1970s to the present, Chile has run a negative balance of payments.[65] Public debt is declining as a factor in future expansion, from US$9.3 to US$7.1 billion in the 1990s; so, the debt crisis of 1982 has become less a factor in future developments. But the nation's total debt is rising and is now about US$25.5 billion. As recently as 1980, it was under US$10 billion. In other words, debt expansion is now outrunning economic growth. It was the explosion of private lending in a speculative bubble that brought down the economy in 1982-84; foreign banks forced Pinochet as a condition of further credit to the government and economy to convert that obligation into a public one. Higher debt levels, as Mexico and the Asian tigers are demonstrating, remain a strategic risk for trade-based nations.

Chile might also be caught up in a regional crisis. At the very best, Chile is an aberration in a heavily indebted region. Latin America owes foreign creditors US$656 billion. Despite having paid on it for years, the debt continues to grow.[66] Mexico holds 27 percent of that debt; Brazil, 25 percent; Argentina, 16 percent; and Venezuela, 5 percent.[67] Mexico bailed out of trouble in 1994-95 with massive infusions of U.S. government funds. It seems unlikely that Chile's conditions can be reproduced elsewhere; none of the other neoliberal regimes is free of staggering social and economic problems.[68] A year after the Mexican bail out, a record US$77 billion in Latin American stocks and bonds were placed on international capital markets.[69] Increasingly, the cycle of international bail outs and ever greater indebtedness, as well as the flow of direct investment into Latin American ventures, is resembling the close of a Ponzi cycle.

Within Chile, as Tomás Moulian has noted, the country has grown silent on issues of underdevelopment and economic justice. The electorate still divides into three groups: left, right, and center. The legacy of the Great Depression remains embedded in political allegiances. The morale and objectives of the left, however, have diminished. One can see this in the many Socialists who spout neoliberal doctrines and in the substantial electoral decline of the Communists. The poor had greater moral authority in the fight against Pinochet than they possess in making any current claims for government help. Writers on present-day Chile report a political *desencanto*, a disinterest in politics.[70] Having accepted the military's economic policies, the Christian Democrats had also accepted a good deal of the military's portrayal of itself and settled for "the politics of what was not possible."[71] In a moving article on political identity, Katherine Hite quotes one Antonio Viera-Gallo, a Chilean Socialist Party congressman, former Speaker of the House, and once a major supporter of Allende:

> Chilean citizens are more modern today. Politics have become relativised, and while still influential, politics has little probability of touching the world of the economy, here businessmen couldn't care less about politics, they go on with their businesses, they export, etc., it's not an issue, and many people, whether they're professionals or well-paid workers, why should they care? Now the problem is that there are many in Chilean society who are poor, who can only emerge and have their demands felt through politics, so parties are somewhat the expression of that part of society, the more backward part of society, not the modern part, because the modern part doesn't need parties.[72]

It is painful to read this, to see the nineteenth-century liberal framework of "modern" and "backward," of "civilized" and "barbaric" repeat itself. From the 1920s to the 1970s, the middle class needed to talk about the poor as a means of improving its own prospects. Now, it gets an improved income and more government jobs even if the poor are ignored.[73] It may be that Chile is simply rebuilding its political life from the long nightmare of the dictatorship. However, this setting is very unlike the 1930s. It is impossible to enter into a discussion about political economy and the legacy of dependence if the middle class ignores or avoids discussing social issues. If the past is any guide, that discussion will revive as part of another crisis of misplaced faith in "savage capitalism."

Endnotes

1. Fernando Henrique Cardoso, "Towards Another Development," *From Dependency to Development: Strategies to Overcome Underdevelopment and Inequality*, Heraldo Muñoz, ed., Westview Special Studies in Social, Political, and Economic Development (Boulder: Westview Press, 1981).

2. Jorge G. Castañeda, *Utopia Unarmed: The Latin American Left after the Cold War* (New York: Vintage Publishers, 1993), 426-27.

3. Osvaldo Sunkel and Pedro Paz Sunkel, *El subdesarrollo latinoamericano y la teoría del desarrollo* (Mexico: Siglo Veintiuno, 1970), 6.

4. Samuel J. Valenzuela and Arturo Valenzuela, "Modernization and Dependency: Alternative Perspectives in the Study of Latin American Underdevelopment," *From Dependency to Development*, Heraldo Muñoz, ed. (1981), cited 25-26.

5. Kay, *Latin American Theories*, 125-64.

6. Vincent A. Mahler, *Dependency Approaches to International Political Economy: A Cross-National Study* (New York: Columbia University Press, 1980), 114, 147.

7. United Nations, Department for Economic and Social Information and Policy Analysis, Statistics Division, *1995 International Trade Statistics Yearbook*, 2 vols. (New York: United Nations, 1996), 1:191.

8. World Bank, *World Tables 1995* (Baltimore: The Johns Hopkins University Press, 1996), 4-5, 9; U.S. Department of Commerce, Office of Latin America and the Caribbean at web site, www.ita.doc.gov/olac/; and United States, Central Intelligence Agency (CIA), *The World Factbook, 1997* (Washington, D.C.: Brassey's, 1996), 85-87 for the current per capita income.

9. David E. Hojman, "Poverty and Inequality in Chile: Are Democratic Politics and Neoliberal Economics Good for You?," *Journal of Interamerican Studies and World Affairs* 38, no. 2-3 (1996), internet 2, table 3.

10. Phyllis Deane, *The State and the Economic System: An Introduction to the History of Political Economy* (Oxford: Oxford University Press, 1989), 187.

11. William Lazonick, "Creating and extracting value: corporate investment behavior and American economic performance," *Understanding American Economic Decline*, Michael A. Bernstein and David E. Adler, eds. (Cambridge: Cambridge University Press, 1994), 108.

12. Eduardo Silva, "Capitalist Coalitions, the State, and Neoliberal Economic Restructuring: Chile 1973-1988," *World Politics* 45, no. 4 (1993), internet 18.

13. Florencia Mallon, "The Promise and Dilemma of Subaltern Studies: Perspectives from Latin American History," *The American Historical Review* 99, no. 5 (1994).

14. H-Latam, "Cultural Studies Debate," (H-Net: Michigan State University, 1997).

15. Stephen Haber, "Introduction: Economic Growth and Latin American Economic Historiography," *How Latin America Fell Behind: Essays on the Economic History of Brazil and Mexico, 1800-1914*, Stephen Haber, ed. (Stanford: Stanford University Press, 1997), 5, 21.

16. Ibid., 10-12.

17. P.J. Cain and A.G. Hopkins, *British Imperialism: Innovation and Expansion, 1688-1914* (London: Longman, 1993), 313-14. See also, P.J. Cain and A.G. Hopkins, *British Imperialism: Crisis and Deconstruction, 1914-1990* (London: Longman, 1993).

18. Donald P. Green and Ian Shapiro, *The Pathologies of Rational Choice Theory: A Critique of Applications in Political Science* (New Haven: Yale University Press, 1994), 7.

19. Ibid., 44-46, 123-28, 170-78.

20. Ibid., 180.

21. Ibid., 188.

22. United Nations, Economic Commission for Latin America, *The Economic Development of Latin America and its Principal Problems*, and Maddison, *Two Crises*, 87.

23. Robert A. Packenham, *The Dependency Movement: Scholarship and Politics in Development Studies* (Cambridge: Harvard University Press, 1992), 110-30, especially 111.

24. William J. Barber, "Chile con Chicago: A Review Essay," *Journal of Economic Literature* 33, no. 4 (1995).

25. David Rock, "War and Postwar Intersections," and Barnard, "Chile," see chap. eight.

26. Patricio Quiroga, ed. *Salvador Allende: obras escogidas (1970-1973)* (Barcelona: Editorial Crítica, 1989); Ignacio González Camus, *El día que murió Allende* (Santiago: CESOC, 1988); United States Senate, Staff Report of the Select Committee to Study Governmental Operations with Respect to Intelligence Activities, "Covert Action in Chile, 1963-1973," (Washington: Government Printing Office, 1975); United States House of Representatives, Subcommittee on Inter-American Affairs of the Committee on Foreign Affairs, "United States and Chile during the Allende Years, 1970-1973," (Washington: Government Printing Office, 1975); Arturo Valenzuela, *The Breakdown of Democratic Regimes: Chile* (Baltimore: Johns Hopkins University Press, 1978); Paul Sigmund, *The Overthrow of Allende and the Politics of Chile* (Pittsburgh: University of Pittsburgh Press, 1977); and Pamela Constable and

Arturo Valenzuela, *Chile under Pinochet: A Nation of Enemies* (New York: W.W. Norton, 1991).

27. Packenham, op cit., 206.

28. Gilbert Ziebura, *World Economy and World Politics, 1924-1931: From Reconstruction to Collapse*, Bruce Little, trans. (Oxford: Oxford University Press, 1990), 17.

29. Rudiger Dornbusch and Sebastian Edwards, eds. *The Macroeconomics of Populism in Latin America* (Chicago: The University of Chicago Press, 1991).

30. Paul Drake, "Comment," *The Macroeconomics of Populism in Latin America*, Rudiger Dornbusch and Sebastian Edwards, eds. (Chicago: The University of Chicago Press, 1991), 35-37.

31. Silva, "Capitalist Coalitions," internet 18, 35. For an economistic view of the regime, which considers its policies reformist and successful, see Sebastian Edwards and Alejandra Cox Edwards, *Monetarism and Liberalization: The Chilean Experiment* (Chicago: University of Chicago Press, 1991).

32. Giovanni Sartori, *Parties and Party Systems* (Cambridge: Cambridge University Press, 1976).

33. Tomás Moulian, "Violencia, gradualismo y reformas en el desarrollo político chileno," *Estudios sobre el sistema de partidos*, Adolfo Aldunate, Angel Flisfisch, and Tomás Moulian, eds. (Santiago: Ediciones FLACSO, 1986); Tomás Moulian, *La forja de ilusiones: el sistema de partidos, 1932-1973* (Santiago: Universidad de Artes y Ciencias Sociales and FLACSO, 1993); Moulian and Torres-Dujisin Moulian, *Discusiones entre honorables*; Moulian and Torres-Dujisin, "Las candidaturas presidenciales de la derecha: 1946"; Yocelevsky R., "El desarrollo de los partidos políticos chilenos hasta 1970"; Leopoldo Benavides, "La formación de la izquierda chilena: relaciones entre el Partido Comunista y el partido Socialista," *FLACSO Documento de Trabajo* (Santiago: FLACSO, 1988); and María Soledad Gómez Ch., "Partido Comunista de Chile (1922-1952)," (Santiago: FLACSO Documento de Trabajo, 1984).

34. Castañeda, op. cit.; O'Brien and Cammack, *Generals in Retreat*, and Smith, *Talons of the Eagle*.

35. Tomás Moulian, *Chile Actual: Anatomía de un mito*, Colección Sin Norte, Serie Punto de Fuga (Santiago: Arcis Universidad, Ediciones Lom, 1997).

36. Hirschman, *Exit, Voice, and Loyalty*; Hirschman, *National Power and the Structure of Foreign Trade*; Habermas, *The Structural Transformation of the Public Sphere*; and Putnam, "Diplomacy and Domestic Politics."

37. Johnson, *Political Change in Latin America*, intro., 184.

38. Boizard B., *Patios Interiores*, 23; Pedro Aguirre Cerda, *El problema agrario* (Paris: 1929), 244; and Infante Barros, *Testigos del treinta y ocho*, 104.

39. Eduardo Frei Montalva, *La política y el espíritu*, 2d, 1st ed. in 1940 ed. (Santiago: Editorial del Pacífico, 1946), 40, 42-43, 50.

40. Iván Jaksíc, *Academic Rebels in Chile: The Role of Philosophy in Higher Education and Politics* (New York: State University of New York, 1989), 89-90.

41. RG 59: 825.50/8-1148, Bowers, no. 532 (1948).

42. Stephen de Vylder, *Allende's Chile: The political Economy of the Rise and Fall of the Unidad Popular* (Cambridge: Cambridge University Press, 1976), chaps. 3, 4; and Sergio Bitar, *Chile: Experiment in Democracy*, Sam Sherman, trans., Inter-American Politics Series, vol. 6 (Philadelphia: Institute for the Study of Human Issues, 1986), chaps. 3, 4.

43. Steven E. Sanderson, *The Politics of Trade in Latin American Development* (Stanford: Stanford University Press, 1992), 203.

44. Constable and Valenzuela, *Chile under Pinochet*; Loveman, *Chile: The Legacy of Hispanic Capitalism*; Genero Arriagada, *Pinochet: The Politics of Power*, N. Morris, V. Ercolano, and K.A. Whitney, trans. (Boston: Unwin Hyman, 1988); Jeffrey M. Puryear, *Thinking Politics: Intellectuals and Democracy in Chile, 1973-1988* (Baltimore: Johns Hopkins University Press, 1994); P. Drake and I. Jaksic, eds. *The Struggle for Democracy in Chile*, 2d ed. (Lincoln: University of Nebraska Press, 1995); Barry Bosworth, Rudiger Dornbusch, and Raul Laban, eds. *The Chilean Economy: Policy Lessons and Challenges* (Washington, D.C.: The Brookings Institution, 1994); Eugenio Ahumada et al., eds. *Chile, la memoria prohibida: las violaciones a los derechos humanos, 1973-1983* (Santiago: Pehuen, 1989); Joseph Collins and John Lear, *Chile's Free-Market Miracle: A Second Look* (Oakland: The Institute for Food and Development Policy, 1995); and Crisóstomo Pizarro, Dagmar Raczunski, and Joaquín Vial, eds. *Políticas económicas y sociales en el Chile democrático* (Santiago: CIEPLAN, 1995).

45. Cathy Lisa Schneider, *Shantytown Protest in Pinochet's Chile* (Philadelphia: Temple University Press, 1995), 132.

46. Paul Drake, *Labor Movements and Dictatorships: The Southern Cone in Comparative Perspective* (Baltimore: The Johns Hopkins University Press, 1996), 132.

47. Lowell S. Jarvis, "The Unravelling of the Agrarian Reform," *Development and Social Change in the Chilean Countryside: From the Pre-Land Reform Period to the Democratic Transition*, C. Kay and P. Silva, eds. (Amsterdam: CEDLA , 1992), 192; and Javier Martínez and Alvaro Díaz, *Chile: The Great Transformation* (Washington, D.C. and Geneva: The Brookings Institution and The United Nations Research Institute for Social Development, 1996), 62.

48. Cristóbal Kay and Patricio Silva, "Rural Development, Social Change and the Democratic Transition," *Development and Social Change in the Chilean Countryside*, Kay and Silva, eds., 293.

348 CHILE

49. José Garrido R., Christián Guerrero Y., and María Soledad Valdés, *Historia de la reforma agraria en Chile*, José Garrido R., eds. (Santiago: Editorial Universitaria, 1988), 182-84.

50. Francisco Vio Grossi, *Resistencia campesina: En Chile y en México* (Santiago: CEAAL, 1990), 184-85.

51. Michael Basch and Ricardo D. Paredes-Molina, "Are There Dual Labor Markets in Chile? Empirical Evidence," *Journal of Development Economics* 50, no. 2 (August 1996).

52. Scott Mainwaring, "Democracy in Brazil and the Southern Cone: achievements and problems," *Journal of Interamerican Studies and World Affairs* 37, no. 1 (1995), internet 17.

53. United Nations, Comisión Económica para America Latina y el Caribe (CEPAL), "Antecedentes estadísticos de la distribución del ingreso Chile, 1940-1982," (Santiago: Naciones Unidas, 1987), 35-36; and Patricio Meller, Raúl O'Ryan, and Andrés Solimano, "Growth, Equity, and the Environment in Chile: Issues and Evidence," *World Development* 24, no. 2 (1996), 262.

54. Stephanie Rosenfeld and Juan Luis Marre, "How Chile's Rich got Richer," *NACLA Report on the Americas* 30, no. 6 (1997 May-June): 20-; as an example of the eulogies to privatized social security, see Suneel Ratan, "How Chile Got It Right," *Time* 145, no. 11 (1995 March 20): 30.

55. Meller, O'Ryan, and Solimano, "Growth, Equity and the Environment in Chile." 262.

56. Scott Mainwaring, "Democracy in Brazil and the Southern Cone," internet 17; Lois Hecht Oppenheim, *Politics in Chile: Democracy, Authoritarianism, and the Search for Development* (Boulder: Westview Press, 1993), 154; Martínez and Díaz, *The Great Transformation*, 136.

57. Osvaldo Sunkel, "Is the Chilean 'Miracle' Sustainable?" *Journal of Interamerican Studies and World Affairs* 37, no. 3 (1995): 1-2.

58. Alejandro Foxley, "Chile: Latin America's middle way (Not Right, Not Left: Thinking About the Alternative)," *New Perspectives Quarterly* 13, no. 4 (1996 Fall): 38; and for Foxley's earlier views of export-led development, see Alejandro Foxley, *Latin American Experiments in Neoconservative Economics* (Berkeley: University of California Press, 1983).

59. Tomás Moulian, *Chile Actual: Anatomía de un mito*, Colección Sin Norte, Serie Punto de Fuga (Santiago: Arcis Universidad, Ediciones Lom, 1997), 18, 40-41, 49, 61.

60. Ibid., 104.

61. Mainwaring, "Democracy in Brazil and the Southern Cone," internet 18; and Pilar Vergara, "In Pursuit of 'Growth with Equity:' The Limits of Chile's

Free-Market Social Reforms," *NACLA Report on the Americas* 29, no. 6 (1996), internet 4, 8.

62. David E. Hojman, "Poverty and Inequality in Chile," intnt. 5, tbls. 4 & 14.

63. Patricio Meller, Raúl O'Ryan, and Andrés Solimano, "Growth, Equity, and the Environment in Chile: Issues and Evidence," *World Development* 26, no. 2 (1996), 262; and Saar Van Hauwermeiren, "Tratados de libre comercio y su impacto sobre el medio ambiente," *El tigre sin selva: consecuencias ambientales de la transformación económica de Chile, 1974-1993*, Rayén Quiroga Martínez, ed. (Santiago: Instituto de Ecología Política, Area de Economía Ecológica, octubre 1994), 456.

64. André Gunder Frank, *ReOrient: Global Economy in the Asian Age* (Berkeley: University of California Press, 1998).

65. Banco Central de Chile, Dirección de Política Financiera, *Indicadores económicos y sociales, 1960-1982* (Santiago: Banco Central de Chile, 1983); James W. Wilkie, Carlos Alberto Contreras, and Catherine Komisarisk, *Statistical Abstract of Latin America*, 2 vols., vol. 1 (Los Angeles: UCLA Latin American Center Publications, 1995), 1:832, and (Banco Central de Chile, 1983), 236.

66. LADB Latin America Data Bank, "New Debt Crisis Looming?" *Latinamerica Press*, 19 Sept. 1996, 3.

67. World Bank, *Global Development Finance: Country Tables*, 2 vols. (Washington, D.C.: World Bank, 1997), 1:166.

68. Mainwaring, "Democracy in Brazil and the Southern Cone," internet 35-36.

69. Carlos Marichal, "The Vicious Cycles of Mexican Debt," *NACLA Report on the Americas* 31, no. 3 (Nov. 1997), 31. Issue is devoted to contemporary problems stemming from the debt crisis of 1982.

70. Ibid., internet 31; Gary Hytrek, "Labor and social development: Costa Rica and Chile," *Journal of Third World Studies* 12, no. 2 (1995): internet 1-3; and Kenneth M. Roberts, "From the Barricades to the Ballot Box: Redemocratization and Political Realignment in the Chilean Left," *Politics and Society 23*, no. 4 (1995): internet 1-5.

71. See the searing portrait of Frei Ruiz-Tagle's inauguration in, Ximena Ortúzar, "Frente a un país sin esperanza, el hijo de Eduardo Frei asumió la presidencia de Chile," *Proceso*, no. 906 (March 14, 1994), 59-61.

72. Katherine Hite, "The formation and transformation of political identity: leaders of the Chilean Left, 1968-1990," *Journal of Latin America Studies* 28, no. 2 (1996): internet 17.

73. Hojman, "Poverty and Inequality in Chile," internet 12.

Fig. 12. Araucanian woman and children, Temuco, Feb. 1933. Native Americans remained victims of land encroachment, outside state concern, well into the twentieth century. Library of Congress.

Fig. 13. The *conventillo* (Santiago) was the dominant form of labor housing in the capital from the 1920s until the spread of shantytowns [*callampas*] in the 1940s. Earl Chapin May, *2000 Miles through Chile: The Land of More or Less* (New York: The Century Company, 1924).

Fig. 14. El Teniente, Rancagua Province, 1918. Braden Copper purchased the mine from Chilean elite and sold it to Guggenheims in 1915. This capital-intensive complex continued as Kennecott Copper Corp. until nationalization in 1970s. U.S. National Archives.

Fig. 15. Coal miners, Lota, early 1930s. Primitive working conditions continued into 1940s. Region's mining uprising halted center-left governments in 1947-48. Library of Congress.

Fig. 16. Steam-driven trucks, hauling wood in the south, early 1930s. Chilean technology remained outmoded. Library of Congress.

Fig. 17. Union Club, downtown Santiago, ca. 1930. The Club was the center of elite male life during the nitrate era and through the 1930s. United States. National Archives.

Fig. 18. Country home, rural scene, ca. 1900. Unidentified, the site is probably just to the south of Santiago. United States. National Archives.

Archives and private papers

Chile

Archivo Nacional. National Library, Santiago. The following ministerial records were consulted.
  Ministerio del Fomento, 1929-1940.
  Ministerio de Hacienda, 1929-1940.
  Ministerio del Interior, 1929-1940.
  Ministerio de Trabajo, 1929-1940.
  Ministerio de Relaciones Exteriores, 1929-1940.
Colección Pedro Aguirre Cerda. National Library, Santiago.

France

Ministere des Affaires Etrangeres. Archives Diplomatiques. L'Amerique, 1918-1940 (B). Quai D'Orsay, Paris.

Great Britain

Antony Gibbs and Sons, Ltd. Archive. Guildhall Library. London.
Archive of the Bank of London and South America. D.M.S. Watson Library. University College, University of London. London.
Archives of the Foreign Office. Public Record Office, Kew Gardens. London.

United States

National Archives, Washington D.C. The following record groups and Department records were consulted:
  Department of Commerce. Record Group 151, 1929-1941.
  Department of State. Records Relating to the Internal Affairs of Chile. Record Group 59, 1929-1949.
  Department of State. Post Records of Embassies. Record Group 84, 1929-1941.
  Export-Import Bank, Credit Files. Record Group 275, 1938.
  War Department. Record Group 165, 1929-1941.
Papers of President Herbert Hoover. Hoover Presidential Library. West Branch, Iowa.
Papers of William S. Culbertson. Library of Congress. Washington, D.C.
Stimson Diaries. Hoover Presidential Library, General Accession. West

Branch, Iowa. This is a microfilm version, the original is in the Yale University Library.

Newspapers, other serial publications, and printed reports of governments and international agencies

Banco Central de Chile, Dirección de Política Financiera. *Indicadores económicos y sociales, 1960-1982.* Santiago: Banco Central de Chile, 1983.

Boletín de la Sociedad de Fomento Fabril. Produced by the Sociedad. Santiago, 1931.

Boletín oficial de la Bolsa de Corredores de Valparaiso. Valparaiso, 1930, 1931.

Cámara de Comercio de Chile. *Memoria.* Santiago, 1932.

Chile. Contraloría General. *Memoria de la Contraloría General correspondiente al año . . . y balance general de la Hacienda Pública.* Santiago, 1932-43.

———. Departamento de Estadística. *Anuario estadístico de Chile.* Santiago, 1928-45.

———. Departamento de Estadística. *Estadística chilena.* Santiago, 1935-43.

———. Dirección General de Estadística. *Censo de agricultura, 1935-36.* Santiago, 1938.

———. Dirección General de Estadística. *Resultados del XX Censo de la Población efectuado el 27 de noviembre de 1930.* Santiago, 1931.

———. Dirección General de Estadística. *Sinópsis estadística.* Santiago, 1933-46.

———. Dirección General de Estadística. *Veinte años de legislación social.* Santiago, 1945.

———. Diputados. *Boletín de sesiones estraordinarios.* Santiago: Congreso, 1931, 1936-37.

———. Diputados. *Boletín de sesiones ordinarios.* Santiago: Congreso, 1930-41.

———. Ministerio de Hacienda. *Hacienda pública.* 1937-39.

Council on Foreign Relations. *The United States in World Affairs: An Account of American Foreign Relations, 1931, 1932.* Walter Lippman in collaboration with William O. Scroggs. New York: Harper and Brothers, 1932, 1933.

Diario Oficial. Santiago, 1931-32.

El Diario Ilustrado. Santiago, 1931, 1935, 1940, 1943.

El Imparcial. Santiago, 1937.

El Mercurio. Santiago, 1930-37, 1939-43.

El Radical. Valparaiso, 1936.

El Sol. Santiago, 1931.

El Sur. Concepción, 1938.

Financial News. London, 1935.

Great Britain. Department of Overseas Trade. *Economic Conditions in Chile*. London: H.M. Stationary Office, 1934.

Hoy. Santiago, 1932-33.

La Crónica. Santiago, 1932.

La Hora. Temuco, 1931.

La Jornada. Mexico City, 1996.

La Nación. Santiago, 1928, 1930-33, 1935-36, 1938.

La Opinión. Santiago, 1932-33, 1935-39.

La Reforma. Mexico City, 1996.

Latinamerica Press. Lima, 1996.

La Unión. Valparaiso, 1938.

League of Nations. *World Production and Prices, 1925-1933*. Geneva: League of Nations, 1933-34.

League of Nations, Secretariat. Financial Section and Economic Intelligence Service, *The Network of World Trade (A Companion Volume to Europe's Trade)*. Geneva: League of Nations, 1942.

League of Nations, Secretariat. Financial Section and Economic Intelligence Service. *Review of World Trade, 1937*. Geneva: Publications Department of the League of Nations, 1938.

NACLA Report on the Americas. New York, 1997.

New York Herald Tribune. New York, 1932.

New York Times. New York, 1931-32.

Proceso. Mexico City, 1994.

The Times. London, 1931-32.

Time. New York, 1995.

United Nations. *Economic Survey of Latin America, 1949*. New York: United Nations, 1950 [original in Spanish, 1949].

____, Comisión Económica para America Latina y el Caribe (CEPAL). *Antecedentes estadísticos de la distribución del ingreso Chile, 1940-1982*. Santiago: Naciones Unidas, 1987.

____, Department for Economic and Social Information and Policy Analysis, Statistics Division. *1995 International Trade Statistics Yearbook*. New York: United Nations, 1996. 2 vols.

United States, Central Intelligence Agency (CIA). *The World Factbook, 1997*. Washington, D.C.: Brassey's, 1996.

____, Department of State. *Papers Relating to the Foreign Relations of the United States, 1931*. Washington, D.C.: Government Printing

Office, 1946-.

United States House of Representatives. Subcommittee on Inter-American Affairs of the Committee on Foreign Affairs. *United States and Chile during the Allende Years, 1970-1973.* Washington: Government Printing Office, 1975.

United States Senate. *Covert Action in Chile, 1963-1973.* Staff Report of the Select Committee to Study Governmental Operations with Respect to Intelligence Activities. Washington: Government Printing Office, 1975.

United States Tariff Commission. *Latin America as a Source of Strategic and Other Essential Materials.* Report no. 144, Second Series. Washington: Government Printing Office, 1941.

Washington Post. Washington, D.C., 1932.

World Bank, *World Tables 1995.* Baltimore: The Johns Hopkins University Press, 1996.

Articles, books, and dissertations

Abel, Christopher and Colin M. Lewis. *Latin America, Economic Imperialism and the State: The Political Economy of the External Connection from Independence to the Present.* London: The Athlone Press, for the Institute of Latin American Studies, University of London, 1985.

Aguirre Cerda, Pedro. *El problema agrario.* Paris: Imprimerie francaise l'edition, 1929.

____. *El problema industrial.* Santiago: Universidad de Chile, 1933.

Ahumada, Eugenio et al., eds. *Chile, la memoria prohibida: las violaciones a los derechos humanos, 1973-1983.* Santiago: Pehuen, 1989.

Alba, Victor. *Politics and the Labor Movement in Latin America.* Stanford: Stanford University Press, 1968.

Albert, Bill. *South America and the First World War: The Impact of the War on Brazil, Argentina, Peru, and Chile.* Cambridge: Cambridge University Press, 1988.

Aldcroft, Derek H. *From Versailles to Wall Street.* London: Allen Lane, 1977.

Alessandri Palma, Arturo. *Historia de América, bajo la dirección superior de Ricardo Levene; Rectificaciones al Tomo IX.* Santiago: Imprenta Universitaria, 1941.

____. *Recuerdos de Gobierno.* 3 vols. Santiago: Editorial Nascimento, 1967.

Alexander, Robert J. *Arturo Alessandri: A Biography.* 2 vols. New

Brunswick, NJ: Rutgers University Latin American Institute, University Microfilms International, 1977.

____. Labor Relations in Argentina, Brazil and Chile. New York: McGraw-Hill Book Co., 1962.

____. Trotskyism in Latin America. Stanford: Hoover Institution Press, 1973.

Aliaga Ibar, Ignacio. "La economía de Chile y la industria del cobre (algunas reflexiones sobre la post-guerra)." Ph.D. diss., Universidad de Chile, 1946.

Allende Gossens, Salvador. La realidad médico-social chilena (síntesis). Santiago: Ministerio de Salubridad, Previsión, y Asisténcia Social, 1939.

Alliende González, Rodrigo. El jefe: la vida de Jorge González von Marées. Santiago: Ediciones Los Castaños, 1990.

Alvarez Andrews, Oscar. Historia del desarrollo industrial de Chile. Santiago: La Ilustración, 1936.

Amin, Samir. Accumulation on a World Scale: A Critique of the Theory of Underdevelopment. Trans. by Brian Pearce. New York: Monthly Review Press, 1974.

____. Unequal Development: An Essay on the Social Formations of Peripheral Capitalism. Trans. by Brian Pearce. New York: Monthly Review Press, 1976.

Anderson, Benedict. Imagined Communities: Reflections on the Origin and Spread of Nationalism. London: Verso, 1983.

Angell, Alan. Politics and the Labour Movement in Chile. Oxford: Oxford University Press for the Royal Institute of International Affairs, 1972.

Antezana-Pernet, Corinne. "Mobilizing Women in the Popular Front Era: Feminism, Class, and Politics in the Movimiento Pro-Emancipación de la Mujer Chilena (MEMCh)." Ph.D. diss., University of California Irvine, 1996.

Araneda Bravo, Fidel. Arturo Alessandri Palma. Santiago: Editorial Nascimento, 1979.

Arancibia Clavel, Patricia, Pablo Bravo Díaz, and Departamento de Historia et al., Universidad Finis Terrae, 1891 visto por sus protagonistas. Santiago: Editorial Fundación, 1991.

Armanet, Daniel. El crédito bancario y el valor de la moneda. Santiago: Editorial Nascimento, 1938.

Arriagada, Genero. The Politics of Power: Pinochet. Trans. by Nancy Morris, Vincent Ercolano, and Dristen A. Whitney. Boston: Unwin Hyman, 1988.

Atria, Raúl. "Tensiones políticas y crisis económica: el caso chileno,

1920-1938." *Estudios Sociales* 10:37 (third trimester 1983).

Aylwin Oyarzún, Mariana, Carlos Bascuñán Edwards, Sofía Correa Sutil, Cristián Gasmuri Riveros, Sol Serrano Pérez, María Tagle Domínguez. *Chile en el siglo XX.* Santiago: Emisión, Ltda., 1986.

Ballesteros, Marto A. and Tom E. Davis. "El crecimiento de la producción y el empleo en sectores básicos de la economía chilena, 1908-1957." *Cuadernos de economía* 2:7 (Sep./Dec. 1965).

Balmori, Diana and Robert Oppenheimer, "Family Clusters: Generational Nucleation in Nineteenth-Century Argentina and Chile." *Comparative Studies in Society and History* 21:2 (Apr. 1979).

Baran, Paul A. *The Political Economy of Growth*, 1957. Reprint. New York: Monthly Review Press, 1967.

Barber, William J. "Chile con Chicago: A Review Essay." *Journal of Economic Literature* 33:4 (1995).

Barker, Ernest. *The Development of Public Services in Western Europe, 1660-1930.* Hamden, CT: Archon Books, 1966.

Barnard, Andrew. "Chile." In *Latin America between the Second World War and the Cold War, 1944-1948.* Ed. by Leslie Bethell and Ian Roxborough. New York: Cambridge University Press, 1992.

____. "Chilean Communists, Radical Presidents and Chilean Relations with the United States, 1940-1947." *Journal of Latin American Studies* 13:2 (Nov. 1981).

____. "The Chilean Communist Party: 1922-1947." Ph.D. diss., University of London, University College, Dec. 1977.

Barría Seron, Jorge I. *El movimiento obrero en Chile; síntesis histórico-social.* Santiago: Ediciones de la Universidad Técnica del Estado, 1971.

Basch, Michael and Ricardo D. Paredes-Molina, "Are There Dual Labor Markets in Chile? Empirical Evidence." *Journal of Development Economics* 50:2 (Aug. 1996).

Bauer, Arnold J. *Chilean Rural Society: from the Spanish Conquest to 1930.* Cambridge: Cambridge University Press, 1975.

Benavides, Leopoldo. "La formación de la izquierda chilena: relaciones entre el Partido Comunista y el Partido Socialista." *FLACSO Documento de Trabajo* no. 389. (Santiago: FLACSO, 1988).

Bergquist, Charles. *Labor in Latin America: Comparative Essays on Chile, Argentina, Venezuela, and Colombia.* Stanford: Stanford University Press, 1986.

Bermúdez Miral, Oscar. *El drama político de Chile.* Santiago: Editorial Tegualda, 1947.

Bernedo, Patricio. "Prosperidad económica bajo Carlos Ibáñez del Campo, 1927-1929," *Historia* 24 (1989).

Bethell, Leslie. "Britain and Latin America in Historical Perspective." In Victor Bulmer-Thomas, ed., *Britain and Latin America: A Changing Relationship*. New York: Cambridge University Press, The Royal Institute of International Affairs, 1989.

Bicheno, H.E. "Anti-Parliamentary Themes in Chilean History," *Government and Opposition* 7:3 (Summer 1972).

Bitar, Sergio. *Chile: Experiment in Democracy*. Trans. by Sam Sherman. Philadelphia: Institute for the Study of Human Issues [ISHI], 1986.

Bizzarro, Salvatore. *Historical Dictionary of Chile*. 2d. ed. Metuchen, NJ: The Scarecrow Press, Inc., 1987.

Blancpain, Jean-Piette. *Les allemands au Chile, 1816-1945*. Koln, Germany: Bohtau Verlag, 1974.

Boizard B., Ricardo. *Cuatro retratos en profundidad: Ibáñez, Lafertte, Leighton, Walker*. Santiago: El Imparcial, 1950.

_____. *Historia de una derrota: 25 de octubre de 1938*. Santiago: Editorial Orbe, 1941.

_____. *La Democracia Cristiana en Chile; un mundo que nace entre dos guerras*. 3d. ed. Santiago: Editorial Orbe, 1963.

_____. *Patios Interiores*. Santiago: Editorial Nascimento, 1948.

Bonilla, Frank and Myron Glazer. *Student Politics in Chile*. New York: Basic Books, 1970.

Borchard, Edwin. *State Insolvency and Foreign Bondholders*. New York: Garland Publishing Inc., 1983. 2 vols. Reprint. New Haven: Yale University Press, 1951.

Bosworth, Barry, Rudiger Dornbusch, and Raul Laban, eds. *The Chilean Economy: Policy Lessons and Challenges*. Washington, D.C.: The Brookings Institution, 1994.

Bowers, Claude G. *Chile through Embassy Windows: 1939-1953*. New York: Simon and Schuster, 1958.

Brandes, Joseph. *Herbert Hoover and Economic Diplomacy: Department of Commerce Policy*. Pittsburgh: University of Pittsburgh Press, 1962.

Bravo Lira, Bernardino. "Chile 1925-1932: de la nueva constitución al nuevo régimen de gobierno." *50 años de vida institucional, 1927-1977*. Santiago: La Contraloría General de la República, 1977.

_____. *Régimen de gobierno y partidos políticos en Chile, 1924-1973*. Santiago: Editorial Jurídica de Chile, 1978.

Brito Peña, Alejandra. "Del rancho al conventillo: Transformaciones en la identidad popular-femenina (Santiago Chile, 1850-1920)." *Voces femeninas y construcción de identidad*. Ed. by Alejandra Brito Peña et al. Buenos Aires: Consejo Latinoamericano de Ciencias Sociales,

CLACSO, 1995.

Brown, Jonathan C. "Jersey Standard and the Politics of Latin American Oil Production, 1911-1930." *Latin American Oil Companies and the Politics of Energy*. Ed. by John D. Wirth. Lincoln: University of Nebraska Press, 1985.

Buchanan, James M., Robert D. Tollison, and Gordon Tullock, eds. *Toward a Theory of the Rent-Seeking Society*. College Station: Texas A&M University Press, 1980.

Buhite, Russell D., and David W. Levy, eds. *FDR's Fireside Chats*. Norman: University of Oklahoma Press, 1992.

Bulmer-Thomas, Victor. *The Economic History of Latin America since Independence*. New York: Cambridge University Press, 1994.

Burbach, Roger Joseph. "The Chilean Industrial Bourgeoisie and Foreign Capital, 1920-1970." Ph.D. diss., Indiana University, 1975.

Burns, E. Bradford. *The Poverty of Progress: Latin America in the Nineteenth Century*. Berkeley: University of California Press, 1980.

Caballero, Manuel. *Latin America and the Comintern, 1919-1943*. Cambridge: Cambridge University Press, 1986.

Cabero, Alberto. *Recuerdos de don Pedro Aguirre Cerda*. Santiago: Imprenta Nascimento, 1948.

Cain, P.J. and A.G. Hopkins. *British Imperialism: Crisis and Deconstruction, 1914-1990*. London: Longman, 1993.

____. *British Imperialism: Innovation and Expansion, 1688-1914*. London: Longman, 1993.

Caravale, Giovanni A., ed. *The Legacy of Ricardo*. London: Basil Blackwell, 1985.

Cárdenas, Enrique. *La industrialización mexicana durante la gran depresión*. Mexico City: El Colegio de Mexico, 1987.

Cardoso, Fernando Henrique. "Towards Another Development." *From Dependency to Development: Strategies to Overcome Underdevelopment and Inequality*. Ed. by Heraldo Muñoz. Westview Special Studies in Social, Political, and Economic Development. Boulder: Westview Press, 1981.

____ and Enzo Faletto. *Dependency and Development in Latin America*. Trans. by Marjory Mattingly Urquidi. Berkeley: University of California Press, 1979.

Carmagnani, Marcello. *Estado y sociedad en América Latina, 1850-1930*. Trans. by P.R. Ferrer from Italian. Barcelona: Editorial Crítica, 1984.

Carriere, Jean. *Landowners and Politics in Chile: A Study of the "Sociedad Nacional de Agricultura," 1932-1970*. Amsterdam: The

Interuniversity Center for Latin American Research and Documentation [CEDLA], Incidentele Publicaties 18, 1980.

Carril Echevarría, José. "Nuestra deuda externa: suspensión y reanudación de sus servicios." Ph.D. diss., University of Chile, Imprenta Relampago, 1944.

Cassell, Gustav. *The Downfall of the Gold Standard.* 1936. Reprint. New York: Augustus M. Kelley, 1966.

Castells, Manuel. *City, Class and Power.* Trans. by Elizabeth Lebas. London: MacMillan Press, 1978.

Castañeda, Jorge G. *Utopia Unarmed: The Latin American Left after the Cold War.* New York: Vintage Publishers, 1993.

Cawson, Alan. *Corporatism and Welfare: Social Policy and State Intervention in Britain.* London: Heinemann Educational Books, 1982.

Cavarozzi, Marcelo José. "The Government and the Industrial Bourgeoisie in Chile." Ph.D. diss., University of California Berkeley, 1975.

____. "El orden oligárquico en Chile, 1880-1940." *Desarrollo económico.* 18:70 (1978).

Ceppi M. de L., Sergio et al. *Chile, 100 años de industria, 1883-1983.* Santiago: Sociedad de Fomento Fabril, 1983.

Chaplin, David, ed. *Peruvian Nationalism: A Corporatist Revolution.* New Brunswick, NJ: Transaction Books, 1975.

Charlin O., Carlos. *Del Avión Rojo a la República Socialista.* Santiago: Empresa Editora Nacional Quimantu, Ltda., 1972.

Chelen Rojas, Alejandro. *Trayectoria del socialismo: apuntes para una historia crítica del socialismo chileno.* Buenos Aires: Editorial Astral, 1967.

Císpedes, Mario and Lelia Garreaud. *Gran diccionario de Chile (biográfico-cultural).* 2 vols. Santiago: Colección Alfa Divulgación, 1988.

Clarke, Stephen V.O. *Central Bank Cooperation, 1924-1931.* New York: Federal Reserve Bank of New York, 1967.

Clayton, Lawrence A. *Grace: W.R. Grace and Co. The Formative Years 1850-1930.* Ottawa, IL: Jameson Books, 1985.

Collier, Ruth Berins and David Collier. *Shaping the Political Arena: Critical Junctures, the Labor Movement, and Regime Dynamics in Latin America.* Princeton: Princeton University Press, 1991.

Collins, Joseph and John Lear, *Chile's Free-Market Miracle: A Second Look.* Oakland, CA: The Institute for Food and Development Policy, 1995.

Constable, Pamela and Arturo Valenzuela. *Chile under Pinochet: A Nation of Enemies.* New York: W.W. Norton, 1991.

Contreras Guzmán, Víctor. *Bitácora de la dictadura: administración Ibáñez, 1928-1931.* Santiago: Imprenta Cultura, 1942.

Correa Prieto, Luis. *El presidente Ibáñez, la política y los políticos; apuntes para la historia.* Santiago: Editorial Orbe, 1962.

Cortes Conde, Roberto and Shane Hunt, eds. *The Latin American Economies: Growth and the Export Sector, 1880-1930.* New York: Holmes and Meier, 1985.

Covarrubias, María Teresa. *1938: La rebelión de los jóvenes.* Santiago: Editorial Aconcagua, 1987.

Cox, Andrew and Noel D. Sullivan, eds., *The Corporatist State: Corporatism and the State Tradition.* Brookfield, VT: Gower Publishing Co., 1988.

Crouch, Colin, ed. *State and Economy in Contemporary Capitalism.* London: Croom Helm, 1979.

Cruz-Coke, Ricardo. *Historia electoral de Chile, 1925-1973.* Santiago: Editorial Jurídica de Chile, 1984.

Davidson, Paul. *International Money and the Real World.* London: MacMillan Press, 1982.

____. *Money and the Real World.* 2d. ed. London: MacMillan Press, 1978.

Deane, Phyllis. *The State and the Economic System: An Introduction to the History of Political Economy.* Oxford: Oxford University Press, 1989.

de Conde, Alexander. *Herbert Hoover's Latin American Policy.* Stanford: Stanford University Press, 1951.

de Secada, C. Alexander G. "Armas, guano y comercio marítimo: Los intereses de W.R. Grace en el Peru, 1865-1885." *Revista latinoamericana de historia económica y social [HISLA],* 7 (first semester, 1986).

De Shazo, Peter. *Urban Workers and Labor Unions in Chile, 1902-1927.* Madison: University of Wisconsin Press, 1983.

de Vylder, Stephen. *Allende's Chile: The political Economy of the Rise and Fall of the Unidad Popular.* Cambridge: Cambridge University Press, 1976.

Dhondt, Jan. "Government, Labour and Trade Unions." *The Great Depression Revisited.* Essays on the Economics of the Thirties. Ed. by Herman van der Wee. The Hague: Nijhoff, 1972.

Dinamarca, Manuel. *La república socialista chilena: orígenes legítimos del partido socialista.* Santiago: Ediciones Documentados, 1987.

Donoso, Armando. *Conversaciones con don Arturo Alessandri.* Santiago: Biblioteca Ercilla, 1934.

Donoso, Ricardo. *Alessandri: Agitador y Demoledor.* 2 vols. Mexico City: Fondo de Cultura, 1954.

Donoso Letelier, Crescente. "Notas sobre el origen, acatamiento y desgaste del régimen presidencial: 1925-1973." *Historia* 13 (1976).

Dornbusch, Rudiger and Sebastian Edwards. "The Macroeconomics of Populism in Latin America." *Journal of Development Economics* 32 (1990).

____, eds. *The Macroeconomics of Populism in Latin America.* Chicago: The University of Chicago Press, 1991.

dos Santos, Theotonio. "The Structure of Dependence." *The American Economic Review* 60:2 (May 1970).

Drake, Paul W. "Comment." *The Macroeconomics of Populism in Latin America.* Ed. by R. Dornbusch and S. Edwards. Chicago: The University of Chicago Press, 1991.

____. "La misión Kemmerer a Chile: Consejeros norteamericanos, estabilización y endeudamiento, 1925-1932." *Cuadernos de historia* 4 (July 1984).

____. *Labor Movements and Dictatorships: The Southern Cone in Comparative Perspective.* Baltimore: The Johns Hopkins University Press, 1996.

____. *Socialism and Populism in Chile, 1932-52.* Chicago: University of Illinois Press, 1978.

____. *The Money Doctor in the Andes: The Kemmerer Missions, 1923-1933.* Durham, NC: Duke University Press, 1989.

____ and Iván Jaksic, eds. *The Struggle for Democracy in Chile.* 2d ed. Lincoln: University of Nebraska Press, 1995.

Duncan, Kenneth and Ian Rutledge, eds. *Land and Labour in Latin America: Essays on the Development of Agrarian Capitalism in the Nineteenth and Twentieth Centuries.* New York: Cambridge University Press, 1977.

Duran Bernales, Florencio. *El Partido Radical.* Santiago: Editorial Nascimento, 1958.

Dyson, Kenneth H.F. *The State Tradition in Western Europe: A Study of an Idea and Institution.* Oxford: Martin Robertson, 1980.

Edwards, Sebastian and Alejandra Cox Edwards. *Monetarism and Liberalization: The Chilean Experiment.* Chicago: University of Chicago Press, 1991.

Edwards Vives, Alberto. *La fronda aristocrática: historia política de Chile.* 4th ed. Santiago: Editorial Pacífico, 1952.

Eichengreen, Barry. *Golden Fetters: The Gold Standard and the Great Depression, 1919-1939.* Oxford: Oxford University Press, 1992.

Ellis, Lewis E. *Republican Foreign Policy, 1921-1933.* New Brunswick,

NJ: Rutgers University Press, 1968.

Ellsworth, Paul T. *Chile: An Economy in Transition*. New York: The Macmillan Company, 1945.

Emmanuel, Arghiri. *Unequal Exchange: A Study of the Imperialism of Trade*. Trans. by Brian Pearce. New York: Monthly Review Press, 1972.

Espinosa, J. Manuel. *Inter-American Beginnings of U.S. Cultural Diplomacy, 1936-1948*. Washington, D.C.: U.S. Department of State, Bureau of Educational and Cultural Affairs, Historical Studies no. 2, 1976.

Evans, Peter B. *Dependent Development: The Alliance of Multinational, State and Local Capital in Brazil*. Princeton: Princeton University Press, 1979.

____, Dietrich Rueschemeyer, and Theda Skocpol, eds. *Bringing the State Back In*. Cambridge: Cambridge University Press, 1985.

____, Dietrich Rueschemeyer, and Evelyne Huber Stephens, eds. *States Versus Markets in the World-System*. Vol. 8, *Political Economy of the World-System Annuals*, edited by Immanuel Wallerstein. Beverly Hills: Sage Publications, 1985.

Faúndez, Julio. *Marxism and Democracy in Chile: From 1932 to the fall of Allende*. New Haven: Yale University Press, 1988.

Fernández, Gonzalo. "Orden, libertad e igualdad, valores básicos de la evolución democrática en Chile hasta 1925." *Estudios sociales* (second trimester, 1983), 10:36.

Findley, Ronald. "On W. Arthur Lewis's Contributions to Economics." *The Theory and Experience of Development: Essays in Honor of Sir W. Arthur Lewis*. Ed. by Mark Gersovitz et al. Boston: George Allen and Unwin, 1982.

Fink, Marvin S. and Staff. *Reports on Electric Power Regulation in Brazil, Chile, Colombia, Costa Rica, and Mexico*. Cambridge: Harvard Law School, 1960.

Fleet, Michael. *The Rise and Fall of Chilean Christian Democracy*. Princeton: Princeton University Press, 1985.

Fleisig, Heywood W. *Long-Term Capital Flows and the Great Depression: The Role of the United States, 1927-1933*. New York: Arno Press, 1975.

Foxley, Alejandro. "Chile: Latin America's Middle Way (Not Right, Not Left: Thinking About the Alternative)." *New Perspectives Quarterly 13* no. 4 (Fall 1996).

____. *Latin American Experiments in Neoconservative Economics*. Berkeley: University of California Press, 1983.

Francis, Michael J. *The Limits of Hegemony: United States Relations with Argentina and Chile during World War II*. Notre Dame: University of Notre Dame Press, 1977.

_____. "The United States and Chile During the Second World War: The Diplomacy of Misunderstanding." *Journal of Latin American Studies* 9:1 (May 1977).

Frank, André Gunder. *Capitalism and Underdevelopment in Latin America: Historical Studies of Chile and Brazil*. New York: Monthly Review Press, 1967.

_____. *ReOrient: Global Economy in the Asian Age*. Berkeley: University of California Press, 1998.

Frei Montalva, Eduardo. *La política y el espíritu*. 2d ed. (1st ed., 1940) Santiago: Editorial del Pacífico, 1946.

French-Davis, Ricardo. "The Importance of Copper in the Chilean Economy: Two Decades of Historical Background." Mimeo from CIEPLAN, 1974. A shortened version appeared in Ernesto Tironi, ed., *El cobre en el desarrollo nacional*. Santiago: Ediciones Nueva Universidad-CIEPLAN, 1974.

Friedman, Milton and Anna Jacobson Schwartz, *A Monetary History of the United States, 1867-1960*. Princeton: Princeton University Press, 1963.

Fuentes, Jordi and Lia Cortes. *Diccionario político de Chile (1810-1966)*. Santiago: Editorial Orbe, 1967.

Fuenzalida, Humberto et al. *Chile: geografía, educación, literatura, legislación, economía, minería*. Buenos Aires: Editorial Losada, S.A., 1946.

Galbraith, John Kenneth. *The Great Crash, 1929*. 3d ed. Boston: Houghton Mifflin, 1972.

García Covarrubias, Jaime. *El partido radical y la clase media: la relación de intereses entre 1888 y 1938*. Santiago: Editorial Andrés Bello, 1990.

Gariazzo, Alicia. "Orígenes ideológicos de los movimientos obreros chilenos y argentinos." *Revista paraguaya de sociología* 18:5 (June/Sep., 1981).

Gardner, Lloyd C. *Economic Aspects of New Deal Diplomacy*. Madison: University of Wisconsin Press, 1964.

Gamonal, Germán. *Jorge Alessandri: el hombre, el político*. Santiago: Holanda Comunicaciones, S.A., 1987.

Garrido R., José, Cristián Guerrero Y., and María Soledad Valdés. *Historia de la reforma agraria en Chile*. Ed. by José Garrido R. Santiago: Editorial Universitaria, 1988.

Gellman, Irwin F. *Good Neighbor Diplomacy: United States Policies in Latin America, 1933-1945*. Baltimore: Johns Hopkins University

Press, 1979.

Gellner, Ernest. *Nations and Nationalism*. Oxford: Blackwell, 1983.

Gil, Frederico C. *The Political System of Chile*. Boston: Houghton Mifflin Co., 1966.

Gilbert, Felix. *The End of the European Era: 1890 to the Present*. New York: W.W. Norton and Co., 1970.

Gómez Ch., María Soledad. "Partido Comunista de Chile 1922-1952." *FLACSO Documento de Trabajo* no. 226. Santiago: FLACSO, 1984.

Góngora Escobar, Alvaro. *La prostitución en Santiago, 1813-1931: Visión de las elites*. Vol. 8, *Colección Sociedad y Cultura*. Santiago: Dirección de Bibliotecas, Archivos y Museos, 1994.

González, Julio Heise. *Historia de Chile. La República Parlamentaria 1861-1925*. 2 vols. Santiago: Editorial Andrés Bello, 1974.

González Camus, Ignacio. *El día que murió Allende*. Santiago: CESOC, 1988.

González Videla, Gabriel. *Memorias*. 2 vols. Santiago: Editora Nacional Gabriel Mistral, 1975.

Gramsci, Antonio. *Letters from Prison*. Trans. by Lynne Lawner. New York: Harper and Row, 1973.

Green, David. *The Containment of Latin America: A History of the Myths and Realities of the Good Neighbor Policy*. Chicago: Quadrangle Books, 1971.

Green, Donald P. and Ian Shapiro. *The Pathologies of Rational Choice Theory: A Critique of Applications in Political Science*. New Haven: Yale University Press, 1994.

Gunther, John. *Inside Latin America*. New York: Harper and Brothers, 1941.

Haber, Stephen. "Introduction: Economic Growth and Latin American Economic Historiography." *How Latin America Fell Behind: Essays on the Economic History of Brazil and Mexico, 1800-1914*. Ed. by Stephen Haber. Stanford: Stanford University Press, 1997.

Habermas, Jürgen. *The Structural Transformation of the Public Sphere: An Inquiry into a Category of Bourgeois Society*. Trans. by Thomas Burger. Cambridge: MIT Press, 1989.

Haglund, David G. *Latin America and the Transformation of U.S. Strategic Thought, 1936-1940*. Albuquerque: University of New Mexico Press, 1984.

Hathaway, Robert M. "1933-1945: Economic Diplomacy in a time of Crisis." *Economics and World Power: An Assessment of American Diplomacy Since 1789*. Ed. by William H. Becker and Samuel F. Wells, Jr. New York: Columbia University Press, 1984.

Hawtrey, R.G. *The Gold Standard in Theory and Practice*. 5th ed. London: Longmans, Green and Co., 1947.

Herfindahl, Orris C. *Copper Costs and Prices, 1870-1957*. Baltimore: Resources for the Future, Inc., and the Johns Hopkins Press, 1959.

Hilton, Stanley E. *Hitler's Secret War in South America: 1939-1945: German Military Espionage and Allied Counterespionage in Brazil*. Baton Rouge: Louisiana State University Press, 1981.

Hirschman, Albert O. *Essays in Trespassing: Economics to Politics and Beyond*. London: Cambridge University Press, 1981.

____. *Exit, Voice, and Loyalty: Responses to Decline in Firms, Organizations, and States*. Cambridge: Cambridge University Press, 1970.

____. *Journeys Toward Progress: Studies of Economic Policy-Making in Latin America*. New York: The Twentieth Century Fund, 1963.

____. *National Power and the Structure of Foreign Trade*. 1945. Reprint. Berkeley: University of California Press, 1980.

H-Latam, "Cultural Studies Debate." H-Net: Michigan State University, 1997.

Hite, Katherine. "The formation and transformation of political identity: leaders of the Chilean Left, 1968-1990." *Journal of Latin America Studies* 28:2 (1996).

Hojman, David E. "Poverty and Inequality in Chile: Are Democratic Politics and Neoliberal Economics Good for You?" *Journal of Interamerican Studies and World Affairs* 38:2-3 (1996).

Hoyt, Jr., Edwin P. *The Guggenheims and the American Dream*. New York: Funk and Wagnells, 1967.

Humud Tleel, Carlos. *El sector público chileno entre 1830 y 1930*. Santiago: Universidad de Chile, 1969.

Hutchinson, Elizabeth Quay. "Working Women of Santiago: Gender and Social Transformation in Urban Chile, 1887-1927." Ph.D. diss., University of California Berkeley, 1995.

Hytrek, Gary. "Labor and social development: Costa Rica and Chile." *Journal of Third World Studies* 12:2 (1995).

Ibáñez Santa María, Adolfo. "Los ingenieros, el estado y la política en Chile. Del Ministerio de Fomento a la Corporación de Fomento, 1927-1939." *Historia* 18 (1983).

Illanes Benítez, Fernando. *La economía chilena y el comercio exterior*. Santiago: Imprenta Chile, 1944.

Infante Barros, Marta. *Testigos del treinta y ocho*. Santiago: Editorial Andrés Bello, 1972.

Jaksic, Iván. *Academic Rebels in Chile: The Role of Philosophy in Higher Education and Politics*. New York: State University of New York, 1989.

James, Marquis. *Merchant Adventurer: The Story of W.R. Grace.* Wilmington, DE: Scholarly Resources, 1993.

Jarvis, Lowell S. "The Unravelling of the Agrarian Reform." In *Development and Social Change in the Chilean Countryside: From the Pre-Land Reform Period to the Democratic Transition.* Ed. by Cristóbal Kay and Patricio Silva. Amsterdam: CEDLA [Centrum voor Studie en Documentatie van Latijns Amerika], 1992.

Jobet, Julio César. *El partido socialista de Chile.* 2 vols. Santiago: Editorial Prensa Latinoamerica, S.A., 1971.

___. *El socialismo chileno à través de sus congresos.* Santiago: Editorial Prensa Latinoamericana, S.A., 1965.

Johnson, John J. *Political Change in Latin America: The Emergence of the Middle Sectors.* Stanford: Stanford University Press, 1958.

Kay, Cristóbal. *Latin American Theories of Development and Underdevelopment.* New York: Routledge, 1989.

___ and Patricio Silva, "Rural Development, Social Change & the Democratic Transition." *Development & Social Change in the Chilean Countryside: From Pre-Land Reform Period to the Democratic Transition.* Ed. by Cristóbal Kay and Patricio Silva. Amsterdam: CEDLA [Centrum voor Studie en Documentatie van Latijns Amerika], 1992.

___. "Transformaciones de la relaciones de dominación y dependencia entre terratenientes y campesinos en el período post-colonial en Chile." *Nueva historia* 2:6 (Oct.-Dec. 1982).

Keller R., Carlos. *La eterna crisis chilena.* Santiago: Editorial Nascimento, 1931.

___. *La locura de Juan Bernales.* Santiago: Editorial Sociedad Amigos del Libro, 1949.

Kindleberger, Charles P. *World in Depression, 1929-1939.* London: Allen Lane, 1973.

King, Roger. *The State in Modern Society: New Directions in Political Sociology.* Basingstoke: Macmillan, 1986.

Kirsch, Henry W. *Industrial Development in a Traditional Society: The Conflict of Entrepreneurship and Modernization in Chile.* Gainesville: The University Presses of Florida, 1977.

Klubock, Thomas Miller. "Class, Community, and Gender in the Chilean Copper Mines: The El Teniente Miners and Working Class Politics, 1904-1951." 2 vols. Ph.D. diss., Yale University, 1993.

Kofas, Jon V. *The Struggle for Legitimacy: Latin American Labor and the United States, 1930-1960.* Tempe: Arizona State University Center for Latin American Studies Press, 1992.

___. "The Politics of Foreign Debt: The IMF, the World Bank and U.S.

Foreign Policy in Chile, 1946-1952." *The Journal of Developing Areas* 31 (Winter 1997).

Krauze, Enrique, Jean Meyer, and Cayetano Reyes. *Historia de la revolución mexicana, 1924-1928*. Vol. 10, *La reconstrucción económica*. Mexico City: El Colegio de Mexico, 1977.

Laclau, Ernesto. "Feudalism and Capitalism in Latin America." *New Left Review* 67 (May-June 1971).

Lafertte, Elías. *Vida de un comunista*. 1957. Reprint. Santiago: Editorial Austral, 1971.

La jefatura de lavaderos de Oro (Su creación, organización administrativa y funcionamiento). Santiago: Dirección General de Prisiones, 1943.

Lambert, Jacques. *Latin America: Social Structures and Political Institutions*. Berkeley: University of California Press, 1967.

Landes, David S. *The Unbound Prometheus: Technological change and Industrial Development in Western Europe from 1750 to the Present*. Cambridge: Cambridge University Press, 1969.

Lane, Frederic C. and Jelle C. Riemersma, eds. *Enterprise and Secular Change: Readings in Economic History*. Homewood, IL: Richard D. Irwin, Inc., 1953.

Lavrin, Asunción. "Women, Feminism and Social Change in Argentina, Chile, and Uruguay, 1890-1940." *Engendering Latin America*. Ed. by Donna Guy, Mary Karasch, and Asunción Lavrin. Lincoln: University of Nebraska Press, 1995.

Lazonick, William. "Creating and Extracting Value: Corporate Investment Behavior and American Economic Performance." *Understanding American Economic Decline*. Ed. by Michael A. Bernstein and David E. Adler. Cambridge: Cambridge University Press, 1994.

Leuchtenburg, William E. *The Perils of Prosperity, 1914-1932*. Chicago: The University of Chicago Press, 1958.

Lewis, W. Arthur. "Economic Development with Unlimited Supplies of Labor." *Manchester School* 22:2 (1954).

Lindberg, Leon N., Robert Alford, Colin Crouch, and Claus Offe, eds. *Stress and Contradiction in Modern Capitalism: Public Policy and the Theory of the State*. Lexington: Lexington Books, 1975.

Lipset, Seymour Martin. "Values, Education and Entrepreneurship." *Elites in Latin America*. Ed. by Seymour Martin Lipset and Aldo Solari. New York: Oxford University Press, 1967.

Loveman, Brian. *El campesino chileno le escribe a su excelencia*. Santiago: ICIRA, 1971.

_____. *Chile: the Legacy of Hispanic Capitalism*. 2d ed. Oxford: Oxford University Press, 1988.

____. *Struggle in the Countryside: Politics and Rural Labor in Chile, 1919-1973*. Bloomington: Indiana University Press, 1976.

Lowi, Theodore J. "Toward a Politics of Economics: The State of Permanent Receivership. *Stress and Contradiction in Modern Capitalism: Public Policy and The Theory of the State*. Ed. by Leon N. Lindberg, Robert Alford, Colin Crouch, and Claus Offe. Lexington: Lexington Books, 1975.

Macchiavello Varas, Santiago. *El problema de la industria del cobre en Chile y sus proyecciones económicas y sociales*. 2 vols. Santiago: Imprenta Fiscal de la Penitenciaria, 1923.

Mack, Macarena, Paulina Matta, and Ximena Valdés Subercaseaux. *Los trabajos de las mujeres entre el campo y la ciudad, 1920-1982*. Santiago: CEDEM, Centro de Estudios de la Mujer, 1986.

Maddison, Angus. *Two Crises: Latin America and Asia, 1929-38 and 1973-83*. Paris: Development Centre of the Organisation for Economic Co-operation and Development, 1985.

Mahdavy, Hossein. "The Problems of Economic Development in Rentier States: the Case of Iran." *Studies in the Economic History of the Middle East from the Rise of Islam to the Present Day*. Ed. by M.A. Cook. London: Oxford University Press, 1970.

Mahler, Vincent A. *Dependency Approaches to International Political Economy: A Cross-National Study*. New York: Columbia University Press, 1980.

Maier, Charles S. *Recasting Bourgeois Europe: Stabilization in France, Germany, and Italy in the Decade after World War I*. Princeton: Princeton University Press, 1975.

Mainwaring, Scott. "Democracy in Brazil and the Southern Cone: achievements and problems." *Journal of Interamerican Studies and World Affairs* 37:1 (1995).

Malaparte, Curzio. *Coup D'Etat: The Technique of Revolution*. Trans. by Sylvia Saunders. New York: E.P. Dutton and Co., Inc., 1932.

Maldonado Prieto, Carlos. "Entre reacción civilista y constitucionalismo formal: las fuerzas armadas chilenas en el periodo 1931-1938." *Contribuciones/Programa FLACSO-Chile* no. 55 (agosto 1988).

____. *La milicia republicana, 1932-1936. Historia de un ejército civil en Chile*. Santiago: Servicio Universitario Mundial, Comité Nacional-Chile, 1988.

Mallon, Florencia. "The Promise and Dilemma of Subaltern Studies: Perspectives from Latin American History." *The American Historical Review* 99:5 (Dec. 1994).

Malloy, James M., ed. *Authoritarianism and Corporatism in Latin*

America. Pittsburgh: University of Pittsburgh Press, 1977.

Mamalakis, Markos J. *The Growth and Structure of the Chilean Economy: From Independence to Allende*. New Haven: Yale University Press, 1976.

____ and Clark W. Reynolds. *Essays on the Chilean Economy*. Homewood, IL: Richard D. Irwin, Inc., 1965.

Mann, Wilhelm. *Chile, luchando por nuevas formas de vida*. Vol 1. Santiago: Editorial Ercilla, 1935-36.

Marichal, Carlos. *A Century of Debt Crises in Latin America: From Independence to the Great Depression, 1820-1930*. Princeton: Princeton University Press, 1989.

____. "The Vicious Cycles of Mexican Debt." *NACLA Report on the Americas* 31:3 (Nov. 1997).

Marrett, Robert. *Peru*. London: Praeger Publishers, 1969.

Marshall, Enrique L. "Régimen monetario actual en Chile y sus antecedentes históricos." *Chile: geografía, educación, literatura, legislación, economía, minería*. Ed. by Humberto Fuenzalida et al. Buenos Aires: Editorial Losada, S.A., 1946.

Marshall R., Jorge. "La nueva interpretación de los orígenes de la industrialización en Chile," Georgetown University, Programa Post-Grado de Economía, ILADES (Instituto de Doctrina y Estudios Sociales), Santiago, Chile, I/10, November, 1988.

Martínez, Javier and Alvaro Díaz. *Chile: The Great Transformation*. Washington, D.C. and Geneva: The Brookings Institution and The United Nations Research Institute for Social Development, 1996.

Mayorga Santana, Ramiro. "Las milicias republicanas." *Revista chilena de historia y geografía* 154 (1986).

McBride, George. *Chile: Land and Society*. New York: American Geographical Society, Research Series no. 19, 1936. Reprint. New York: Octagon Books, 1971.

McCaa, Robert. *Marriage and Fertility in Chile: Demographic Turning Points in the Petorca Valley, 1840-1976*. Boulder: Westview Press, 1983.

Means, Gardiner C. "The Growth in the Relative Importance of the Large Corporation in American Economic Life." *Enterprise and Secular Change: Readings in Economic History*. Ed. by Frederic C. Lane and Jelle C. Riemersma. Homewood, IL: Richard D. Irwin, Inc., 1953.

Meller, Patricio, Raúl O'Ryan, and Andrés Solimano, "Growth, Equity, and the Environment in Chile: Issues and Evidence." *World Development* 24:2 (1996).

Middlemass, Keith. *Politics in Industrial Society: The Experience of the British System Since 1911*. London: A. Deutsch, 1979.

Miller, Rory. *Britain and Latin America in the Nineteenth and Twentieth Centuries*. New York: Longman, 1993.

Minsky, Hyman P. *John Maynard Keynes*. New York: Columbia University Press, 1975.

____. *Can "It" Happen Again? Essays on Instability and Finance*. New York: M.E. Sharpe, Inc., 1982.

____. *Stabilizing an Unstable Economy*. New Haven: Yale University Press, 1986.

Moggridge, D.E. *Return to Gold 1925: The Formulation of Economic Policy and its Critics*. Cambridge: Cambridge University Press, 1969.

Molineu, Harold. *U.S. Policy Toward Latin America: From Regionalism to Globalism*. 2d ed. Boulder: Westview Press, 1990.

Monckeberg, Gustavo. *Análisis del problema de la valorización de Santiago y del pago de las expropriaciones de terrenos por causa de utilidad pública*. Santiago: Editorial Nascimento, 1937.

Monteón, Michael. *Chile in the Nitrate Era: The Evolution of Economic Dependence, 1880-1930*. Madison: University of Wisconsin Press, 1982.

____. "Latin America, Underdevelopment, and the Rentier State." *Crítica* 2:2 (Fall, 1990); Spanish version in *Economía* [Lima] 13:25 (June, 1990).

Moran, Theodore H. *Multinational Corporations and the Politics of Dependence: Copper in Chile*. Princeton: Princeton University Press, 1974.

Morgan-Webb, Charles. *The Rise and Fall of the Gold Standard*. New York: The Macmillan Company, 1934.

Moulian, Tomás. *Chile Actual: Anatomía de un mito*. Colección Sin Norte, Serie Punto de Fuga. Santiago: Arcis Universidad Ediciones Lom, 1997.

____. *La forja de ilusiones: el sistema de partidos, 1932-1973*. Santiago: Universidad de Artes y Ciencias Sociales and FLACSO, 1993.

____. "Violencia, gradualismo y reformas en el desarrollo político chileno." *Estudios sobre el sistema de partidos, edited by Adolfo Aldunate, Angel Flisfisch and Tomás Moulian*. Santiago: Ediciones FLACSO, 1986.

____ and Isabel Torres-Dujisin. *Discusiones entre honorables: las candidaturas presidenciales de la derecha entre 1938 y 1946*. Santiago: Facultad Latinoamericana de Ciencias Sociales [FLACSO], 1987.

____ and Isabel Torres-Dujisin. "Las candidaturas presidenciales de la derecha: 1946." *FLACSO Documento de Trabajo* no. 339. Santiago: FLACSO, June 1987.

Muñoz G., Oscar. *Crecimiento industrial de Chile, 1914-1965.* 2d ed. Santiago: Universidad de Chile, 1971.

Myrdal, Gunner. *An Approach to the Asian Drama: Methodological and Theoretical.* New York: Vintage Books, 1970.

Nunn, Fredrick M. *The Military in Chilean History: Essays on Civil-Military Relations, 1810-1973.* Albuquerque: University of New Mexico Press, 1976.

O'Brien, Philip and Paul Cammack, eds. *Generals in Retreat: the Crisis of Military Rule in Latin America.* Manchester: Manchester University Press, 1985.

O'Brien, Thomas F. "'Rich beyond the Dreams of Avarice': The Guggenheims in Chile." *Business History Review* 63 (Spring 1989).

____. *The Revolutionary Mission: American Enterprise in Latin America, 1900-1945.* New York: Cambridge University Press, 1996.

O'Conner, James. *The Fiscal Crisis of the State.* New York: St. Martin's Press, 1973.

O'Connor, Harvey. *The Guggenheims: The Making of an American Dynasty.* New York: Covici, 1937.

O'Donnell, Guillermo A. *Modernization and Bureaucratic-Authoritarianism: Studies in South American Politics.* Berkeley: University of California, Institute of International Studies, 1973.

Olavarría Bravo, Arturo. *Chile entre dos Alessandri: Memorias políticas.* 3 vols. Santiago: Editorial Nascimento, 1962.

Olson, Mancur. *The Rise and Decline of Nations: Economic Growth, Stagflation, and Social Rigidities.* New Haven: Yale University Press, 1982.

Oppenheim, Lois Hecht. *Politics in Chile: Democracy, Authoritarianism, and the Search for Development.* Boulder: Westview Press, 1993.

Ortega Martínez, Luis. "Acerca de los orígenes de la industrialización chilena, 1860-1879." *Nueva historia* no. 2 (1981).

____. "Change and Crisis in Chile's Economy and Society, 1865-1879." Ph.D. diss., University of London, 1979.

____, Carmen Norambuena Carrasco, Julio Pinto Vallejos, and Guillermo Bravo Acevedo. *Corporación de Fomento de la Producción: 50 años de realizaciones, 1939-1989.* Santiago: Corporación de Fomento de la Producción, 1989.

Ortíz, Eduardo. *La gran depresión y su impacto en Chile.* Santiago: Vector, Centro de Estudios Económicos y Sociales, 1982.

Packenham, Robert A. *The Dependency Movement: Scholarship and*

Politics in Development Studies. Cambridge: Harvard University Press, 1992.

Palma, J. Gabriel. "Chile 1914-1935: de economía exportadora sustitutiva de importaciones." *Nueva historia: revista de historia de Chile* 2:7 (Jan.-Mar. 1983).

____. "From an Export-led to an Import-substituting Economy: Chile 1914-39." *Latin America in the 1930s: The Role of the Periphery in World Crisis*. Ed. by Rosemary Thorp. New York: St. Martin's Press, 1984.

Palma Zuñiga, Luis. *Historia del partido radical*. Santiago: Editorial Andrés Bello, 1967.

____. *Pedro Aguirre Cerda: maestro, estadísta, gobernante*. Santiago: Editorial Andrés Bello, 1963.

____ and Julio Iglesias Meléndez. *Presencia de Juan Antonio Ríos*. Santiago: Editorial Universitaria, 1957.

Partido Radical, *El Partido Radical ante el "Acuerdo de Caballeros," Ross-Calder Discursos de los Diputados Radicales*. Santiago: Empresa El Imparcial, 1936.

Petras, James. *Politics and Social Forces in Chilean Development*. Berkeley: University of California Press, 1969.

Phelps, Dudley M. *Migration of Industry to South America*. 1939. Reprint. Westport: Greenwood Press, 1969.

Pike, Frederick B. *Chile and the United States, 1880-1962: The Emergence of Chile's Social Crisis and the Challenge to United States Diplomacy*. Notre Dame: University of Notre Dame Press, 1963.

____. *FDR's Good Neighbor Policy: Sixty Years of Generally Gentle Chaos*. Austin: University of Texas Press, 1995.

____ and Thomas Stritch, eds. *The New Corporatism: Social and Political Structures in the Iberian World*. Notre Dame, 1974.

Pinto Lagarrigue, Fernando. *Crónica política del siglo XX: desde Errázuriz Echaurren hasta Alessandri Palma*. Santiago: Editorial Orbe, 1972.

Pinto Santa Cruz, Aníbal. *Chile: un caso de desarrollo frustrado*. Santiago: Editorial Universitaria, 1959.

Pitts, Mary A. *Economic Development in Chile Under Two Growth Strategies, 1925-1968*. New York: Garland Publishing, Inc., 1987.

Pizarro, Crisóstomo. *La huelga obrera en Chile, 1890-1970*. Santiago: Ediciones Sur, 1971.

____, Dagmar Raczunski, and Joaquín Vial, eds. *Políticas económicas y sociales en el Chile democrático*. Santiago: CIEPLAN, 1995.

Poblete Troncoso, Moisés. *Labor Organizations in Chile*. Bulletin of Labor Statistics no. 461. Washington, D.C.: United States Government Printing Office, Oct. 1928.

———. *El derecho del trabajo y la seguridad social en Chile: sus realizaciones, panorama américano, XXV años de legislación social.* Santiago: Editorial Jurídica, 1949.

Polanyi, Karl. *The Great Transformation: The Political and Economic Origins of Our Time.* Boston: Beacon Press, 1944.

Pollack, Benny. "Class and Mass in the Chilean Socialist Party." *Mobilization and Socialist Politics in Chile.* Ed. by Benny Pollack. Liverpool: Centre for Latin-American Studies, Monograph Series no. 9, 1980.

——— and Hernán Rosencranz. *Revolutionary Social Democracy: The Chilean Socialist Party.* London: Frances Pinter, 1986.

Pollard, Robert A. and Samuel F. Wells, Jr. "1945-1960: The Era of American Economic Hegemony." *Economics and World Power: An Assessment of American Diplomacy Since 1789.* Ed. by William H. Becker and Samuel F. Wells, Jr. New York: Columbia University Press, 1984.

Ponce Molina, Homero. *Historia del movimiento asociativo laboral chileno.* Vol. 1, Período 1838-1973. Santiago: Editorial ALBA, 1986.

Potashnik, Michael. "Nacismo: National Socialism in Chile, 1932-1938." Ph.D. diss., University of California Los Angeles, 1974.

Puryear, Jeffrey M. *Thinking Politics: Intellectuals and Democracy in Chile, 1973-1988.* Baltimore: Johns Hopkins University Press, 1994.

Putnam, Robert D. "Diplomacy and Domestic Politics: the Logic of Two-Level Games." *International Organization* 42:3 (Summer 1988).

Quiroga, Patricio, ed. *Salvador Allende, obras escogidas (1970-1973).* Barcelona: Editorial Crítica, 1989.

Rabe, Stephen G. *Eisenhower and Latin America: The Foreign Policy of Anticommunism.* Chapel Hill: University of North Carolina Press, 1988.

Remmer, Karen L. *Party Competition in Argentina and Chile: Political Recruitment and Public Policy, 1890-1930.* Lincoln: University of Nebraska Press, 1984.

"Reportaje Conservador, al jefe del nacismo." Santiago: ca. 1936. Mimeo.

Ricardo, David. *The Works and Correspondence.* 10 vols. Vol. 1. Ed. by Piero Sraffa and Maurice H. Dobb. New York: Cambridge University Press, 1951.

Richards, Alan R. "The Political Economy of Commercial Estate Labor

Systems: a Comparative Analysis of Prussia, Egypt, and Chile." *Comparative Studies in Society and History* 21:4 (Oct. 1979).

Rippy, J. Fred. *Globe and Hemisphere: Latin America's Place in the Postwar Foreign Relations of the United States*. Chicago: H. Regnery Co., 1958.

Roberts, Kenneth M. "From the Barricades to the Ballot Box: Redemocratization and Political Realignment in the Chilean Left." *Politics and Society* 23:4 (1995).

Rock, David. "War and Postwar Intersections, Latin America and the United States." *Latin America in the 1940s: War and Postwar Transitions*. Ed. by David Rock. Berkeley: University of California, 1994.

Roddick, Jackie. "The Failure of Populism in Chile: Labour Movement and Politics Before World War II." *Boletín de estudios latinoamericanos* 31 (Dec. 1981).

Rojas Flores, Jorge. *El sindicalismo y el estado en Chile (1924-1936)*. Santiago: Colección Nuevo Siglo, 1986.

____, Alfonso Murua Olguin, Gonzalo Rojas Flores. *La historia de los obreros de la construcción*. Santiago: Programa de Economía del Trabajo, 1993.

Rosemblatt, Karin Alejandra. "Gendered Compromises: Political Cultures, Socialist Politics, and the State in Chile, 1920-1950." 2 vols. Ph.D. diss., University of Wisconsin, 1996.

Sáez, Sebastián. *La economía política de una crísis: Chile, 1929-1939*. Santiago: CIEPLAN, Notas Técnicas no. 130, May 1989.

Sáez Morales, (General) Carlos. *Recuerdos de un soldado: el ejército y la política*. 3 vols. Santiago: Biblioteca Ercilla, 1934.

Sánchez, Luis Alberto. *Visto y vivido en Chile: Bitacora chilena, 1930-1970*. Lima: Editoriales Unidas, 1975.

Sanderson, Steven E. *The Politics of Trade in Latin American Development*. Stanford: Stanford University Press, 1992.

Santa Cruz, Lucia et al. *Tres ensayos sobre la mujer chilena, Siglos XVIII-XIX-XX*. Santiago: Editorial Universitaria, 1978.

Sartori, Giovanni. *Parties and Party Systems*. New York: Cambridge University Press, 1976.

Sater, William F. "The Abortive Kronstadt: The Chilean Naval Mutiny." *Hispanic American Historical Review* 60:2 (May 1980).

Scott, Joan. "Gender: A Useful Category of Historical Analysis." *American Historical Review* 91:5 (Dec. 1986).

Schmitter, Philip. "Still the Century of Corporatism?" *Review of Politics* 36 (Jan. 1974).

Schneider, Cathy Lisa. *Shantytown Protest in Pinochet's Chile*. Philadelphia: Temple University Press, 1995.

Schott, Kerry C. *Policy, Power and Order: The Persistence of Economic Problems in Capitalist Societies.* New Haven: Yale University Press, 1984.

Segall, Marcelo. *Desarrollo del capitalismo en Chile: Cinco ensayos dialécticos.* Santiago: Editorial Pacífico, 1953.

Seguel C., José M. *La industria eléctrica ante la legislación chilena.* Santiago: Imprenta de los Talleres Leblanc, 1941.

Sen, Amartya. *Poverty and Famines: an essay on entitlement and deprivation.* Oxford: Oxford University Press, 1981.

Sheahan, John. *Patterns of Development in Latin America: Poverty, Repression, and Economic Strategy.* Princeton: Princeton University Press, 1987.

Sigmund, Paul. *The Overthrow of Allende and the Politics of Chile.* Pittsburgh: University of Pittsburgh Press, 1977.

Silva, Eduardo. "Capitalist Coalitions, the State, and Neoliberal Economic Restructuring: Chile 1973-1988." *World Politics* 45:4 (1993).

Silva, Patricio. "State, Public Technocracy, and Politics in Chile, 1927-194." *Bulletin of Latin American Research* 13:3 (Sep. 1994).

Silva Bascuñán, Alejandro. *Una experiencia social cristiana.* Santiago: Editorial del Pacífico, 1949.

Skelton, Alex. "Copper." *International Control in the Non-Ferrous Metals.* Ed. by William Yandell Elliott. New York: The Macmillan Company, 1937.

Skidmore, Thomas E. "Workers and Soldiers: Urban Labor Movements and Elite Responses in Twentieth-Century Latin America." *Elites, Masses, and Modernization in Latin America, 1850-1930.* Ed. by Virginia Bernard. Austin: University of Texas Press, 1979.

Scully, Timothy R. "Chile." *Building Democratic Institutions: Party Systems in Latin America.* Ed. by Scott Mainwaring and Timothy R. Scully. Stanford: Stanford University Press, 1995.

Smith, Brian H. *The Church and Politics in Chile: Challenges to Modern Catholicism.* Princeton: Princeton University Press, 1982.

Smith, Gaddis. *The Last Years of the Monroe Doctrine, 1945-1993.* New York: Hill and Wang, 1994.

Smith, Peter. *Talons of the Eagle: Dynamics of U.S.-Latin American Relations.* New York: Oxford University Press, 1996.

Smith Millar, Silas. *El comercio ante la crisis económica.* Santiago: n.p., 1932.

Snow, Peter G. *Radicalismo chileno: historia y doctrina del partido radical.* Santiago: Editorial Francisco de Aguirre, 1972.

Snyder, J. Richard. "William S. Culbertson in Chile: Opening the Door to a Good Neighbor, 1929-1933." *Inter-American Economic Affairs* 26:1 (Summer, 1972).

Somervell, Philip. "Naval Affairs in Chilean Politics, 1910-1932," *Journal of Latin American Studies* 16:2 (Nov. 1984).

Somjee, A.H. *Development Theory: Critiques and Explorations.* New York: St. Martin's Press, 1991.

Spalding Jr., Hobart. *Organized Labor in Latin America: Studies of Workers in Dependent Societies.* New York: New York University Press, 1977.

Sraffa, Piero. *Production of Commodities by Means of Commodities.* Cambridge: Cambridge University Press, 1951.

Stallings, Barbara. *Class Conflict and Economic Development in Chile, 1958-1973.* Stanford: Stanford University Press, 1978.

____. *Banker to the Third World: U.S. Portfolio Investment in Latin America, 1900-1986.* Berkeley: University of California Press, 1987.

Stemplowski, Ryszard. "Chile y las compañías petroleras, 1931-1932. Contribución al estudio del entrelazamiento dominación-dependencia." *Ibero-Amerikanisches Archiv* 4:1 (1978).

Stepan, Alfred C. *The State and Society: Peru in Comparative Perspective.* Princeton: Princeton University Press, 1978.

Stevenson, John Reese. *The Chilean Popular Front.* 1944. Reprint. Westport: Greenwood Press, 1970.

Steward, Dick. *Trade and Hemisphere: the Good Neighbor Policy and Reciprocal Trade.* Columbus: University of Missouri Press, 1975.

Stickell, Arthur L. "Migration and Mining: Labor in Northern Chile, 1880-1930." Ph.D. diss. University of Indiana, 1979.

Stone, Lawrence. "England's Financial Revolution." Review of *The Sinews of Power: War, Money and the English State, 1688-1783*, by John Brewer. *New York Review of Books* (15 Mar. 1990), 51.

Strawbridge, George. *Ibáñez and Alessandri: The Authoritarian Right and Democratic Left in Twentieth-Century Chile.* Buffalo: Special Studies Council on International Studies, State University of New York at Buffalo, September 1971.

Sunkel, Osvaldo. "Is the Chilean 'Miracle' Sustainable?" *Journal of Interamerican Studies and World Affairs* 37:3 (1995).

____ and Pedro Paz Sunkel. *El subdesarrollo latinoamericano y la teoría del desarrollo.* Mexico: Siglo Veintiuno, 1970.

Super, Richard R. "The Seguro Obrero massacre." *The Underside of Latin American History.* Ed. by John F. Bratzel and Daniel M. Masterson. East Lansing: Latin American Studies Center, Michigan State University, 1977.

Sznajder, Mario. "A Case of Non-European Fascism: Chilean National Socialism in the 1930s." *Journal of Contemporary History* 28 (1993).

Tapia-Videla, Jorge. "The Chilean Presidency in a Developmental Perspective." *Journal of Inter-American Studies and World Affairs* 19:4 (Nov. 1977).

Taylor, A.J.P. *English History.* New York: Oxford University Press, 1965.

Temin, Peter. *Did Monetary Forces Cause the Great Depression?* New York: W.W. Norton and Company, Inc., 1976.

Thomas, Jack Ray. "Marmaduke Grove: A Political Biography." Ph.D. diss., Ohio State University, Columbus, 1962.

Thorp, Rosemary, ed. *Latin America in the 1930s: The Role of the Periphery in World Crisis.* London: MacMillan, in association with St. Antony's College, Oxford, 1984.

Tilly, Charles. *Coercion, Capital, and European States, AD 900-1990.* Cambridge: Cambridge University Press, 1990.

Timoshenko, Vladimir P. *World Agriculture and the Depression.* Michigan Business Studies 5:5 (1933). Ann Arbor: University of Michigan School of Business Administration.

Tironi, Eugenio. *El liberalismo real: la sociedad chilena y el régimen militar.* Santiago: Ediciones Sur, 1986.

Tixier, Adrien Pierre. "The Development of Social Insurance in Argentina, Brazil, Chile and Uruguay." *International Labour Review* 32 (Nov. 1935).

Troncoso, Moisés Poblete and Ben G. Burnett. *The Rise of the Latin American Labor Movement.* New York: Bookman Associates, 1960.

Tulchin, Joseph S. *The Aftermath of War: World War I and U.S. Policy Toward Latin America.* New York: New York University Press, 1971.

Universidad de Chile. *Desarrollo económico de Chile, 1940-1956.* Santiago: Universidad de Chile, 1956.

Universidad de Chile. Facultad de Ciencias Sociales, Instituto de Economía. *La economía de Chile en el período 1950-1963.* 2 vols. Santiago: Universidad de Chile, 1963.

Urzúa Valenzuela, Germán. *La democracia práctica: Los gobiernos radicales.* Santiago: Editorial Melquíades for CIEDES, 1987.

___. *Historia política de Chile y su evolución electoral (desde 1810 a 1992).* Santiago: Editorial Jurídica de Chile, 1992.

Usher, Dan. *The Economic Prerequisite to Democracy.* New York: Columbia University Press, 1981.

Valdés Subercaseaux, Ximena. *Mujer, trabajo, y medio ambiente: los nudos de la modernización agraria.* Santiago: CEDEM, Centro de Estudios para el Desarrollo de la Mujer, 1992.

___, Loreto Rebolledo G. Angélica Willson A., *Masculino y femenino en la hacienda chilena del siglo XX.* Santiago: FONDART-CEDEM, Fondo de Desarrollo de la Cultura y las Artes, Ministerio de Educación, and Centro de Estudios para el Desarrollo de la Mujer, 1995.

Valdivia Ortíz de Zárate, Verónica. *La milicia republicana. Los civiles en armas. 1932-1936.* Santiago: Dirección de Bibliotecas Archivos y Museos. Centro de Investigaciones Diego Barros Arana, 1992.

___. "Los civiles en armas: La milicia republicana, 1932-1936." Master's thesis, Universidad de Santiago de Chile. 1989.

Valdivieso, Fernando Bravo, Francisco Bulnes Serrano, and Gonzalo Vial Correa. *Balmaceda y la guerra civil.* Santiago: Editorial Fundación, 1991.

Valenzuela, Arturo. *The Breakdown of Democratic Regimes: Chile.* Baltimore: Johns Hopkins University Press, 1978.

___. *Political Brokers in Chile: Local Government in a Centralized Polity.* Durham: Duke University Press, 1977.

Valenzuela, Samuel J. *Democratización via reforma: la expansión del sufragio en Chile.* Buenos Aires: Ediciones del IDES, 1985.

___ and Arturo Valenzuela, eds. *Military Rule in Chile: Dictatorship and Oppositions.* Baltimore: Johns Hopkins University Press, 1986.

___ and Arturo Valenzuela. "Modernization and Dependency: Alternative Perspectives in the Study of Latin American Underdevelopment." *From Dependency to Development: Strategies to Overcome Underdevelopment and Inequality.* Ed. by Heraldo Muñoz. Westview Special Studies in Social, Political and Economic Development. Boulder: Westview Press, 1981.

Van Hauwermeiren, Saar. "Tratados de libre comercio y su impacto sobre el medio ambiente." *El tigre sin selva: consequencias ambientales de la transformación económica de Chile, 1974-1993.* Ed. by Rayén Quiroga Martínez. Santiago: Instituto de Ecología Política, Area de Economía Ecológica, Oct. 1994.

Véliz, Claudio. "La mesa de tres patas." *Desarrollo económico* 3 (1967).

Vial Correa, Gonzalo. *Historia de Chile (1893-1973): Historia del Régimen Parlamentario (1891-1920)* and *Arturo Alessandri y los golpes militares (1920-1925).* 3 vols. Santiago: Editorial Fundación, 1981-1986.

____. *Historia de Chile (1891-1973): La dictadura de Ibáñez (1925-1931)*. Vol. 4. Santiago: Editorial Fundación, 1996.

____, Pablo Valderrama Hoyl, and David Vasquez Vargas, *Historia del Senado de Chile*. Santiago: Editorial Andres Bello, 1995.

Villalobos, Sergio et al. *Historia de Chile*. 4 vols. Santiago: Editorial Universitaria, 1974-76.

Vitale, Luis. *Interpretación marxista de la historia de Chile*. 3 vols. Santiago: Ediciones de Prensa Latinoamericana, 1967-71. 2 vols.: 4, 5. Vol. 5. Barcelona: Fontamara, 1980.

Vio Grossi, Francisco. *Resistencia campesina: En Chile y en México*. Santiago: CEAAL [Consejo de Educación de Adultos de América Latina], 1990.

Wagner, Gert. "Trabajo, producción y crecimiento. La economía chilena, 1860-1930." Santiago: Pontifícia Universidad Católica de Chile, Instituto de Economía, Documento de Trabajo no. 150 (Oct. 1992).

Wee, Herman van der, ed. *The Great Depression Revisited. Essays on the Economics of the Thirties*. The Hague: Nijhoff, 1972.

Whynes, David K. and Roger A. Bowles. *The Economic Theory of the State*. Oxford: Martin Robinson, 1981.

Wiarda, Howard J. *Corporatism and Comparative Politics: the other great "ism"*. New York: M.E. Sharpe, 1997.

____. *Corporatism and National Development in Latin America*. Boulder: Westview Press, 1981.

____ and Harvey F. Klein, eds. *Latin American Politics and Development*. 4th ed. Boulder: Westview Press, 1996.

Williams, John H. "The Crisis of the Gold Standard." *Enterprise and Secular Change: Readings in Economic History*. Ed. by Frederic C. Lane and Jelle C. Riemersma for the American Economic Association and the Economic History Association. Homewood, IL: R.D. Irwin, 1953.

Wilson, Joan Hoff. *American Business and Foreign Policy, 1920-1933*. Lexington: University Press of Kentucky, 1971.

Winn, Peter. *Weavers of Revolution: The Yarur Workers and Chile's Road to Socialism*. Oxford: Oxford University Press, 1986.

Wood, Bryce. *The Making of the Good Neighbor Policy*. New York: W.W. Norton, 1961.

Wright, Thomas C. *Landowners and Reform in Chile: The Sociedad Nacional de Agricultura, 1919-1940*. Urbana: University of Illinois Press, 1982.

Würth Rojas, Ernesto. *Ibáñez: caudillo enigmático*. Santiago: Editorial del Pacífico, S.A., 1958.

Yocelevsky R., Ricardo A. "El desarrollo de los partidos políticos chilenos hasta 1970." *FLACSO Cuadernos de Trabajo* no. 102. Santiago: FLACSO, 1986.

Young, George F.W. "Jorge González von Marées: Chief of Chilean Nacism." *Jahrbüch für geschichte von staat, wirtschaft und gesellschaft lateinamerikas* 11 (1974).

Young, Lowell T. "Franklin D. Roosevelt and the Expansion of the Monroe Doctrine." *North Dakota Quarterly* (Winter, 1974).

Zañartu Prieto, Enrique. *Hambre, miseria e ignorancia*. Santiago: Editorial Ercilla, 1938.

Zeitlin, Maurice. *The Civil Wars in Chile (Or the Bourgeois Revolutions That Never Were)*. Princeton: Princeton University Press, 1984.

____ and Richard Earl Ratcliff. *Landlords and Capitalists: The Dominant Class of Chile*. Princeton: Princeton University Press, 1988.

Zemelman M., Hugo. "El movimiento popular chileno y el sistema de alianzas en la década de los treinta." *América latina en los años treinta*. Ed. by Luis Antezana E. et al. Mexico City: Instituto de Investigaciones Sociales, Universidad Nacional Autónoma de México, 1977.

Ziebura, Gilbert. *World Economy and World Politics, 1924-1931: From Reconstruction to Collapse*. Trans. by Bruce Little. Oxford: Oxford University Press, 1990.

Index

ers in 180; Wachholtz in 257;
wages in 176; White Guard in
185; women in 58; women work-
ers in 40; worker warehouses in
33, 38, 74, 178
Sartori, Giovanni 330-31, 346
Schnake Vergara, Oscar 82, 183,
232, 238, 283-85, 290, 299, 305,
307
Schwartzenberg, Julio 185-86
Sen, Amartya 5, 13, 95, 192
Sevier, U.S. Ambassador Hall 55,
161-62, 165, 167, 208-209, 212
Shapiro, Ian 321, 345
Shell-Mexico Oil 30, 36, 76, 224,
263, 266
Singer Sewing Machine Company
77, 96
Skidmore, Thomas E. 209, 212
Small Business Association 221
Smith, E.A. Cappelen 32, 79
Smoot-Hawley Tariff 43, 71
Snow, Peter G. 97, 304, 306, 311
social question 169
social security 109, 195, 228, 233,
236, 338, 342, 348
Social-Democratic Party 181
Social-Republican Party 181
Socialist Militia 232, 238
Socialist Republic 83, 183, 185, 195,
225
Society for Industrial Development
[Sociedad de Fomento Fabril, SO-
FOFA] xii, 39, 54, 71, 114, 117,
128-29, 191, 221, 257, 279, 304,
306, 325
Society for Industrial Promotion 43
Society for Tourism and Hotels 117
Solís, Juan S. 203
South American Frutera Company
148-50
South American Power Company
29, 152, 154
South Korea 339
Soviet Union, and:
Chilean Communists 197, 301;
Chilean elite 290; collapse of 313-

15; Great Depression 331; Latin
Americans 294; Nazi invasion of
286; exports oil 76, 150
Spain, and:
compensation trade 135; government 144; Great Depression 331;
Popular Front 204, 219, 331
Spalding, Hobart Jr. 212
Spanish Civil War 227
Standard Oil of New Jersey 28, 30,
36, 76, 151, 224, 263, 292
Stannard, Earl T. 255, 270, 308-309,
312
State Mortgage Bank [Caja de
Crédito Hipotecario] xii, 43, 69,
80, 156, 244, 257, 280
Stimson, Secretary of State Henry
53, 59, 84, 93, 96, 99
strikes 5, 39, 83, 108, 184, 190-94,
199, 203-204, 217, 233, 261-65,
280, 293-301, 332
bakers 39; coal mine 301; consumer 227; copper mine 236;
general 108; illegal 199, 217,
296; labor 88, 170, 184, 191; lawyers 83; metal workers 199;
movement for 199, 302; of
(1936), (1940), and (1943) 281-
82; port 198; professionals 81;
railroad 171, 201, 203-204; rent
199, 236; retailers 108; rolling
298, 301; rural 236; student 46;
teachers 197; U.S. mining firm
238; white-collar 302
students
demonstrations 45; left-wing 79,
184; loyal to government 197;
medical 81; movement 45; organize civic guard 46; strike 46;
university 44, 46, 91, 229
subaltern studies 318, 344
suffrage 41
movement 194
Sweden, and compensation trade 135
Switzerland, and compensation trade
135
synthetic nitrates 25, 32, 255, 292-93

Associate Professor at the University of California San Diego,
Michael Monteón was born in 1946 in Mason City, Iowa,
where he recieved his early education. His parents came from
the states of Jalisco and Guanajuato, Mexico. He earned
advanced degrees from the University of Denver (B.A.) and
Harvard University (M.A. and Ph.D.).

Distinguished author of articles on the history and politics
of Argentina, Chile, and Mexico, Dr. Monteon specializes on
the history of political economy and of labor relations. Prior
to this current work, *Chile and the Great Depression*, he
published *Chile in the Nitrate Era: The Evolution of Economic Dependence, 1880-1930* (Wisconsin, 1982) and coedited the publication *Engendering Wealth and Well Being: Empowerment for Global Change* (Westview, 1995).